Human Diversity

Edison J. Trickett
Roderick J. Watts
Dina Birman

editors

Human Diversity

Perspectives
on People in Context

Jossey-Bass Publishers • San Francisco

Substantial discounts on bulk quantities of Jossey-Bass books are available to corporations, professional associations, and other organizations. For details and discount information, contact the special sales department at Jossey-Bass Inc., Publishers. (415) 433-1740; Fax (415) 433-0499.

For sales outside the United States, please contact your local Paramount Publishing International office.

The epigraph by Edward O. Wilson opening Chapter Nineteen is reprinted by permission of the publishers from *The Diversity of Life* by Edward O. Wilson, Cambridge, Mass.: The Belknap Press of Harvard University Press, Copyright © 1992 by the President and Fellows of Harvard College.

The epigraph by Charles Taylor opening Chapter Nineteen is reprinted from *Multiculturalism and the Politics of Recognition*. Princeton, N.J.: Princeton University Press, 1992, p. 73.

Gloria Negri's excerpt in Chapter Eight is from Negri, G. (1988, Nov. 4). After 60 years, he's still dedicated. *Boston Globe*, p. 2. Reprinted courtesy of *The Boston Globe*.

Library of Congress Cataloging-in-Publication Data

Human diversity : perspectives on people in context / Edison J.
  Trickett, Roderick J. Watts, Dina Birman, editors. — 1st ed.
       p.   cm. — (The Jossey-Bass social and behavioral science
  series)
    Includes bibliographical references and index.
    ISBN 0-7879-0029-X
    1. Ethnopsychology.   2. Difference (Psychology).   3. Identification
  (Psychology).   4. Pluralism (Social sciences).   I. Trickett, Edison J.
  II. Watts, Roderick J.   III. Birman, Dina, date.
  IV. Series.
  GN502.H87   1994
  155.8 — dc20   94-17753
                                                                CIP

FIRST EDITION
HB Printing   10 9 8 7 6 5 4 3 2 1   *Code 94109*

The Jossey-Bass
Social and Behavioral
Science Series

Contents

**Part IV: Applying Paradigms and
Concepts of Human Diversity: Conducting
Diversity-Conscious Research and Creating
Settings Supportive of Diversity**

Preface

Diversity has become both a critical and an elusive concept in U.S. society, as changing demographics force a self-examination of what this country can and should be. It is elusive because, like any popular phrase, it can become trivialized or can be used to signify a superficial attachment to certain social values without serious consideration of the implications of those values for interpersonal behavior or social policy. However, it is critical because so much rests on how we attempt to balance an appreciation of the differences inherent in diversity with the need for a common culture that is necessary for any society to remain coherent.

Social sciences in general, and psychology in particular, have in recent years been increasingly involved in the larger discussion and debate about diversity and its multiple meanings. Much of this participation has involved what might be called constituency politics, focusing on the concerns of particular groups who have become organized over time in self-defense. We applaud the commitments they represent. However, within our own field of psychology, we have been struck by the relatively parallel but nonoverlapping nature of the scholarship on various groups participating in the larger conversation. The accumulating knowledge relevant to both understanding diversity and making the world safe for it is too often a piecemeal knowledge that evolves independently rather than interdependently across various groups. What is needed is an effort to provide the kind of dialogue that can, over time, allow both an appreciation of difference and an understanding of common cause among those seeking to develop a psychology of diversity. *Human Diversity: Perspectives on People in Context* was born of this need.

The underlying idea behind the book is to accentuate the theme of both similarities and differences by presenting perspectives that have evolved in different areas of diversity scholarship. The intent is not to ensure that every organized group has an opportunity to be represented, though this is not an unworthy goal. The point is somewhat different: to provide grist for the intellectual mill of furthering the ideas on which a psychology of human diversity can be based. The goal is to think about diversity more than about how to do specific work such as culturally competent therapy. As the title implies, we believe that furthering this dialogue requires an emphasis on understanding people in a historical and sociocultural context.

Although in recent years, other attempts to unite the diverse themes of distinct groups have been embraced under the diversity concept, none have focused explicitly on the crosscutting themes that unite the distinct scholarship on each of these groups. The present book raises the question of whether the concepts used in minority mental health, the psychology of women, gay and lesbian psychology, the psychology of disability, and other areas represent similar ideas, or whether quite different meanings are attached to these concepts in different contexts. In this way, the book raises the discussion of diversity to a new level of analysis and, in so doing, explores the meanings of frequently used concepts such as oppression, culture, and identity in greater depth than is generally the case in writings on this subject. Moreover, such a perspective on the issues allows us to consider the psychology of all human beings as being rooted in their particular cultural and sociopolitical context. Thus, the ideas explored in this book form the tools for a psychology of human diversity that includes the majority as well as the minority, the privileged as well as the oppressed.

The goal of the book is to allow for exploration of the similarities and differences in the experiences of diverse groups and to stimulate cross-fertilization of ideas in the field. To that end, we have constructed the book in a way that accentuates the broad cross-cutting themes inherent in all scholarship on various aspects of human diversity. First, we focus on the paradigms and conceptual frameworks that different scholars bring to this field. Second, we have selected key concepts in the field that are salient for scholarship on all groups embraced by the diversity concept. These include the concepts of oppression, culture, and identity as they are dealt with in the psychology of diverse groups. Third, we explore the application of these varied approaches to diversity to the research process and to the question of how we create academic and other settings that reflect the values of diversity. Finally, we provide a concluding chapter that integrates and highlights the issues of similarity and difference found earlier in the book. The outcome is a book that offers a different perspective on psychology, rooted in the contextual experience of diverse groups.

We have allowed for individual contributors' preferences with respect to terminology such as *Afro American or African American,* white or White, and so on, because specific usage often has a larger significance that the contributors are referring to.

Overview of the Contents

The authors who have prepared chapters for this book include notable scholars whose areas of expertise inform the discourse on diversity. While most of the authors come from various areas of psychology such as social, community, and cross-cultural psychology, sociology and anthropology are also represented. This range of contributors has greatly enhanced the breadth of paradigmatic perspectives relevant to a psychology of human diversity.

The book's twenty chapters are organized into four parts. Part One presents an overview of the concept of diversity within psychology and some of the many constraints to its becoming central to discourse in psychology. Part Two outlines various specific paradigms that have emerged in the diversity area over time and that will continue to define inquiry in the near future. Part Three focuses on three key concepts that cut across different areas of diversity: oppression and intergroup dynamics, culture, and identity. Part Four addresses two topics relevant to applying the diversity perspectives described thus far: carrying out research and creating social settings supportive of diversity. A concluding chapter presents the implications of the book for the future of theory and research on diversity.

In covering such a broad and important topic, we were not able to devote adequate attention to all the areas of scholarship relevant to the topic or to solicit contributions from many whose work and perspective could have enriched the book. However, we believe that the following chapters address the clear need in the field to develop a broad and integrative perspective on the theory and research of human diversity that promotes the investigation of both similarity and difference.

Audience

This book is directed at graduate students, academics, and practitioners who deal with diversity in the course of their endeavors. However, we emphasize that the current demographics of the United States make this book relevant to all, not just those who specialize in diversity. For those who are unfamiliar with the particular areas of inquiry represented here, this book can serve as an overview of the issues, offering examples of different frameworks for understanding diversity. For those who are involved in the field, the chapters contained herein offer a new look at the issues. Each of the authors has written about the group or field he or she knows best, but with an understanding of the overarching concept of the book. In that way, chapters speak to specific topics in the context of the broader theme of diversity.

While the book is not explicitly directed at practitioners, we believe, with Lewin, that there is nothing so practical as a good theory, and we are confident that practitioners will find in the following pages many useful ways of thinking about their work with diverse clients in varied communities. Indeed, the paradigms and concepts explored in this volume highlight the differences in the way people frame and understand issues of diversity and may explain differences and disagreements between members of provider agencies and the communities they serve. In light of this, there may be few better long-range pragmatic outcomes than learning different ways of approaching the many aspects of the diversity issue.

Acknowledgments

Our first debt of gratitude is to the contributors represented in the following chapters who worked with us to develop the book. Their intellectual contributions and willingness to work within the constraints of the volume made this book possible. With few exceptions, each author was a contributor to a conference held in October 1988 at the University of Maryland, College Park. That conference, bearing the same title as this book, was supported by the University of Maryland's General Research Board and Department of Psychology. We gratefully acknowledge their contribution to what turned out to be a springboard for this book. In addition, several conference participants who did not contribute directly to this book nonetheless helped shape its ideas through their conference contributions. We wish to thank Adrienne Asch, Hussein Bulhan, Michelle Fine, Linda Garnets, Doug Kimmel, Gloria Levin, Jean Baker Miller, Amado Padilla, Manuel Ramirez, Joe Trimble, Melba Vasquez, Teena Wax, and Irving Kenneth Zola for their influence on our work. A special thanks is due Stanley Sue, one of the conference participants, for his introductory remarks.

In addition, we appreciate the guidance of Rebecca McGovern, social and behavioral science editor at Jossey-Bass, who provided both support and useful feedback as the book progressed. Wilma Holdway provided timely secretarial assistance at various stages of the project.

August 1994   Edison J. Trickett
                                                          Brookeville, Maryland

                                                          Roderick J. Watts
                                                          Oak Park, Illinois

                                                          Dina Birman
                                                          Brookeville, Maryland

The Editors

Edison J. Trickett is professor of psychology at the University of
Maryland and is currently serving as special assistant on sociocultural processes in mental health at the National Institute
of Mental Health. He received his B.A. degree (1963) from
Trinity College, Hartford, Connecticut, in psychology and his
M.A. (1965) and Ph.D. (1967) degrees from Ohio State University in clinical psychology.

　　Trickett's current work extends the ecological perspective
on diversity underlying this book to issues of diversity and multiculturalism in public schools. He deals with these issues as editor
of the *American Journal of Community Psychology*. He has also written
extensively about ecology as a framework for research and intervention in community psychology. His books include *Living
an Idea: Empowerment and the Evolution of an Alternative Public School*
(1991) and *Community Consultation* (1983, with Patrick O'Neill).

　　Trickett conducted postdoctoral research at the Social Ecology Laboratory at Stanford University and taught at Yale University before joining the faculty at the University of Maryland. He
is a past president of Division 27 of the American Psychological
Association and the Society for Community Research and Action.

Roderick J. Watts is a community psychologist and a licensed clinical psychologist currently working as associate professor of psychology at DePaul University in Chicago. He began his college education at Fisk University in Nashville and received his B.A. degree (1977) at Oberlin College in psychology. Watts received his M.A. (1980) and Ph.D. (1984) degrees from the University of Maryland in psychology.

His research interests include human diversity, racism, racial identity, and manhood development. He has served as a consultant to governmental organizations, schools, foundations, research and public policy organizations, universities, and other nonprofit organizations. Watts has held positions at the Consultation Center at Yale University and the Institute for Urban Affairs and Research at Howard University.

Dina Birman is a psychologist at the Refugee Mental Health Branch in the Center for Mental Health Services, which is part of The Substance Abuse and Mental Health Services Administration of the U.S. Public Health Service. She received her B.S. degree (1983) from the School of Foreign Service at Georgetown University in international politics and her M.A. (1988) and Ph.D. (1991) degrees from the University of Maryland in clinical/community psychology.

Birman's interests in cross-cultural psychology are derived from personal experience as a refugee to the United States from the former Soviet Union and include issues of ethnic and racial identity, acculturation and biculturalism, and the psychology of women. In her work, she provides consultation and technical assistance on mental health issues to federal, state, and private refugee resettlement agencies. She is involved in developing culturally sensitive primary prevention initiatives in resettlement sites throughout the country, including mental health intervention programs for Evangelical Christian and Jewish refugees from the former Soviet Union, former political prisoners from Vietnam, and Bosnian refugees. Her research focuses on acculturation processes and adaptation of refugees and immigrants.

List of Contributors

Clayton P. Alderfer
Rutgers University

L. Seán Azelton
University of Illinois at
Chicago

Martha E. Bernal
Arizona State University

John W. Berry
Queens University

Dina Birman
Substance Abuse and Mental
Health Services Administration
U.S. Public Health Service

Rebecca G. Burzette
University of Illinois at Chicago

Brian Cotton
University of Southern
California

Amy J. Dabul
Arizona State University

Anthony R. D'Augelli
Pennsylvania State
University

Margaret Gatz
University of Southern
California

Lev S. Gonick
Wilfrid Laurier University

Janet E. Helms
University of Maryland

James M. Jones
University of Delaware

James G. Kelly
University of Illinois at
Chicago

Walter J. Lonner
Western Washington
University

Lynne O. Mock
University of Illinois at
Chicago

Linda James Myers
Ohio State University

Isaac Prilleltensky
Wilfrid Laurier University

Julian Rappaport
University of Illinois at
Urbana-Champaign

Shulamit Reinharz
Brandeis University

Nancy Felipe Russo
Arizona State University

Jessica Scheer
National Rehabilitation
Hospital Research Center

Suzette L. Speight
Loyola University Chicago

Edison J. Trickett
University of Maryland

Forrest B. Tyler
University of Maryland

Roderick J. Watts
DePaul University

Human Diversity

Introduction

Stanley Sue

Throughout history and in every society, people have had to deal with human diversity of all kinds. That issues of diversity have not been resolved is apparent. Violence because of ethnic, religious, gender, and sexual orientation has continued; prejudice and discrimination on the basis of diversity are common in all parts of the world; and growth and development are sometimes restricted because one is somehow different from others. In addition to issues that touch every society, we encounter more local issues such as affirmative action, inclusion of diversity topics in the curriculum, and culturally effective means of intervening to enhance the lives of individuals.

I find *Human Diversity: Perspectives on People in Context* bold and challenging. The book itself is diverse because of the inclusion of chapters on a wide range of issues concerning different groups and populations. Unlike other books that focus on only one group, this book discusses a number of different topics, including ethnic minorities, gender, sexual orientation, and disability. Because of this wide range of topics, it would be easy to view the book as a hodgepodge of special interests, as the voice of "political correctness," or as an attack on white males.

1

This would be a mistake. Rather than being a book of special-interest concerns, it covers common themes: oppression because of differences, the inability to fully understand and appreciate human nature because of cultural blinders, well-intentioned but often misguided efforts at intervention that fail to take into account the diversity of people, and the need to more thoroughly conceptualize and study diversity. Furthermore, labeling efforts to promote diversity as political correctness has the unfortunate effect of hindering discussion and analysis, by dismissing opposing views without examining their merits. Finally, the culprit is not white males. I have no illusions that, if the dominant group were Chinese or women, the world would necessarily be better. What really matters is the way we think about human beings. Diversity should be appreciated and nurtured rather than used as a basis for oppression.

Personal and cultural values are challenged by diversity. In addressing the challenge, we must develop an appreciation of variations among human beings, even if the differences may be antagonistic to our own values and beliefs. Does this mean that all views or cultural values are equally valid? The dilemma raised by this question can be illustrated by the conflict over human rights. At the 1993 United Nations World Conference on Human Rights held in Vienna, a number of Asian countries asserted that the Universal Declaration on Human Rights was culturally bound, defined by the West, and inappropriate to many non-Western countries. Singaporean officials felt that Asian tradition placed greater emphasis on consensus than on competition, so that Western, competitive-style democracy was a cultural misfit for non-Western countries. Officials from several countries argued that religious and cultural traditions justify a limited freedom of expression and a reduced social role for women. Others believed that the attacks on the declarations as being Western in origin would threaten human rights principles in general and attempts to gain equality for women in particular.

Is such equality a biased, Western concept or a universal right? Without directly addressing this question, let me say that appreciation of different values does not mean that we must accept all views or values as relative. Nevertheless, if nations, societies, groups, and individuals have erred, it has probably been in an egocentric and ethnocentric direction in which personal and cultural values are promoted as universally desirable. The task for social scientists is to understand the cultural basis for their own views and the consequences of these views.

As a step in this understanding, we must develop a positive appreciation for diversity and multiculturalism, valuing human diversity and realizing that it is an essential part of existence. Over a five-year period, I regularly taught in mainland China. What bothered me was that I rarely saw any non-Chinese except for occasional encounters with white tourists. I missed seeing the African Americans and Latin Americans whom I regularly saw in Los Angeles. (It is not that the Chinese lack diversity; rather, I yearned to see different ethnic and racial groups.) In the United States, we often perceive diversity as a problem, and we fail to find strength in it. When we see racially and ethnically different Americans winning medals in the Olympics, we have a sense of pride in the achievements of our nation. When the Olympics are over, we again see diversity as a source of problems.

Part of the difficulty in appreciating diversity is the fact that our collective efforts to address the issue have been motivated in part by political, legal, and social pressures; a sense of fairness and equity; social desirability; fear; guilt; and obligation. Given these mixed motives, it is difficult to develop an affirming and positive sense of appreciation. Compliance and the social desirability of appearing nonracist may hinder a strong affirmation of the value of diversity. I say this despite research that demonstrates that legislating changes can influence our hearts and that certain conditions, as originally outlined by Gordon Allport, can result in the development of positive attitudes and reduce racial discrimination (for example, providing members of different ethnic groups with equal-status contacts, engaging in cooperative rather than competitive tasks, and operating under norms or authorities that discourage prejudice). My fear is that we may have compartmentalized our efforts and separated compliance from real attitudinal change.

In conclusion, we must understand the cultural blinders that we wear and begin to truly appreciate diversity. Our notions of diversity should be broadened beyond ethnicity, gender, sexual orientation, and social class. It is true that these characteristics have often resulted in oppression and minority-group status. Nevertheless, to define diversity in these terms will only perpetuate the view that something has to be done for the oppressed. My belief is that diversity should not be embraced because it helps the oppressed; instead, we will all be served by affirming diversity. Cultural diversity is part of the nature of human beings, and it should be part of the nature of our science and practice in the social sciences.

PART I

Overview

A Psychology
of Human Diversity

Toward an Overarching
Framework for Diversity

Edison J. Trickett,
Roderick J. Watts, Dina Birman

Today the concept of diversity has become central in the national debate about the current and future hopes for our society. It has emerged in dicussions of immigration policies, educational practices, and whether or not certain life-styles are acceptable. It has been caricatured in arguments about political correctness, embodied in issues of affirmative action and the related imagery of quotas, and viewed as a criterion for assessing the equity of social policies and practices. Attention to diversity has created both heat and light about what kind of country we are, raised awareness of our history of incorporating different immigrant groups into the broader culture, yielded critical examination of our social policies and the assumptions about diversity on which they are built, and provided the grist for self-examination of the ideas on which the country was founded.

Why this movement has become so pervasive in national debate in recent years can be traced to at least two additive sets of factors. The first set involves changing demographics. During the past several decades, the United States has become an increasingly multicultural society because of an influx of immigrants and refugees, particularly those from Southeast Asia

and Central and South America. The impact of these migra-
tions is nowhere more evident than in the public schools, where,
in some urban areas, English is not the native language of a
majority of the students. While many ethnic communities have
coalesced to provide resources and support for their members,
reports of the quality of life in such communities often paint
a portrait of stress (Loo, 1991), and ethnic conflicts between
immigrant or refugee groups and native-born U.S. groups are
not unusual. Struggles for scarce resources and conflicts over
access to education are two of the ways in which the changing
demographics of the country are rippling through its communities and institutions.

    The second set of factors stems from an earlier time when,
as now, the country was engaged in a national debate about
its nature. The time was the 1960s, and the debate involved
power, disenfranchisement, and the latent and manifest ways
in which groups of individuals were oppressed and denied equal
access to resources. The civil rights movement, and later the
women's movement, arose from the social unrest of the time
to become consciousness-shaping forces. Though movements
organized to counter racism and sexism had previously existed,
this period changed U.S. society and the social sciences in several
important ways. The concepts of oppression, group identity,
and empowerment emerged at this time as critical to understanding and changing the social context. Over time, new groups were
organized around similar issues, presenting a new set of voices
in the political arena. These groups, representing people of color,
women, gays and lesbians, individuals with disabilities, and the
aged, collectively altered the consciousness of the country by
directing attention to the ways in which policies and practices
discriminated against groups in the workplace, the public schools,
the home, and the community. From internal forces as well as
immigration, the concept of diversity gained momentum.

    In the context of these larger social forces, psychology has
also been challenged by the diversity of the people whose behavior it seeks to understand. This diversity has challenged the
foundations of psychology by suggesting that traditional psychology is particularistic rather than universal and that its the-

ories reflect the worldviews and attending limitations of those who created them and the social context in which they were created. Proponents of these newer perspectives argue that theory and practice must be understood in the contexts of the environment, culture, and population in question.

As a consequence, psychology is currently struggling to incorporate human diversity into the theories, perspectives, methodologies, and practices of the field. This struggle is taking place in many areas, ranging from recruitment practices to curricular transformation to theory development. It is seen in efforts to promote cross-cultural competence among practitioners and researchers, the increased publication of books focusing on specific populations, and the inclusion in ethics codes of attention to and appreciation of the full range of human diversity.

Most importantly, the challenge of diversity for psychology is a paradigmatic one: to develop ways of thinking that can illuminate the notion of diversity as a psychological and sociopolitical aspect of people's lives. Such a task involves a confrontation with much of the history of how psychology has developed as a social science and who developed it. It demands the creation of different perspectives from those that have dominated earlier psychological research and practice. This chapter provides the contours of what some of those alternative perspectives might include.

As the psychological study of human behavior unfolds, two contrasting sets of images of people and how they are understood are emerging. These emphases involve more broadly a series of correlated, though by no means isomorphic, processes of development in the field. One image emphasizes the biological or genetic contributions to behavior: the value of isolating and studying basic processes, the rigor of experimental design and quantitative understanding, and a critical-realist philosophy of science that regards the goal of social science as one of successive though incomplete approximations of accurate description of the world. The other emphasizes quite different images. Here, the emphasis is on people in context. Social and contextual contributions to individual behavior are the object of study: processes are understood only in relation to the contexts in which they occur, multiple types of designs and methods are seen as preferable ways of capturing the multiple realities of individuals in differing social contexts, and philosophies of science are more likely to reflect a concern with understanding how to capture the multiple realities of people in varied contexts. This second perspective has emerged both independent of and in response to the challenges posed by human diversity to psychology and related fields.

The purpose of this chapter is to develop the concept of human diversity by drawing on the implications of this second perspective. Doing so requires us to trace how organized psychology has conceptualized the notion of diversity and how that notion has changed over time. Such a recounting sets the stage for the meaning and definition of our preferred term, *human diversity*. As the meaning of the diversity concept has changed, so have the philosophies of science that are relevant to its study. For just as attending to the diversity of individuals and groups led to a focus on new questions about human behavior, so the emergence of new philosophies of science has provided ideas for new ways of knowing. Thus, we also pay explicit attention to the emergence of new philosophies of science that promote both diverse and contextual epistemologies on which to base a psychology of human diversity.

Evolution of the Concept of Diversity in the Twentieth Century

While a complete explication of how the concept of diversity has been played out in psychological research, practice, and policy is beyond the scope of the present chapter, certain broad themes are recognizable in the dominant literature of the field over time. These changing themes represent an important aspect of the context of psychology within which a psychology of human diversity now fits.

The Early Years: Diversity as Inferiority

Perhaps the most salient image of the concept of diversity during the early part of the twentieth century involved the notion that diversity meant deviance from the norm, and deviance meant inferiority. During these years, the potential of mental measurements, particularly the assessment of intelligence, captured much energy in the psychological community. Then, as today, psychologists were eager to apply their science to the realm of social policy. Drawing on the potential value of the intelligence test developed for therapeutic and placement purposes by Théodore Simon and Alfred Binet, psychologists sought to extend their influence through use of mental testing. Their primary tasks focused on screening potential soldiers for World War I and assessing the relative intelligence of varied immigrant groups who, during the early 1900s, were entering the United States at an unprecedented rate. The upshot of the latter activity was to provide scientific data supportive of exclusionary social policies with respect to immigrants. Many scientific explanations, primarily genetic, were invoked in the service of these social policies, lending credence to the use of science as a justification for political decisions.

The history of these efforts, as well as of previous ones in the nineteenth century, is documented in varied sources. Gould (1981), for example, in *The Mismeasure of Man,* provides a telling historical account of how science, through the concept of mental measurements, served the political goals of defining diversity, both racial and gender, as inferiority. Kamin (1974), in *The Science and Politics of IQ,* eloquently reiterates the historical masking of political agendas through the use of scientific evidence and experts. More recently, both Nobles (1986) and Albee (1992) review the social role of psychology in the early twentieth century and arrive at a similar conclusion. Psychology, without explicit acknowledgment, was inextricably linked to a specific sociopolitical agenda supportive of ethnocentrism, racism, and sexism.

To be sure, some social philosophers and psychologists provided an alternative set of perspectives on the field. W.E.B. Du Bois (1935) and Franz Fanon (1967), for example, articulated perspectives on oppression and society that, by implication, devastated the dichotomy between psychology and politics maintained by influential psychologists of the time. George Sanchez (1932, 1934) wrote convincingly of the discriminatory nature of IQ tests when used with Mexican American children, a critique comparable to that provided by African American scholars.

Such critiques of the dominant paradigms and social implications of the field were not confined to people of color, however. Movements also existed within the predominantly white mainstream psychology. Of special note is the Society for the Psychological Study of Social Issues, which was founded in the 1930s and was energized by the rise of Nazi Germany. This group has, since that time, served as an organized force that focuses explicitly on the role of psychology in understanding and attempting to resolve social problems related to race and discrimination, and, more broadly, in emphasizing the social responsibility of the profession.

These varied efforts notwithstanding, the dominant image of diversity by psychology in the early years was one that supported the notion that to be different was to be inferior.

The Later Years: A Foot in the Door and the Deficit Model

It was not until the social turmoil of the 1960s, following the progress of the civil rights movement in effecting changes in both laws and expectations, that the issue of diversity surfaced as a major concern of organized psychology. Two central developments during this time were the increased access to influence of previously excluded groups of psychologists and the reemergence of diversity as deficit. Now, however, environmental determinants tended to override genetic explanations as reasons for the underlying deficit.

Access for New Voices. During the 1960s, one set of critiques of organized psychology focused on the ways in which the demographics of the field reflected broader social inequalities. Pressure was exerted on the American Psychological Association by black psychologists to promote more inclusionary practices, and the association responded with considerable efforts to integrate black psychologists into its organizational structure through participation on boards and committees. In the late 1960s, the Association of Black Psychologists was formed as an independent group to further their interests and to serve as a visible reminder to organized psychology of its accountability and constituents. These early efforts by black psychologists were soon followed by efforts by women; members of other racial and ethnic minority groups, such as Hispanic and Asian American psychologists; and later gays, lesbians, and the disabled. Each mounted critiques of the field from a distinctive vantage point, and each demanded a voice in the debate.

The dominant agenda underlying these inroads into the field was political — that is, how to gain power, affirmation, and voice. Unless each group was an influential player in the game, members had no institutional mechanism to gain credibility and to influence the more substantive aspects of the field — its theories, methods, and choice of problems. Access was thus a necessary precondition for further developments.

The Deficit Model of Diversity. During this period, the predominant conception of diversity within psychology focused on the poor and the disenfranchised. Conceptually, emphasis was placed on what has come to be called a deficit model (Ryan, 1971; Sue, Ito, & Bradshaw, 1982; White & Parham, 1990), the assumption, often implicit, that poor and minority individuals lacked the genes, culture, or personality to live a successful life. Thus, the normative standard of evaluation remained the same as in earlier years, that is, the dominant culture. However, the causes focused increasingly on sociopolitical factors such as oppression rather than on the genetic inferiority claims that had predominated fifty years earlier.

The deficit model focused attention on the needs of disenfranchised and underserved people and aided in mobilizing resources to help them. However, it relied on an environmental determinism and an implicit acceptance of the values of the dominant culture that would later form the basis for its critique.

Beyond the Deficit Model: Cultural Pluralism and an Affirming Cultural Identity

The deficit model did not fundamentally alter earlier conceptions of diversity as inferiority. However, it did provide some concepts and energy that have subsequently transformed the notion of diversity. The focus on social oppression legitimated the concept of oppression as a topic of concern for psychologists. Grier and Cobb's *Black Rage* (1968), for example, provides a vivid narrative of the implications of oppression for black well-being. The oppression concept has subsequently become fundamental to one of the primary paradigms of diversity that has developed, the sociopolitical paradigm (see Watts, 1992, Chapter Three of this volume).

Another reaction to the notion of difference as deficit was the development of perspectives highlighting the positive value of cultural and group identity rather than a deficit orientation. The black-consciousness movement with its slogan, "Black Is Beautiful," turned the notion of deficit on its head and provided the impetus for a second perspective on diversity that would evolve over time, what Watts (Chapter Three of this volume) called population-specific psychologies. *Black Psychology* (R. L. Jones, 1972) and *Chicano Psychology* (Martinez, 1977) represent examples of efforts to understand the experience of specific groups on their own terms rather than according to criteria defined by the dominant culture.

The focus on oppression influenced another key area of great relevance to the diversity field as well — identity theory. While seeing racial and ethnic identity as a topic of concern and inquiry had been long-standing (Clark & Clark, 1947; see also "Psychological Nigrescence," 1989), theorizing in the early 1970s clarified a particular role for oppression as a critical force in shaping the stages of black identity development. Thus, Cross (1971, 1978), in outlining his stage theory of black racial identity, emphasizes the fundamental nature of the encounter with the white normative standard in the evolution of this identity.

Cutting across many of the developments since the "diversity as deficit" days is another critical aspect of the evolution of the diversity concept: the contribution of culture to the human experience. Specifically, the positive aspects of culture were celebrated as topics of inquiry, and the imagery of cultural diversity replaced the earlier image of difference as deficit. With this development, the image of the United States as a melting pot has been contrasted with a "salad bowl" ideal, sometimes known as cultural pluralism (Sue & Moore, 1984).

Thus, over time, difference as deficit has been countered by various paradigms that emphasize the distinctive and positive aspects of difference. These newer models shift from an exclusive emphasis on minority status to include both culture and oppression as key concepts. They attend to and appreciate the competencies and resilience of people adapting to disenfranchising social realities. Most importantly, they provide an increasingly complex set of ideas that locate individuals in their sociocultural contexts and that consider the varied opportunities and constraints operating in them. J. M. Jones (1990) has characterized the totality of these changes as a shift from affirmative action to affirmative diversity: "Affirmative diversity is defined as the affirmation of the fundamental value of human diversity in society, with the belief that enhancing diversity increases rather than diminishes quality. . . . Human diversity is better embodied in the concept of affirmative diversity than in the concept of affirmative action. Although affirmative action addresses questions of social justice, it fails to acknowledge cultural differences (except in a pejorative way) and usually fails to accommodate to implications of these differences in culture for students, faculty, career goals, and the content and development of training" (pp. 18–20).

Perspectives on People in Context: Diversity and Majority Groups

The above perspective broadens considerably the ways in which we view diversity as being context- and culture-bound. First, such a perspective counteracts the tendency to view various groups primarily as political special-interest groups that scholars and practitioners can marginalize and focuses on the implications of diversity for the substance of psychology itself. Thus, the study of diversity per se is now acknowledged as an area of relevance to both theory and intervention. This in turn pushes for a more inclusive and less segregated place for diversity within the field.

Second, the positive emphasis on pluralism and on the cultural distinctiveness of ethnic and racial minorities has helped focus attention on the structure, values, norms, and attitudes present in the dominant culture from which all these groups differ. Within the cultural-pluralism perspective, everyone has a culture, a race, a gender, a sexual orientation, and a place in the social order. Thus, whites, men, heterosexuals, and the wealthy join those who were once considered special-interest groups as subjects of inquiry. Graham (1992), for example, discusses the image of men in this society from a historical perspective and, in the more popular literature, Bly (1990) has received considerable credit for stimulating the men's movement. Helms (1984, 1986) has set forth a theory of the development of white racial identity as an alternative to the theory of the development of black racial identity. Indeed, in a recent publication, she has even suggested that "a race is a nice thing to have" (1992).

Such theories increasingly support the value of understanding diversity within a perspective that explicitly focuses on people in context (Trickett, Watts, & Birman, 1993). This contextual perspective underlies our chosen term, *human diversity*. Before discussing that term more precisely, let us turn to another set of influences on our definition: the increasing diversity of the philosophies of science that emerged during the period when the concept of diversity was itself changing.

The Liberating Role of Multiple Methodologies and Philosophies of Science

In discussing the relation between feminism and methodology, Harding (1987) distinguishes between three related concepts: method, methodology, and epistemology. *Method* is defined as "techniques for gathering evidence," *methodology* as "a theory and analysis for how research should proceed," and *epistemology* as a theory of knowledge, which includes such questions as "Who can be a knower?" and "What tests must beliefs pass in order to be legitimated as knowledge?" (p. 2). In separating these interrelated concepts, Harding provides a useful frame for discussing the liberating role of multiple methodologies and underlying philosophies of science as they pertain to the study of diversity. She does so by reminding us that, as Kuhn (1970) has so forcefully argued, the specific methods used in conducting science are themselves embedded in and reflective of underlying worldviews that guide not only choice of method, but adequacy of method, choice of problem, and interpretation of data. She further demonstrates how viewing science primarily in terms of method alone can itself be oppressive.

Just as the meaning of the diversity concept has evolved over the past thirty years, so have the methods, methodologies, and epistemologies that guide social science research. As has been documented elsewhere (Shweder & Fiske, 1986), psychology's early history drew heavily on paradigms of the physical sciences. These paradigms emphasized control, the value of the laboratory as a setting for creating manipulable conditions, and the assumption that the investigator does not influence the phenomenon being investigated. Further, the scientist alone had the power to define the problem, construct the conditions under which data were gathered, and interpret the meaning of the data. Taken as a general paradigm, these procedures provided justification for the development of psychology as an ahistorical, acultural, and acontextual endeavor intended to discover basic psychological laws (Sarason, 1981). The positivistic philosophy of science supporting these methods underscored the notion that psychology, like the natural sciences, would adopt a building-block approach to the development of enduring generalizations about human behavior.

Beginning in the 1960s, however, this dominant paradigm came under attack from a variety of quarters. The concept of paradigm crisis was used to assess discontent within such areas as social psychology (Rosnow, 1981), child development (Bronfenbrenner, 1979), and clinical psychology (Sarason, 1981). Considerable critical work was done to unearth the latent assumptions of the basic paradigms in psychology, particularly concerning the personological bias of the field. Thus, Ryan (1971) described how the practice of psychology resulted in blaming the victim. In a similar vein, Caplan and Nelson (1973), using as an exemplar research on African Americans, suggested that because most psychological research on social problems focused on the personal qualities of those defined as having or being the problem, most policy implications addressed person-fixing rather than context-changing.

Critiques of the dominant paradigms underlying psychological research also included other issues central to the development of a psychology of human diversity. One such critique challenged the objectivity of the field's research by asserting a link between the substance of the field and the demographics of its representatives. Nobles (1986), for example, argued that, by tradition and membership, mainstream psychology was not equipped to study ethnicity among people of color because it was developed by European Americans of a different culture and social status, whose worldview differed from those of many ethnic minorities. This dominant worldview of primarily white, male, heterosexual, relatively wealthy, able-bodied people, in turn, affected the definition of problems, psychological practices, and the research process. Similar critiques were voiced in the development of the psychology of women and, more recently, of gay and lesbian psychology and the psychology of disability (Chodorow, 1978; Gilligan, 1982; Fine & Asch, 1988; Rich, 1983).

A second and related critique focused on the implausibility of ignoring the effect of the relationship between the investigator and the respondent on the nature and validity of the data. Cronbach (1986), in contrasting the natural science–based positivistic paradigm with one more appropriate for the social sciences, summed up the difference best. "Although particles are attracted to other particles," he wrote, "they don't fall in love" (p. 85). More recently, this issue has perhaps been best advanced by writings in feminist psychology, where such exemplars as Gilligan's *In a Difference Voice* (1982), Belenky, Clinchy, Goldberger, and Tarule's *Women's Ways of Knowing* (1986), and Reinharz's *Feminist Methods in Social Research* (1992) offer concrete examples of how research may benefit from adopting a different perspective on the research relationship than is captured by the historical research traditions of the field.

The Specific Role of a Social-
Constructionist Philosophy of Science

These above-mentioned critiques of the dominant paradigm have helped to legitimate the evolution of multiple ways of knowing in psychology in general and in the promotion of diversity in particular. Thus, qualitative and ethnographic research approaches are receiving increasing attention (Strauss & Corbin, 1990; Agar, 1985). With respect to diversity, Howard (1991), drawing on anthropology and ethnography, proposes a narrative or storytelling approach to understanding human action. "We are lived by the stories of our race and place," he writes. "We are, each of us, locations where the stories of our place and time become partially tellable" (p. 192).

The emergence of such perspectives as that voiced by Howard owes much to the rise of a social-constructionist philosophy of science during the same time period when the concept of diversity was evolving. This movement can be viewed as a reaction to the hegemony of method, methodology, and epistemology present in the 1960s. As the term *constructionist* implies, this approach begins with a vastly different premise about the nature of reality than is contained in logical positivism or critical realism (Cook & Campbell, 1979). Rather than attempting to discover successive approximations of objective reality, social constructionism begins with the importance of understanding how individuals construct their world through social exchange processes.

The constructionist position is well stated by Gergen (1985): "The degree to which a given form of understanding prevails or is sustained across time is not fundamentally dependent on the empirical validity of the perspective in question, but on the vicissitudes of social processes (e.g. communications, negotiation, conflict, rhetoric)" (p. 268). Within this perspective, emphasis centers on the processes through which information is gathered, the relationship among those participating in these exchange processes, issues of reciprocal influence and accommodation, the values of all parties in the interactions, and the place in the social order of those involved in the construction of reality. Here, individuals are active creators and definers of their realities, not passive respondents or victims of environmental circumstance.

More specifically, such a perspective suggests that social constructions reflect the social niches and ideological interests of their constructors. Therefore, the constructions of powerful people and interests can play a critical role in maintaining the current social order. The philosophical foundations of this perspective are captured by Paulo Freire (1990):

> The normal role of human beings in and with the world is not a passive one. . . . [They] participate in the creative dimension as well; men can intervene in reality in order to change it. . . . *Integration*[,] as distinguished from *adaptation*, . . . results from the capacity to adapt oneself to reality *plus* the critical capacity to make choices and to transform that reality. To the extent that man loses his ability to make choices and is subjected to the choices of others[, that is,] from external prescriptions, he is no longer integrated. Rather, he is adapted. He has "adjusted" [p. 4; emphasis in original].

Within this perspective, the construction of reality is a political act compounded by the degree to which it is imposed on one population by another. Thus, the development of critical consciousness to recognize worldviews is an essential part of the process of social change. Social constructionism has thus served as an intellectual critique of the positivist position that truth is objective and unrelated to the relationship between the knowledge provider and the knowledge gatherer. Applied to issues of diversity, it has served as a reminder that the dominant methods of psychological research, the problems selected as important to pursue, and the demographics of the data gatherers have conspired against developing a psychology of individuals that emerges from the experiences and perspectives of those who occupy different places in the social order. It not only opens up the role of qualitative inquiry as an essential component of understanding but promotes a variety of questions both about individuals in varied social contexts and about the relationship of researchers to those individuals.

Walsh (1987), in a paper discussing the research relationship in community psychology, captures nicely the spirit of constructionist imagery in conducting community research. In so doing, he amplifies on Harding's perspective that methods themselves can be oppressive or empowering (see also Rappaport, 1990). According to Walsh:

> Active control and responsibility for one's social and mental health, basic values in the subdiscipline [community psychology], imply that community psychologists must engage in democratic action *with* citizens, not bureaucratic action *for* them. . . . The communal approach to research is harmonious not only with the profession's ethical values but also with the revised philosophy of science. . . . In the natural sciences tradition . . . the underlying epistemology is that rigorously objective detachment is essential to insure reliability and validity and that gathering knowledge does not affect nor is affected by the human context in which the investigation occurs. . . . By contrast, in the revised philosophy of science . . . human inquiry is essentially transactional in nature. It is distinguished by reciprocal influence between any given investigation and the particular social context in which it is embedded. . . . Knowledge-gathering is an inherently interpersonal process that enhances, not detracts from, objectivity, since a research relationship of exchange strengthens both the internal and external validity of the investigation. . . . This epistemological framework, therefore, is more suited to community psychology than the natural sciences paradigm [pp. 783–784].

Perspectives on People in Context:
Dimensions of the Concept of Human Diversity

Taken together, the above-mentioned changes in the diversity
concept and accompanying ways of knowing over the past thirty
years provide a framework for the development of a psychology of human diversity. This framework places diversity in a
social context and includes the following orienting ideas. First,
it extends beyond the frequently used terms *cultural, ethnic,* and
racial to stress that issues of oppression and disenfranchisement
extend beyond cultural or ethnic groups to include people discriminated against for reasons other than their race or ethnicity. Thus, discrimination based on age, gender, or sexual orientation is explicitly included. In so doing, the framework looks
for both similarities and differences in the experiences of varied
groups. Further, while neither denying nor minimizing the importance of individual differences within groups, the framework
asserts the importance of understanding group identity and
group identification not only as potentially important aspects
of group life, but also as markers that affect experience in the
broader society as well. A human diversity perspective does not,
however, imply that the history or depth of oppression for these
populations is equivalent, because the ranges and foci of different groups' experiences are distinct.

Second, the term *diversity* offers some advantages over the
terms *minority, oppressed,* and *disadvantaged* because it conveys a
positive regard for human differences. It further encourages a
focus on culture, resilience, and strength as well as on the consequences of oppression. Third, because we are all people in
context, the diversity concept is extended to include members
of the so-called dominant culture as well. The concept of the
dominant culture thus becomes an object of deconstruction that
not only takes into account its oppressive aspects but also places
the varied group and cultural identifications of whites in context. The notion of diversity promotes an inclusive exploration
of people in context and mitigates against developing a psychology that marginalizes nonprivileged groups as special interests.

In the human diversity paradigm, *all* populations and world-views are subject to inquiry.

Conclusion

Together, these emphases highlight the importance of concepts such as oppression, culture, intergroup relations, and identity as being central to the development of a psychology of human diversity. They suggest the value of understanding how our multiple group identifications become activated in varied social settings, and how the history of our field and culture is reflected in current policies, structures, and norms. In sum, they suggest a central emphasis on research and practice that conceptualizes diversity in a contextual framework.

Yet the human diversity perspective also underscores the importance of methodology in understanding how diversity is expressed. It affirms that methods used to generate information should be congruent with the value assumptions underlying the diversity concept. Thus, it supports methods that can appreciate diversity from the inside out and applauds those kind of collaborations that empower rather than objectify the people we wish to understand. As the concept of human diversity is elaborated, let it include attention to both the content and the process by which we proceed.

References

Agar, M. (1985). *Speaking of ethnography.* Newbury Park, CA: Sage.

Albee, G. (1992, Aug.). Psychological origins of the white male patriarchy. In I. Prilleltensky (Chair), *Discrimination and antidemocratic forces in the history of American psychology.* Symposium conducted at the annual meeting of the American Psychological Association, Washington, DC.

Belenky, M. F., Clinchy, B. M., Goldberger, N. R., & Tarule, J. M. (1986). *Women's ways of knowing.* New York: Basic Books.

Bly, R. (1990). *Iron John*. New York: Vintage Books.

Bronfenbrenner, U. (1979). *The ecology of human development: Experiments by nature and design*. Cambridge, MA: Harvard University Press.

Caplan, N., & Nelson, S. D. (1973). On being useful: The nature and consequences of psychological research on social problems. *American Psychologist, 28,* 199–211.

Chodorow, N. J. (1978). *The reproduction of mothering*. Berkeley: University of California Press.

Clark, K. B., & Clark, M. P. (1947). Racial identification and preference in Negro children. In T. M. Newcomb & E. L. Hartley (Eds.), *Readings in social psychology* (pp. 169–178). Troy, Mo.: Holt, Rinehart & Winston.

Cook, T. D., & Campbell, D. T. (1979). *Quasi-experimentation: Design and analysis issues for field settings*. Boston: Houghton Mifflin.

Cronbach, L. J. (1986). Social inquiry by and for earthlings. In D. W. Fiske & R. A. Shweder (Eds.), *Metatheory in social science: Pluralisms and subjectivities* (pp. 83–107). Chicago: University of Chicago Press.

Cross, W. (1971). The Negro to black conversion experience. *Black World, 20,* 13–27.

Cross, W. (1978). The Thomas and Cross models of psychological nigrescence: A review. *Journal of Black Psychology, 5,* 13–31.

Du Bois, W.E.B. (1935). *Black reconstruction*. Orlando, FL: Harcourt Brace Jovanovich.

Fanon, F. (1967). *Black skin, white masks*. New York: Grove Press.

Fine, M., & Asch, A. (Eds.). (1988). *Women with disabilities*. Philadelphia: Temple University Press.

Freire, P. (1990). *Education for a critical consciousness*. New York: Continuum.

Gergen, K. (1985). The social constructionist movement in modern psychology. *American Psychologist, 40,* 266–275.

Gilligan, C. (1982). *In a different voice*. Cambridge, MA: Harvard University Press.

Gould, S. J. (1981). *The mismeasure of man*. New York: W.W.Norton.

Graham, S. R. (1992). What docs a man want? *American Psychologist, 47,* 837–841.

Grier, W. H., & Cobb, P. M. (1968). *Black rage.* New York: Basic Books.

Harding, S. (1987). Is there a feminist method? In S. Harding (Ed.), *Feminism and methodology.* Bloomington: Indiana University Press.

Helms, J. E. (1984). Towards a theoretical explanation of the effects of race on counseling: Black/white interactional model. *The Counseling Psychologist, 12*(4), 153–165.

Helms, J. E. (1986). Expanding racial identity theory to cover counseling process. *Journal of Counseling Psychology, 33,* 62–64.

Helms, J. E. (1992). *A race is a nice thing to have.* Topeka, KS: Content Communications.

Howard, G. S. (1991). Culture tales: A narrative approach to thinking, cross-cultural psychology, and psychotherapy. *American Psychologist, 46,* 187–197.

Jones, J. M. (1990). Who is training our ethnic minority psychologists and are they doing it right? In G. Stricker and others (Eds.), *Toward ethnic diversification in psychology education and training.* Washington, DC: American Psychological Association.

Jones, R. L. (Ed.). (1972). *Black psychology.* New York: Harper-Collins.

Kamin, L. J. (1974). *The science and politics of IQ.* Hillsdale, NJ: Erlbaum.

Kuhn, T. H. (1970). *The structure of scientific revolutions.* Chicago: University of Chicago Press.

Loo, C. (1991). *Chinatown: Most time, hard time.* New York: Praeger.

Martinez, J. L., Jr. (Ed.). (1977). *Chicano psychology.* San Diego, Calif.: Academic Press.

Nobles, W. (1986). *African psychology.* Oakland, CA: Black Family Institute.

Psychological nigrescence. (1989). *The Counseling Psychologist, 17*(2) [Special issue].

Rappaport, J. (1990). Research methods and the empowerment social agenda. In P. Tolan, C. Keys, F. Chertok, & L. Jason

(Eds.), *Researching community psychology: Issues of theory and methods*. Washington, DC: American Psychological Association.

Reinharz, S. (1992). *Feminist methods in social research*. New York: Oxford University Press.

Rich, A. (1983). Compulsory heterosexuality and the lesbian experience. In E. Abel & E. Abel (Eds.), *The Signs reader: Women, gender, and scholarship*. Chicago: University of Chicago Press.

Rosnow, R. L. (1981). *Paradigms in transition*. New York: Oxford University Press.

Ryan, W. (1971). *Blaming the victim*. New York: Vintage Books.

Sanchez, G. I. (1932). Group differences in Spanish-speaking children: A critical view. *Journal of Applied Psychology, 16,* 549–558.

Sanchez, G. I. (1934). Bilingualism and mental measures. *Journal of Applied Psychology, 18,* 765–772.

Sarason, S. B. (1981). *Psychology misdirected*. New York: Free Press.

Shweder, R. A., & Fiske, D. W. (Eds.). (1986). *Metatheory in social science: Pluralisms and subjectivities*. Chicago: University of Chicago Press.

Strauss, A., & Corbin, J. (1990). *Basics of qualitative research*. Newbury Park, CA: Sage.

Sue, S., Ito, J., & Bradshaw, C. (1982). Ethnic minority research: Trends and directions. In E. E. Jones & S. J. Korchin (Eds.), *Minority mental health* (pp. 37–58). New York: Praeger.

Sue, S., & Moore, T. (1984). *The pluralistic society*. New York: Human Sciences Press.

Trickett, E. J., Watts, R., & Birman, D. (1993). Human diversity and community psychology: Still hazy after all these years. *Journal of Community Psychology, 21,* 264–279.

Walsh, R. T. (1987). The evolution of the research relationship in community psychology. *American Journal of Community Psychology, 15,* 773–788.

Watts, R. (1992). Elements of a psychology of human diversity. *Journal of Community Psychology, 20,* 116–131.

White, J., & Parham, T. (1990). *The psychology of blacks*. Englewood Cliffs, NJ: Prentice-Hall.

2

Our Similarities
Are Different:
Toward a Psychology
of Affirmative Diversity

James M. Jones

When he was asked to compare himself with his famous father Yogi, Dale Berra observed: "I am a lot like him, only our similarities are different!" I was quite taken with this observation, because on its surface, it appears to be nonrational, but in its essence, it defines a major issue in the debates about diversity. Specifically, the apparent nonrationality of this statement is so judged because of our cultural penchant for dichotomous, absolute logical thinking. When we address issues of diversity, we are forced to deal with an either/or option that pits similarity against difference. This oppositional stance leads many to conclude that "celebrating diversity" emphasizes differences and, by so doing, diminishes the common ground we share. The real task before us is to find a way to advance difference and similarity simultaneously!

It is my contention that the approach of psychology toward understanding human behavior has been flawed because it has made the assumption that similarities between people are opposite from the differences between them. Our conceptual, methodological, and statistical approaches operate so that the more difference we discover, the less similarity we posit. Conversely, the more alike things are, the less different they are. The result of this way of thinking inevitably pits difference against similarity.

This chapter will argue for a synthetic approach to diversity that emphasizes the simultaneity of similarity and difference. I will use the field of experimental social psychology to illustrate the limitations of traditional psychological approaches and to suggest how they can be modified and extended to improve the prospects for an emergent psychology of human diversity.

Marilynn Brewer's theory of optimum differentiation (1991) makes an excellent start in this direction. She postulates twin human needs for uniqueness (difference) and belonging (similarity), which we attempt to balance over time through a self-correcting hydraulic mechanism. When extremes of uniqueness lead to aloneness, we seek belonging and the companionship of others. When extremes of belonging cause us to lose our identity and self-awareness, we emphasize our uniqueness. These mechanisms modulate over time to create a dynamic balance between similarity and difference, belonging and uniqueness.

A similar perspective is voiced by Vernon Dixon (1976) in his assessment of the cultural basis of African American behavior. In his analysis of the nature of worldview, he suggests two critical concepts: (1) symbolic affective imagery as the basis of acquisition and utilization of personal knowledge and (2) "di-unitality," the union of opposites as a logical structure that enables knowledge to represent the duality of life processes — life and death. In the epistemology of African cultural philosophy, good is not opposed to evil; instead, the two are obverse aspects of a single reflection of being. As with Brewer's analysis, opposing processes are linked, united, or combined into one dynamic process or structural whole.

This dynamic goal is represented by the dialectal processes through which a status quo or thesis is challenged by a new way of thinking that seeks to negate or undo it — to use the Hegelian discourse, the antithetical argument. The antithesis makes possible a new vision that challenges the power base of the traditional way, whether we speak of scientific tradition or the hegemony of scientific method and discourse. Defenders of the status quo fight to preserve the tradition; the revolutionaries fight to change, undo, or usurp it. The consequence of this dynamic process is a new synthetic outcome that combines both viewpoints but diverges from each of them.

The challenge of a psychology of diversity is, in my mind, the challenge of this synthetic possibility. Virtually all approaches to formulating a psychology of human diversity begin with a deconstructionist attack on the status quo that may be, to borrow from Watts's cogent analysis (1992), population-specific, sociopolitical, cross-cultural, or ecological. A political Maginot Line is drawn in this battle when the status quo is radically deconstructed to nothingness — the baby follows the bathwater down the drain. Perhaps the insecurity of facing attack and potential loss of power causes defensive reactions by the traditionalists. Maybe their passionate belief in the demonstrated success of the traditional scientific paradigm commands loyalty. But the more assertively the traditionalists defend, the more aggressively the revolutionaries attack.

In this chapter I will first discuss some of the problems with the dominant paradigm of psychological theory and research when it is applied to questions of race, ethnicity, gender, and other dimensions of diversity. Second, I will briefly review the issues to be considered in creating a psychology of human thought and behavior that takes human diversity into account. Third, and finally, I will synthesize these remarks in an approach I call affirmative diversity.

Problems with the Paradigm of Psychology as It Relates to Human Diversity

The basic, overriding problem with the dominant paradigm of psychology is the overvaluation of the experimental scientific paradigm with its correlated nomothetic, theory-driven, hypothetico-deductive methodologies. I do not argue that this positivist theme should be replaced but, instead, that if it is considered the *only* legitimate means of acquiring knowledge it will do a disservice to developing a psychology of human diversity. Let me list some aspects of this approach and reasons why it can be problematic.

Race as a Variable

The experimental paradigm subjects race and (and other demographic or social-status variables) to second-class status as an
experimental variable. When I was in graduate school, two comments of colleagues and mentors stood out. The first was that
we experimental social psychologists were not interested in people but in variables. The second was that race was not a variable. Since we cannot manipulate race (that is, randomly assign
subjects to racial conditions), it is less interesting theoretically.
For a young, black would-be psychologist, who went to graduate school to learn the techniques of a discipline I thought offered
promise as a means of better understanding and ultimately
ameliorating race relations in this country, this was sobering
indeed.

The Psychosocial Aspects of Race

When we do treat race as an independent variable, it is on the
basis of phenotypical categorical aspects, not the psychosocial
dimensions of experience. The biology of race is probably its
least important aspect but its most prominent feature in the
paradigm of psychological science. I (Jones, 1991) and many
others (for example, Zuckerman, 1990) have noted the relative
insignificance of a biological basis of race, and indeed, the politics
of race emphasize much more the sociological, social, perceptual, and cultural aspects (Jones, 1991). Research that purports
to be about race but fails to capture the individual, interpersonal, and cultural dimensions is likely to be simple-minded.
    For example, Sagar and Schofield (1980) sought to test
the idea that blacks were perceived to be more aggressive than
whites. Ambiguous acts (tapping on the back with a pencil,
bumping someone in the hall, asking for a piece of cake) were
associated by photograph randomly with a black or white sixth-
grade boy. Black and white sixth-grade boys were asked to judge
the extent to which the acts were aggressive and/or a cause for
fear. The research design was a 2 × 2 factorial, using the race
of the actor and the race of the judge. The results showed two

main effects: black actors were judged to be more aggressive and white judges perceived actors generally to be more aggressive. The absence of an interaction led the authors to conclude that there was a generalized tendency for both black and white boys to perceive black boys as more aggressive.

I offered an alternative cultural interpretation of these findings (Jones, 1983) that emphasized within-group judgments as a baseline and other-group judgments as deviations from the baseline. Within-culture black judgments of black actors and white judgments of white actors were almost identical, with means of 8.4 and 8.3, respectively. However, by comparison, black judges' between-culture ratings of white actors were significantly lower (7.4), while white judges' between-culture ratings of black actors were significantly higher (9.0) than the corresponding within-culture ratings. This suggests that each group saw its own members as similarly aggressive, with blacks seeing whites as less so and whites seeing blacks as more so.

The authors' interpretation of these results supported a universal stereotype of black boys being more aggressive. In so doing, they exaggerated the differences between these boys, because subjects were divided into black and white on the basis of phenotypical social categories, and their experience was perceived as nonoverlapping. However, in my reinterpretation, I made a cultural assumption and found that black and white subjects were similar in their judgments of in-group members. Once a baseline of similarity was established, the *real* differences could be exposed. This example illustrates the fact that both similarities and differences can be uncovered and both advance our understanding of the complexity of human diversity.

Reliance on biological conceptualization of race leads to a failure to embed race in the experience that creates its sociopolitical and cultural aspects. For example, one explanation for why research findings may confirm racial stereotypes is the self-fulfilling prophecy. Word, Zanna, and Cooper (1974) showed that the behavior of people who occupy a salient social status is partially a function of the expectancies others have for their behavior. In their study, white Princeton University subjects treated black high school students differently from white high school students with respect to certain nonverbal cues of liking. These authors subsequently showed that when white college students were treated in similarly different ways (that is, in nonverbal ways that suggested liking or not-liking), performance in a job interview deteriorated for those treated negatively relative to those treated positively. This experiment was thus able to show that a biased white person could produce the inferior behavior she or he expects, which would then validate that person's expectation and legitimate a negative hiring decision. This analysis takes us below the superficial factors of skin color and identifies underlying psychological processes that *explain* behavior (see Snyder, Tanke, & Berscheid, 1977, for an aspect of this for women).

Further, we fail to account for ways in which the cultural expectancies of members of the social-status group affect their behavior. If I expect that you expect me to fail, I may be inclined to fail. Moreover, my perceptions of myself may also depend in part on my expectations of you. Crocker and Major (1989) capture this idea in their research on attributional ambiguity. In their research, negative feedback had an adverse impact on the self-esteem of blacks, but only if the whites providing that feedback were *unaware* of the target's racial identification. When blacks believed that whites were aware of their race, negative feedback did not have diagnostic value and correspondingly had little impact on self-esteem. Crocker and Major argue that this psychological dynamic can explain why blacks do not show massive lowered self-esteem in the face of widely documented stigmatization.

Avoiding Person-Blame Explanations

The individual level of analysis often leaves us to explain problem behaviors in terms of individuals rather than interactional or social structure influences. Social psychology has been concerned with race in part because it has been a consistent, pernicious, and ubiquitous social problem in America for centuries. The social action legacy, tied to the empirical and theoretical base of the discipline, is responsible for some of the most significant advances we have made. However, some perhaps unintended consequences of this focus yield a lose-lose proposition.

In trying to right social wrongs, the tendency is to focus on the deficiencies of both the so-called perpetrators of the problem, such as prejudiced personalities and biased cognitive processes, and the so-called victims, such as self-hatred, dysfunctional families, and the culture of poverty. The scientific goal of this research becomes one of identifying these deficiencies for the sake of changing the debilitating behavior. Instead, it is important to find concepts and procedures with which to address social problems that do not automatically assume the worst in people. Such approaches must focus on both the strengths of individuals and the ways in which social processes and structures can be the object of inquiry and change. This, in my mind, is one of the big challenges in a psychology of human diversity — to be an instrument not only for the amelioration of human social problems, but for the elevation of the good qualities of human beings.

Avoiding Cross-Cultural Generalizations

Generalizing scientific findings often works against understanding and learning from the diversity of human beings. The idea that certain traits or human capacities are universal and normally distributed can be used to mean that individuals or groups who fall below the mean in this distribution have less of the attribute. For those attributes thought to make positive contributions to society, this can translate to the idea that some individuals are inherently inferior.

William McDougall addressed this issue in his 1921 book, *Is America Safe for Democracy?* McDougall's premise was evaluated by considering the basis for the ascendancy of nations to world domination. There were two rival hypotheses: (1) the economic thesis, which proposed that favorable conditions such as access to sea lanes and natural resources created ideal conditions that were exploited by a people to achieve dominant world status, and (2) the anthropological thesis, which suggested that the genetic composition of a people caused them to rise to exalted levels, thus conferring biological and characterological superiority on them. McDougall opted for the anthropological explanation, citing Africa as an example of a continent with superior economic opportunities that nevertheless failed to produce world dominance. The title of his book addressed the question of whether America could afford to be genetically democratic and thus possibly sow the seeds of its own dissolution. The attributes that he felt made America great (introversion, curiosity, providence, and intellectual capabilities) were precisely those he found wanting in immigrant groups and indigenous groups such as African Americans.

When we assess the variables that rise to the top today as measures of capacity or desirable functioning, we find that they are remarkably similar to those suggested by McDougall. Will (control), providence (hoarding or delay of gratification), introversion (individualism, lack of sociability), curiosity (need cognition), and, of course, intelligence describe not only McDougall's list of superior attributes or temperament, but contemporary psychological analysis. Generalizing the desirability of these attributes across human groups leads inexorably to differential valuation and assignment of competence. A psychology of diversity is, at best, hampered by the form and substance of this sort of analysis.

In an effort to demonstrate the limitations of such cross-cultural generalizations, one study (Chinese Culture Connection, 1987) sought to determine if the typical finding that Western-derived constructs can explain non-Western patterns of behavior could be reversed. That is, could a construct developed in a non-Western culture explain any meaningful Western behavior? Indeed, a Chinese Value Survey developed in Hong Kong with Chinese subjects who had no regard for Western concepts produced four factors: integration (broadly interactive, stabilizing culture of trust, noncompetition, tolerance, and harmony), Confucian work dynamism (thrift, persistence, order, and shame), human-heartedness (kindness, patience, and courtesy) and moral discipline (moderation, purity, and denial). Three of these factors were highly correlated with Western value concepts derived by Hofstede (1980), suggesting comparability across cultures.

The point of this example is to show that it is possible to discover universally meaningful characteristics by considering one culture from the emic perspective of another. However, as this study so creatively illustrated, any culture can be used as a standard from which universal characteristics are investigated, not just the Western societies that have traditionally compared other cultures to their own on their own terms.

The Limitations of Scientific Methods

Scientific methods and statistical procedures are generally better suited for demonstrating differences than discerning similarities. The notion of normal distributions and central-tendency comparisons interacts with the tendency to dichotomize ends of a continuum as separate and distinct. Black-white IQ differences are a full standard deviation apart on average, but there is nevertheless an 80 percent overlap between blacks and whites in their IQ scores. By emphasizing differences, we fail to appreciate the preponderant effects of similarity.

The null hypothesis is designed to work best when it can make an unequivocal claim of difference. Statistical "success" occurs when such a claim can be made. Because difference is what we seek, we establish a low cutoff for statistical probabilities to protect against a Type I error — claiming difference when we really do not have it.

The significance of human diversity rests, in my judgment, in both the similarities and differences that exist between and among human beings. Our statistics are designed to detect our differences, but our similarities may be the basis for our common humanity. In general, our statistics do not help us to make these claims very well.

Summary

The questions raised by this general critique and analysis concern the nature of the problem with the current scientific paradigm. This critique includes the limitations of the individual level of analysis for understanding the diversity of human experience.

It also cautions against considering social status in superficial, demographic terms without considering in depth the context and meaning of each individual's social niche. It cautions against generalizations that can cover up important differences and, conceptually, patterns of similarity as well. Finally, the variables we study are, in fact, culture-specific and culturally defined. In the absence of translations across cultures that establish parity and similarity, we end up with a kind of cultural hegemony that establishes a comparative paradigm with certain culturally defined variables at the apex. Deviations across human groups, by this analysis, almost always become the basis for assessing deficiency or incapacity. We will achieve greater success and a more inclusive understanding of human behavior when we learn from the diversity of human experience, rather than stifling it by forcing it into cultural templates that we think represent superior forms of human behavior.

Implications for a Psychology of Human Diversity

In developing a psychology of diversity, it is clearly not possible to take into account each of the many dimensions on which human beings differ. However, as William McGuire has observed, "If you have a pretzel shaped world, you need pretzel shaped theories to explain it" (McGuire, personal communication, September 1990). The paradigm of Western psychology is not sufficiently pretzel-like because it has not looked systematically at some of the most obvious dimensions upon which humans differ or, rather, it has not looked at them in a useful way. Diversity introduces error in a neat science of nomothetic generalizations.

There are two ways in which the limitations of the traditional scientific paradigm have implications for a science of diversity. First, the role of culture and context is seen as critical in understanding and explaining the diversity of human behavior. Second, alternative methodological approaches are necessary that will emphasize multiple sources of causality and more in-depth analysis. So where should a science of diversity look for data and how would the search be organized?

Cultural and Contextual Effects on Human Diversity

Culture and context are emerging again as conspicuous candidates for explaining human behavior. Among recent volumes in social psychology, culture is a dominant theme (Triandis, 1994; Smith & Bond, 1994; Lonner & Malpass, 1994; Matsumoto, 1994; Moghaddam, Taylor, & Wright, 1993). Context has been conceptualized by Cohen and Siegel (1991) as social systems, physical environment, the thing in which individuals function, and the evolution over time of all three. Context cannot ultimately be distinguished or disconnected from the individuals who function in it. The transactional, ecological approach to behavior is what has perhaps evolved into our contemporary concern with context.

Diversity is an element of this evolution into culture and context. However, diversity is often viewed primarily as a political process and therefore is often presumed on its face to be illegitimate science. To ultimately build a science of diversity will require that we get past this trivialization of diversity and embed the arguments in the substantive concepts and methods of inquiry into things like culture and context, structure and change over time, ecologies, and transactions. These contexts include different levels of analysis, such as the family, the community, and the larger society.

Family Socialization

Efforts to understand within-family socialization must be rooted in the diverse ecologies of different groups. Some psychological findings seem to apply across diverse cultural groups, such as the findings that firstborns differ from other children on numerous dimensions, that gender roles can be established within the first few months of life, and that lower-income families use physical punishment more than middle- and higher-income families. However, differences exist among people who are products of similar families and larger ecologies. In poor urban settings, some children emerge with psychic strength and a will to overcome, while others seem to give up and place themselves at the

mercy of extant destructive forces. Such similarities and differences are both instructive about human dynamic processes.

Moore (1986) showed that black middle-class adoptive
children in white homes had higher IQ scores than black children in black adoptive homes, suggesting that the IQ tests reflect,
in part, cultural differences represented along racial lines. Do
black mothers socialize their children racially (Peters, 1988) and,
if so, how does this relate to the so-called generalized capacities
of abstract thought and analysis? We need to understand the
role that within-family socialization plays in the unfolding of
human behavior across diverse cultures and ethnic groups.

Community Socialization

An emphasis on within-community socialization rests on the assertion that factors beyond biology and family contribute significantly to human behavior. Plomin and colleagues have advanced the provocative notion of unshared social environments
to show that familial siblings acquire over 50 percent of their
characteristics from interactions they do not share with their
brothers and sisters. They assert that about 40 percent are linked
to inherited qualities, 10 percent to commonly shared socialization and experience, and 50 percent to experiences unique to
each. The point is that diversity of unshared environments is
the norm and accounts for much of the variance in human behavior. We may routinely overinterpret the common effects of similar contexts and environments and thus fail to appreciate the
uniqueness that each person experiences. The more generalizations we make, the more we may miss the important influences
in individual lives. One implication of this perspective is that you
cannot expect a universal racial or socioeconomic label to fully
capture the shared experience. We must represent this element
of diversity in our models and schemes of human behavior in
ways that capture the richness and true diversity of experience.

Subcultural and Cultural Influences

Culture influences behavior in a myriad of important ways that
determine the style, the tools, and the expectancies that drive

human behavior (Triandis, 1994; Smith & Bond, 1994). For example, research on social loafing (Latane, Williams, & Harkins, 1979) in this country suggests that individuals work less hard in group situations, where their individual level of effort is more difficult to discern than when they are working alone. However, the opposite tendency is observed in other cultures; individuals work harder in group settings than in individual settings (Gabrenya, Wang, & Latane, 1985).

It has also been found that students in the United States are most happy when they achieve individual success, but in Japan, happiness is intimately linked to engagement with others and mutual outcomes (Markus & Kitayama, 1991).

Intercultural Contact

The interaction of individuals and groups from different cultural contexts affects people individually as well as the groups to which they belong. The nature of intercultural contact can influence the development of cultural values and strategies, as well as the adaptational requirements for individuals. Describing a pattern of intercultural contact in the hometown of his youth, a former university president noted to a group of black faculty, "I did not grow up learning to hate blacks, there weren't many of them around. I learned to hate Polacks."

Diversity means that people who are different will interact with each other with outcomes that are not always easy to predict. Contact itself may sow the seeds of conflict or compassion. The net effect is that our models of human interaction cannot be one-sided or one-dimensional. We cannot study prejudice among whites, for example, by only looking at whites! We have done that for several decades, and now, when increasingly large numbers of whites profess a desire to rid themselves of bias and bigotry, they come up against historical victims who do not accept their good intentions. By looking at reciprocal influences, we find that "solutions" inspired by decades of research, which indicate decategorization, individuation, and the like as a means of breaking down group-based stereotypes and corresponding conflicts, may not work. Intergroup relations must be transacted, not dictated. Our science of diversity must accurately reflect the experiences of *all* parties, not just those who, for whatever reason, are placed at center stage.

Psychosocially Meaningful Variation

The self-fulfilling prophecy clearly shows that stereotypical expectations can cause behavior in a target person that, in turn, reinforces the stereotypical expectation originally held. This recursive process can sustain behaviors over a long period of time. Thus, to understand diversity, we must also understand not only the development of socialization effects that emerge from particular identifiable contexts such as family, community, and culture, but the interactive and reciprocal dynamics to which we respond. People differ in the extent to which the self-fulfilling prophecy may influence their behaviors. Its effects can operate in both negative and positive ways. Therefore, one strategy for change could well be to simply modify expectations and observe changes in behavior.

I have focused on elements of diversity that have a broad impact on behavior and that could greatly benefit through the application of analytic paradigms focusing on the impact of diversity on behavior. It should be clear that each of these factors interacts with the others. Any final epistemological approach must discover ways of looking at overlapping and reciprocal influences across these domains and levels of analysis.

Methodological Implications for Issues of Human Diversity

Undertaking a complex analysis of human diversity necessitates a modification of our primary methodological strategies and assumptions. I see three areas in which this can be important: the variables we study, the analytic approaches we take, and the statistical procedures and underlying assumptions we employ.

Variables We Study

The independent and dependent variables thought to be important in psychology derive from the questions we believe it is important to answer. If we ask different questions, we are likely to formulate different variables to study. Among the prominent variables in standard psychological investigations are performance, expectations, values, goals, abilities, personality, and motivation. For the most part, they are framed from the perspective of how they contribute to successful adaptation (mainstream functioning in this society) or unsuccessful adaptation (deficient performance in mainstream society). To do this we need to add variables that reflect political perspectives that are adopted and adapted to living as a political minority (in a power sense), where one's social status is demeaned at the same time that universal messages of opportunity are extolled. This double-bind or conflict situation can be understood as a psychosocial variable with behavioral consequences. To some extent, acculturation is a variable that addresses it.

We also need to explore variables that reflect adaptation to particular ecological environments. Successful functioning can and does occur in environments that are not typical of the normative or mainstream environments represented in much of our theorizing and research. How do intelligent people negotiate these environments and what attributes do they utilize in doing so?

Analytic Approaches

The analytic approaches we employ must be responsive to the diversity, complexity, and multifaceted nature of our experience. First, models for these analyses should include dialectical discourse in which conflict production and resolution are seen as part of the process of growth and development. The dialectic between conflict and resolution is central to many stage theories of development (Erikson, 1968). However, with respect to diversity, the dimensions of in-group, out-group, and we-they are of central importance as conflicting driving forces that require resolution. The goal of such analyses is a synthetic understanding of how diverse aspects of social status, culture, socialization, gender, and other areas are integrated in the psychological makeup of people. Further, we want to know the behavioral consequences of such integration. Concepts such as androgyny and biculturalism reflect this dialectical-discourse model.

Second, with respect to research design, longitudinal tracking and cohort analysis are necessary to tease out the relative influences of diverse experiences on human behavior. As cultural contexts and influences change, specific socialization effects unfold, and the effects of the self-fulfilling prophecy accumulate, we need to employ designs capable of understanding behavior as the result of all these forces.

Third, the dialectic referred to above assumes that causation is bidirectional and caused by multiple factors. The development of methods for assessing such interactions and multiple influences is a critical methodological and conceptual issue. Conceptual frameworks and statistical methods that reflect either/or dichotomous thinking should be expanded to include techniques that do not presume unidirectional causality or bipolar, intraindividual accounts of human nature. Our variables must be constructed from the range of contexts and enviro ments that influence behavior. The goal is to discover patter of influence that affect a range of behaviors over time and across situations, rather than to find single cause-and-effect relationships between single unit variables and specific behaviors. Diversity of influence may also be revealed in diversity of behavior, so we must be able to detect behavioral variability as well.

Finally, it is necessary to avoid *main-effect* comparisons of groups defined solely by nominal categories if we are to understand the dynamic influences of diversity. What does it mean to compare a sample of men and a sample of women in a Psychology 101 class? What about all the other ways in which they may differ or be similar? Such main-effect comparisons oversimplify complex factors of diversity and thus mislead people into stereotypical judgments.

Conclusion

Let me close by suggesting a perspective that captures the spirit and essence of my previous comments: affirmative diversity. Affirmative diversity is the focused attempt to discover ways in which the diversity of experience of human beings contributes to resilience and strength and to improved capacities of performance within both individuals and groups. Within individuals, we look for ways in which adapting to conflicting or hostile environments, integrating competing values, and finding instrumental ways of achieving success can broaden the spectrum of behavioral possibilities and create a stronger, more resilient, human being.

Affirmative diversity addresses the possibility that collectivities or groups are strengthened by the diversity of their individual members. It seeks to develop strategies for implementing institutional decision making consistent with that proposition — that human diversity is a positive value in institutional development and performance.

To achieve affirmative diversity, we must continually struggle with the dialectic between similarity and difference with which I began this chapter. That our similarities are different means that we do the same things differently. We all raise children to be bearers of our culture; we seek self-esteem and a sense of validation. But we do it in different ecological realities, responding to local rather than universal challenges that lend a distinctiveness to our adaptation and survival. The task of affirmative diversity is to discover the universal without demanding uniformity and to affirm that this difference is positive while acknowledging a potential common sense of humanity. Doing so will avoid the trap of radical cultural relativism and allow us to widen the envelope of human capacities and potentials without requiring an invidious comparison of difference to dominant cultural norms.

We have given much lip service to the notion of human diversity as a value and a good in society and in the world. But we have not, through disciplined inquiry, demonstrated exactly how diversity confers strengths to us as individuals and as a society. The goal of affirmative diversity is to legitimate and promote this inquiry and the values underlying it.

References

Brewer, M. B. (1991). The social self: On being the same and different at the same time. *Personality and Social Psychology Bulletin, 17,* 475–482.

Chinese Culture Connection. (1987). Chinese values and the search for culture-free dimensions of culture. *Journal of Cross-Cultural Psychology, 10,* 143–164.

Cohen, R., & Siegel, A. W. (Eds.). (1991). *Context and development.* Hillsdale, NJ: Erlbaum.

Crocker, J., & Major, B. (1989). Social stigma and self-esteem. *Psychological Review, 96,* 608–630.

Dixon, V. J. (1976). World views and research methodology. In L. M. King, V. J. Dixon, & W. W. Nobles (Eds.), *African philosophy: Assumptions and paradigms for research on black persons.* Los Angeles: Fanon Center Publications.

Erikson, E. (1968). *Identity: Youth and crisis.* New York: Norton.

Gabrenya, W. K., Wang, V. E., & Latane, B. (1985). Social loafing on an optimizing task: Cross-cultural differences among Chinese and Americans. *Journal of Cross-Cultural Psychology, 16,* 223–242.

Hofstede, G. (1980). *Culture's consequences: International differences in work-related values.* Newbury Park, CA: Sage.

Jones, J. M. (1983). The concept of race in social psychology: From color to culture. In L. Wheeler & P. Shaver (Eds.), *Review of Personality and Social Psychology* (Vol. 4). Newbury Park, CA: Sage.

Jones, J. M. (1991). Psychological models of race: What have they been and what should they be? In J. Goodchilds (Ed.), *Psychological perspectives on human diversity in America.* Washington, DC: American Psychological Association.

Latane, B., Williams, K., & Harkins, S. (1979). Many hands make light the work: Causes and consequences of social loafing. *Journal of Personality and Social Psychology, 37,* 822–832.

Lonner, W. J., & Malpass, R. (1994). *Psychology and culture.* Needham Heights, MA: Allyn & Bacon.

McDougall, W. (1921). *Is America safe for democracy?* New York: Scribner's.

Markus, H., & Kitayama, S. (1991). Culture and the self: Implications for cognition, emotion, and motivation. *Psychological Review, 98,* 224–253.

Matsumoto, D. (1994). *People: Psychology from a cultural perspective.* Pacific Grove, CA: Brooks/Cole.

Moghaddam, F. M., Taylor, D. M., & Wright, S. C. (1993). *Social psychology in cross-cultural perspective.* New York: W. H. Freeman.

Moore, E. (1986). Family socialization and the IQ test performance of traditionally and transracially adopted black children. *Developmental Psychology, 22,* 317–326.

Peters, M. F. (1988). Parenting in black families with young children: A historical perspective. In H. P. McAdoo (Ed.), *Black families* (2nd ed.). Newbury Park, CA: Sage.

Plomin, R., Reiss, D., Hetherington, E. M., & Howe, G. W. (1994). Nature and nurture: Genetic contributions to measures of the family environment. *Developmental Psychology, 30,* 32–43.

Sagar, A., & Schofield, J. W. (1980). Racial and behavioral cues in black and white children's perceptions of ambiguously aggressive acts. *Journal of Personality and Social Psychology, 39,* 590–598.

Smith, P. B., & Bond, M. H. (1994). *Social psychology across cultures: Analysis and perspectives.* Needham Heights, MA: Allyn & Bacon.

Snyder, M., Tanke, E. D., & Berscheid, E. (1977). Social perception and interpersonal behavior: On the self-fulfilling nature of social stereotypes. *Journal of Personality and Social Psychology, 35,* 656–666.

Triandis, H. (1994). *Culture and social psychology.* New York: McGraw-Hill.

Watts, R. (1992). Elements of a psychology of human diversity. *Journal of Community Psychology, 20,* 116–131.

Word, C., Zanna, M. P., & Cooper, J. (1974). The non-verbal mediation of self-fulfilling prophecies in interracial interaction. *Journal of Experimental Social Psychology, 10,* 109–120.

Zuckerman, M. (1990). Some dubious premises in research and theory on racial differences. *American Psychologist, 45,* 1397–1403.

PART II

Human Diversity

Philosophical and
Paradigmatic Tenets

3

Paradigms
of Diversity

Roderick J. Watts

As noted in Chapter One of this volume and elsewhere (Trickett, Watts, & Birman, 1993; Watts, 1992), a psychology of human diversity owes much to the anger, frustration, and disillusionment of African Americans and other populations of color, European American women, gay and lesbian psychologists, and others who have felt disenfranchised by the dominant perspectives in psychology. Their critiques have been the impetus for a reexamination of the dominant models in psychology.

Although no progress can be made until critique gives way to creativity, it is instructive to summarize the criticisms of conventional psychological theory. A review of the criticisms clarifies the issues that are most in need of attention. Following a brief outline of the recurrent criticisms of dominant models (see also Jones, Chapter Two of this volume), this chapter will consider how existing social science paradigms can serve as a point of departure for a new psychology of human diversity. These paradigms include concepts such as oppression, identity, and intergroup processes that other authors in this volume consider in greater detail.

According to critics (for example, D. W. Sue, 1981; White &

49

Parham, 1990; Nobles, 1986; Albee, 1988), a psychology of human diversity faces numerous challenges:

1. Ethnocentric theory (including sexist and ageist theory) that understands the distinctive attributes of nondominant populations as psychosocial defects. Harry Stack Sullivan's interpretations of African American behavior are a good illustration of ethnocentric bias. His conclusions were filtered through the lens of European cultural history, which includes puritan and Victorian sensibilities. He said: "I judge that there are many definitely promiscuous people [among blacks] and that this laxity arises from factors of personality development as well as from a permissive culture" (Sullivan, 1964, pp. 103–104, quoted in Nobles, 1986, p. 13).

2. Genetic or constitutional-deficiency models for explaining population differences. History provides many examples of viewing population differences in IQ as evidence of one population's inherent superiority over another (rather than, for instance, as a problem of context, theory, or measurement). Recent consistent evidence that people of Asian descent have higher IQ scores than whites has not led researchers to seriously consider a genetic explanation, however (S. Sue & Okazaki, 1990). According to researchers, socialization is the culprit (Stevenson, 1992). Unlike U.S. parents, parents in racially homogeneous Japan see effort as more important than genes in academic performance. Apparently, their children reap the benefits of parental emphasis on hard work (Stevenson, 1992).

3. Cultural-deficit models for explaining differences. Until recently, theorists used the notions of cultural deprivation and the culture of poverty to explain population differences in behavior. Nourished by the zeitgeist, these theories often rose high before they became discredited. But as old theories pass, new ones arise. For example, after the Los Angeles uprising in 1992, then vice president Dan Quayle attributed the unrest to a "poverty of values." Current theorizing about an underclass and hip-hop culture risks becoming the latest version of cultural deficit.

An underlying belief in cultural superiority (Ramirez, 1983) and the ongoing search for the origins of "deficits" have prevented many social scientists from asking a more basic question: How does one account for environment and culture when distinguishing pathology from distinctiveness? Other shortcomings of dominant perspectives in the United States include a largely apolitical or status quo approach to psychological work (Albee, 1988; Prilleltensky, 1989) that separates sociopolitical and psychological phenomena and marginalizes psychologists who are interested in social oppression and social change.

Paradigms of Diversity

At least four paradigms are relevant to a psychology of human diversity. Each offers a different lens from which to view social, political, and psychological phenomena. In the spirit of pluralism, none are put forward as better than the others in all situations. Their utility can only be assessed through application. The four paradigms are (1) population-specific psychologies (PSPs), (2) cross-cultural psychology, (3) sociopolitical psychology, and (4) intergroup theory. Although each paradigm differs in emphasis, they all share a value on the primacy of context in understanding human behavior. PSPs and cross-cultural theory emphasize cultural context, sociopolitical perspectives focus on historical and political contexts, and intergroup theory stresses the influence of group membership and dynamics. Although this chapter does not consider the ecological perspective in community psychology, it too is consistent with diversity-conscious psychology (Watts, 1992; Trickett, Watts, & Birman, 1993). The ecological paradigm sees humans as elements of a dynamic environmental and social system. Like each of the proverbial blind men who attempted to describe an elephant from the one part they had touched, each of these paradigms gives us a different insight into the psychology of human diversity.

Several key terms require definitions before proceeding. *Distinctive populations* share a unique pattern of historical experience, physical attributes, beliefs, or practices. Members identify, to varying degrees, with others in the population. *Culturally distinctive populations* have worldviews based on ethnicity or nationality; transmission of worldview is familial, vertical (from the old to the young through social roles), and generational as well as horizontal (that is, between peers). I am a member of a culturally distinct group (African Americans), as are Polish Americans and Choctaws. (See Lonner, Chapter Ten of this volume, for a detailed discussion of culture.) My African American life experience, identity, and worldview led to the use of more examples from African American culture than from other cultures. These factors also contributed to a personal affinity for PSPs and sociopolitical perspectives.

Socially Distinctive Populations

Socially distinctive populations are defined by intracultural variation instead of ethnicity or nationality. Nonetheless, they have distinctive patterns of beliefs and behavior. Transmission of worldview relies on nonfamilial and horizontal methods as much as or more than vertical methods. Social forces and oppression typically play a major role in making these populations self-conscious. Examples include gays, lesbians, and populations based on age and social class.

Worldview

This is the pattern of beliefs, behavior, and perceptions that is shared by a population based on similar socialization and life experiences. Whereas heredity or simple self-declaration may grant someone membership in a distinctive population, cognitive and behavioral patterns define psychological membership. Like population membership, these psychological patterns are grounded in history. For example, part of a cultural pattern for Mexican Americans is the consumption of corn in various forms, a preference historically grounded in Mexican–Native American culture. However, worldview is not a personality trait for two reasons. First, it does not follow that loving potatoes and hating corn disqualifies a person from claiming a Mexican American worldview. The key word in the definition is *pattern* — not a presence or absence of discrete characteristics. Second,

I define worldview as a predisposition, not a trait; it changes substantially depending on the ecological context. For example, specific African American religious behavior may differ radically in the Southern and Northwestern areas of this nation, but it would still be wise to seek out churches, whatever the region, if one is interested in identifying important community institutions for blacks. Worldview is part of the deep structure of groups and their members, what Ibrahim (1985) calls "existential categories." Although the pattern that defines worldview is often synonymous with culture, this chapter frequently uses the term *worldview* because the distinctiveness of some populations is not a result of their culture.

Finally, *groups* are subsets of populations that coalesce in specific settings; for example, laborers and managers in a steel mill are groups.

Population-Specific Psychologies

PSPs focus on understanding a single population rather than on comparative analysis. For populations with a history of oppression, PSPs overlap with sociopolitical perspectives as theorists seek to debunk negative images that rationalize racism, sexism, and other forms of oppression.

Figure 3.1 highlights the major elements in the evolution of most PSPs. At the base of the diagram is the researcher's explicit acknowledgment of her or his cultural values and worldview. In reaction to the unstated worldview that undergirds most social science scholarship, feminists and people of color are typically explicit about their frame of reference. Even the titles of books and articles make their stance explicit, for example, Reinharz and Davidman's *Feminist Methods in Social Research* (1992). This practice compels us to "unpack" or deconstruct scholarship with implicit worldviews but without modifiers. Books simply titled *Research Methods* may come under greater scrutiny. Is the author talking about masculinist, logical-positivist, or European American research methods? Taken to extremes, this practice reinforces the factional divides in social science, but it also increases our awareness of how personal characteristics and context influence professional work.

Figure 3.1. Population-Specific Perspectives.

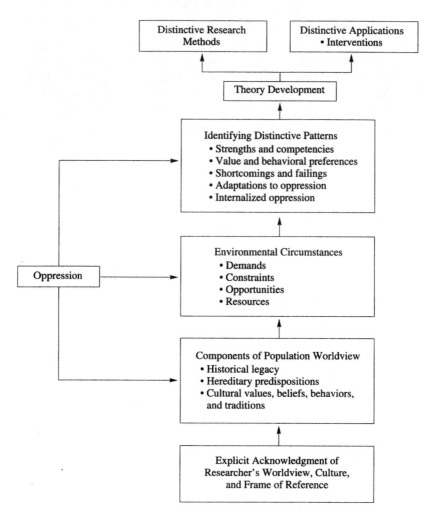

Worldview

The researcher is at the base of the diagram because self and the context of self are the root of all theory and practice. One step up from this is worldview. For many PSP theorists, initial efforts are on the discovery, construction, and articulation of a population's distinctive worldview or culture. PSP theorists see the pattern of values, beliefs, attitudes, historical experience, and hereditary predispositions that constitute a worldview as a primary determinant of human behavior and professional practice (for example, Belenky, Clinchy, Goldberger, & Tarule, 1986; Ramirez, 1983; Nobles, 1986; D. W. Sue, 1981).

An understanding of worldview provides information needed to create theories (Jones, 1986) and methods (for example, Ramirez, 1983) consistent with it. Ramirez's writings (1983) on mestizo psychology (*mestizo* means mixed — of European, indigenous, and African ancestry) illustrate the construction and discovery process involved in formulating a population's worldview. He says, "The mestizo worldview stresses the importance of ecology[;] it had its origins in the native peoples of the Americas (Lee, 1976). Indian cultures view the person as an open system which both affects and is affected by his or her surroundings. Harmony with the environment, both physical and social, is thus of primary concern in psychological adjustment" (p. 8). Similarly, James Myers & Speight (Chapter Five of this volume) construct "optimal theory" from explicit Afrocentric and woman-centered worldviews.

As PSP theorists sharpen distinctions between worldviews, traditional models will face fresh challenges. Sometimes the sharpening leads to insights about racism, ethnocentrism, homophobia, or sexism in theories built on certain worldviews. People begin to challenge the idea that only one sexual orientation is normal, they question the existence of histrionic disorders with no corresponding macho disorders, and so on. Professionals who do not reveal or examine their most important tool (themselves) will forever be subject to post hoc efforts by others to uncover their biases. Unfortunately, there are no guidelines for identifying and describing the key attributes of a researcher-practitioner-

as-instrument. Moreover, scholars are often unsophisticated
about the impact of their worldview and ill-prepared by their
training to consider it (Unger, Draper, & Pendergrass, 1986).

Environmental Circumstances

Environmental opportunities and constraints regulate the expression of distinctive population characteristics. For example,
if a young Asian American woman's cultural heritage predisposes
her to value group achievement as much as individual achievement and her environment restricts nonacademic pathways to
success, then her group orientation is likely to express itself and
serve as a resource for her scholastic behavior; perhaps it may
manifest itself as a preference for, and proficiency in, group
studying strategies. This scenario was constructed from S. Sue
and Okazaki's description (1990) of the high educational attainment of Asian Americans. They postulate that culture is influential but mediated by societal opportunities and restrictions.

    As Sue and Okazaki note, "restrictions" often take the form
of oppression. The presence of oppression complicates our understanding of culture and worldview because it is often unclear
whether a characteristic of a population reflects an aspect of culture or an effort to combat oppression. Why not consider adaptations to oppression as just another part of culture? Because
to do so would require the culture's members to identify with
elements of their behavior or values that are a consequence of
exogenous, exploitative human forces rather than the evolution
of their own heritage. Confusing culture with the by-products
of oppression helped spawn the now-discredited "culture of
poverty" hypothesis. Adaptations to oppression may continue
as a pattern while oppression exists, but labeling all patterns
as cultural patterns veils important distinctions.

Identifying Distinctive Patterns

A population's behavioral, value, and competency patterns are
central attributes of PSPs. Patterns are constructed from research, reviews of research, and history. Jones's TRIOS theory

(1986) is a particularly good example because it presents distinctive patterns of cultural values and behavior that can be positive. Jones identifies time perception, rhythm, improvisation, oral tradition, and spirituality as patterns and themes of black personality. Rhythm is evident in the call-and-response cycle black pastors establish with their congregations in many African American churches, as distinct from the one-way, nonrhythmic communication between priest and congregation in a typical Catholic Mass. Griots (oral historians) in old West Africa were part of this tradition as are their modern counterparts, the rap musicians of today. Improvisation is as integral to classical African American music (jazz) as the recital of written music is to European classics. Jones's theory illustrates the interplay between empirical research, history, and theory development in PSPs.

Theory

Theory is shaped by all the elements beneath it in the diagram and revised by the elements above it. In turn, it produces demands for new methods and suggests new interventions. For example, Ramirez's mestizo theory (1983) is holistic instead of reductionistic, because of its Native American cultural context. The methods required are similarly context-rich. Ramirez describes The Multiple Autobiography in a Single Family as a family assessment tool that is consistent with the mestizo worldview: "Each member of the family tells his own life story in his own words. [Sessions are audiotaped.] . . . The independent versions of the same incidents given by the various members provide a built-in check upon the reliability and validity of much of the data[;] unskilled, uneducated, and even illiterate persons can talk about themselves . . . in an uninhibited, spontaneous and natural manner" (Lewis, 1961, pp. xi, xii, xxi, quoted in Ramirez, 1983, p. 76).

The method generates a great deal of data and a demand for analytic techniques that can identify themes and patterns. As the elements in Figure 3.1 interact over time, researchers create a body of literature and action on the population under study.

The preceding review presented several strengths of the population-specific perspective: explicit worldviews, positive affirmation of distinctiveness, a competency (rather than deficit) orientation, and alternative methodologies. There are potential weaknesses as well. For example, what is to prevent the emergence of parallel psychologies ad infinitum? Will a Native American psychology suffice, or is there a need for separate psychologies for each Native American population? Will factions diverge to a point where we create a Tower of Babel in psychology devoid of shared concepts? Although the proliferation of population psychologies may seem daunting to scholars and practitioners alike, an optimum balance between mergers and separations ought to occur over time. A population's sociopolitical salience will determine if a new psychology emerges, and (if it is given fair consideration) the successes and failures of theory, research, and application will determine if it survives.

Although PSPs are generally associated with disenfranchised groups, the creation of PSPs is also essential for populations such as European American men who have not, as a population group, experienced systematic oppression. Members of many other populations write about white men, but there are few self-conscious insider views of the white, male worldview. Historically, when European American men viewed themselves as a distinctive population, it was often as civilizers of the world (see Jordan, 1974; Kovel, 1970). More recently, in light of the fledgling men's movement, feminist social critique, and increased public awareness of "the browning of America" (Henry, 1990), new thinking is emerging about what it means to be a white man. Much of this discourse takes place in the popular press, but the work of Alderfer (Chapter Nine of this volume) and Helms (1990; also see Chapter Thirteen of this volume) testifies to a growing interest in the deconstruction of whiteness and a self-conscious white, male psychology.

The Cross-Cultural Perspective

Although PSPs give us a rich, detailed understanding of a particular population, they give us less insight into the *shared* human experience or the complexities of multicultural research and action. Because a multicultural society inevitably leads to intergroup dynamics and comparative research to explore the similarities and distinctiveness of populations, valid cross-cultural methods are essential to a psychology of human diversity. Moreover, cross-cultural concepts can alert us to ethnocentric theory and methodology and to the misuse of comparative data. Anthropology's notion of cultural relativism (Ebel, 1986; Stein, 1986) helps to check ethnocentric thinking. The value of cultural relativism, according to Wagner (1981), is that it "poses a constant question, keeps a persistent radical doubt. . . . [It serves] . . . as a critique of ethnocentrism and scientific imperialism" (quoted in Stein, 1986, p. 169). It also helps us to appreciate and protect the myriad of solutions populations devise to solve the common problems of human existence. Extreme "vulgar" relativism, on the other hand, where all actions and perspectives are viewed as equally legitimate, can undermine sociopolitical action and promote nihilism (Ravn, 1991; Prilleltensky & Gonick, Chapter Seven of this volume) and provide a ready rationale for any evil imaginable.

Researchers and Their Discipline

Cross-cultural psychologists seek to (1) identify and understand unique and universal cultural attributes through comparison, (2) determine the influence of these attributes on attitudes and behavior, and (3) understand and intervene in intercultural settings. Cultural and ethnic psychology as described by Berry in Chapter Six of this volume overlaps considerably with the cross-cultural pespective. Cross-cultural psychologists usually take no explicit and consistent ideological stance aside from cultural relativity; in actual practice, research efforts are much more likely to seek the cross-cultural validation of psychological concepts derived from the study of dominant populations than to test concepts revealed from the study of nondominant populations (Jahoda, 1980). Thus, as shown in Figure 3.2, discipline and a priori theory play a fundamental role.

Like anthropology, cross-cultural psychology emerged

Figure 3.2. The Cross-Cultural Perspective.

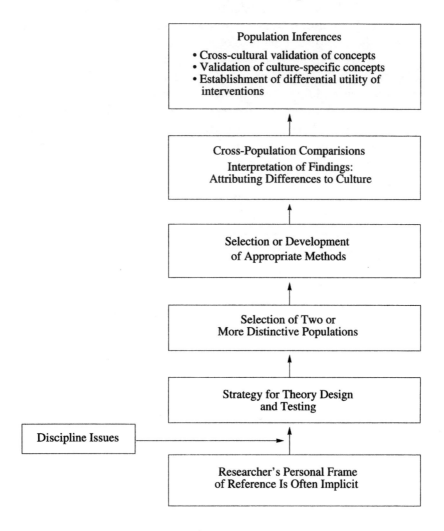

from Europeans' efforts to study and understand populations different from their own (Nencel & Pels, 1991). Unlike PSPs, the worldviews of cross-cultural researchers are often unstated. Although many PSP theorists are critical of dominant perspectives and labor to develop alternatives, cross-cultural psychologists may be personally invisible in their work.

Strategy for Theory Design and Testing

The first explicit objective in cross-cultural work is to determine the theory or intervention activities of interest. For example, Berry (Chapter Six of this volume) describes cognitive performance as one "core problem in cultural and ethnic psychology." Berry also describes the need for a testing strategy—in his words, a means of conceptualizing and assessing the construct of interest. Thus, in cross-cultural psychology, the search for universals is as important as understanding specific populations.

Selecting Populations

A cross-cultural test requires sampling of at least two distinct populations. There must be a cultural boundary to identify and cross in order to test the research questions. As Lonner points out in Chapter Ten of this volume, this quest creates a host of problems associated with ensuring that a given sample of people from a population actually represents that distinctive population. As noted in the definitions that began this chapter, nominal population members may not share the psychological patterns of beliefs and behavior that define their group, and if there is no measure of psychological membership, the researcher will not know how representative the sample is. Can we assume that a sample of Hopi who respond to a university's request for Native American research subjects *represent* Hopi culture? These challenges are daunting. They require cross-cultural researchers to focus on careful operationalization of concepts such as ethnic or racial identity, so that they can define their sample. The value of the findings hinges on the assumption that the compared groups represent their respective populations. As Lonner notes, many of these problems stem from an effort to use culture and ethnicity as an independent variable, a problem cultural anthropologists and PSP researchers avoid by confining their work to a search for definitive patterns within a population.

Selecting Methods

As Berry notes in Chapter Six and as Lonner notes in Chapter Ten, methods and instrumentation interact with the culture of the research participants. If oral communication is as important to African American culture as Jones (1986) contends, the use of surveys may not be the optimal approach. Ramirez (1983) would make a similar argument against surveys and in favor of the use of interviews or other research methods when working with Latin Americans. Such cultural differences complicate the work of cross-cultural researchers, because these researchers must resolve problems of measurement strategy as well as construct validity. On the other hand, exploring and resolving these problems can lead to greater understanding of cultural distinctiveness.

Attributing Meaning

Lambert, Weisz, and Knight's cross-cultural study of Jamaican and U.S. adolescents (1989) is an example of the complexities of designing and interpreting cross-cultural research. Basing their study on a review of clinical data in both countries, they concluded "that characteristics of a culture (for example, values, expectancies, and childrearing practice) may *suppress* the development of certain types of child behavior and foster . . . others" (p. 470; emphasis added). They found that Jamaicans tended to have more "overcontrol" disorders (for example, fearfulness, sleep problems, or somatic disorders) and fewer of the "undercontrol problems" (for example, fighting, disobedience, or stealing) typical of U.S. youth.

Lambert, Weisz, and Knight's test of control as the cultural variable of importance may be misleading, despite their results. The conclusion that control is a key theme in emotional life may be culture-bound and not culturally universal. In Anglo-American culture, emotions are often seen as something to control, lest irrationality and disorder prevail. According to Kochman (1981), "whites conceive of and practice self-control as repression, checking impulses from within before they are released. Once such impulses are released, whites feel that self-control has been lost" (p. 31). White and Parham (1990) and Kochman (1981) suggest that for African Americans, channeling and expressing emotions effectively — not controlling them — is the cultural imperative. White and Parham (1990) cite the call-and-response interplay in black churches as an example of a ritual structure that governs or channels emotional expression. In certain African American church settings, participants can express themselves intensely while enjoying the security of agreed-upon boundaries and protocols for behavior. Thus, investigators with a priori concepts of interest such as the notion of control may get significant results, yet miss or distort a group's distinctive cultural attributes.

Inferences

Unless we know what the patterns of cultural difference are, it is difficult to respect them and incorporate them into psychology. Cross-cultural psychology is uniquely positioned to search for distinctive and common cultural attributes. We need this paradigm to understand how behavior and intervention strategies are influenced by culture, and none of the other paradigms have the methods needed to produce these inferences.

The pitfall of the cross-cultural perspective is that of the struggle for pluralism in general. How do we recognize and value distinctive cultural patterns while building a foundation for unity based on shared universals? Part of the answer to this difficult question lies in developing strong traditions of both population-specific and cross-population studies. PSPs help us understand and value distinctiveness without filtering it through concepts of interest to another population. Cross-cultural research creates a knowledge base for exchange between populations.

The Sociopolitical Perspective

Sociopolitical analysis has received a great deal of attention by PSP theorists, whose populations of interest — African Americans, women, and so on — experience oppression. Sociopolitical perspectives are essential to a psychology of human diversity, because social inequity is associated with a host of negative health and mental health outcomes (McCord & Freeman, 1990; Bulhan, 1988; Albee, 1980). Moreover, the formulation of effective policy requires an understanding of social, political, and institutional processes, because policy implementation is a systems intervention. Thus, it is perilous to ignore sociopolitical forces. Sociopolitical analysis is also compatible with many other concepts in human diversity that are on a similar level of analysis. Examples include culture, ecology, institutions, and social systems. As shown in Figure 3.3, the foundation stone of the sociopolitical perspective is an awareness of injustice or oppression. To bear fruit, however, this awareness requires methods that can illuminate, document and ultimately challenge oppression.

Sociopolitical Theory and Methods

Most authors highlight ideology, power, oppression, and empowerment as key concepts in sociopolitical theory (Fanon, 1963; Rappaport, 1981; Serrano-García, 1984; Prilleltensky & Gonik, Chapter Seven of this volume; Albee, 1988). As noted in Figure 3.3, all sociopolitical perspectives have a systems focus that gives much more weight to the power elite's policies and institutions than to individuals in determining human behavior and social position. Albee's critique of the intelligence construct in "The Politics of Nature and Nurture" (1988) argues that social forces, not science or meaningful group differences, define intelligence. Albee grounds his analysis in history as is typical of sociopolitical theorists. Similarly, Fanon (1963) views historical analysis as essential in his discussion of colonization and the oppression it wrought: "[Decolonization] cannot become intelligible or clear to itself except in the exact measure that we can discern the movements which give it historical form and content" (p. 36). Critical analysis of traditional psychology by Albee and others such as Prilleltensky (1989) is designed to uncover the role professional work plays in society and the status quo.

Sociopolitical perspectives are often polemical, polarizing, and, for some, emotionally energizing. Oppressors and victims are defined dialectically. Stokely Carmichael put it succinctly: "If you are not part of the solution, you're part of the problem" (Carmichael, 1970).

Ideology and Oppression

Sociopolitical psychologists have used the concept of ideology to illuminate the interests of the powerful in society while critiquing the role of psychology in serving the interests of these powerful groups (Wallston, 1981; King, Moody, Thompson, & Bennett, 1983). Hare-Mustin and Marecek (1988) and other feminist writers have used deconstruction as a mean of uncovering latent ideology and bias in psychological theory. The impact of oppressive ideology, and methods for countering it, are a concern of many sociopolitical writers. Similarly, Puerto Rican psychologist Irma Serrano-García (1984) sought to counter oppressive ideology in her homeland by including the "construction of a more critical comprehension of the social and political forces which comprise one's daily life world" (Keiffer, 1982, p. 14) in her intervention.

On one level, oppression is a *process;* it is the unjust exercise of power by one group over another to control ideas and desirable resources. This process serves to maintain an asymmetrical distribution of resources among socially meaningful groups such as racial and gender groups. As Moss (1991) notes, oppression, or "depowerment," is the exercise of options available to one group at the expense of other more vulnerable groups. Depowerment by the powerful restricts the options, choices, and opportunities for less powerful competitors. As an *outcome,* oppression consists of the circumstances that result from a long-term and consistent denial of essential resources. Brittan

Figure 3.3. Sociopolitical Perspectives.

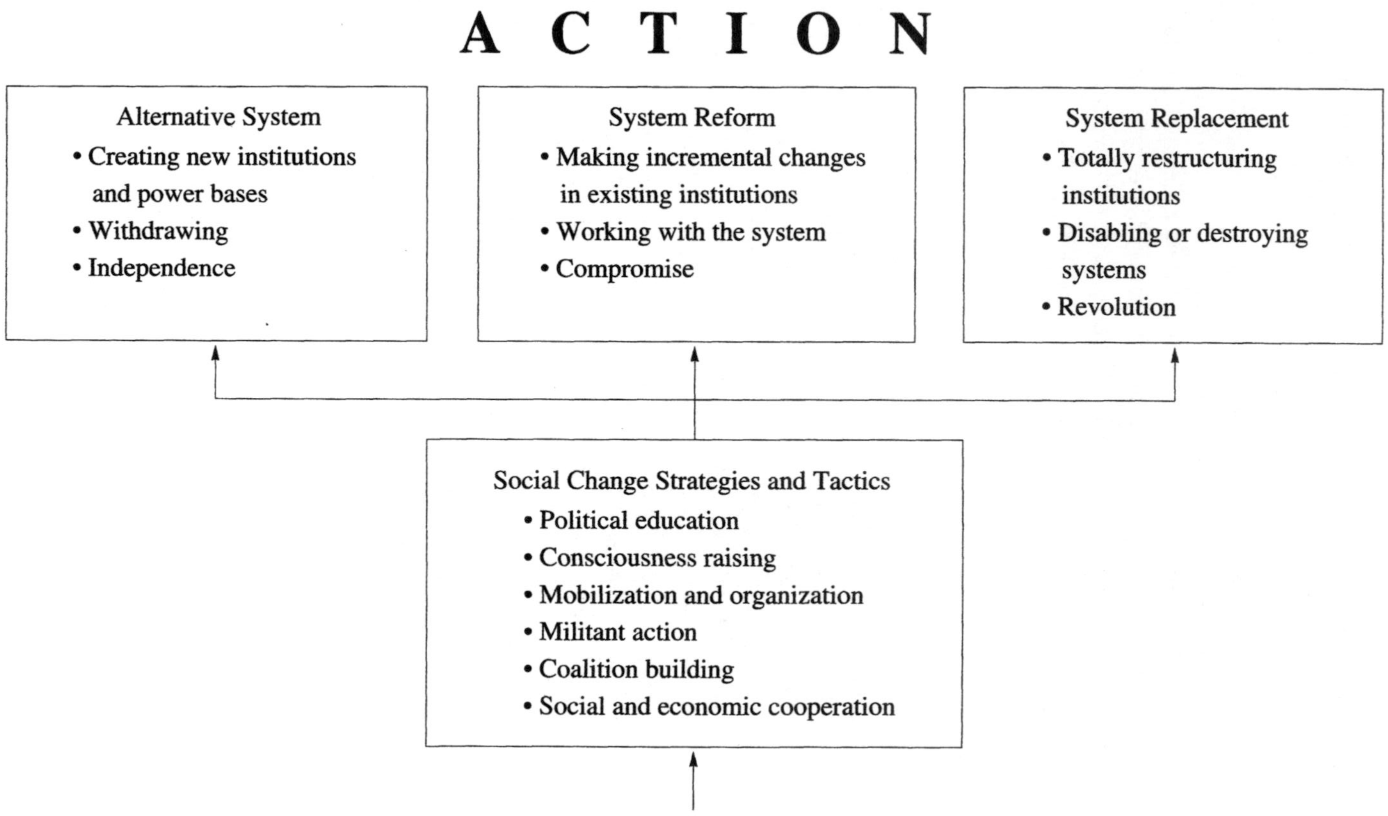

A C T I O N

Alternative System

- Creating new institutions and power bases
- Withdrawing
- Independence

System Reform

- Making incremental changes in existing institutions
- Working with the system
- Compromise

System Replacement

- Totally restructuring institutions
- Disabling or destroying systems
- Revolution

Social Change Strategies and Tactics

- Political education
- Consciousness raising
- Mobilization and organization
- Militant action
- Coalition building
- Social and economic cooperation

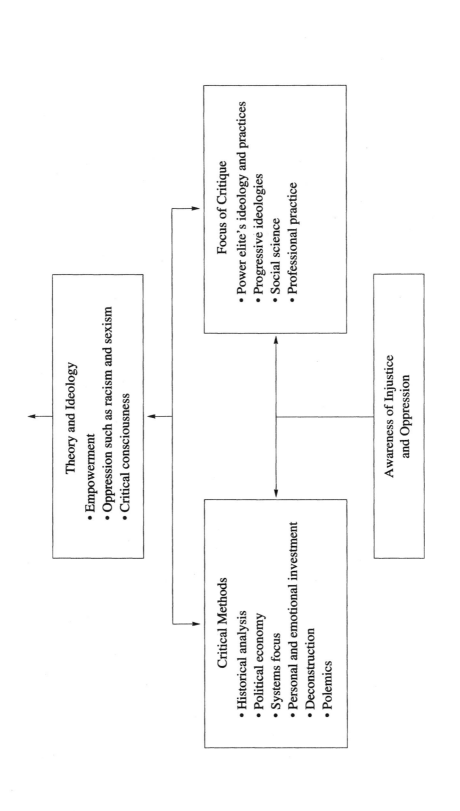

Theory and Ideology

- Empowerment
- Oppression such as racism and sexism
- Critical consciousness

Focus of Critique

- Power elite's ideology and practices
- Progressive ideologies
- Social science
- Professional practice

Critical Methods

- Historical analysis
- Political economy
- Systems focus
- Personal and emotional investment
- Deconstruction
- Polemics

Awareness of Injustice and Oppression

and Maynard (1984) speak to outcomes in their definition of "primary" oppression. They define primary oppression as the consequences of disparities in the possession of cultural and social resources.

For example, oppression may be an alternative way of understanding certain instances of depression or adjustment reactions. The diagnostic criteria of the *Diagnostic and Statistical Manual of Mental Disorders–Revised (DSM III-R)* (American Psychiatric Association, 1987) for dysthymia — a personality disorder characterized by depression — include feelings of hopelessness and low self-esteem, which are the emotional components of subjugation and low personal power. Similarly, the animal model of learned helplessness that is frequently cited as an analogue to human depression (Seligman, 1975) may also be considered a model of oppression and its consequences: people can be overcome by hopelessness and helplessness when pain is inflicted repeatedly, irrespective of personal actions or efforts.

Oppressive ideologies can produce psychological harm in varying ways. Some power-holder ideologies do damage by attributing success and failure to individual abilities (that is, person blame) while failing to implicate social forces (Caplan & Nelson, 1973). In other cases, ideology justifies oppression by attributing failure to an inherent inferiority of the oppressed population.

Racism and sexism are special cases of oppression. Both represent historically grounded, institutionalized discrimination rewarded by material gain and rationalized by an ideology of superiority (Jones, 1972; Dovidio & Gaertner, 1986; Jones, 1986). Some argue that racism is an international, superordinate concept that is best described as white supremacy (Akbar, 1991). Theorists base their assertion on the long history of national and international policies supporting the subjugation of people of color by Europeans (for example, slavery, segregation and internment, colonialism, and the destruction of indigenous populations in the Americas). Just as the confluence of sociopolitical and population-specific perspectives produced white supremacy from racism in the black psychology literature, the analysis of sexism has given rise to the concept of patriarchy. Patriarchy, like white supremacy, puts sexism in a much broader ideological and cultural context.

Implications for Action

The links that race, gender, and other human attributes have to oppression suggest that PSPs and sociopolitical perspectives can be joined to create culture-specific (or worldview-specific) models of empowerment. Abdul-Adil's content analysis of radical rap music (1992) provides evidence of a distinctive worldview among young African Americans in impoverished, central-city environments. Radical rap is an intensely political and culturally oriented form of rap that urges social action as it dramatizes inner-city experience. Abdul-Adil and I (Watts & Abdul Adil, in press) have developed an intervention for young African American men called *Young Warriors* that uses rap videos to develop critical thinking about manhood and social injustice. Youngsters who think critically may be less likely to emulate the predatory and antisocial behavior modeled in mass culture, while exposure to politically conscious rap gives them new ways of understanding their social condition. Critical consciousness, or "conscientization," as described by Freire (1968, 1990) is a natural area for psychosocial researchers and community psychologists to pursue (Montero, 1990). Conscientization helps to reveal ideologies, pulling them out of the background and into the foreground. It clarifies how ideologies maintain the status quo, thereby creating new options for empowerment.

The major strengths of the sociopolitical perspective are its unfailing historical and systemic approach to human behavior. Sociopolitical theorists critique psychology and the professional practice of psychology in the context of power relations and oppression. This orientation is a counterpoint to the person-centered approach traditional to psychology. Because so little action research based on a sociopolitical perspective is published, the disadvantages of the approach are not yet apparent. As the area develops, weaknesses will appear. For example, ideology can become dogma, research a pseudonym for advocacy, and polarization of groups the norm.

The Intergroup Perspective

In contrast to cross-cultural and PSPs that deal with the properties of populations, intergroup theory deals with general processes governing the operation of groups that coalesce in a wide
range of specific circumstances. Key concerns of intergroup theory relevant to human diversity are:

- The circumstances that lead to the formation of groups, their
  structural aspects (for example, boundaries and roles), and
  their developmental cycle
- The effect of population membership, group membership,
  and intergroup dynamics on cognition (especially prejudice)
  and behavior
- Identity, power, conflict, and social comparisons in groups
- The dynamics of intergroup contact (for example, parallel
  process)

Unlike the sociopolitical perspective, ideology-based social change is not central. Nor are attributes specific to a single
group of great interest, as is the case for PSPs. Understanding
general principles takes precedence. Further, the intergroup approach calls for much greater scrutiny of process and the role
of the researcher-practitioner than does the cross-cultural approach. When practitioners or researchers make contact with
others, intergroup theory can help them to anticipate issues that
emerge. In addition, intergroup theory can help professionals
to assemble and creatively manage the conflicts within heterogeneous groups. Alderfer (Chapter Nine of this volume) provides additional information on the theoretical aspects of intergroup relations.

A specific example will help to illustrate the practical
value of the intergroup perspective. Suppose that two European
American women received funding to run a teenage-pregnancy-
prevention program in a working-class Mexican American
community. They had previously collaborated on a pregnancy-
prevention program for youngsters in a mostly white, middle-
class community and wished to demonstrate their model's effec-

tiveness in a different setting. Because of their limited knowledge of Mexican American culture, they interviewed several
Mexican Americans for the position of project director. They
hired a second-generation, upper-middle-class, Mexican American woman with a degree in public health.

A variety of overlapping group memberships and intergroup dynamics come into play in this scenario, as depicted in
Figure 3.4. The two senior researchers (principal investigators,
or PIs) and the project director are part of the newest group,
the research team. The project's goals and the women's shared
identities as social science practitioners form the boundary for
this group. Within the group, however, is a dyad, formed by
the preexisting relationship between the two PIs. They, in turn,
are part of a larger population of second-generation, upper-

Figure 3.4. The Intergroup Perspective.

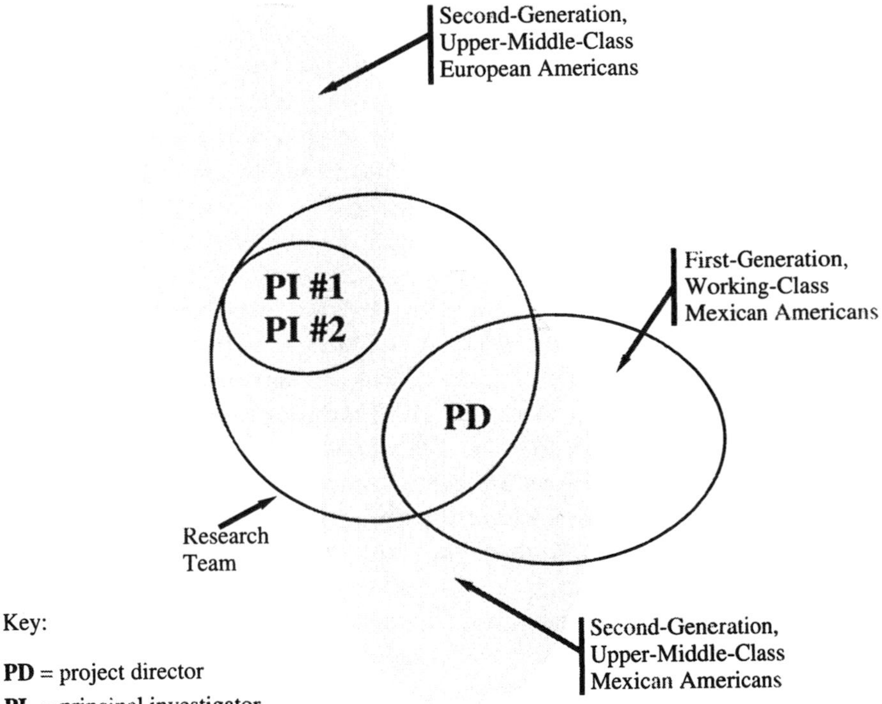

Key:

PD = project director
PI = principal investigator

middle-class European Americans (the shaded upper ellipse). The project director, on the other hand, has ties to the population of second-generation, upper-middle-class Mexican Americans (the shaded lower ellipse). Because of a shared class background and Mexican American acculturation, the ellipses overlap, but only partially. The target population, first-generation, working-class Mexican Americans (the unshaded ellipse), overlaps with the project director's group-of-origin because of their common culture, but the overlap is incomplete as a result of the difference in generations, social class, and probably acculturation.

The intergroup perspective offers some guidance and predictions that could benefit this team. The diagram reveals how the project director may experience conflict because (1) she has less power in the research team as a project director than if she were a PI, (2) she has no history of professional experience with either PI, (3) she has cultural differences with the PIs, and (4) she has class and possibly acculturation differences with the target population. The historical legacy of relations between Europeans and Mexicans comes into play as well; local and historical tensions (or goodwill) between the two populations may predispose group members to replay these conflicts in project-related discussions. The likelihood of this depends in part on the personal qualities of the PIs and the project director and on their willingness to acknowledge the cultural dynamics.

Additional hazards arise when the project team contacts the target population. The project director was hired because of her knowledge of the target population, but if she identifies strongly with this group, despite class and generational differences, she may adopt the interests of the targets at the expense of the research team's agenda. This weakens the research team's group boundary. She would then become an advocate for the targets and not a team resource who helps to reconcile the project's design with the target population's needs. If team members witness intercultural conflict in the target community (for example, objections to school birth-control policies by Mexican American Catholics), they may find this conflict replicated in the research team. In intergroup dynamics terminology, this is *parallel process* (Alderfer, Chapter Nine of this volume).

Parallel processes are themes and conflicts from one group that are absorbed by, or projected onto, another group. If the research team is unaware of the parallel process, it can be destructive, especially when it recapitulates cultural conflicts that exist in society. The team thinks it is debating only project issues, but the energy of the conflict suggests otherwise. The team absorbs the excess energy from the school conflict, which triggers unconscious feelings and associations based on personal ethnicity. Fortunately, if parallel process is recognized, the team has a here-and-now opportunity to explore personal racial and cultural dynamics as well as the community events that brought them to the surface. They can then use these feelings to devise constructive solutions to project problems.

Alternatively, if the project director identifies fully with the research project and her professional worldview, strengthening the research team's boundary, members of the target population may reject her as part of the out-group. This is already a risk because of differences between the project director and the targets in generation and class status. Either way, it is apparent from Figure 3.4 that the project director can be pulled in different directions by her membership in three distinct groups. The senior researchers have the advantages of a preexisting relationship with one another and the power to define the group's objectives, but they must process their concerns openly with the project director or risk strengthening their dyad and isolating her further.

Few groups use intergroup theory to profit from the advantages of diversity. In this example, if the PIs hired the Mexican American project director out of political correctness, they were practicing tokenism. When this happens, a special set of intergroup dynamics becomes active and, as Laws (1975) describes, the token is likely to face pressure to trade identity for increased power and group status. If the PIs hired the woman for her knowledge about Mexican American culture and her links to that community, the PIs must determine if her membership in the culture is more than nominal. If it is nominal, she adds little to the project; if her identity is strong, then culturally charged parallel processes may develop and require management.

A willingness to manage parallel processes and other intergroup dynamics is part of diversity-conscious practice in psychology. Power relations are significant too. Research or practice controlled by European Americans but managed by and targeted to people of color is not uncommon, but it is not ideal, even if parallel processes and other dynamics are expertly managed. Awareness of the larger sociopolitical forces that create scenarios like the one in Figure 3.4 should not be overshadowed by efforts to manage intergroup processes. Thus, what follows is an intergroup intervention, not a systems intervention. It cannot alter the basic power relations of the situation.

What the PI Staff Can Do

Set a tone for the open exchange of personal feelings and experiences about culture. Have group members see themselves as research-intervention tools that must constantly be examined for validity. This is the clinical (Lowman, 1988) and constructivist approach (Gergen, 1985) to professional activity. Acknowledge that intellectual knowledge is not a substitute for experiential knowledge. Cede power to superior life experiences as well as to intellectual and institutional authority because they are in the project's interest. Practice humility. Jacobson (1988) argues that competent cross-cultural work requires personal experience with the client's culture. Beware of prejudices and urges to retreat to preexisting subgroup alliances. Strive for mutual accommodation; a multicultural—not monocultural—style should characterize your team's work. Rather than designating the project director as a "buffer" who is responsible for all cultural issues, actively attempt to build personal experience with the target population. By becoming personally knowledgeable about a new culture, you will gain a more intuitive sense of workable interventions.

What the Project Director Can Do

Avoid using superior personal experience as a weapon for exposing ignorance or producing guilt. Instead, use it as a power base to expand role-based power restrictions. At the same time, do not permit the senior staff to avoid personal bicultural development. Challenge concepts that distort the worldview of the target population. Deal directly with any feeling that subgroup boundaries in the project group are undermining its identity. Maintain vigilance about feelings of alienation, cooptation, and conflict between group memberships. Avoid the recapitulation of population-level dynamics at the group level, such as exploitive relationships, racism, and pressures to relinquish cultural identity to gain status or power.

This extended, practical example of intergroup theory covered several of its advantages. Alderfer considers the underlying theory in more detail later in this volume. The shortcomings of this approach are similar to those of laboratory social psychology, the individual-differences paradigm, and theories based on intrapsychic phenomena: it rests on the assumption that group and intergroup processes are universal and not setting- or population-specific. The differential effects of history, culture, and ecology are not given a central role in theory. This is particularly true of the intergroup literature in the United States, where laboratory research and theory development have been emphasized over practical applications to the problems of society (Moghaddam, 1987). As noted previously, intergroup analysis may not have any influence on the structural power relations between groups. At its worse, this encourages people to accommodate to injustice by simply managing the conflict it produces.

Conclusion

This chapter reviewed four perspectives relevant to a psychology of human diversity. Each perspective emphasizes different methods and concepts, but they all assign an important role to the social and environmental context of behavior.

Although the perspectives overlap, each offers unique insights into a given situation. They can be compared to the multicolored set of filters a photographer uses to deal with different lighting conditions and artistic aims. No one filter captures all elements of a scene and no one rendering of a scene is ideal for all purposes. As with good photography, a good understanding of the dynamics of human diversity is gained by those with the capacity to view a situation through several filters. When different perspectives are united by a desire for social justice, they enrich one another and contribute to our understanding of the human condition.

References

Abdul-Adil, J. (1992). *Rap music: Toward a culture-specific model of empowerment*. Unpublished master's thesis, Department of Psychology, DePaul University, Chicago.

Akbar, N. (1991). Paradigms of African American research. In R. Jones (Ed.), *Black psychology* (3rd ed.). Berkeley, CA: Cobb & Henry.

Albee, G. (1980). A competency model must replace the defect model. In L. Bond & J. Rosen (Eds.), *Competence and coping during adulthood* (pp. 75–102). Hanover, NH: University Press of New England.

Albee, G. (1988). The politics of nature and nurture. *American Journal of Community Psychology, 10,* 4–28.

American Psychiatric Association. (1987). *Diagnostic and statistical manual of mental disorders–Revised* Washington, DC: Author.

Belenky, M., Clinchy, B., Goldberger, N., & Tarule, J. (1986). *Women's ways of knowing: Development of self, voice, and mind.* New York: Basic Books.

Brittan, A., & Maynard, M. (1984). *Sexism, racism, and oppression.* New York: Basil Blackwell.

Bulhan, H. (1988). *Franz Fanon and the psychology of oppression.* New York: Plenum.

Caplan, N., & Nelson, S. (1973). The nature and consequences of psychological research on social problems. *American Psychologist, 28,* 199–211.

Carmichael, S. (1970). "We are going to use the term 'black power' and we are going to define it because black power speaks to us." In J. Bracey, A. Meier, & E. Rudwick (Eds.),

Black nationalism in America (pp. 470–475). New York: Bobbs-Merrill.

Dovidio, J. F., & Gaertner, S. L. (Eds.). (1986). *Prejudice, discrimination and racism.* San Diego, CA: Academic Press.

Ebel, H. (1986). The strange history of cultural relativism. *Journal of Psychoanalytic Anthropology, 9,* 177–183.

Fanon, F. (1963). *The wretched of the earth.* New York: Grove Press.

Freire, P. (1968). *Pedagogy of the oppressed.* New York: Seabrook Press.

Freire, P. (1990). *Education for a critical consciousness.* New York: Continuum.

Gergen, K. (1985). The social constructionist movement in modern psychology. *American Psychologist, 40,* 266–275.

Hare-Mustin, R., & Marecek, J. (1988). The meaning of difference: Gender theory, post-modernism and psychology. *American Psychologist, 43,* 455–462.

Helms, J. E. (1990). An overview of racial identity theory. In J. E. Helms (Ed.), *Black and white racial identity: Theory, research, and practice* (pp. 9–32). Westport, CT: Greenwood Press.

Henry, W. (1990, April 9). Beyond the melting pot. *Time,* pp. 28–31.

Ibrahim, F. (1985). Effective cross-cultural counseling and psychotherapy: A framework. *Counseling-Psychologist, 13,* 625–638.

Jacobson, F. M. (1988). Ethnocultural assessment. In L. Comas-Diaz & E. F. Griffith (Eds.), *Clinical guidelines in cross-cultural mental health* (pp. 135–148). New York: Wiley.

Jahoda, G. (1980). Theoretical and systematic approaches in cross-cultural psychology. In H. Triandis & J. Draguns (Eds.), *Handbook of cross-cultural psychology* (Vol. 6, pp. 69–141). Needham Heights, MA: Allyn & Bacon.

Jones, J. M. (1972). *Prejudice and racism.* Reading, MA: Addison-Wesley.

Jones, J. M. (1986). Racism: A cultural analysis of the problem. In J. F. Dovidio & S. L. Gaertner (Eds.), *Prejudice, discrimination and racism.* San Diego, CA: Academic Press.

Jordan, W. (1974). *The white man's burden: Historical origins of racism in the United States.* New York: Oxford University Press.

Keiffer, C. (1982). The development of empowerment: The development of participatory competence among individuals in citizen organizations. *Division 27 Newsletter* (American Psychological Association), *16,* 13–15.

King, L., Moody, S., Thompson, O., & Bennett, M. (1983). Black psychology reconsidered: Notes toward curriculum development. In J. Chunn, P. Dunston, & F. Ross-Sheriff (Eds.), *Mental health and people of color.* Washington, DC: Howard University Press.

Kochman, T. (1981). *Black and white styles in conflict.* Chicago: University of Chicago Press.

Kovel, J. (1970). *White racism: A psychohistory.* New York: Pantheon Books.

Lambert, M. C., Weisz, J. R., & Knight, F. (1989). Over- and undercontrolled clinic referral problems of Jamaican and American children and adolescents: The culture general and the culture specific. *Journal of Consulting and Clinical Psychology, 57,* 467–472.

Laws, J. (1975). The psychology of tokenism: An analysis. *Sex Roles, 1,* 51–67.

Lowman, R. (1988). What *is* clinical method? In D. Berg & K. Smith (Eds.), *The self in social inquiry* (pp. 173–187). Newbury Park, Calif: Sage.

McCord, C., & Freeman, H. P. (1990). Excess mortality in Harlem. *New England Journal of Medicine, 322,* 173–177.

Moghaddam, F. M. (1987). Psychology in the three worlds: As reflected by the crisis in social psychology and the move toward indigenous third-world psychology. *American Psychologist, 42,* 912–920.

Montero, M. (1990). Ideology and psychological research in Third World contexts. *Journal of Social Issues, 36,* 43–55.

Moss, J. (1991). Hurling oppression: Overcoming anomie and self-hatred. In B. Bowser (Ed.), *Black male adolescents: Parenting and education in community context.* Lanham, MD: University Presses of America.

Nencel, L., & Pels, P. (1991). *Constructing knowledge: Authority and critique in social science.* London: Sage.

Nobles, W. (1986). *African psychology.* Oakland, CA: Black Family Institute.

Prilleltensky, I. (1989). Psychology and the status quo. *American Psychologist, 44,* 795–802.

Ramirez, M. (1983). *Psychology of the Americas: Mestizo perspectives on personality and mental health.* Elmsford, NY: Pergamon Press.

Rappaport, J. (1981). In praise of paradox: A social policy of empowerment over prevention. *American Journal of Community Psychology, 9,* 1–26.

Ravn, I. (1991). What should guide reality construction? In F. Steier (Ed.), *Research and reflexivity* (pp. 96–112). Newbury Park, CA: Sage.

Reinharz, S., & Davidman, L. (1992). *Feminist methods in social research.* New York: Oxford University Press.

Seligman, M. (1975). *Helplessness.* New York: W. H. Freeman.

Serrano-García, I. (1984). The illusion of empowerment: Community development within a colonial context. *Prevention in Human Services, 3,* 173–200.

Stein, H. (1986). Cultural relativism as the central organizing resistance in cultural anthropology. *Journal of Psychoanalytic Anthropology, 9,* 157–175.

Stevenson, H. (1992). Learning from Asian schools. *Scientific American, 267,* 70–76.

Sue, D. W. (1981). *Counseling the culturally different: Theory and practice.* New York: Wiley.

Sue, S., & Okazaki, S. (1990). Asian-American educational achievements: A phenomenon in search of an explanation. *American Psychologist, 45,* 913–920.

Trickett, E., Watts, R., & Birman, D. (1993). Human diversity and community psychology: Still hazy after all these years. *American Journal of Community Psychology, 21,* 264–279.

Unger, R., Draper, R., & Pendergrass, M. (1986). Personal epistemology and personal experience. *Journal of Social Issues, 42,* 67–79.

Wagner, R. (1981). *The invention of culture.* Chicago: University of Chicago Press.

Wallston, B. (1981). What are the questions in psychology of women? A feminist approach to research. *Psychology of Women Quarterly, 5,* 597–614.

Watts, R. (1992). Elements of a psychology of human diversity. *Journal of Community Psychology, 20,* 116–131.

Watts, R., & Abdul-Adil, J. (in press). Psychological aspects of oppression and sociopolitical development. In R. Newby & T. Manley (Eds.), *The poverty of inclusion, innovation, and interventions: The dilemma of the African-American underclass.* Rutgers, NJ: Rutgers University Press.

White, J., & Parham, T. (1990). *The psychology of blacks.* Englewood Cliffs, NJ: Prentice-Hall.

4

Feminism and Psychology: A Dynamic Interaction

Nancy Felipe Russo
Amy J. Dabul

Psychology—through its theories, methods, and practices—both reflects and shapes the larger sociocultural context (Russo, 1983). Carolyn Wood Sherif (1979, p. 127) expressed it well in the following words: "What goes on in our laboratories, clinics, and classrooms must be seen for what it is, cultural phenomena and events where we can learn about individuals, provided we understand the times and the larger societies of which they are part." Feminism has been part of that larger context. This chapter summarizes some challenges of feminism to the science of psychology and highlights selected contributions of feminist researchers in making the field more responsive to issues of diversity.

American science has long been viewed as a tool for implementing democratic ideals and values. As Cattell (1978) pointed out in his presidential address at the fourth meeting of the American Psychological Association in 1875: "Selected representatives of science in England and America . . . hold that science had an adequate end in the satisfaction of intellectual curiosity. On the other hand, [Benjamin] Franklin, the father of American science, speaks of new discoveries as important only because they tend to extend the power of [human beings] over

matter, avert or diminish . . . evils . . . , or augment . . . enjoyments" (p. 60).

This aspect of psychology's history is important to remember because it suggests that a tradition of service in the public
interest has been incorporated into the cultural norms and activities of the science of psychology from its inception. This tradition
is institutionalized in the bylaws of the American Psychological
Association (APA), founded in 1892 "to advance psychology as
a science and profession and as a means of promoting human
welfare" (American Psychological Association, 1985, p. xxi).

The important question for American scientists, then, has
not been whether science (and by implication, psychology)
should serve larger values. It is, rather, *whose* values? A feminist
analysis of this statement would emphasize that definitions of
"evils" and "enjoyments" depend on one's standpoint. Extend-
ing the power of human beings "over matter" can be interpreted
either as domination and oppression or as nurturance and
growth.

To feminist psychologists, in society and in psychology,
those values and perspectives have too often been androcentric;
power and control have connoted domination and oppression
rather than agency and efficacy. Actions that devalue and discriminate against women are viewed as antithetical to the welfare of all people. To understand the commitment of feminist
psychologists to diversity, the values, goals, and principles of
feminists must first be understood.

Feminism: Definitions, Goals, and Principles

Feminism is defined as "the theory that women should have political, economic, and social rights equal to those of men" and
"the movement to win such rights for women" (*Webster's New
World Dictionary of the American Language*, College Edition, 1968,
p. 534). This definition oversimplifies the diverse definitions,
ideologies, frameworks, and analyses of the conditions of women
that constitute political, economic, and social inequalities (Donovan, 1992; Tong, 1989) and that are encompassed by the con-

cept of feminism. Feminist theories differ in their attempts to define and explain these inequalities, as well as in the goals and strategies for prevention, intervention, and amelioration of their effects (Anderson & Collins, 1992; Donovan, 1992). Indeed, the widely ranging theories, goals, techniques, and strategies may even conflict with one another (Unger, 1989).

Feminist psychologists, however, have a shared purpose: to search for knowledge that can direct us to sociopolitical and personal change congruent with feminist goals, however they are defined. For feminist psychologists, this goal of empowering women has inevitably led to critiques of all stages of the research process (Denmark, Russo, Frieze, & Sechzer, 1988; McHugh, Koeske, & Frieze, 1986; Grady, 1981; McKenna & Kessler, 1977; Russo, 1990).

The specific goals of feminism have been a reaction to the particular forms of sexism and inequities that exist at a particular moment in a particular context. As Spelman (1988) has stated, "All women are women, but there is no being who is only a woman" (p. 102). Feminist psychologists struggle to deal with the multiple realities for women created by the interaction of gender, ethnicity, social class, sexual orientation, age, degree of being able-bodied, and other social categories. Actions to eliminate social, economic, and political inequalities must be constructed around the multiple forms of those inequalities — forms that depend on many cross-cutting social categories. The ideals of feminist psychology thus mandate inclusivity and awareness of issues of diversity in theory, research, and practice (Brown & Root, 1990; Comas-Díaz, 1991; Reid & Comas-Díaz, 1990; A. Smith & Stewart, 1983).

The ideal of incorporating diversity into feminist theory and research has yet to be consistently and fully attained (Fine, 1985, 1992). The goals and agendas of particular feminist activities have too often emphasized the issues, concerns, and contexts of white, middle-class feminists to the exclusion of those of women in other social categories. Breaking the glass ceiling for women in middle management, for example, is not a priority for single mothers on welfare who cannot find jobs and who are concerned about having a roof over their heads and food for their children. "Liberating" women to pursue careers does not speak to African-American women, who have always worked outside the home. Concerns about sexist concepts in psychotherapy, which has primarily served middle- and upper-class consumers, have not been priorities for women of color who do not have access to basic health care for themselves and their families.

Yet the feminist movement within psychology has had strong, articulate, ethnic minority women who have played critical roles in shaping the definitions, norms, and institutions of feminist psychology. Their contributions continue to expose deficiencies and provide alternative models for evolution, even revolution, in feminist theories, methods, and applications (Amaro & Russo, 1987; Brown & Root, 1990; Comas-Díaz, 1991; Comas-Díaz & Greene, in press; Murray & Scott, 1982; Rabinowitz & Sechzer, 993; Reid & Comas-Díaz, 1990). Issues of diversity have gone beyond ethnicity, however (Comas-Díaz, 1991), to include degree of being able-bodied (Fine & Asch, 1988), age (Datan, 1989; Rodeheaver & Datan, 1988), class (Belle, 1990), and sexual orientation (Boston Lesbian Psychologies Collective, 1987; Brown, 1989; Wilkinson & Kitzinger, 1993).

The Link Between Diversity and Feminist Thought

As Dale Spender (1985) has pointed out, "Feminist knowledge is based on the premise that the experience of all human beings is valid and must not be excluded from our understandings, whereas patriarchal knowledge is based on the premise that the experience of only half the human population needs to be taken into account and the resulting version can be imposed on the other half." Although the specific goals and strategies of feminists are diverse, there are some basic principles for developing a knowledge based on a feminist perspective. These include rejecting the androcentric view of the male as the norm, putting women's experiences and meanings at the center of the analysis, and emphasizing sociocultural origins and definitions of

gender. Feminists of all disciplines have worked to expose the
ways in which an androcentric choice of concepts, interpretations, and language for describing women's experiences has
devalued women (Bleier, 1986; Fausto-Sterling, 1985; Farnham,
1987). This rejection of the male as the norm and the female
as a devalued "other" leads to recognition of psychological knowledge as being socially constructed. Once that leap is made,
diverse standpoints reflecting the convergence of multiple social categories can be envisioned, and the questions generated
by feminist researchers and theorists become transformed (Bohan, 1990; Crawford & Marecek, 1989; Sherif, 1979).

Rather than viewing women as deviants, problems, or
victims, a feminist perspective considers women as active agents
with positive strengths, who construct knowledge with self-
awareness, creativity, and intelligence and invest meaning in
their experiences that reflects their diverse social identities. Simple mechanistic or deterministic models do not explain the complex realities that interest feminists. According to Wine (1985),
"The categories, hierarchies, structure, and research methods
developed to describe male experience are simply not adequate
to the task of describing ours" (p. 187).

Shedding old paradigms, however, is not easy. Kahn and
Yoder (1989), for example, argue that the individualistic orientation of American psychology and society becomes reproduced
in the field of the psychology of women, displacing feminist psychologists from their goals of women's empowerment and societal change. Theories that presume essential differences between
men and women (whether inherent, biological, or a product of
early socialization) imply that such differences are permanent
and resistant to change. Thus, although the analyses posed by
such theories seek to portray differences in a positive light (Gilligan, 1982; Belenky, Clinchy, Goldberger, & Tarule, 1986),
they can nonetheless undermine efforts to improve women's status (Mednick, 1989; Kahn & Yoder, 1992).

Fine and Gordon (1989) also emphasize difficulties in implementing feminist ideals. After reviewing articles published
in the *Psychology of Women Quarterly* in 1985–86, they reported
that feminist psychology in that journal did "reform the samples,

methods, and questions of psychology as well as broaden the scope of interpretation." However, they also concluded that "most feminist psychologists have yet to declare questions of power primary; to establish white, patriarchal control as central to relations and representations of gender; and to take seriously the spaces that women create as retreats, as celebrations, as moments of resistance, and as the closets for our social transformation" (p. 151).

Nonetheless, most feminist psychologists do consider women's behaviors and cognitions to be socioculturally determined adaptations to their diverse social environments (Ricketts, 1989; Unger, 1989). Feminist psychologists emphasize that attributing women's thoughts and actions to inherent personal attributes rather than to women's interactions with their gendered sociocultural environments is fallacious (Ricketts, 1989). Thus, they are working to develop new, integrative paradigms that will both recognize individuals as conscious agents of change and view sociocultural factors as defining situations and shaping contingencies, identities, outcomes, and possibilities for action (Deaux, 1993; Fine, 1992).

Deaux and Major (1987), for example, have developed a model of gender conceptualized as a component of ongoing interactions. In their interactive model, perceivers communicate expectations, targets negotiate their own identities, and the resulting behavior is shaped by the immediate context in which the interaction takes place. If gender role expectations of either or both parties are salient in a particular situation, they can guide the interaction.

Feminist psychology thus requires going beyond pointing out gaps in current knowledge within narrow traditional boundaries. Feminists must claim the power to name issues and problems in new ways, from alternative perspectives, and for new audiences (Stimpson, 1979). In this process of redefining boundaries and constructing new knowledge, feminists emphasize that knowledge evolves and changes as the sociocultural context evolves and changes. Issues of diversity thus become integral keys to understanding women's lives and make the quest for new theories and methods of conceptualizing and studying the interaction of people with their situations over time and across cultures essential for progress in feminist research (Adler, 1993; Denmark & Paludi, 1993; Hare-Mustin & Marecek, 1990; O'Connell & Russo, 1991; Unger, 1989).

Contemporary feminist psychology is now an active, organized subfield of psychology. Feminist psychologists are working in a variety of areas that broaden psychological understanding of the pervasive impact of sociocultural institutions on the individual. They are in the forefront of cross-disciplinary collaboration in psychology and are playing important roles in establishing and expanding structures, such as women's studies programs, designed to nourish such collaborations. Their activities reflect a hundred-year heritage of feminist activity in psychology.

Feminist Psychology: Linking Theories and Methods

Because theory and method are interrelated, building a feminist knowledge base has required extensive questioning of methods in psychology. If the goal of feminist research is to empower women, are some methods more suited for achieving that goal? This question has stimulated substantial discussion and debate in the field (Allen & Baber, 1992; Fine, 1992; Landrine, Klonoff, & Brown-Collins, 1992; Reinharz, 1992).

Feminists have argued that "dominant beliefs about the proper ways to pursue knowledge have made psychological research peculiarly prone to bias in its conception, execution, and interpretation" (Sherif, 1979, p. 99). These beliefs, which are interrelated, generally derive from what has been called psychology's "physics envy" (Keller, 1985). They include adopting reductionism from the physical sciences as a model, narrowly defining the parameters of the investigation, masking bias in the guise of "objectivity," and privileging knowledge gained through the experimental method over knowledge gained from other types of research (Sherif, 1979). The detrimental impact of these beliefs is seen in the distorted pictures of women's lives that have been generated by the flawed measures and techniques traditionally used in psychological research.

Measures and Techniques Used
in Psychological Research

Many of the current measures and techniques used in psychology
have been criticized by feminist scholars as being reductionistic
and constructed from an androcentric perspective (Sherif, 1979;
O'Connell & Russo, 1991). Lewin and Wild (1991) provide a description of sexism in the construction of a variety of psychological
tests of measurements, particularly the Minnesota Multiphasic
Personality Inventory (MMPI). They describe how measures have
used male content, such as sports, in test items used to assess
academic skills, never considering alternatives to the assumption
that this content was equally valid for men and women as an indi-
cant of academic ability. They also demonstrate how deficiencies
in conceptualization become reflected in deficiencies in operationalization. Thus, the makers of the MMPI, who conceptualized
gay sexual orientation in males as identical to femininity in
women, validated the test's measure of femininity on a criterion
group of gay men. The latest revision of the MMPI rectified this
problem, but it now includes a "masculinity-femininity scale" that
is of mysterious origin (the test makers do not explain its construction) and lacks face validity (Lewin & Wild, 1991).

Another approach is found in the work of Landrine,
Klonoff, and Brown-Collins (1992), who demonstrated that ethnic minority women and majority women responded similarly
on an objective test of self-definition but looked significantly
different on subjective measures of the self. This finding demonstrates the importance of exploring differences in the meanings
of experiences in general (and test items in particular) before
assuming that objective tests are measuring the same thing when
they are used with research participants from different sociocultural backgrounds or social statuses.

In the area of life-events research, life-event scales that
purport to assess sources of stress in people's lives do not adequately cover rape, battering, and sexual harassment. Such
omissions mean that sources of stress for men and women become obscured, creating a picture of women's psychological distress as reflecting women's higher psychological vulnerability

rather than their greater exposure to negative life events (New-mann, 1984). Women's strengths and coping strategies in the face of great adversity are overlooked, and their weaknesses and deficiencies are emphasized.

Instruments to measure depression have not always separated the expression of sadness (dysphoric mood) from other depressive symptoms (Klerman, 1980). The gender difference in total depression scores appears to reflect greater levels of sadness expressed by women, which is in keeping with their gender role norms (Newmann, 1984). Ironically, although self-disclosure of such feelings is generally considered to be protective for psychological distress, women's greater expression of sadness on such measures is considered a signal of psychological disorder.

The implication of measurement in all of these areas is that feminist science needs to question and reconceptualize the way concepts are operationalized in research so that they reflect the experiences of women's lives and the meanings women assign to those experiences. Women's behaviors and coping strategies must be understood in their sociocultural context, with full recognition of the choices and options open to them, so that their strengths can be understood and appreciated. The powerful impact of gender role norms — norms that vary with a woman's other social dimensions, including ethnicity and class — in shaping women's options across situations must never be forgotten.

Sexism in Research: Research on Conformity

Research on conformity provides a number of illustrations of the way norms associated with differential gender roles and status in the larger society might influence psychological research. First, consider the name of the variable: conformity. Selecting the word *conformity* (as opposed to *interpersonal responsiveness, communal sensitivity,* or *team playing*) to describe the research topic may influence the attitudes and expectations that investigators bring to their work.

The conformity label has negative connotations for men; independence and autonomy are central values in male gender roles in this society. These values do not hold for traditional conceptualizations of women's roles, where the stereotype has been that women are more suggestible and conforming than men. Although the findings are inconsistent, in general, women do appear slightly more likely to conform than men (Eagly, 1987). How might these results be explained by other than internal personal attributes (that is, men being seen as strong and independent, women as weak and suggestible)?

A feminist perspective might offer alternative explanations rooted in the differential roles of men and women that intrude into the experimental setting. Such explanations could emphasize that concern with interpersonal relationships, a tendency to treat other people more democratically, and responsiveness to the social environment are all features associated with women's gender role that may be engaged in a conformity experiment (Eagly, 1987). The merit of seeking an explanation rooted in the larger social context rather than in gender-related personal attributes is further supported by the fact that when researchers are male, gender differences are larger and females more conforming (Eagly & Carli, 1981).

Explanations for the impact of experimenter gender in conformity research illustrate the great variety of subtle ways by which gender can potentially influence the research process. First, male researchers might choose topics more in keeping with the interests or expertise of their own gender or design research settings that make males feel more at ease (and thereby less likely to be influenced). Female researchers might be more likely to report a failure to find gender differences (perhaps because they are pleased to find that the stereotype of the suggestible women is greatly exaggerated), while male researchers might be more likely to consider nonsignificant results uninteresting and discard them. Lower-status people are more likely to conform, and gender differences in status may carry over to the laboratory. Competitive male gender role norms may be operating in the experimental situation as well, so that males and females may both be conforming in the experiment, but to different things. Thus, in the presence of a male experimenter, males may be more likely to conform to the competitive norms of the male sex role and act independently rather than conforming to the norms of the experimental group.

In any case, the impact of the gender of the experimenter reminds us that the experimental setting is a social context, and that norms, roles, and expectations governing social behavior in our society intrude on that context. How sociocultural norms of the larger context distort the research process is much more difficult to conceptualize.

Is an Objective Psychology
Antithetical to Feminist Goals?

Objective science has been equated with value-free science, which feminists have exposed as a political myth. Significant work requires some sort of theory or perspective behind it, however rudimentary. Because choosing a theory requires defining who is to be the knower and who is to be known, that choice, by definition, is a political act (Hess & Ferree, 1987). Cloaking scientific activity in impersonal language and a neutral style of discourse only obscures the impact of the perspective; it does not eliminate it (D. Smith, 1979).

But is an objective psychology totally antithetical to feminist goals? Is the charge that "feminist psychology" is an oxymoron a fair one? Psychologists recognize that knowledge of the world comes by way of selective processing and interpretation of information gained through our senses. Psychological research and theory explore links between cognition, affect, motivation, and the interpersonal context. Some of the most compelling documentation of the complexity of human subjectivity comes from "objective" psychological research (Fiske & Taylor, 1991).

As a science, psychology emphasizes the development of *empirical* knowledge. It is assumed that there is a "real" world that lies outside the thoughts and feelings of the particular psychologist and is discoverable by clearly specifying definitions and procedures so that methods and findings can be reproduced, verified, and critiqued by individuals holding diverse value systems. The use of empirically measurable definitions and clearly specified procedures to know this real world distinguishes psychology from the "common sense" that encompasses the unsystematic observations, intuitions, guesses, and cultural myths used to devalue women and denigrate their activities. Objectivity means that such common sense can be challenged through methods that yield public and reproducible findings. Although the critiques of the construction of objectivity are important, it must also be recognized that scientific ideology that has valued reason and objectivity has been a powerful tool in the hands of feminist scientists for exposing misinformation, myths, and shibboleths about women and their lives and circumstances.

The recent efforts of antiabortion forces to construct a "postabortion syndrome" provide an example of the power of scientific methods used in the service of feminist goals. Such forces have used anecdotal accounts, "qualitative methodology," and inappropriate application of empirical research methods to argue that access to abortion should be denied because it constitutes a significant mental health risk in the form of postabortion syndrome (Speckhard & Rue, 1992). In contrast, research using scientific methods has shown the fallaciousness of the postabortion-syndrome concept. Although a woman may indeed have psychological problems after having an abortion, a voluntarily chosen *legal* abortion, particularly if it is conducted in the first trimester, is rarely associated with psychological distress that is patterned and severe enough to characterize it as a syndrome (Adler and others, 1992).

Further, such research has shown that simply attributing a woman's problems to having an abortion is inappropriate. A woman's responses after resolving her pregnancy are complex, depend on the circumstances surrounding the abortion (for example, its legality, the length of gestation of the pregnancy, and social support for the woman's decision), involve both positive and negative emotions, and reflect the woman's social and financial context as well as her prepregnancy physical and psychological status (Adler and others, 1992; Major & Cozzarelli, 1992; Russo, 1992; Russo & Zierk, 1992).

Suggesting that objectivity has merit as an ideal in psychology does not imply lack of recognition for the impact of values on the research process — such an impact is an objective fact! But even if diverse psychologists agree that particular methods are appropriate and findings are "real," they may interpret the findings in different ways, depending on their values. For example, the finding that women and minorities use fewer individualistic strategies to cope with tragedy has been interpreted by some as a demonstration of ineffective coping and/or learned helplessness. However, these same findings have been reinterpreted by feminists who suggest that in an oppressive context it may be adaptive to ignore individualistic strategies and take control through other methods such as collective change (Fine, 1992).

Alternatively, gender differences in expectations and attributions for success and failure have been explained by focusing on negative characteristics of women, such as fear of success and self-derogatory biases. But these gender differences can also be explained by focusing on negative characteristics of men, such as their fear of failure and/or other self-enhancing biases (Levine, Reis, Sue, & Turner, 1976). Depending on which group is the standard, differences between groups can be interpreted to each other's advantage or disadvantage.

As an alternative, feminist empiricists advocate a "conscious partiality" (Hess & Ferree, 1987, p. 12), whereby the values and perspectives underlying the research are made explicit for all to examine and critique. This perspective highlights the intellectual advantage of diversity. From this standpoint, strategies that encourage men and women of diverse ethnic backgrounds and cultural experiences to become psychologists are also strategies for stimulating intellectual evolution and the development of alternative paradigms in the field.

Feminist concerns with representing women's experiences in their sociocultural context have required the use of innovative research designs and data collection procedures that are not amenable to traditional laboratory approaches. For example, understanding the pervasiveness and impact of rape, battering, incest, and other forms of violence against women, and the cumulative effects of "minor" events and acts that undermine and degrade women on a daily basis, cannot be assessed in a laboratory setting. Nor could the complexity of a sexual harassment situation in the workplace, which could include any number of possible factors—changes in power dynamics, the social context, the working climate, the impact of harassment on career stability and chances for upward mobility, and various other psychological and stress-related mental health consequences. Researchers in the area of sexual harassment have begun to recognize the importance of using a variety of new research designs to understand the complexity of women's lives and the processes that affect them.

Conclusion

Given the evolution, issues, and activities of feminist psychology, is there an answer to the question, How can the feminist perspective be integrated into the theories and methods of psychology to enrich the science of psychology and empower women in all of their diversity?

It appears that this can be done in three ways. First, it is important to create opportunities for feminist employment in academic institutions, where knowledge is constructed and transmitted to future generations. Without a continued line of diverse feminist scholars, feminist contributions can be reattributed, rendered invisible, and ignored. Feminist psychologists who have worked in applied settings have influenced the field in important ways, but their contributions have been even less likely to be preserved and transmitted.

Second, women's history is vital for preserving and transmitting our feminist heritage. Women's history in psychology reveals the role of social institutions and networks in building careers and defining what is a meritorious contribution and what is not. Only after the emergence of the field of women's history in psychology were the contributions of early feminist foremothers in psychology rediscovered and publicized. Nor surprisingly, the male-centered and male-dominated academic institutions did not preserve the history of feminist challenges to their basic values and assumptions.

Finally, the roles and status of women in the larger social context have an influence on both the subject matter of psychology and the roles and status of women psychologists. The contours of the feminist critique of psychology have reflected the contours of sexism and racism in psychology and society. Further, when societal priorities place an emphasis on areas traditionally considered to be the "women's sphere," such as child development, cooperation and empathy, and even women's health, the fortunes of feminist psychologists prosper — a reflection of the fact that social priorities cannot be achieved without feminist knowledge. When societal problems stemming from women's devalued status become urgent (for example, increased social and health care costs resulting from violence against women or unintended pregnancy), programs and actions that enhance women's status become of greater interest.

Given that sexism and racism persist in many quarters of society, it should not be surprising that psychological knowledge continues to be used to support the status quo. Feminist psychologists still need to rebut the myths and shibboleths used to justify a disadvantaged status for women and minorities. But the increased diversity of the United States, the increasing power and influence of women and minorities in psychology and society, and the changing attitudes of men toward their traditional roles give us hope. Psychology in the twenty-first century may continue to be a tool to justify a sexist and racist status quo, but the use of psychological knowledge for those purposes will be challenged.

References

Adler, L. L. (Ed.). (1993). *International handbook on gender roles.* Westport, CT: Greenwood Press.

Adler, N. E., & others. (1992). Psychological factors in abortion: A review. *American Psychologist, 47,* 1194–1204.

Allen, K. R., & Baber, K. M. (1992). Ethical and epistemological tensions in applying a postmodern perspective to feminist research. *Psychology of Women Quarterly, 16,* 1–15.

Amaro, H. A., & Russo, N. F. (Eds.). (1987). Hispanic women and mental health. *Psychology of Women Quarterly, 11* (Whole No. 4).

American Psychological Association. (1985). Bylaws of the American Psychological Association. *Directory of the American*

Psychological Association (pp. xxi–xxvii). Washington, DC: Author.

Anderson, M., & Collins, P. H. (1992). *Race, class, and gender.* Belmont, CA: Wadsworth.

Belenky, M. F., Clinchy, B. M., Goldberger, N. R., & Tarule, J. M. (1986). *Women's ways of knowing: The development of self, voice, and mind.* New York: Basic Books.

Belle, D. (1990). Poverty and women's mental health. *American Psychologist, 45,* 385–389.

Bleier, R. (Ed.). (1986). *Feminist approaches to science.* Elmsford, NY: Pergamon Press.

Bohan, J. (1990). Contextual history: A framework for replacing women in the history of psychology. *Psychology of Women Quarterly, 14,* 213–227.

Boston Lesbian Psychologies Collective (Eds.). (1987). *Lesbian psychologies: Explorations and challenges.* Urbana: University of Illinois Press.

Brown, L. (1989). New voices, new visions: Toward a lesbian/gay paradigm for psychology. *Psychology of Women Quarterly, 13,* 445–458.

Brown, L. S., & Root, M.P.P. (Eds.). (1990). *Diversity and complexity in feminist therapy.* New York: Haworth Press.

Cattell, J. M. (1978). The progress of psychology as an experimental science. Address of the President of the American Psychological Association, 1895. In E. R. Hilgard (Ed.), *American psychology in perspective: Addresses of the presidents of the American Psychological Association — 1892–1977.* Washington, DC: American Psychological Association.

Comas-Díaz, L. (1991). Feminism and diversity in psychology. *Psychology of Women Quarterly, 15,* 597–609.

Comas-Díaz, L., & Greene, B. (Eds.). (in press). *Women of color and mental health.* New York: Guilford Press.

Crawford, M., & Marecek, J. (1989). Psychology reconstructs the female: 1968–1988. *Psychology of Women Quarterly, 13,* 147–165.

Datan, N. (1989). Aging women: The silent majority. *Women's Studies Quarterly, 17,* 12–19.

Deaux, K. (1993). Reconstructing social identity. *Personality and Social Psychology Bulletin, 19,* 4–12.

Deaux, K., Major, B. (1987). Putting gender into context: An interactive model of gender-related behavior. *Psychological Review, 94,* 369–389.

Denmark, F. L., & Paludi, M. (Eds.). (1993). *Handbook on the psychology of women.* Westport, CT: Greenwood Press.

Denmark, F. L., Russo, N. F., Frieze, I., & Sechzer, J. (1988). Guidelines for avoiding sexism in psychological research. *American Psychologist, 43,* 582–585.

Donovan, J. (1992). *Feminist theory: The intellectual traditions of American feminism* (2nd ed.). New York: Continuum.

Eagly, A. H. (1987). *Sex differences in social behavior: A social role interpretation.* Hillsdale, NJ: Erlbaum.

Eagly, A. H., & Carli, L. L. (1981). Sex of researchers and sex-typed communications as determinants of sex differences in influenceability: A meta-analysis of social influence studies. *Psychological Bulletin, 90,* 1–20.

Farnham, C. (Ed.). (1987). *The impact of feminist research in the academy.* Bloomington: Indiana University Press.

Fausto-Sterling, A. (1985). *Myths of gender: Biological theories about women and men.* New York: Basic Books.

Fine, M. (1985). Reflections on a feminist psychology of women. *Psychology of Women Quarterly, 9,* 167–183.

Fine, M. (1992). *Disruptive voices: The possibilities of feminist research.* Ann Arbor: University of Michigan Press.

Fine, M., & Asch, A. (Eds.). (1988). *Women with disabilities: Essays in psychology, culture, and politics.* Philadelphia: Temple University Press.

Fine, M., & Gordon, S. M. (1989). Feminist transformations of/Despite psychology. In M. Crawford & M. Gentry (Eds.), *Gender and thought: Psychological perspectives.* New York: Springer-Verlag.

Fiske, S. T., & Taylor, S. E. (1991). *Social cognition* (2nd ed.). New York: McGraw-Hill.

Gilligan, C. (1982). *In a different voice: Psychological theory and women's development.* Cambridge, MA: Harvard University Press.

Grady, K. E. (1981). Sex bias in research design. *Psychology of Women Quarterly, 5,* 628–636.

Hare-Mustin, R., & Marecek, J. (1990). *Making a difference:*

Psychology and the construction of gender. New Haven, CT: Yale University Press.

Hess, B. B., & Ferree, M. M. (Eds.). (1987). *Analyzing gender: A handbook of social science research*. Newbury Park, CA: Sage.

Kahn, A. S., & Yoder, J. D. (1989). The psychology of women and conservatism: Rediscovering social change. *Psychology of Women Quarterly, 13,* 417–432.

Kahn, A. S., & Yoder, J. D. (Eds.). (1992). Women and power. *Psychology of Women Quarterly, 16* (Whole No. 4).

Keller, E. F. (1985). *Reflections of gender and science.* New Haven, CT: Yale University Press.

Klerman, G. (1980). Overview of affective disorders. In H. I. Kaplan, A. M. Freedman, & B. I. Sadock (Eds.), *Comprehensive textbook of psychiatry III* (Vol. 2, pp. 1305–1319). Baltimore, MD: William & Wilkins.

Landrine, H., Klonoff, E. A., & Brown-Collins, A. (1992). Cultural diversity and methodology in feminist psychology. *Psychology of Women Quarterly, 16,* 145–163.

Levine, R., Reis, H. T., Sue, E., & Turner, G. (1976). Fear of failure in males: A more salient factor than fear of success in females? *Sex Roles, 2,* 389–398.

Lewin, M., & Wild, C. (1991). The impact of the feminist critique on texts, assessment, and methodology. *Psychology of Women Quarterly, 15,* 581–598.

McHugh, M. C., Koeske, R. D., & Frieze, I. H. (1986). Issues to consider in conducting nonsexist psychology: A review with recommendations. *American Psychologist, 41,* 879–890.

McKenna, W., & Kessler, S. J. (1977). Experimental design as a source of sex bias in social psychology. *Sex Roles, 3,* 117–128.

Major, B., & Cozzarelli, C. (1992). Psychosocial predictors of adjustment to abortion. *Journal of Social Issues, 48,* 121–142.

Mednick, M.T.S. (1989). The politics of psychological constructs: Stop the bandwagon, I want to get off. *American Psychologist, 44,* 1118–1123.

Murray, S. R., & Scott, P. B. (Eds.). (1982). Special issue on black women. *Psychology of Women Quarterly, 6* (Whole No. 3).

Newmann, J. (1984). Sex differences in symptoms of depression: Clinical disorder or normal distress? *Journal of Health and Social Behavior, 25,* 136–159.

O'Connell, A. N., & Russo, N. F. (Eds.). (1991). Women's heritage in psychology: Origins, developments, and future directions [Centennial Issue]. *Psychology of Women Quarterly, 15* (Whole No. 4).

Rabinowitz, V. C., & Sechzer, J. A. (1993). Feminist perspectives on research methods. In F. L. Denmark & M. Paludi (Eds.), *Handbook on the psychology of women* (pp. 23–66). Westport, CT: Greenwood Press.

Reid, P., & Comas-Díaz, L. (1990). Gender and ethnicity: Perspectives on dual status. *Sex Roles, 22,* 397–407.

Reinharz, S. (1992). *Feminist methods in social research.* New York: Oxford University Press.

Ricketts, M. (1989). Epistemological values of feminists in psychology. *Psychology of Women Quarterly, 13,* 401–415.

Rodeheaver, D., & Datan, N. (1988). The challenge of double jeopardy: Toward a mental health agenda for aging women. *American Psychologist, 43,* 648–654.

Russo, N. F. (1983). Psychology's foremothers: Their achievements in context. In A. N. O'Connell & N. F. Russo (Eds.), *Models of achievement: Reflections of eminent women in psychology* (pp. 9–24). New York: Columbia University Press.

Russo, N. F. (1990). Reconstructing the psychology of women. In M. T. Notman & C. Nadelsen (Eds.), *Women and men: New perspectives on gender* (pp. 43–62). Washington, DC: American Psychiatric Press.

Russo, N. F. (1992). Psychological aspects of unwanted pregnancy and its resolution. In J. D. Butler & D. F. Walbert (Eds.), *Abortion, medicine, and the law* (4th ed., pp. 593–626). New York: Facts on File.

Russo, N. F., & Zierk, K. L. (1992). Abortion, childbearing, and women's well-being. *Professional Psychology: Research and Practice, 23,* 269–280.

Sherif, C. W. (1979). Bias in psychology. In J. A. Sherman & E. T. Beck (Eds.), *The prism of sex: Essays in the sociology of knowledge* (pp. 93–134). Madison: University of Wisconsin Press.

Smith, A., & Stewart, A. J. (1983). Approaches to studying racism and sexism in black women's lives. *Journal of Social Issues, 39,* 1–15.

Smith, D. (1979). A sociology for women. In J. A. Sherman & E. T. Beck (Eds.), *The prism of sex: Essays in the sociology of knowledge* (pp. 135–188). Madison: University of Wisconsin Press.

Speckhard, A. C., & Rue, V. (1992). Postabortion syndrome: An emerging public health concern. *Journal of Social Issues, 48,* 95–120.

Spelman, E. V. (1988). *Inessential women: Problems of exclusion in feminist thought.* Boston: Beacon Press.

Spender, D. (1985). *For the record: The meaning and making of feminist knowledge.* London: Women's Press.

Stimpson, C. R. (1979). The power to name: Some reflections on the avant-garde. In J. Sherman & E. T. Beck (Eds.), *The prism of sex: Essays in the sociology of knowledge.* Madison: University of Wisconsin Press.

Tong, R. (1989). *Feminist thought: A comprehensive introduction.* Boulder, CO: Westview Press.

Unger, R. K. (1989). Explorations in feminist ideology: Surprising consistencies and unexamined conflicts. In R. K. Unger (Ed.), *Representations: Social constructions of gender* (pp. 203–211). Amityville, NY: Baywood.

Wilkinson, S., & Kitzinger, C. (1993). *Heterosexuality: A feminism and psychology reader.* London: Sage.

Wine, J. D. (1985). Models of human functioning: A feminist perspective. *International Journal of Women's Studies, 8*(2), 183–192.

5

Optimal Theory and the Psychology of Human Diversity

Linda James Myers
Suzette L. Speight

As technology advances, the world shrinks and global crises are exacerbated by our inability to understand and appreciate one another. The prevailing worldview fosters alienation, competition, and the need for oppression. Several authors have pointed to the void in Western psychology that is created by the lack of a comprehensive framework for understanding how gender, race, ethnicity, age, sexual orientation, class, and other aspects of human diversity are integral to the field of psychology in general and community psychology in particular (Graham, 1992; Watts, 1992; Yee, Fairchild, Weizmann, & Wyatt, 1993). Optimal Theory (Myers, 1988) offers a coherent framework for realizing the unity within the varieties of human diversity and a method for accounting for individual and community action. Optimal Theory encourages an examination of human behavior through socially defined diversity markers such as race, ethnicity, gender, and physical ability. This chapter examines the value of Optimal Theory as a system of reasoning that avoids and transforms oppositional thinking by creating spaces that support the psychology of human diversity. We will consider the principles and tenets of Optimal Theory as they apply to issues of human diversity, particularly its implications for oppression and social change.

Introduction to Optimal Theory

Optimal Theory draws from the philosophical parameters of ancient traditions of African culture (Amen, 1990; Asante & Asante, 1990; Chernoff, 1990; Jahn, 1961; Karenga, 1989; Mbiti, 1970; Nobles, 1980; Myers, 1988; Sproul, 1979). Philosophically, the interrelatedness, interconnectedness, and interdependence of all humanity is assumed, given current archaeological evidence of a single gene pool (Cann, Stoneking, & Wilson, 1987). Accordingly, each human being is seen as the individual and unique expression of a systematic (naturally ordered), self-perpetuating, and self-correcting life energy that is manifested in various ways. The notion of human diversity within this context is critical because the diversity markers (for example, race, ethnicity, gender, and physical ability) symbolizes the nature, form, and organization of life energy, reflecting many levels of meaning and significance.

Optimal Theory emerged in the late seventies. Although it shares ideas with what are now called the Africentric (or Afrocentric) and transpersonal schools of thought, Myers (1981) sought to go beyond a critique of the hegemony of the Western worldview in social science, with the aim of introducing a paradigm that reflected African cultural realities. Key elements of philosophy from the beginnings of human civilization in Africa were used to create a worldview and conceptual system consistent with African common sense, modern Western physics, and Eastern philosophy. Optimal Theory emphasizes spirituality, which is missing in most Western models of human functioning and development (Myers, 1984). Maslow predicted a "fourth force" in psychological inquiry concerned with consciousness, health, and well-being beyond ego and personality (Walsh & Vaughn, 1980). Optimal Theory is consistent with this fourth force.

Optimal Theory holds that humankind is of one life energy, and each individual is the unique creation of this life force. This energy is self-organizing and ordered, functioning maximally under the natural equilibrium, harmony, and unity. Human beings are the expression of what can be defined as energy, spirit, consciousness, or god/goddess. Traditions within African, Native American, feminist, Eastern, and creation spirituality also acknowledge this spiritual unity of humankind. According to Myers and others (1991), "A key tenet of optimal psychology and these other alternate worldviews is the inseparability of the spiritual and the material aspects of reality in which all is seen as the individual and unique manifestation of infinite spirit" (p. 58). In Optimal Theory, identity is seen as the individuated expression of a unified consciousness.

When people become alienated from the unity of consciousness and begin to perceive themselves solely as an individuated self separate from the creative life energy, the estrangement spreads to other aspects of being. As a result, a sense of connection to others is lost and a proclivity for the oppression of others grows. Fragmented, alienated consciousness also creates disharmony and imbalance in the environment and exacerbates insecurity, isolation, and fear. In this suboptimal sociocultural context, individuals base their sense of themselves on material and other external criteria, believing themselves to be how they appear, the clothes they wear, their incomes, their position, the model of car they drive, and so on. Anxiety, insecurity, and fear emerge as they recognize the finite and limited nature of the material possessions on which their fragile self-concept has been built. In the suboptimal worldview, the chief problem is that identity is bound to individual form and disconnected from previous and future generations, nature, and the community. As Sampson (1985) describes it, "The peculiar feature of the Western view is its search for an autonomous, fully integrated entity in itself, defined by its separateness and distinctiveness from other people and the rest of nature" (p. 1204). Sampson (1989) says that industrialization and technology have contributed to the development of a "self-contained individual," detached, alienated, and separate from the community.

In an optimal sociocultural context, the self is "multidimensional, encompassing the ancestors, those yet unborn, nature, and community" (Myers and others, 1991, p. 56). Self-worth is assumed to be intrinsic, independent of external form (Myers, 1981, 1988). Human beings are the individual and unique manifestation of a single life energy regardless of how they appear. A spiritual connection with all of life is acknowledged. Interrelatedness, interdependence, and cooperation characterize human relationships. Life is seen as a process of integrating and expanding one's sense of self to discover its spiritual essence. This sense of connection and relatedness may be a theoretically significant higher development of identity (see, for example, Gilligan, 1988; Sampson, 1985, 1989). According to Hoare (1991), "Mature identities must extend beyond an individualistic self to a generative caring for other groups and for the entire human species" (p. 51). Myers and others (1991) contains a more comprehensive treatment of Optimal Theory applied to issues of identity development.

Human Diversity and Optimal Theory

Culture, a people's way of life, reflects and reinforces the belief system held by a people about themselves and their world. Reality and experience are determined by the nature of the assumptions and beliefs held within the prevailing conceptual system. To the extent that cultures utilize differing conceptual systems, the social realities created and the behaviors manifested will differ accordingly.

Within an optimally constructed culture, it is possible to examine interrelationships. This global vision allows a society to see beyond the superficial, apparent differences to the spiritual unity of all of life. In Optimal Theory, differences between people are seen to emerge from their belief systems, which may be based on suboptimal or optimal conceptual systems. Within an optimal framework, individuals are seen as unique configurations of spiritual energy that are manifested in a myriad of ways, including skin color, ethnicity, size, age, sexual orientation, and gender. These external realities do not diminish the spiritual essence uniting all of life.

In contrast, a suboptimal conceptual system creates an

essentially faulty assumption about an individual's true identity and relationship to the cosmos, which influences human relationships. Whenever people have been socialized to believe in their alienation from the unifying life energy and begin to define themselves through the more superficial aspects that are apparent to the five senses, their way of life will reflect increasing chaos, disharmony, and disorder: "Because worth is not intrinsic, individuals are left to rely on external realities for feelings of self-worth. Hence, one's skin color, class, sex, age, physical or mental abilities, income, education, occupation, and ethnicity all become critical factors in defining individuals" (Speight, Myers, Cox, & Highlen, 1991, p. 31).

A suboptimal conceptual system will yield dichotomous thinking in hierarchical terms (either this or that is better). White skin or male gender become criteria that automatically make some people better. This approach to life promotes societal "-isms" and materialism. Big business (material gain) becomes the primary institution influencing policy, rather than religion or other social values. A "might makes right" orientation emerges and the blindness of the powerful prevents consideration of alternate points of view. Alienation from any conscious sense of unity with the life force brings further alienation from self and others. The need to feel superior, to control, to dominate, and to acquire objects is a natural outcome of this alienation, as is the separation of mind, body, spirit, and nature. According to Myers and others (1991): "Whenever one upholds a segmented conceptualization of the world, oppression is the natural consequence" (p. 62).

It is within this social context that the need for a psychology of human diversity emerges. Optimal Theory provides a basis for transcending apparent differences and understanding the more critical values, attitudes, emotions, and experiences. An optimal conceptual system grants a concurrent examination of individual uniqueness and spiritual unity. Optimal Theory uses the cultural frame of reference of a particular population (ancient Africans) from which to derive its philosophical tenets. However, we argue that the theory's universality is inherent, since all people are African people if they go back far enough into their ancestry to the beginnings of human civilization in the Lake Victoria region of East Africa. Hence, Optimal Theory is holistic and unifying. The perspective of our collective ancestors makes possible a better understanding of the unity of humanity, creating a clear foundation on which to build knowledge of human diversity.

Optimal Theory is not population-specific in the sense that it is relevant to only a particular group of people. It is quite interesting that most of the psychological literature in the West is actually white, male, middle-class psychology. But because of the hegemony of white, middle-class males, this work has been neither defined nor delimited as population-specific; instead, it has been presented as universal, establishing itself with an intellectual imperialism that forces those who attempt to understand human behavior from divergent frames of reference to define themselves as separate and distinct. Typically, these alternate perspectives are categorized by common human diversity markers such as African or Africentric psychology or women's psychology. The long-standing inability of white, middle-class male psychologists to acknowledge their own human diversity markers, and their role in defining not only the issues studied but also the methodology, analyses, and conclusions drawn, exemplifies the serious flaw with most of Western scholarship and society's inherent difficulties with issues of human diversity.

Watts (1992) has called for a network of human diversity that encompasses a multiplicity of convergent and divergent theories related to human diversity. A system of interrelated theories is proposed to address the psychology of diversity. Optimal Theory transforms the assumed separateness of the cross-cultural, population-specific, and sociopolitical perspectives identified by Watts. According to Watts, there are typically three areas of emphasis in population-specific psychologies: (1) the principal elements of the population's culture or worldview (Belenky, Clinchy, Goldberger, & Tarule, 1986; Myers, 1988; Nobles, 1986; Ramirez, 1983), (2) efforts to use knowledge of culture, ethnicity, or worldview to understand, predict, or change behavior (Dasen, Berry, & Sartorius, 1988; Myers, 1988), and (3) explorations of the interaction between worldview, culture, and oppression (Bulhan, 1988; Myers, 1988; Myers and others, 1991). Optimal Theory incorporates these elements in its philosophical assumptions (Myers, 1988). According to Speight, Myers, Cox, and Highlen (1991), the best approach to multiculturalism is derived from a blending of the particular and the universal. An integrated synthesis and balance are required. Optimal Theory has two important strengths: (1) it is a model for theory building because it attends to previously ignored aspects of human experience and diversity and (2) it is a spiritually grounded theory based on humanistic ideals (Watts, personal communication, June 1993).

Oppression and Social Change

According to Optimal Theory, oppression is the logical result of a suboptimal conceptual system. For example, under the hegemony of the suboptimal frame of reference, the near annihilation of Native Americans took place, the enslavement of Africans occurred, and the exploitation of people of color continues today throughout the world. Myers (1981, 1984, 1988), in an attempt to comprehend the prevalence of "-isms" (racism, sexism, classism, heterosexism) within our society, concludes that it is the very nature of the dominant societal worldview that is oppressive. Within the suboptimal conceptual system, oppressing others or being oppressed becomes a characteristic feature of the society. The suboptimal philosophical assumptions that structure the way we view the world are themselves faulty because they are self-alienating and result in alienation from others. To be oppressed, therefore, is to be socialized into a conceptual system that leads to a fragmented sense of self. As stated in Myers and others (1991), "All people who adopt the Suboptimal conceptual system are oppressed" (p. 56).

Oppression is the result of giving over power to forces outside oneself and allowing such external forces to determine and define one's reality. This external orientation is rooted at its deepest levels in the conceptual system shaping one's thoughts and feelings about self, others, and ultimately one's relationship to the world. Within an optimal framework, typical distinctions between the oppressor and the oppressed are not viable, since all those who internalize a fragmented worldview will be oppressed.

Paulo Freire's seminal work, *Pedagogy of the Oppressed,* (1992) explored the reciprocal nature of oppression: "Once a situation of violence and oppression has been established, it engenders an entire way of life and behavior for those caught up in it — oppressors and oppressed alike. Both are submerged in this situation, and both bear the marks of oppression" (p. 44). Freire calls this mark of oppression "dehumanization." Those whose humanity was stolen and those who stole it are both dehumanized. An oppressor's belief system, according to Freire, perceives everything as an object of domination, resulting in a materialistic concept of existence. The oppressed often cannot perceive the oppressive system and instead end up identifying with their oppressor. They may internalize the opinion the oppressor holds of them. When a culture has defined certain criteria to be marks of superiority (for example, white skin, male gender, thinness, and youth) and individuals do not meet these criteria, they often internalize oppression, accepting their espoused inferiority, and seek to become more like the oppressor in any way possible. They may rely on acquisition of the superficial external criteria as the basis for bolstering a fragile sense of self.

This internalized oppression, in effect, supports the oppressive system, and the oppressed become positioned as a participant in their own oppression. Goldenberg (1978), in a discussion of the ideological schema that mediates oppression within American society, explores the "doctrine of personal culpability" (p. 11): "It is, in short, the kind of doctrine through which those who have been purposefully contained, made to feel expendable, or otherwise manipulated are now encouraged to view their condition as not only inevitable, but also traceable to some mysterious personal deficiency. The result is the transformation of social injustice into a perverted form of poetic justice: the myth is maintained by making the victim believe himself to be the principal author of his own victimization" (p. 12).

Oppression is not a one-way process, for despite any concerted efforts by one individual to oppress another, oppression cannot take place unless the other allows it, by yielding her or his consciousness and power to the oppressor's definition of reality. However, Optimal Theory should not be interpreted as blaming the victim for his or her own oppression or acquiescence. To the contrary, if the oppressed have no part in their oppression, then they can have no part in their liberation. Freedom is not a gift bestowed from one to another. Instead, it is acquired through responsible and constant deliberate action (Freire, 1992). To Freire, liberation is a transformational process of becoming more completely human: "Although the situation of oppression is a dehumanized and dehumanizing totality affecting both the oppressors and those whom they oppress, it is the latter who must, from their stifled humanity, wage for both the struggle for a fuller humanity; the oppressor, who is himself dehumanized because he dehumanizes others, is unable to lead this struggle" (p. 32).

Liberation occurs when the need to find a more valid, stable, intrinsic sense of identity propels the individual to move beyond externalized criteria to a self-definition that empowers rather than disempowers. According to Optimal Theory, liberation is a struggle to regain that original connection with the infinite life force. The individual must engage in a "battle to reconquer . . . a surrendered identity" (Erikson, 1968, p. 297). One must truly go within to rediscover the true nature of the self.

The South African leader Nelson Mandela is a miraculous testimony to the capacity of the mind and soul to rediscover the true nature of power. Imprisoned for over twenty-five years, the ultimate example of oppression on the material plane, Nelson Mandela arose wholly liberated and free. His sense of self had certainly transcended the material prison in which he languished. This capacity to transform material circumstances is grounded in a spiritual reality, a connection with the ultimate life energy.

Just as a suboptimal conceptual system will foster intolerance and a devaluing of difference, an optimal conceptual system provides a mechanism for freeing oneself from mental bondage and integrating difference into a holistic picture of the self and others.

Applications of Optimal Theory

Optimal Theory is sociopolitical in that it identifies the fundamental importance of notions of power and oppression in shaping the experience of diverse groups. Using Optimal Theory, we are able to trace the roots of the oppression dynamic (the cyclical roles of oppressor and victim) to a place within the individual human psyche itself. Getting to the core of the dynamic, liberation and empowerment are made possible through a cognitive restructuring process that enhances individuals' capacity to control their thoughts and feelings through reconnection with a more authentic sense of identity.

Optimal Theory has significant implications for research methodologies. The dynamics of cultural contexts can be explored from an optimal frame of reference without compelling the investigator to pretend that she or he operates from the worldview of the population being studied. Rather, the analysis of conceptual systems provides a framework for identifying the underlying assumptions of both the investigators and the research participants. Research from an optimal theoretical perspective does not strive for illusory "objectivity" by falsely distancing itself from a particular worldview. Instead, the researcher brings into conscious awareness the set of assumptions underlying his or her own worldview. This reduces distortions concerning the group under investigation resulting from the researcher's preconceived assumptions. Instead of claiming detachment and interpreting phenomena, the researcher becomes immersed and consciously aware of the assumptions she or he has been using and has a framework for understanding the assumptions used by others. This process frees the researcher from the constraints of a false objectivity.

Furthermore, the research methodologies proposed by Optimal Theory provide an opportunity to integrate the etic and emic approaches to multicultural research. The etic approach refers to a universal perspective. It emphasizes the development of explanatory constructs applicable to all cultures (Lonner, 1985). The emic approach refers to a culture-specific perspective that attempts to examine cultural groups in their own terms rather than contrasting them to other reference groups (Lonner, 1985). The dichotomy between the etic and emic approaches to research is a manufactured one, an artifact of the suboptimal perspective. Speight, Myers, Cox, and Highlen (1991) state: "Both universal and culturally specific approaches are limited in their exclusivity when researching the complex nature of humans, in that they either underestimate or overestimate the influence of culture" (p. 34).

Optimal theory sanctions the development of a hermeneutic perspective that goes beyond the etic-emic distinction, allowing examination of and focus on the interpretation of the phenomenon itself. This expansion of psychology's scientific worldview sheds new light on how research is conceptualized, conducted, and analyzed (Lincoln & Guba, 1985). With the optimal conceptual system as a guiding framework, knowledge can be gained about the scientific process so that the process itself becomes the subject of scrutiny, leading to an increased understanding of the self and others.

Conclusion

Optimal Theory offers a framework and basis for understanding the impact of race, gender, class, age, and all the other diversity markers identifiable among human beings, by unifying the differences while insisting upon the significance of the articulation. Much of the capacity to comprehensively meet the challenges ahead lies in the fact that the optimal perspective is holistic enough to break through the limits of dichotomous (either/or) thinking and bring into focus diunital (both/and) logic. Human beings are the same and different simultaneously. They are the same because of the underlying unifying spiritual essence and different in the forms they take.

Three important principles can be identified relative to a psychology of human diversity: (1) contingent on one's conceptual system, responses to difference will vary; (2) when a suboptimal set of assumptions is adhered to, its fragmented nature sets in place alienation within the self, from nature, causing insecurity and resistance to that which is experienced as "other"; and (3) human diversity will be fully valued and appreciated when the schism created by the suboptimal construction of reality is bridged. Optimal theory provides instructions for bridging the schism. Additionally, the schism itself can be seen as necessary to the self-knowledge process of positive identity development (Myers and others, 1991).

Stated differently, the alienation perceived and experienced by the individual and collective can, if used for purposes of edification toward greater self-knowledge, provide the impetus for growth, health, and unity. For instance, when the human diversity markers possessed by individuals put them at risk for the development of a false identity, a special opportunity for growth is also created. This challenges commonly held beliefs about what it means to be "different" within a cultural context that is intolerant of diversity. Exploring the roles of culture, identity, and oppression in human diversity can help us to grow toward wholeness individually and collectively. In our growth, we will place less emphasis on the superficial diversity markers and focus more on the substantive aspects of humanity having to do with who we are in terms of our character, ethics, values, and morals, rather than with the way we superficially appear. Optimal theory furnishes a new perspective that incorporates diversity as an integral part of understanding human behavior.

References

Amen, R. (1990). *Metu Neter*. Bronx, NY: Khamit Corporation.

Asante, M., & Asante, K. (1990). *African culture: The rhythms of unity*. Trenton, NJ: Africa World Press.

Belenky, M., Clinchy, B., Goldberger, N., & Tarule, J. (1986). *Women's ways of knowing: Development of self, voice, and mind*. New York: Basic Books.

Bulhan, H. (1988). *Franz Fanon and the psychology of oppression*. New York: Plenum.

Cann, R. L., Stoneking, M., & Wilson, A. C. (1987). Mitochondrial DNA and human evolution. *Nature, 325*, 31–36.

Chernoff, J. (1990). *African rhythm and African sensibility*. Urbana, Ill.: University of Illinois Press.

Dasen, P., Berry, J., & Sartorius, N. (1988). *Health psychology: Towards application.* Newbury Park, CA: Sage.

Eisler, R. T. (1987). *The chalice and the blade: Our history, our future.* New York: HarperCollins.

Erikson, E. (1968). *Identity: Youth and crisis.* New York: Harper-Collins.

Freire, P. (1992). *Pedagogy of the oppressed.* New York: Continuum. (Original work published 1970)

Gilligan, C. (1988). Remapping the moral domain: New images of self in relationship. In C. Gilligan, J. V. Ward, & J. M. Taylor (Eds.), *Mapping the moral domain* (pp. 3–19). Cambridge, MA: Harvard University Press.

Goldenberg, I. I. (1978). *Oppression and social intervention.* Chicago: Nelson-Hall.

Graham, S. (1992). "Most of the subjects were White and middle class": Trends in published research on African-Americans in selected APA journals, 1970–1989. *American Psychologist, 47,* 629–639.

Hoare, C. H. (1991). Psychosocial identity and cultural others. *Journal of Counseling and Development, 70,* 45–53.

Jahn, J. (1961). *Muntu: African culture and the Western World.* New York: Grove Press.

Karenga, M. (1989). Toward a sociology of Maatian ethics. *Journal of African Civilization, 10,* 352–395.

Lincoln, Y. S., & Guba, E. G. (1985). *Naturalistic inquiry.* Newbury Park, CA: Sage.

Lonner, W. (1985). Issues in testing and assessment in cross-cultural counseling. *Counseling Psychologist, 13,* 599–614.

Mbiti, J. (1970). *African religions and philosophy.* New York: Doubleday.

Myers, L. J. (1981). The nature of pluralism and the African American case. *Theory into Practice, 20,* 3–6.

Myers, L. J. (1984). The psychology of knowledge: The importance of world view. *New England Journal of Black Studies, 4,* 1–12.

Myers, L. J. (1988). *Understanding an Afrocentric world view: Introduction to an optimal psychology.* Dubuque, IA: Kendall/Hunt.

Myers, L. J., and others. (1991). Identity development and

world view: Toward an optimal conceptualization. *Journal of Counseling and Development, 70,* 54–63.

Nobles, W. (1980). *African psychology: Toward its reclamation, reascension, and revitalization.* Oakland, CA: Black Family Institute.

Nobles, W. (1986). *African psychology.* Oakland, CA: Black Family Institute.

Ramirez, M. (1983). *Psychology of the Americas: Mestizo perspectives on personality and mental health.* Elmsford, NY: Pergamon Press.

Sampson, E. E. (1985). The decentralization of identity: Toward a revised concept of personal and social order. *American Psychologist, 40,* 1203–1211.

Sampson, E. E. (1989). The challenge of social change for psychology. *American Psychologist, 44,* 914–921.

Speight, S. L., Myers, L. J., Cox, C. I., & Highlen, P. S. (1991). A redefinition of multicultural counseling. *Journal of Counseling and Development, 70,* 29–36.

Sproul, B. (1979). *Primal myths.* New York: HarperCollins.

Walsh, R. N., Vaughan, F. (Eds.). (1980). *Beyond ego: Transpersonal dimensions in psychology.* Los Angeles: Jeremy P. Tarcher.

Watts, R. (1992). Elements of a psychology of human diversity. *Journal of Community Psychology, 20,* 116–131.

Yee, A. H., Fairchild, H. H., Weizmann, F., & Wyatt, G. E. (1993). Addressing psychology's problems with race. *American Psychologist, 48,* 1132–1140.

6

An Ecological Perspective on Cultural and Ethnic Psychology

John W. Berry

The task of cross-cultural psychology has typically been to describe and explain human psychological diversity as a function of cultural diversity. The term *culture* usually includes notions that are both broader than culture (such as ecology) and less broad (such as ethnicity). That is, a range and a network of contexts for human development and behavior need to be understood in interpreting human psychological functioning. This complex includes whole ecosystems (physical environments in which humans and other animals engage in an endless process of cultural and biological adaptation), nation-states and societies with comprehensive economic and political institutions, ethnocultural groups with cultural traditions transmitted over generations, and evolving relationships between these contexts. The essence of this diverse enterprise is captured in the following definition: "Cross-cultural psychology is the study of similarities and differences in individual psychological functioning in various cultural and ethnic groups; of the relationships between psychological variables and socio-cultural, ecological and biological variables; and of ongoing changes in these variables" (Berry, Poortinga, Segall, & Dasen, 1992, p. 2).

115

In this chapter, I present a summary of this perspective, as it applies both to the cultures of autonomous national populations and to ethnocultural groups within such populations. The terms *cultural* and *ethnic* will be used to signify these two areas of interest. The chapter begins with a presentation of an ecological and cultural framework within which human psychological development and behavior take place. This is followed by a comparison of the goals and activities of cultural psychology and ethnic psychology and then by an outline of a methodological framework for carrying out research in both areas. The chapter ends with a discussion of the application of these ideas to understanding some specific aspects of psychological functioning both across and within cultures.

An Ecological Framework

An ecological framework for cross-cultural psychology is presented in Figure 6.1. This framework is a conceptual scheme derived from earlier models I proposed (Berry, 1975, 1976, 1986), where it was called an "ecocultural model." However, its roots go back to the views of Kardiner and Linton (1945) and Whiting (1974) in the field of culture and personality.

The framework distinguishes between the *population* level and the *individual* level of analysis. The flow of the framework is from left to right, with population-level variables (on the left) conceived of as influencing individual outcome (on the right). This general flow is intended to correspond to the interests of cross-cultural psychology; we wish to account for individual and group differences in psychological characteristics as a function of population-level factors. However, it is obvious that a full model, one that attempts to completely specify relationships in the real world, would have many more components and numerous feedback arrows, representing reciprocal influences between components and by individuals on other variables in the framework.

The notion of feedback recognizes the individual as an actor and avoids viewing the developing and behaving individual as a mere pawn. For ease of presenting the framework, the

Figure 6.1. An Ecological Framework for Cross-Cultural Psychology.

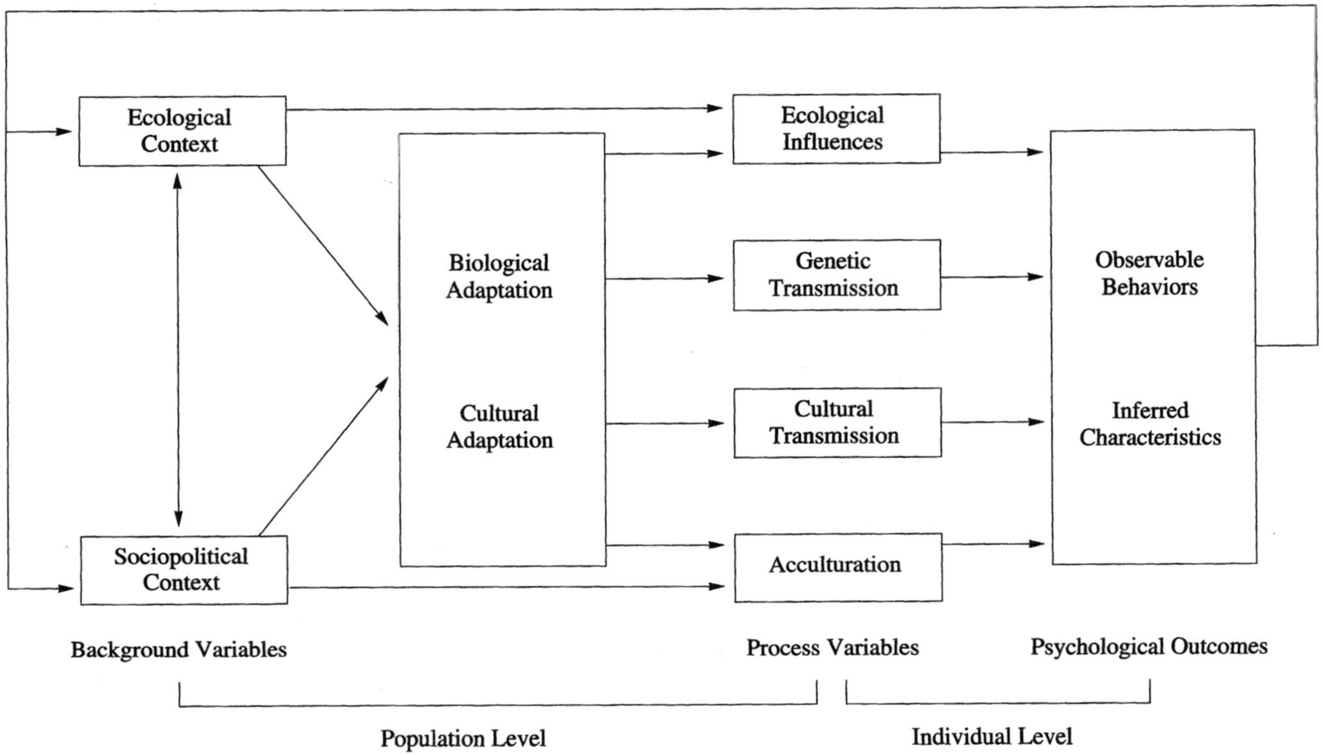

two feedback relationships illustrated in Figure 6.1 (individuals influencing their ecological and sociopolitical contexts) are used to signal feedback in the framework more generally.

At the extreme left are two major classes of influence (background variables of ecological and sociopolitical context), while at the extreme right are the psychological characteristics that are usually the focus of psychological research (including both observable behaviors and inferred characteristics such as motives, abilities, traits, and attitudes). The two middle sets of variables (the process variables) represent the various forms of transmission or influence from population variables to individuals. For completeness, both biological and cultural factors are included; however, the usual emphasis in cross-cultural psychology is on cultural influences.

The ecological context is the setting in which human organisms and the physical environment interact. It is best understood as a set of relationships that provide a range of life possibilities for a population. Such an interactive point of view is the essence of an ecological approach and avoids the pitfalls of earlier approaches, such as that of environmental determinism (Berry, 1976; Feldman, 1975). Since the organism interacts with its habitat primarily to exploit resources in order to sustain individual and collective life, the basic feature of this ecological context is *economic activity*. This variable involves nonindustrial cultural groups that are rated with respect to their degree of reliance on five kinds of economic activity: hunting, gathering, fishing, pastoralism, and agriculture. Urban-industrial societies have a way of life in which other dimensions of economic activity have emerged and that is rated on those dimensions, the most common being socioeconomic status. However, each form of economic activity implies a different kind of relationship between the local human population resources of the habitat. These relationships in turn imply varying cultural, biological, and psychological outcomes.

With respect to adaptation at the population level, individual behavior can be understood across cultures only when both cultural and biological features are taken into account. This joint interest in cultural and biological influences on behavior appears necessary because the exclusion of cither as a factor in the explanation of human psychological variation makes little sense (Boyd & Richerson, 1985). Culture is transmitted by the processes of *enculturation* and *socialization,* which are the central concepts used to describe this cultural transmission.

However, not all outcomes are necessarily the result of ecological relationships. Also depicted in Figure 6.1 is the view that culture and individual behavior are affected by influences stemming from cultural contact in the sociopolitical context of one's group. These influences form the basis for *acculturation,* resulting from such historical and contemporary experiences as colonial expansion, international trade, invasion, and migration.

Not all relationships between the two major background variables and psychological outcome are mediated by cultural or biological adaptation. Some influences are direct and rather immediate, such as environmental learning in a particular ecology (leading to a new performance), nutritional deficiency during a famine (leading to reduced performance), or a new experience with another culture (leading to new attitudes or values). Since individuals can recognize, screen, appraise, and alter all of these influences, whether they are direct or mediated, there are likely to be wide individual differences in the psychological outcomes.

Cultural and Ethnic Psychology

In cross-cultural psychology, it is possible to discern a characteristic dimension for understanding human diversity. At one end, the ideal, human diversity is viewed in anthropological terms, where all cultures are equally valued and equally valid collective expressions of human life; at the other end, unfortunately, the frequent practice is for human diversity to be treated as a set of deviant variations on one's own form of cultural life, (usually Euro-American, urban, and industrialized). This dimension is used in both branches of the discipline: the long-standing concern with geographically dispersed, autonomous national cultures (cultural psychology) and the newer concern with ethnocultural groups in pluralistic societies (ethnic psychology) (see Berry, 1985).

Cultural psychology seeks to discover systematic relationships between cultural and behavioral variables, asking whether individuals growing up in culture A tend to develop that culture's psychological qualities. The hallmark of cultural psychology is the attempt to understand individual psychological functioning in the cultural context in which it developed.

Many psychologists who are interested in the role of culture in human behavior have pursued the relationship comparatively, in order to introduce some variability in cultural experience. They ask whether individuals growing up in culture A tend to develop culture A's psychological qualities more than those growing up in culture B develop culture B's psychological qualities. In this definition, culture is conceived of as a relatively full-scale and independent way of life that generally surrounds the developing individual and provides a broad enculturation context for psychological development. For this enterprise, the term *cross-cultural psychology* has typically been employed (Berry, Poortinga, Segall, & Dasen, 1992).

The field of *ethnic psychology* poses a similar question: Does an individual growing up in ethnocultural group P develop group P's psychological qualities, and does this happen more than among persons growing up in ethnocultural group Q? However, ethnocultural groups usually do not provide a full-scale or independent cultural surround: an individual developing in such a group is usually primarily enculturated by his or her own ethnocultural group but is also acculturated by some other group (either a host culture or another ethnocultural group).

The key aspects compared in these two psychologies are shown in Table 6.1. The numbers refer to the blocks of information that are typically sought.

Cultural Psychology

The central features of cultural psychology are as follows. First, substantial contextual data are gathered about the cultural group we are working in (1), including ecological adaptation, economic base, social structure, language, and child rearing practices,

Table 6.1. Cultural Psychology and Ethnic Psychology:
A Comparison of Information Required in Research Studies.

Aspects Being Compared	Cultural Psychology	Ethnic Psychology
Population (independent) variables	1. Characteristics of cultural group in which the individual develops	6. Characteristics of ethnocultural group in which the individual develops or of which he or she becomes a member
		7. Characteristics of other groups with which the developing individual is in contact
		8. Characteristics of the interactions between the groups in contact
Individual (dependent) variables	2. Psychological qualities of individuals developing within a cultural group	9. Psychological qualities of individuals developing within, or becoming members of, an ethnocultural group
General goal	3. To discover systematic relationships between independent and dependent variables	10. To discover systematic relationships between independent and dependent variables
Explanatory constructs	4. Enculturation and socialization	11. Enculturation and acculturation
Use of comparative method	5. To discover psychological similarities and differences between individuals developing under different and independent cultural conditions, and to link these conditions to psychological variation	12. To discover psychological similarities and differences between individuals developing in, or becoming members of, different ethnocultural groups, and to link the group conditions to psychological variation

taking care to assess those of particular theoretical importance for the study. Then an attempt is made (2) to assess the psychological qualities of interest; historically, these have been in the areas of perception, cognition and personality, but they now run the full gamut of psychological functions and processes. The general goal (3) is to discover systematic relationships between the background cultural, or independent, variables and the psychological, or dependent, variables. The preferred explanatory construct for these relationships in cultural psychology (4) has tended to be one based on the obvious teaching and learning activities (cultural transmission) that take place in every culture (enculturation or socialization); however, biological constructs (genetic inheritance) and biological factors (for example, nutrition) remain as plausible alternative, or interactive, mechanisms in many cases. When researchers seek to increase variation in the independent and dependent variables by using the comparative method (5), patterns of similarities as well as greater differences usually become apparent.

Ethnic Psychology

While we did not attend earlier to the definition of a cultural group, we need to come up with a working definition of an ethnocultural group. First, the group must be an identifiable set of individuals who socially interact and who maintain themselves over time; there also needs to be some social structure and some system of norms governing the conduct of members. Thus, people who merely share a common origin — for example, all people living in Brazil whose ancestors came from Italy — do not sufficiently define an ethnic group. Second, the group needs to be ethnic in character. What constitutes *ethnic* is not easy to define precisely; however, two necessary aspects generally appear in most definitions. The *objective* facet refers to descent from an original cultural group in two distinct senses: being offspring and being derivative. People who are biological and cultural offspring of members of a group can usually be defined by objective indicators such as name and genealogy; ethnocultural group life can usually be studied objectively by social scientists to demonstrate that such things as food, dress, language, and religion are not exact replicas of original cultural phenomena, generation after generation, but are derivative versions modified over time and space. The *subjective* aspect involves a sense of identity with or attachment to the group; people feel they belong and work to maintain the ethnocultural group and their membership in it.

What are the important characteristics of an ethnocultural group for researchers (6)? In general, these parallel, but are more complicated than, the characteristics of a cultural group (1). This is so because an ethnocultural group is not in charge of defining itself; both other groups with which it is in contact (7) and the nature of the group interactions (8) influence the characteristics of the particular ethnocultural group, in addition to influences derived from its own cultural heritage.

To begin, we need to carry out an inventory of the nature of the group (6), including its name, size, location, organization, languages, socieconomic status, and demographic stability; this parallels the ethnographic work usually done for a cultural group (1). This inventory goes well beyond the simplistic practice of just naming an ethnocultural group (for example, "Hispanic"), which assumes that the contents of the package are completely known by its label.

Other groups (7) may be important contributors to the psychological development of an individual; a Breton is almost inevitably influenced by French culture just as a French Canadian is by English-Canadian compatriots. If this is the case, then these other groups' characteristics need to be equally studied, emphasizing the same variables that were attended to earlier (6).

The relationships between the focal and other groups (8) are also important topics for study in ethnic psychology. Here we must confront the issue of minority. The terms *ethnic* and *minority* are not identical; there can be nonethnic minorities, like children and people with disabilities, and ethnocultural groups who are not minorities, like the Flemish in Belgium. At the simplest level, *minority* refers to a group that is small in number, or at least not the majority in a society. However, it has also come to refer to groups that are both relatively powerless (subordinate) and objects of discrimination. These latter two characteristics, however, depend on the characteristics of other groups (7), such as their willingness to share privilege and status, and on the relations between groups in a society (8), including their mutual tolerance. In open, pluralist societies that espouse a multicultural ideology (Berry, Kalin, & Taylor, 1977), it is possible in principle to have no minorities, only ethnocultural groups.

An exclusive focus on a particular ethnocultural group (like guest workers in Germany or Chicanos in the United States) *as a minority* tends to define the issues in terms of the group's characteristics (6), rather than in terms of the other important sets of variables, for example, the broader social and political context (7) and the complex pattern of relationships between this context and the particular group of concern (8). The pairing of *ethnic* with *minority* in psychological research predetermines the conceptual and empirical approaches that may be taken and usually biases the research in substantial ways.

These biases arise because of the ethnocentrism inherent in the use of the term *minority* rather than *ethnocultural group*. The latter term directs our attention to the numerous features of a group that give it uniqueness, substance, and vitality. The use of the term *minority,* however, places a group in a subservient position and defines it only in relation to a dominant group, rather than in its own terms. When we believe that all we need to know about a minority group is its current name, we are likely to define that group with our stored (and often stereotypical) information. Referring to a group as ethnocultural should stimulate our obligation to attend fully to the group's cultural qualities.

The list of possible dependent variables in ethnic psychology (9) includes all those relevant to cultural psychology. Moreover, this rather full list can be supplemented by another set of psychological variables arising from the complexity of the individual's context. Specifically, in addition to developing in the ethnocultural group's own context (6), the individual is influenced by other groups (7), giving rise to potentially contradictory learning situations with respect to what is to be learned and what is reinforced and to a set of divergent and possibly conflictual group relations (8). Moreover, individuals may *be-*

come members of an ethnocultural group after initial development in their original cultural group, by experiencing the process
of acculturation. All of these factors give rise to a new set of
behaviors that need to be attended to: identity confusion, feelings of marginality, depression, anxiety, and many others, collectively termed *acculturative stress* (Berry, Kim, Minde, & Mok,
1987). Other research topics also become important, including
bilingualism, cognitive test and school performance, ethnic identity, intergroup relations, and attitudes toward the process of
acculturation itself (Berry and others, 1989). Thus, both the independent and dependent variables become more complex when
moving from cultural psychology to ethnic psychology.

I see, in principle, no fundamental difference between the
general goals of ethnic (10) and cultural (3) psychology: to discover systematic relationships between the context and the psychological characteristics that appear between individual members of the group. They may be more difficult to discover in
ethnic psychology, given the complexity of the parts, and they
may be less well advanced, given the newness of the field, but
they are not different in any fundamental way.

The major explanatory construct (11) of enculturation,
or socialization, discussed in relation to cultural psychology remains important in ethnic psychology: a child is primarily enculturated into her or his own group. However, in addition,
the individual is also *acculturated* to other contexts: his or her own
group may be converted to an ethnocultural group through interaction with other more powerful groups (6), contact with other
groups (7) brings new behaviors to master, and the individual
has to learn to manage the day-to-day aspects of group relations (8).

Acculturation as a process always involves contact, often
involves conflict, and usually results in some form of adaptation by the individual and group; moreover, changes often occur in both the groups in contact. For many researchers, work
on the nature of acculturation has become the core of our interest in ethnic psychology (Berry & Annis, 1988). It is now
clear that the outcome of acculturation will vary dramatically
depending on a variety of factors, including the nature of the

ethnocultural group (6), of other groups in contact (7), of intergroup relations (8), and of many psychological characteristics of the individuals in the ethnocultural group (9).

Four possible outcomes for ethnocultural groups and their individual members are conceptualized in Figure 6.2: *assimilation* (in which an ethnocultural group disappears by absorption), *separation* (in which an ethnocultural group sets out on its own), *integration* (in which an ethnocultural group establishes itself distinctively as an integral component of a pluralistic society), and *marginalization* (in which an ethnocultural group becomes marginalized and its members become demoralized) (Berry and others, 1989). Each category in this fourfold classification is considered to be an acculturation strategy or option available to individuals and groups in pluralist societies, and toward which individuals may hold attitudes.

Assignment to one of these categories rests on how the acculturating individual answers two questions. One asks whether or not the individual's own cultural identity and customs are of value and should be retained. The other asks whether interethnic contact is desirable and whether relations with other groups in the larger society are of value and to be sought.

Figure 6.2. Model of Possible Outcomes of Acculturation.

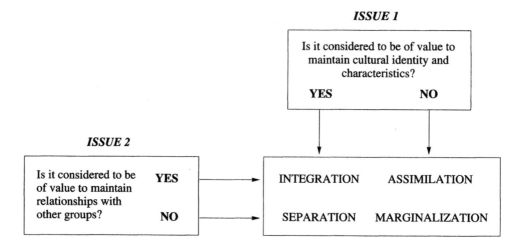

When the answer to the first question is no and the answer to the second is yes, the assimilation option is defined — that is, relinquishing one's cultural identity and moving into the larger society. This can take place by way of absorption of a nondominant group into an established dominant group, or it can occur through the merging of many groups to form a new society, as in the "melting pot."

The integration option implies maintenance of the cultural integrity of the group, as well as movement by the group to become an integral part of a larger societal framework. In this case, a large number of distinguishable ethnocultural groups cooperate within a larger social system, resulting, for example, in the "mosaic" that is promoted in Canada.

When there are no relations with the larger society and ethnic identity and traditions are maintained, another option is defined. Depending upon whether the dominant or nondominant group controls the situation, this option may take the form of either segregation or separation. When the pattern is imposed by the dominant group, classic segregation to keep people "in their place" appears. On the other hand, when a group has the power and desire to lead an existence outside full participation in the large society, the separatist option occurs. Segregation and separation differ primarily with respect to which group or groups have the power to determine the outcome.

Finally, an option exists that is difficult to define precisely because it is accompanied by a good deal of collective and individual confusion and anxiety. In the marginalization option, groups lose cultural and psychological contact with both their traditional culture and the larger society. They characteristically strike out against the larger society and experience feelings of alienation, loss of identity, and acculturative stress. When such a pattern is stabilized in a nondominant group, it constitutes the classic situation of marginality, as described by Stonequist (1937). When marginalization is imposed by the larger society, it is tantamount to ethnocide.

These variations in acculturation strategies and outcomes imply a wide variation in behaviors among members of ethnocultural groups living in pluralist societies. Those seeking assimilation will shift their behaviors in one direction, while those seeking separation will move in the opposite direction. These contrasts in acculturation strategies can create conflicts within families and communities, leading to increased acculturative stress and to increased rates of psychological and social problems (Berry & Kim, 1988). As a strategy, integration is generally the most successful, not only in societies like Canada's where cultural maintenance is officially encouraged and supported (Berry, 1991), but also in societies like that of the United States, where pressures toward assimilation are relatively strong (Krishnan & Berry, 1992). The least successful strategy, in terms of social and mental health, is widely acknowledged to be marginalization, a condition most often associated with ascribed membership in a minority group.

A Nested Methodological Framework

Whether working within cultural or ethnic psychology, it is necessary to link the background contextual, or independent, variables to the psychological outcome, or dependent, variables. A framework to assist in this endeavor is presented in Figure 6.3.

The goals of the framework (modified from Berry, 1980) are (1) to link psychological effects or outcomes (on the right) to their contexts (on the left) across the scheme; (2) to do so at four distinct levels, ranging from naturalistic forms of research (at the top) to controlled forms of research (at the bottom); and (3) to link the four levels of contexts by "nesting" each one in the level above it.

Looking at the contexts, the *ecological context* is the "natural-cultural habitat" of Brunswik (1957) or the "preperceptual world" of Barker (1968). It consists of all the relatively stable and permanent characteristics of the environment and the population that provide the context for human action and includes the population-level variables identified in Figure 6.1 — the ecological context, the sociopolitical context, and the cultural and biological adaptations made by the group.

Nested in this ecological context are two levels of the "life space" or "psychological world" of Lewin (1936). The *learning*

Figure 6.3. A Framework for Linking Contextual Variables to Effects.

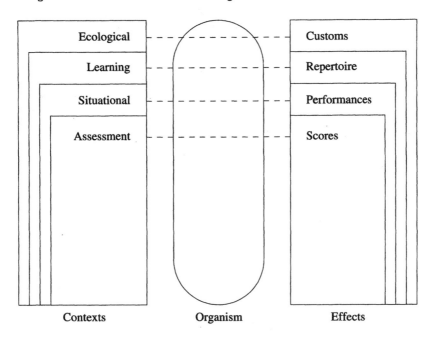

| Contexts | Organism | Effects |

context is the pattern of recurrent experiences that provides a basis for individual learning: the set of independent variables that operate in a particular habitat during cultural transmission and the development of behavioral characteristics. The *situational context* is the limited set of environmental circumstances (the "setting" of Barker, 1968) that may account for particular behaviors at a given time and place. They include such features of a setting as specific roles or social interactions, which influence a person's response to the setting.

The *assessment context* represents any environmental characteristics, such as test items or stimulus conditions, designed by the psychologist to elicit a particular response or test score. The degree to which the assessment context is nested in the first three contexts represents the degree of ecological validity of the task being faced by an individual.

Paralleling these four contexts are four behavioral outcomes. *Customs* refers to the complex, long-standing, and developed behavioral patterns in the population or culture that occur as an adaptive response to the ecological context. They include established, collective, and shared patterns of behavior discovered in a cultural or ethnocultural group.

Repertoire is the relatively stable complex of behaviors that have been learned by an individual over time in the recurrent experiential or learning context. Included are the skills, traits, and attitudes that have been nurtured in particular roles or acquired by specific training or education, whether formal or informal. The third effect, *performances*, connotes those behaviors that appear in response to immediate stimulation or experience. In contrast to a person's repertoire, they are not so much a function of role experience or long-term training; instead, they appear in reply to immediate situational experiences.

Scores is composed of the behaviors that are observed, measured, and recorded during psychological assessments such as experiments, interviews, or testing. If the assessment context is nested in the other contexts, then the scores may be representative of both the repertoire of the individual and the customs of the population.

The relationships between the environmental contexts and the behavioral outcomes can be traced across the scheme (the dotted lines). The top level is concerned with the life situation in physical, environmental, and cultural terms and its relationship to daily customs and practices in the population. The second level ties together the recurrent training and learning experiences of individuals and their characteristic repertoire of behaviors. The third level concerns specific acts as a function of immediate and current experiences; when the setting is right, the performance takes place. And the fourth level is devoted to the systematic study of the relationships between stimuli and scores obtained by individuals.

There are obvious parallels between the methodological framework in Figure 6.3 and the more conceptual presentation in Table 6.1. Most importantly, they both identify the need to obtain a complete picture of cultures and ethnocultural groups before attempting to understand and interpret any psychological data obtained from them. Only when tests and experimental tasks and outcomes (or scores) are understood in terms of their relationship with variables in the three upper levels of the scheme will cross-cultural psychologists grasp the meaning of their data.

Application of Frameworks to the Study of Cognition

How can these various frameworks enable us to better understand psychological similarities and differences in cultural and ethnocultural groups? To answer this question, we can try to apply them to a core problem in cultural and ethnic psychology: the conceptualization and assessment of cognitive performance in cultural and ethnocultural groups.

The most common problem in the study of cognition is that the dominant society insists on understanding the cognitive life of members of ethnocultural groups in terms that may not make any sense to members of the group itself. This is often a particular problem in the acculturation arenas of formal schooling and work, and in cognitive assessment for these domains.

One way to avoid this problem is to work with a cultural or ethnocultural group to discover its members' own views about the goals and qualities of cognitive development. This approach has become known as "indigenous cognition" (Berry, Irvine, & Hunt, 1988); it stands in sharp contrast to the more usual style of assessment found in standardized testing that is dominated by Western industrialized societies' views about cognitive competence.

The study of indigenous cognition is part of a current trend in cognitive psychology that can be identified by the notions of "everyday cognition" (Goodnow, 1980; Rogoff & Lave, 1984), "practical intelligence" (Sternberg & Wagner, 1986), and "savoirs quotidiens" (Dasen & Bossel-Lagos, 1989). In these theoretical and empirical statements, a focal concern is how individuals develop and display their cognitive activity in mundane, nonformal, and nonacademic situations, such as being on the job, doing the shopping, playing games, or waiting on tables. Such situations provide the opportunity to observe cognitive activity in natural settings and in a wider variety of contexts than psychologists have traditionally employed in their research. Two of the obvious consequences of this approach are, first, that while such studies are likely to be more generalizable to others within a culture, they may also be less comparable across cultures, and second, that more difficulties are encountered in making inferences from the data.

To avoid idiosyncrasies based on a single informant, the study of indigenous cognition must also attend to local cultural or collective interpretations. Cognitive life is not merely an individual phenomenon; it is also influenced by the cultural norms and practices with which one grows up. Hence, collective cultural values and goals for cognitive development need to be studied and drawn into the interpretation of the data obtained. Such an approach is an emic one, in which indigenous views are extremely useful in interpreting psychological data.

Cognitive Values

By *cognitive values* is meant the set of cognitive goals that are collectively shared and toward which children are socialized in a particular society. It is essential to understand these goals, since we cannot assess how far a person has gotten unless we understand where she or he is going. Studies of the meaning of intelligence in differing cultures (Berry, 1984a), and of socialization more generally (Segall, Daren, Berry, & Poortinga, 1990) constitute an important set of data in our attempt to understand the kinds of cognitive competence toward which children are directed. These studies exhibit a wide and diverse set of cognitive goals, often diverging sharply from the Western "quick, analytic, abstract" cluster so deeply inculcated by the Western school system and so thoroughly incorporated in standard assessment devices.

Cognitive Development

Once goals have been identified, it is possible to discover how far individuals have traveled toward them. Since, in the perspective of indigenous cognition, groups may have radically different goals, these goals can be diagrammed as being radially different. Figure 6.4 attempts to capture this variation by drawing paths from a common, underlying, universal cognitive process toward varying goals along a number of radii. While no diagram can capture the complexity of natural phenomena, Figure 6.4 shows in graphic form the varying goals and the extent of development toward them that may be reached. The essential point is that serious underestimation of cognitive development will occur if assessment focuses on progress toward a goal that ecological or cultural evidence informs us is not one toward which the culture directs individuals.

To make this view more concrete, evidence from reviewing cultural definitions of intelligence (Berry, 1984b; Serpell, 1989) shows that in some groups, holistic rather than analytic problem solving is culturally valued, and that deliberation

Figure 6.4. Paths from Cognitive Processes Toward Goals.

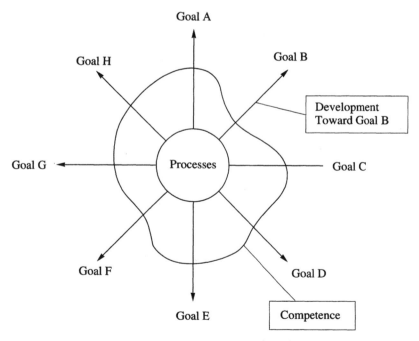

rather than haste is the proper course of action; moreover, collective discussion, rather than individual reflection, may be the preferred mode of thinking about a problem. In a society with this cluster of cognitive values, an individual confronted with a standardized Western psychological test may exhibit "minimal development" toward the analytic-fast-individualistic criterion but may be maximally developed toward the holistic-reflective-collectivistic criterion. The tragedy is that most psychologists would not discover this source of the "problem," given their lack of recognition of alternative cognitive goals.

Cognitive Competence

To continue, the cognitive competence of an individual in a particular culture or ethnocultural group may be conceived of as actual progress toward a number of culturally valued cognitive goals. In Figure 6.4, the distance out from the center along a culturally valued radius is the measure of development and thus implies competence of a particular sort. Because competencies are usually multiple, the full picture of an individual's competence would be presented by a space enclosed by a line joining the various points of development on each radius (indicated by the globular form in Figure 6.4). In this example, developed competence in ability C is substantially greater than in ability B.

An Empirical Example

The ecological approach to understanding cognitive development and cognitive competence is the most appropriate way to understand and explain the cognitive life of both cultural and ethnocultural groups. This approach can be used to examine, for example, groups that have established themselves in a distinctive way over generations within pluralist societies, such as African Americans or Hispanics, as well as more recently settled groups (such as Vietnamese refugees or South Asian immigrants.

Our recent work among the Cree of Northern Ontario, Canada (Berry & Bennett, 1991) has focused on the relationship of literacy to cognitive development. One result of this project has been the realization that there is a need for a more fine-grained and locally based (emic) understanding of how the Cree themselves conceive of cognitive competence, how they identify it and transmit it to their children, and how they know when it has been successfully inculcated in the matured individual.

In our study (Berry & Bennett, 1992), we used both ethnographic and psychometric procedures to uncover what the Cree understand by notions such as *intelligent, smart, clever, able,* and *competent.* The first stage was to work with a small set of key informants to elicit Cree concepts for those and similar terms and to seek their linguistic and contextual elaborations. We collected a list of twenty words dealing with cognitive competence through a series of very loosely structured interviews conducted with Cree speakers in the community of Big Trout Lake, in Northern Ontario. These speakers varied in their level of education and were equally divided between males and females.

The twenty words were written out on cards in the Cree syllabic script and participants were asked to sort the cards on the basis of similarity of meaning. Multidimensional scaling revealed two dimensions (see Figure 6.5). Reading from left to right on the horizontal axis, there is movement from a negative to a positive evaluation. The words on the left side of the figure are not only disliked (*stupid* and *crazy* are not traits that are positively valued), but some are probably considered to be morally reprehensible as well (for example, *cunning* and *backwards knowledge*).

The vertical dimension of the figure is more difficult to interpret. At one extreme are two words for *mentally tough,* in the sense of being brave and having courage or fortitude. At the other extreme are *religious* and *understands new things.* This dimension may have something to do with openness or sensitivity. The paucity of words in the lower half of the figure makes it difficult to be more specific.

In the figure, there is a cluster of words on the right side and slightly above center (in other words, both sensitive and morally good), containing the words we have rendered in English

Figure 6.5. Multidimensional Scaling of Card Sorting for Competence Terms.

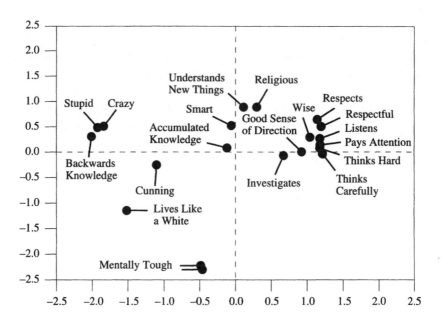

as *wise, respects, respectful, listens, pays attention, thinks hard* and *thinks carefully.* This cluster, we suggest, constitutes the core meaning of cognitive competence among the Cree.

The word most directly opposite the core cluster, and therefore most distant from it in terms of being insensitive and morally bad, is rendered as *lives like a white,* in the sense of behaving, thinking, and comporting oneself like a white person. It is tempting to regard this as the Cree version of being a "klutz," particularly since clumsy boorishness features in so many stories of white men in the bush. Its closeness to words like *cunning, stupid, crazy,* and *backwards knowledge*—wisdom turned to the service of disruption and disharmony—should alert us to look for meanings of negative moral content and insensitivity.

In discussions of the words in the core cluster, three very strong emphases were found—taking time, being self-sufficient, and allowing abilities to develop:

1. *Taking time*. There is an emphasis in all "good thinking" on
    going slowly and thoroughly and eschewing rapid action
    and decision, what in English we might call deliberation.
    Patience is also frequently mentioned as an attribute of good
    thinking but it is patience with a heavy admixture of per-
    severance. The patient person is one who sticks with a task,
    who doesn't give up when he or she starts feeling "lazy,"
    and who is hardworking but not in a hurry.
2. *Independence and self-sufficiency*. The goal of traditional sociali-
    zation is to make people self-sufficient so that they can sur-
    vive without being a drain upon others. The theme of sur-
    vival is a constant one in discussions of Cree traditional
    ways of life. Unnecessary dependence upon others is seen
    as irresponsible and immature behavior.
3. *Development*. "Good thinking" is seen as something that de-
    velops within each individual. A person can hinder, or even
    misdirect, this development (using knowledge for evil or
    disruptive purposes, for instance), but in the proper cir-
    cumstances, for ordinary people, knowledge will grow in
    its own good time. There is a sense here of allowing expe-
    rience to work on you, of not closing yourself off from your
    own wisdom. There is also a sense of trust in the process
    that reinforces a social predilection among the Cree for let-
    ting people go about things in their own way and not con-
    stantly trying to supervise, direct, and interfere.

This empirical example is only one of many explorations
of indigenous conceptions of cognitive competence now being
carried out within the conceptual framework of cultural psychology. It has taken this field a long time to move from a singular (and mainly Western ethnocentric) notion of intelligence
to study patterns of cognitive abilities both in context and with
culturally informed psychometric procedures (Berry, Irvine, &
Hunt, 1988). Because of this, we remain a long way from attaining a pan-human understanding of cognitive functioning.

In contrast, this way of understanding cognitive competence has not really begun at all with ethnocultural groups. In
my view, this culturally sensitive approach is rejected because

of the biases inherent in the notion of minority; the assimilationist ideology of most institutions, and especially formal schools, in the dominant society; and the strong belief by most psychologists that they already know what intelligence is and how to measure it. Many potential improvements would result by understanding, assessing, and using the ecological approach and indigenous notions of competence, and of most other psychological phenomena, with ethnocultural groups. Without such a change, psychologists perpetuate the marginalization of such groups and must bear some responsibility for the social and political consequences.

Conclusion

This chapter has attempted to show how an ecological approach to cross-cultural psychology can put our research activities into value-neutral terms, make it more culturally sensitive, and make our applications more appropriate and useful. While the bulk of the evidence for this claim can be found in cultural psychology, I believe that it is equally true for ethnic psychology. This position is advocated, not only for the field of cognition, but potentially for many other areas of psychological interest. In particular, in individual and group development work and in health studies, the ecological approach has considerable merit for the understanding of human diversity both across and within human populations.

References

Barker, R. (1968). *Ecological psychology*. Stanford, CA: Stanford University Press.

Berry, J. W. (1975). An ecological approach to cross-cultural psychology. *Nederlands Tijdschrift voor de Psychologie, 30,* 51–84.

Berry, J. W. (1976). *Human ecology and cognitive style: Comparative studies in culture and psychological adaptation*. London: Sage.

Berry, J. W. (1980). Ecological analyses for cross-cultural psychology. In N. Warren (Ed.), *Studies in cross-cultural psychology* (Vol. 2, pp. 157–189). London: Academic Press.

Berry, J. W. (1984a). Cultural relations in plural societies: Alternatives to segregation and their socio-psychological implications. In M. Brewer & N. Miller (Eds.), *Groups in contact* (pp. 11–27). San Diego, CA: Academic Press.

Berry, J. W. (1984b). Towards a universal psychology of cognitive competence. *International Journal of Psychology, 19,* 335–361.

Berry, J. W. (1985). Cultural psychology and ethnic psychology: A comparative analysis. In I. Reyes-Lagunes & Y. Pooratinga (Eds.), *From a different perspective* (pp. 3–15). Lisse, The Netherlands: Swets and Zeitlinger.

Berry, J. W. (1986). The comparative study of cognitive abilities: A summary. In S. E. Newstead, S. H. Irvine, & P. L. Dann (Eds.), *Human assessment: Cognition and motivation* (pp. 57–74). Dordrecht, The Netherlands: Nijhoff.

Berry, J. W. (1991). Understanding and managing multiculturalism: Some possible implications of research in Canada. *Psychology and Developing Societies, 3,* 17–49.

Berry, J. W., & Annis, R. C. (Eds.). (1988). *Ethnic psychology: Research and practice with immigrants, refugees, native peoples, ethnic groups and sojourners.* Lisse, The Netherlands: Swets & Zeitlinger.

Berry, J. W., & Bennett, J. A. (1991). *Cree syllabic literacy: Cultural context and psychological consequences* (Tilburg University Press Monographs in Cross-Cultural Psychology). Tilburg, The Netherlands: Tilburg University Press.

Berry, J. W., & Bennett, J. A. (1992). Cree conceptions of cognitive competence. *International Journal of Psychology, 27,* 73–88.

Berry, J. W., Irvine, S. H., & Hunt, E. B. (Eds.). (1988). *Indigenous cognition: Functioning in cultural context.* Dordrecht, The Netherlands: Nijhoff.

Berry, J. W., Kalin, R., & Taylor, D. (1977). *Multiculturalism and ethnic attitudes in Canada.* Ottawa, Canada: Minister of Supply and Services.

Berry, J. W., & Kim, U. (1988). Acculturation and mental health. In P. Dasen, J. W. Berry, & N. Sartorius (Eds.), *Cross-cultural psychology and health: Towards applications.* Newbury Park, CA: Sage.

Berry, J. W., Kim, U., Minde, T., & Mok, D. (1987). Comparative studies of acculturative stress. *International Migration Review, 21,* 491–511.

Berry, J. W., Kim, U., Power, S., Young, M., & Bujaki, M. (1989). Acculturation attitudes in plural societies. *Applied Psychology, 38,* 185–206.

Berry, J. W., Poortinga, Y., Segall, M., & Dasen, P. (1992). *Cross-cultural psychology: Research and applications.* New York: Cambridge University Press.

Boyd, R., & Richerson, P. J. (1985). *Culture and the evolutionary process.* Chicago: University of Chicago Press.

Brunswik, E. (1957). Scope and aspects of the cognition problem. In A. Gruber (Ed.), *Cognition: The Colorado Symposium.* Cambridge, MA: Harvard University Press.

Dasen, P. R., & Bossel-Lagos, M. (1989). L'étude interculturelle des savoirs quotidiens: Revue de la litérature. In J. Retschitzky, M. Bossel-Lagos, & P. R. Dasen (Eds.), *La recherche interculturelle* (pp. 98–114). Paris: L'Harmattan.

Feldman, D. (1975). The history of the relationship between environment and culture in ethnological thought: An overview. *Journal of the History of the Behavioural Sciences, 110,* 67–81.

Goodnow, J. (1980). Everyday concepts of intelligence and its development. In N. Warren (Ed.), *Studies in cross-cultural psychology* (Vol. 2, pp. 191–219). London: Academic Press.

Kardiner, A., & Linton, R. (1945). *The individual and his society.* New York: Columbia University Press.

Krishnan, A., & Berry, J. W. (1992). Acculturative stress and acculturation attitudes among Indian immigrants to the United States. *Psychology and Developing Societies, 4,* 187–202.

Lewin, K. (1936). *Principles of topological psychology.* New York: McGraw-Hill.

Rogoff, B., & Lave, J. (Eds.). (1984). *Everyday cognition: Its development in social context.* Cambridge, MA: Harvard University Press.

Segall, M., Daren, P., Berry, J. W., & Poortinga, Y. (1990). *Human behavior in global perspective: An introduction to cross-cultural psychology.* Elmsford, NY: Pergamon Press.

Serpell, R. (1989). Dimensions endogènes de l'intelligence chez les A-chewa et autres peuples africains. In J. Retschitzky, M. Bossel-Lagos, & P. R. Dasen (Eds.), *La recherche intercul-turelle* (pp. 164–179). Paris: L'Harmattan.

Sternberg, R., & Wagner, R. (Eds.). (1986). *Practical intelligence: Origins of competence in the everyday world.* New York: Cambridge University Press.

Stonequist, E. V. (1937). *The marginal man.* New York: Charles Scribner's Sons.

Whiting, J. W. (1974). A model for psychocultural research. *Annual report.* Washington, DC: American Anthropological Association.

PART III

Key Concepts
in Human Diversity

Oppression and
Intergroup Dynamics,
Culture, and Identity

7

The Discourse of Oppression
in the Social Sciences:
Past, Present, and Future

Isaac Prilleltensky
Lev S. Gonick

We find ourselves writing about oppression from a position of privilege. As middle-class, white, young males with academic jobs, we struggle with the paradox of criticizing the oppressive structures of society and benefiting from their existence at the same time. Furthermore, we are painfully aware of the distance between the written word and the courageous act of self-sacrifice for social change. This tension cannot be easily resolved. As citizens, our integrity cannot be judged merely on our moral pronouncements, but on the sincerity of our actions to reduce conditions of oppression. This statement is not intended as a self-exculpatory preface to a business-as-usual academic oration. Rather, it is part of contending with the contradictions inherent in writing about oppression from the comfort of an office. Having said that, we hope that our effort will help people in academic circles to move the discourse of oppression to a more useful, value-explicit, and relevant plane.

Note: An interdisciplinary grant from the Research Office of Wilfrid Laurier University in Waterloo, Ontario, Canada, facilitated the completion of this chapter. We wish to thank the capable research assistants who helped us in this project: Rich Janzen, Heather Potter, Tammie Thibault, and Melanie Wilson.

We believe that a project that claims to reintroduce the concept of oppression in the social sciences is essential to the infusion of moral values in human discourse. In contrast to prevailing approaches, we believe that future approaches to oppression should be marked by an interdisciplinary epistemology, by a moral philosophy of praxis, by increased attention to oppression in the global context, and, finally, by a commitment to support marginalized communities in strengthening their positions of influence. All these directions are subsumed under a call for moral philosophy in the social sciences. Once the morality of studying oppression, domination, and resistance is fully comprehended, it will be more difficult to rationalize inaction in obtaining social justice.

But how is the concept of oppression helpful in human diversity? Our assumption is that issues of power, resistance, and domination are central to the promotion of human diversity (Bartky, 1990; Sampson, 1993; Taylor, 1992; Watts, 1992). This is why we offer here an interdisciplinary interpretation of the condition of oppression. Individually and together we have come to realize that our intellectual heritages are painfully ill-equipped to assist us in reclaiming the language of oppression. Finding an emancipatory language to challenge and construct alternatives to oppression demands partnerships between several intellectual traditions whose separation is neither natural nor necessary. Coming from the disciplines of political science (Lev Gonick) and psychology (Isaac Prilleltensky), we wish to be sensitive to oppression that is political as well as psychological. We consider both external sources and internal manifestations of oppression. It is our position that while students of politics, economics, and sociology are more likely to turn to forms of external-structural analysis, such as imperialism, the market, the balance of power, racism, and patriarchy, those in psychology are more likely to turn to forms of internal-psychosocial analysis. Both sets of perspectives focus on human action and interaction. But whereas the internal-psychosocial view relates action to the agent's capability, the external-structured view sees action as a function of the agent's position in the politico-economic context. Assumptions and practices blind the perspectives to one another (Etzioni, 1991).

We begin by identifying a matrix of values that guide our inquiry subsumed in the concept of reciprocal empowerment. We then define human diversity and oppression. Following the introduction of these central concepts, we delineate a historically informed framework for reviewing and understanding the discourse of oppression in the social sciences. Finally, we present a model for enacting emancipatory principles in our disciplines.

Reciprocal Empowerment, Diversity, and Oppression: A Value-Based Approach

The term *reciprocal empowerment* embodies our prescription for promoting human welfare. This involves the allocation of self-determination, distributive justice, collaboration, and democratic participation of the self and others. The promotion of human diversity entails the affirmation of the values of reciprocal empowerment, despite the existence of differences. Under oppression, people are deprived of these values. Table 7.1 offers a summary of the place of values in reciprocal empowerment, human diversity, and oppression.

**Table 7.1. Reciprocal Empowerment,
Human Diversity, and Oppression: A Value-Based Approach.**

Values	Reciprocal Empowerment	Human Diversity	Oppression
Self-determination	The power to give to oneself and others the ability to define identity	Celebration of uniqueness and affirmation of identity despite differences	Externally produced and internalized negative view of oneself
Distributive justice	The power to give to oneself and others sufficient resources	Recognition of diversity as a resource and fair allocation of goods and burdens despite differences	Externally produced and internalized view of oneself as not deserving more resources
Collaboration and democratic participation	The power to give to oneself and others a voice in society	Equal participation in decision-making processes despite differences	Externally produced and internalized view of one's own voice as unimportant

Reciprocal Empowerment

In general terms, empowerment refers to the degree of control people exercise over their lives (Prilleltensky, 1994; Rappaport, 1981, 1987). Marginalized individuals or communities are those that remain vulnerable precisely because of the absence of power to frame their personal and structural relations vis-à-vis the other. However helpful the concept of empowerment may have been in legitimating the demand for more power on the part of vulnerable populations, we suggest that the unqualified pursuit of power may degenerate into a new version of personal or collective self-interest, where the individual or the group seeking more power may do so at the expense of other, more vulnerable people or groups (Riger, 1993). The demand for autonomy and personal freedom needs to be tempered with the value of interdependence, for we not only are dependent on others for our well-being, but we also define ourselves in relation to others (Sampson, 1993; Taylor, 1992). Hence, we propose the idea of reciprocal empowerment, where the pursuit of personal or collective power is moderated by the ethical imperative to give power and control to others who are in a less advantageous position.

Believing in the fundamental value of the equality of all human beings (Singer, 1993; Taylor, 1992), we argue that human diversity should not be an obstacle in the equal application of the principles of reciprocal empowerment. In fact, like Hamilton and Barrett (1986), we affirm the need to support a "political culture built on the recognition rather than the denial of division and differences between people" (p. 2). Our approach to human diversity celebrates the affirmation of self-determination, distributive justice, and collaborative and democratic participation in recognizing the existence of differences in socioeconomic status, culture, race, ethnicity, ability, age, gender, or sexual orientation. It is a testament to the human spirit of many oppressed groups that, despite harsh conditions of oppression, they develop strategies for resisting or overcoming domination.

The philosophy of reciprocal empowerment is, however,

a never-ending struggle that calls for efforts on the part of those already empowered to (1) strive to depower those who resist sharing resources and (2) share their power with vulnerable communities. The twin strategies of advocating the relative depowering of privilege while supporting space for marginalized individuals or communities to reappropriate their own power and identity are essential elements in our understanding of collaborative democracy. Often, marginalized groups are minority groups. However, the concordance between the two "imagined communities" (Anderson, 1983) is hardly perfect. Indeed, many have cross-cutting identifications that temporally and spatially coalesce.

The risk in a nonreciprocal concept of empowerment is that some social groups may regard themselves as always having less power than others, and they may therefore neglect other groups that may be in an even weaker position. People in the middle class can always maintain that they are powerless in comparison to the upper classes, but they should not forget that there are other, more deprived, groups that experience even higher degrees of powerlessness. Reciprocal empowerment, then, should be about creating and supporting interventions, institutions, communities, and programs of action that maximize the capacity of self-defined groups to empower themselves.

Self-determination, distributive justice, and collaborative and democratic participation are the three pillars of empowerment (Prilleltensky, 1994). The reformulation of empowerment that we suggest retains these essential values but emphasizes the element of interdependence that is so crucial for human coexistence. These values apply to individuals as well as groups and can potentially be experienced by people from any social group. However, it is extremely difficult to rise above the collective disempowerment of one's reference community to enjoy these rights, because the individual's ability to claim self-determination, justice, and a voice is tied to the group's capacity to secure these values. Thus, we can talk of an *individual's* ability to reach a fulfilling level of self-determination, but his or her prospects are heavily influenced by the *collective* standing of his or her community (Etzioni, 1991).

Self-Determination. Self-determination is "the individual's ability to pursue chosen goals without excessive frustration" (Olson, 1978, p. 45). For Rawls (1972), the capacity to carry out one's objectives in life is "perhaps the most important primary good" (p. 440). According to Ortega y Gasset, "to live is to constantly decide what we are to become" (1983, p. 190). In the context of human diversity, self-determination implies the ability of each member of society to develop a personal identity without fearing discrimination — that is, to affirm her or his identity despite differences from dominant societal norms.

Proper recognition of one's identity is, according to Taylor, "not just a courtesy we owe people. It is a vital human need" (1992, p. 26). The concept of identity, Taylor argues, refers to people's "understanding of who they are, of their fundamental defining characteristics as a human being" (1992, p. 25). Identity and recognition are intimately tied, for people validate their identity on the basis of recognition from others. Needless to say, this ideal of recognition is far from reality for many people. Taylor says, "A person or group of people can suffer real damage, real distortion, if the people or society around them mirror back to them a confining or demeaning or contemptible picture of themselves. Nonrecognition or misrecognition can inflict harm, can be a form of oppression, imprisoning someone in a false, distorted, and reduced mode of being" (p. 25).

Under conditions of oppression, social and political forces impose barriers on the ability of people to develop self-acceptance and self-esteem. Messages that reject a person's culture, heritage, or unique diversity can erode personal pride and lead to alienation (Collier, 1977; Montero, 1992; Nobles, 1976). If those rejecting messages are incorporated by the oppressed person or group, feelings of humiliation and shame may emerge, restricting further the prospects of self-determination. Although we wish to affirm the need to define oneself in connection to others, a position long held by feminists (Zanardi, 1990), "some have more power to set the terms of co-construction than others" (Sampson, 1993, p. 143), therefore limiting the chances of the weaker partner to construct an identity to his or her liking. Unless power imbalances are rectified, the dominant person will obstruct the self-determination of the "other."

Distributive Justice. Distributive justice is the principle invoked to guide the fair and equitable allocation of burdens and resources in society (Facione, Scherer, & Attig, 1978; Miller, 1978). It may be defined as *"suum cuique,* to each his due" (Miller, 1978, p. 20). This value puts forth "principles from which we may work out an ideally just distribution of rights and privileges, burdens and pains, among human beings as such" (Sidgwick, 1922, p. 274).

Yet as an analytic perspective, distributive justice is inseparable from economic structures and social institutions. Economically powerful countries or classes severely limit the access of weaker counterparts to resources and opportunities (Gonick & Rosh, 1988; Weisband, 1989), thus perpetuating their dominant position. Systemic exploitation is deeply structured within the dominant capitalist mode of production. We are mindful of Pettman's warning that, under capitalism, "the notion of a more 'just' *distribution* is a mere palliative. . . . To tinker only with the *distributive* terms of such a system would be worse than useless; indeed, it would be 'unjust'" (1979, pp. 88–95; emphasis in original). The challenge of moral economy thus becomes inextricably linked with distributive justice. To promote empowerment, people must have material and psychological resources. Consequently, mindful as we are of the realities of political economy, actions to advocate and realize moral economy are made concrete in empowering interventions that remove barriers to goods.

In the context of human diversity, distributive justice requires that interventions promote the equitable distribution of resources and opportunities to all members of society, regardless of their defining characteristics. Resources can be distributed in society according to various criteria, such as merit and need. Depending on the circumstances, one or another may be more appropriate (Facione, Scherer, & Attig, 1978). In the case of marginalized groups, the reality of discrimination demands that resources and opportunities be reallocated on the basis of the criterion of need, because these groups are equally deserving of resources but have been systematically deprived of them by dominant sectors of society. This is the rationale for programs such as affirmative action, where a wrong is addressed by promoting access for disadvantaged groups. In essence, then, distributive justice calls for the allocation of resources to members of marginalized groups in order to reach a balance between the resources and opportunities enjoyed by dominant and marginalized communities.

Collaboration and Democratic Participation. The principles of self-determination and distributive justice should be enacted through a collaborative and democratic process. Democracy, as Lummis reminds us, is a word that "joins 'the people' and 'power.' This means that it is not the name of any particular political system or arrangement of institutions; rather, it is a situation that a political system may or may not help to bring about. [It is] not a historically existing institution, but a historical project" (1982, pp. 9–10). Collaboration and democratic participation reflects best the ideal that individuals should be equal partners in any decision-making process affecting their lives. This principle, regarded by Riessman (1986) as central to the empowerment agenda, is a defining characteristic of empowering social, political, and scholarly pursuits (Rappaport, 1990).

Diversity

Collaboration supports the vision of a pluralist society that seeks unity and harmony in diversity. Unity, argues Fals Borda (1991), "is sought in diversity, in respect for the right to be different and in the dialectical convergence of contraries" (p. 30). Ways must be found to catalyze the creative resources of diverse people into fostering harmonious communities. The importance of building democracy through participation is not missed by Fals Borda. He claims that "participative pluralism, respectful and tolerant of internal diversities and convergences, is also conducive to designing *democratic or collective forms of conducting movements*" (Fals Borda, 1991, p. 30; emphasis in original).

At present, marginalized voices encounter many obstacles to democratic participation. Privilege and domination are upheld by either force or psychological manipulation. Gramsci (1971) referred to the latter as cultural and political hegemony.

Hegemony is maintained by civil institutions such as the legal
system, schools, and the media, which defend the status quo
by means of persuasion (Femia, 1981; Kiros, 1985). Although
there are no legal restrictions preventing people from expressing their opinion in most Western countries, there are cultural
barriers. In many other countries, censorship of dissenting voices
is brutal and violent. Whatever the case may be, the end result
is that structural arrangements of power limit the possibilities
for oppressed classes and groups to have a participative role in
issues affecting their lives. There cannot be a meaningful celebration of human diversity unless all members of society, regardless of gender, age, ability, sexual orientation, or ethnic background, can express their voices in equal participation despite
their differences (Watts, 1992; Sampson, 1993).

Oppression

For us, oppression entails a state of asymmetric power relations
characterized by domination, subordination, and resistance,
where the dominating people exercise their power by restricting access to material resources and by implanting in the subor-
dinated people self-deprecating views about themselves. It is only
when the latter can attain a certain degree of conscientization
(critical social and political awareness) that resistance can begin (Bartky, 1990; Fanon, 1963; Freire, 1972; Memmi, 1968;
Montero, 1992; Pheterson, 1986). Oppression, then, is a series
of asymmetrical power relations between individuals, genders,
classes, communities, nations, and states. These power relations
lead to conditions of alienation, misery, inequality, and social
injustice among human beings and to conditions of exploitation, fragmentation, and marginalization.

    The dynamics of oppression are internal as well as exter-
nal. External forces deprive individuals or groups of the benefit
of self-determination, distributive justice, and democratic participation (Barrett, 1988; Brittan & Maynard, 1984; Bulhan,
1985; Weisband, 1989). Frequently, these restrictions are internalized and operate at a psychological level as well, where
the person acts as her or his own censor (Bosmajian, 1983;

Collier, 1977; Goldenberg, 1978; Lerner, 1991; Montero, 1992; Pheterson, 1986). The dual nature of oppression is captured in the following quote from Bartky (1990):

> When we describe a people as oppressed, what we have in mind most often is an oppression that is economic and political in character. But recent liberation movements, the black liberation movement and the women's movement in particular, have brought to light forms of oppression that are not immediately economic or political. It is possible to be oppressed in ways that need involve neither deprivation, legal inequality, nor economic exploitation; one can be oppressed psychologically — the "psychic alienation" of which Fanon speaks. To be psychologically oppressed is to be weighed down in your mind; it is to have a harsh dominion exercised over your self-esteem. The psychologically oppressed become their own oppressors; they come to exercise dominion over their own self-esteem. Differently put, psychological oppression can be regarded as the "internalization of intimations of inferiority" [p. 22].

Oppression, as the antithesis of reciprocal empowerment, curtails self-determination, perpetuates social injustice, and suppresses the voices of vulnerable individuals.

In summary, we view oppression as a condition where externally produced deprivation of rights and privileges leads to either internal representations of self-dejection or psychological immobility. Attaining consciousness of the psychological internalization of oppression is a meaningful step in eradicating this abject condition. Consciousness, needless to say, is not sufficient to change oppressive realities, but it is a very important step. Both political and psychological interventions will be needed in order to eliminate conditions of oppression. The psychological cannot do without the political and vice versa.

The Discourse of Oppression:
A Descriptive and Prescriptive Framework

Having defined oppression and its connection to human diversity, we turn to the role of mainstream social science in eliminating or reinforcing oppression. There are many ways in which human discourse can either promote or obstruct self-determination, distributive justice, and democratic participation of marginalized or oppressed groups. We next identify and discuss four dimensions of social scientific discourse that can be instrumental in either fostering or thwarting the promotion of these values.

Philosophical Orientation

By philosophical orientation, we mean the emphasis placed on either epistemology or moral philosophy. Discourses that singularly stress the need for the pursuit of knowledge, regardless of its moral-philosophical implications, risk constructing theories that do not answer the needs of people in the community. Worse yet, they may develop harmful knowledge. Orientations that promote moral philosophy as part of their theory building are very sensitive to the potential use and application of knowledge for the promotion of human welfare. In their extreme, one orientation seeks pure knowledge, the other human welfare. As we shall see in our analysis of historical trends in the social sciences, both orientations predominated at one point or another. Our position, which places epistemology in the service of moral philosophy, will be described later as part of our view of the future.

Admittedly, our terminology for this and subsequent dimensions is derived from Western social thought. It may very well be that other cultures reject the very division between knowledge and socially useful action. We advocate for the subordination of the former to the latter, but this conception may be inadequate to express the worldviews of other peoples. In African philosophy, for instance, it has been claimed that the boundaries between ontology, epistemology, and ethics are much more fluid than in Western philosophy (Onyewuenyi, 1991). Akan morality shares many of the tenets of Western humanism but differs from it in that Akan philosophy "is not supernaturalistic. On the contrary, it maintains a rigid supernaturalistic metaphysics that is rejected by Western humanism" (Gyekye, 1987, p. 143).

We are aware that many African philosophers reject the entire Western philosophical edifice for its conspiracy in the European colonization of their continent (Serequeberhan, 1991). Conradie (1980) states that "to accept Western philosophy as 'philosophy' is thus to accept the epistemology of colonialism" (p. 396). Although our choice of terms like *epistemology* and *moral philosophy* is an obvious reflection of our own background, it is not intended to deny the existence of other philosophies that may question this conceptualization. Our selection is based, not only on our own biases, but also on the fact that the scientific tradition we wish to examine has been informed by this terminology.

Disciplinary Boundaries

Scholarship can be fragmented or integrative. The particular kind adopted will have repercussions for the realization of self-determination, distributive justice, and democracy. For instance, a discourse that seeks to understand and reduce oppression in strictly psychological terms is bound to fail. It will degenerate into a blame-the-victim mentality if the political and economic realities of domination are ignored. On the other hand, a deterministic political analysis that ignores elements of human agency is equally invalid. We will explore below some of the historical trends that account for permeability or rigidity in the social sciences.

Geocultural Focus

The geocultural bias of a discourse influences how it promotes or inhibits social interests. The establishment of Eurocentric norms and parameters by definition discriminate against people from other backgrounds. In addition, the choice of population to be studied will also have an impact on oppressed groups, either by ignoring certain groups altogether or by studying them with tools and concepts that perpetuate their victimization. The application of Eurocentric norms to the lives of people in developing nations perpetuates the intellectual domination exerted by Western discourses over other countries (Brittan & Maynard, 1984; Bulhan, 1985; Nobles, 1976; Turner & Singleton, 1978). Potentially, the discourse of oppression can focus on global norms and issues or on specific, regional ones.

Representation of Marginalized Voices

Representation of marginalized voices deals directly with the issue of meaningful participation in societal affairs. The interests of marginalized groups can be represented in human discourse or strategically excluded from scholarly and public debates. As the concerns of oppressed groups can be only minimally advanced by members of other groups, it is crucial that members of marginalized communities hold positions of influence from which they can meaningfully serve their communities. Although academic discourse is only one way of promoting the cause of oppressed and minority groups, it is very useful in placing issues of importance on the public agenda.

The four analytic dimensions presented will help us in reviewing the discourse of oppression in mainstream social science and our own prescription for change. We advocate a *decentered dialogue* (see Table 7.2) that may put forth a more useful idiom, one that is more inclusive of other people's perspectives. The descriptions and prescriptions advanced here reflect our experience, and, as such, they embody our contributions as well as our limitations.

Historical Analysis

In our brief analysis, we review three major historical phases. The first one spans from the 1860s to the 1920s, the second one from the 1920s to the 1960s, and the third one from the 1960s

Table 7.2. Dominant Trends Influencing the Discourse of Oppression in Mainstream Social Sciences.

Trend	Phase 1 1860–1920	Phase 2 1920–1960	Phase 3 1960–Present	Phase 4 Present–Future
Philosophical orientation	Balance between epistemology and moral philosophy	Epistemology of technical rationality	Increased emphasis on moral philosophy	Epistemology at the service of moral philosophy
Disciplinary boundaries	Somewhat permeable due to grand theorizing	Rigid due to rise of professions	Flexible due to systems theory	Minimally required
Geo-cultural focus	Rigid Eurocentric focus	Rigid division with North-American focus	Somewhat reduced division and increased global dialogue	Decentering and global dialogue required
Representation of minority voices	Some indirect representation	Excluded from mainstream	Some recognition within mainstream	End of mainstream
Discourse of oppression	Largely political, yet reductionistic	Technical and apolitical	Technical but more political	Political and more differentiated

till the present. Phase 4 is our prescription for the future. Table 7.2 offers a summary of the major trends in the social sciences influencing the intellectual treatment of oppression. Although we focus on our respective areas of specialty, namely political science and psychology, we also pay attention to developments in economics and sociology.

The First Generation: 1860–1920

To a large degree, the philosophical orientation of early thinkers such as Karl Marx, Emile Durkheim, Sigmund Freud, Benedetto Croce, Vilfredo Pareto, and Henri Bergson combined epistemological and moral concerns. The Marxist conception of praxis, as the unity of theory and action, was still quite prevalent. Because Marx and his contemporaries had a philosophical as well as a scientific education, they drew no clear line of demarcation between social science and social philosophy. Durkheim, for instance, found his professional calling informed by "his desire to contribute to the moral consolidation of the Third Republic" (Alpert, 1939, p. 15). Durkheim's unwavering militancy in advocating democratic and humanitarian values places him in sharp relief against the scorn of Pareto and the skepticism of Croce and Gaetanu Mosca. For Durkheim, a product of the Enlightenment, science reinforced democracy, and democracy science.

Most of these intellectuals were brought up in the humanist tradition of broad scholarship. The grand theorizing of scholars such as Croce, Freud, and Pareto precluded rigid boundaries between the fledgling social disciplines. Although this led to permeable disciplinary boundaries, it also fostered discrete intellectual traditions that would soon lead to the solidification of distinct professional groups. While neither Freud nor Max Weber, for example, were oblivious to the existence of sociological and psychological factors in oppression, each helped found schools of thought that would promote a narrow orientation toward psychology or sociology.

Freud's use of psychological terms to explain oppression furnished capitalism with a powerful ideological strategem — the attribution of personal unhappiness to intrapsychic conflict. His opinion that "women's inferior capacity for sublimation" (Freud, 1961) stemmed from an underdeveloped superego did not escape supporters of patriarchy (Lerman, 1986; Unger & Crawford, 1992). On the other hand, Freud's strongest legacy to the eradication of oppression lies in what Abramson (1984) called "personal liberation." This is the process whereby individuals free themselves from intrapsychic conflicts that may elicit inhibitions, anxieties, and fears. Few thinkers have assisted so much in promoting such therapeutic mentality. The risks of focusing on personal liberation to the exclusion of politics notwithstanding, it would be unfortunate to discredit en bloc individual therapy. Unless individuals liberate themselves from personal fears, repression, and so on, they may lack the energy for social transformation. Nonetheless, Freud was more of a personal than a social liberator.

If Freud's legacy undermines political and social factors in oppression, Weber's writings underestimate the psychological realm (Parsons, 1949). Weber, the Prussian, upper-class German idealist, placed the politics of oppression front and center through his *Herrschaftssoziologie* (sociology of domination). Weber was preoccupied with the concepts of power and domination (*Herrschaft*). He defined power as the "probability that one actor within a social relationship will be in a position to carry out his own will despite resistance" and domination as "the probability that a command with a given specific content will be obeyed by a given group of persons" (Weber, 1966, p. 154). His work illuminated some of the bureaucratic, organizational, and structural dynamics of oppression. As opposed to Freud, Weber's chief intellectual weakness lay in the field of psychology. Under Freud and Weber, an initially broad interpretation of oppression became increasingly narrower, as they developed grand psychological and sociological theories, respectively.

From our vantage point, the primary geocultural focus of this intellectual generation was Eurocentric, and oppressed voices were represented indirectly by spokespersons from the middle or upper classes. In addition, there was a defining tension between grand theorizing and a concern for praxis, on the one hand, and the creation of reductionistic discourses and "scientistic" tendencies on the other (Ross, 1991). In the end, it would appear that the intellectual exercise of dissecting the human condition proved to be more compelling than actions designed to improve it. In the following period, disciples of Weber and Freud further narrowed the subject matter. The postwar period, particularly in North America, saw an embrace of Cartesian positivism. In the next era, the agenda of the oppressed was nearly expunged from mainstream social science.

The Second Generation: 1920–1960

Our second generation of social science emerged when psychology and political science adopted the ontological, epistemological, and methodological assumptions of the natural sciences (Berman, 1981; Wolfe, 1989), a trend sometimes called scientism (Ross, 1991). Ross says, "The Rockefeller Foundation massively entered the scene in the early 1920s. They wanted to help solve social problems in a way that would spare the family name controversy and spare the country more radical changes. For their purposes, the emerging scientific idiom of social science was attractive, promising both distance from political controversy and knowledge that would allow the real control of social change" (p. 400).

The philosophical orientation of this generation is characterized by an epistemology of technical rationality. Moral, social, and political problems were seen in technical-scientific terms. Social injustice, discrimination, and exploitation were temporary predicaments, waiting to be solved by advanced social science. As Riger (1992) puts it: "Modern science conceives itself as a search for knowledge free of moral, political, and social values. The application of scientific methods to the study of human behavior distinguished American psychology from philosophy and enabled it to pursue the respect accorded the natural sciences" (p. 730).

Thus, in this period, technical rationality flourished at the expense of moral philosophy. Requests for psychological input came from every corner of society, and psychology eagerly served government, the military, education, industry, and business (Danziger, 1990). Psychology's uncritical acceptance of instrumental rationality was not without a heavy moral cost. In making their services available to dominant sectors of society with much fervor, psychologists effectively became highly sophisticated agents of social control. Psychology helped to persuade victims of oppression that they were to blame for their suffering (Prilleltensky, 1994). Riger (1992) states: "By stripping behavior of its social context, psychologists rule out the study of sociocultural and historical factors, and implicitly attribute causes to factors inside the person" (p. 731). This was the prevailing logic of the times.

The second generation of political scientists and sociologists were likewise ensnared by the logic of technical rationality. The result was an effort to devise propositions about humans and social phenomena in general. In North America, the dominant form of political theorizing was initiated by a self-styled school of "rational idealism" (Neumann, 1957, p. 372). Rational idealists shared beliefs in the rationality of humans (particularly male decision makers), the harmony of interests among people, and the continuing spread of democratic institutions. The fading of rational idealism during the interwar years fostered a status quo-oriented political science that was concerned with equilibrium, balance, and order. A strong, white, North American geocultural focus predominated in both psychology and political science during this period. Social science was to mimic white, North American culture. Individuals from other cultures were measured and classified according to white, North American parameters and were said to desire the same goods North Americans pursued. The imperialist policies of the United States had an effect on social scientists, who began treating people from dominated groups, other nations, and other ethnic backgrounds as inferior (Brittan & Maynard, 1984; Collier, 1977; Nobles, 1976; Pepitone, 1989; Turner & Singleton, 1978; Young, 1991).

The Third Generation: 1960 to the Present

From the 1960s to the early 1990s, a growing number of intellectuals advocated social change from within the academy and sought to make the politics of social science explicit. This related to the rise of social liberation movements during the 1960s (Franklin, 1969; Potts, 1993; Turner & Singleton, 1978; Young, 1991). In large measure, the social sciences used the experience of social liberation struggles as part of their general critique of "value-free" social science. Psychologists (Albee, 1986; Fox, 1993; Goldenberg, 1978; Rappaport, 1977, 1981), sociologists (Bottomore, 1975; Horowitz, 1971), economists (Baran & Sweezy, 1966; Mermelstein, 1975), and political scientists (Fox-Piven & Cloward, 1971; Huberman & Sweezy, 1968; Parenti, 1977) all began to reexamine the morality of their discourses, resulting in numerous calls for social action.

The discourse of the 1960s was direct and action-oriented. African American leaders talked bluntly about the "demands of previously oppressed peoples to be free of their oppression. . . . The existing systems of the dominant, oppressive group—the entire spectrum of values, beliefs, traditions and institutions—will have to be challenged and changed" (Carmichael & Hamilton, 1967, pp. 178–179).

The women's movement found in consciousness raising a successful vehicle for the popular education of women on the sources and effects of sexism. This "systematic program of education was among the Women's Movement's highest priorities. Social change was not possible, it was argued, until women clearly understood why they were oppressed and how" (Shreve, 1989, p. 14). Shreve notes that the benefits were shared not only by those who directly participated in the groups but also by millions of women who were influenced by feminist thinking. Lesbians, who "were oppressed on the basis of their sexuality more than heterosexual women—doubly oppressed and doubly outcast" (Burns, 1990, p. 145), worked within feminist organizations to end their discrimination by both heterosexual women and men.

It is astonishing that the revolutionary thinking advanced by people like Martin Luther King, Jr., and others had relatively little effect on the social responsiveness of universities. Although women's studies and African American studies were evidence of the penetration of liberation ideologies, these new additions to the academy often served to keep the new ideas contained and isolated from established scholarship. Despite some erosion in the divide between epistemology and moral philosophy, we would argue that universities in North America did not share or reflect the need for social change as advocated by grass-roots groups (Harries-Jones, 1991). For historical reasons associated with the tenuous status of the social sciences in North American universities since the beginning of the century, disciplines like psychology, sociology, and political science did not risk manifest involvement with social causes for fear of being accused of partiality, lack of objectivity, and the like (Heyworth, 1991). Today's milder pattern of social involvement by universities in the form of community outreach seems to be determined more by the need to be accountable to the public than by an ethical commitment to promote social justice.

In contrast, many social scientists in Latin America have closer alliances with social movements (Fals Borda, 1991). In their role as facilitators of popular education and community mobilization, social scientists assist in the formation of regional educational, political, and cultural groups with an emancipatory orientation. Influenced by the work of Paulo Friere, and through participatory research, adult education workshops, and consciousness raising, social scientists advance the "aspirations of the underprivileged and downtrodden classes in each locality" (Fals Borda, 1991, p. 22).

While Paulo Freire was pioneering consciousness raising through popular education in South America, Myles Horton was doing similar things in his popular Highlander Folk School in the Appalachian mountains of Tennessee. Horton held adult education classes and racial integration workshops for whites and African Americans. Rosa Parks, who was instrumental in initiating the famous bus boycott in Montgomery, Alabama, in 1955 to end racial segregation in public transportation, is said to have been deeply affected by her stay a few months earlier at Highlander (Burns, 1990).

Although parallels exist in the discourse on oppression in South and North America, progressive Western intellectuals are faced with the severe challenge presented by deconstructionism in all of its guises. Deconstruction is the quintessential reflexive school of thought. Advanced initially as a form of literary criticism, it has become a powerful tool for analyzing the subjectivity embedded in texts. As such, it challenges the claims to impartiality and rationality that are implicitly invoked in most forms of human discourse (Parker, 1992). It aspires to uncover internal contradictions of writing and the dynamics of power relations at work in the structuring of text (Parker & Shotter, 1990).

Deconstruction does offer a methodology capable of dislodging the cultural-myths responsible for the reproduction of many social ills. However, deconstructionism as a method, and postmodernism as a school of thought, are by their very ontological makeup ambivalent toward ethical commitments. According to Wolfe (1989), "Postmodern 'deconstructive' consciousness . . . is distrustful of the binding power of any moral rules" (p. 6). Its capacity to contribute to the eradication of oppression is doubtful. It can drift into a form of moral relativism that offers no meaningful alternatives, or challenges, to the societal status quo.

Burman (1990) goes further in her critique of deconstruction. She states that "the overall problem concerns the approach's inability to ally itself with any explicit political position; and following from this, a deliberate 'distancing' and 'deconstruction' of any progressive political program" (pp. 210–211). Furthermore, she argues that "deconstruction is fundamentally committed to a liberal pluralism which renders each of its deconstructive readings equally valid, and paralyzes political motivation" (pp. 214–215). From our perspective, the extent to which moral philosophy informs a theory should become the principal evaluative criterion for social science discourse. Thus, it could be claimed that the progress attained by feminist and allied approaches is attenuated by certain forms of deconstructionism.

In contrast to the previous era, and related to the rise of systems theory (Bertalanffy, 1968), we witness in this era flexible disciplinary boundaries. Increased dialogue among these social disciplines, in part a reaction to explanations proposed by biological, cultural, psychological, or economic reductionism (Brittan & Maynard, 1984; Laclau & Mouffe, 1985; Turner & Singleton, 1978), has influenced the discourse of oppression.

Scholars are addressing the multiple levels of oppression by employing phrases such as "double jeopardy" and "layers of oppression" to describe the complex nature of oppression (Abberley, 1987; Morris, 1992). For example, feminist theorists incorporate the economic, political, sociological, and psychological sources and consequences of women's oppression (Bartky, 1990; Barrett, 1988). Another example of an interdisciplinary approach to oppression is liberation theology (Pottenger, 1989). Confronted with the domination suffered by vast numbers of South Americans, theologians resorted to political and economic analysis to understand and change the social realities of their people. This doctrine, very influential in South America, has also taken hold in African American communities in the United States (Potts, 1993).

In the United States, community psychology emerged as a formal subdiscipline of psychology in the 1960s and is another example of a field committed to an ecological approach to social problems (Rappaport, 1977). The ecological model in community psychology seeks to incorporate individual, group, institutional, community, and societal variables in its analysis of oppression (Goldenberg, 1978). It rejects the victim-blaming stance implicit in several reductionist approaches (Albee, 1981; Prilleltensky, 1994).

Individual authors have also fostered cross-cutting discourses related to the issue of oppression. Lerner (1991), author of *Surplus Powerlessness,* conducted a comprehensive inquiry into personal and societal oppression. "Surplus powerlessness," or a sense of hopelessness beyond what is dictated by structural determinants, originates in an individualistic economic and cultural environment where misfortune or success is the sole responsibility of the self. Kovel, in *White Racism* (1984), combines political economy with cultural psychology or psychohistory in explaining the oppression of white racism. Another social thinker attempting to provide a comprehensive understanding of oppression is Bulhan (1985). He states: "In reality, few human encounters are exempt from oppression of one kind or another. For by virtue of our race, sex, or class, each of us happens to be a victim and/or perpetrator of oppression. Racism, sexism, and class exploitation are the most salient forms of oppression in the contemporary world. But there also exists oppression on the grounds of religious belief, political affiliation, national origin, age, and physical and mental handicap" (p. vii).

The work of Memmi (1967, 1968) and Fanon (1963) on colonized people captured the attention of many social scientists. These authors drew a great deal of attention to the psychological internalization of subjugating conditions. They documented the emotional pain and personal metamorphoses occurring in the psyche of the colonized and others.

More so than ever before, marginalized voices are gaining a forum for their concerns. The new social movements representing their voices "focus on issues of oppression and domination [and] they usually seek democratization of institutions and practices, to bring them under more direct popular control" (Young, 1991, p. 83). Many voices can now be heard: homosexuals and bisexuals (Kallen, 1989; Neisen, 1990), psychiatric survivors (Chamberlin, 1990), the physically challenged (Abberley, 1987), African Americans (Franklin, 1969), aboriginals (Richardson, 1989), and women (Hooks, 1984). The common cause of these grass-roots organizations continues to be liberation from political and economic restraints and from stereotypes that obstruct human potential (Fals Borda, 1991; Taylor, 1992).

Despite these developments, it would be a mistake to assume that interdisciplinary moral discourses on oppression prevail. In the main, the examples we have enumerated remain marginalized and in the minority, albeit a vocal minority. Similarly, the main agenda and geocultural focus of the social sciences remains European and North American. The social sciences continue to reflect, by and large, one narrow and distorted conception of the world that is deeply rooted in capitalism and patriarchy. Brittan and Maynard (1984) call this "Western projection," a bias in which "Western scientific discourse is universalized as the yardstick of understanding and investigation. Accordingly, when commentators consider instances of oppression in other contexts they immediately try to assimilate these instances to a general theory of oppression which is assumed to have universal applicability" (p. 208).

In summary, the discourse of oppression of this generation is characterized by an attempt to overcome reductionistic
explanations of domination based on either endogenous or exogenous determinism. Furthermore, the discussion of oppression has become more political than ever before, prompting
renewed appreciation for the role of moral philosophy in the
social sciences. Finally, although it has not received nearly
enough attention, the plight of oppressed communities has
received much more attention than in the past.

The Fourth Generation: Our View of the Future

The surge of dissenting groups over the past twenty years has
challenged the hegemonic reductionism and moral disinterest
of the social sciences (Wolfe, 1989; Young, 1991). These groups
have questioned the many walls erected by positivism: the
dichotomy between epistemology and moral philosophy, disciplinary boundaries, and barriers to the expression of different,
nonmainstream voices. Nonetheless, these walls still exist. To
reduce oppression, the social sciences must change their philosophical orientation, increase interdisciplinary dialogue, expand their geocultural focus, and increase the representation
of marginalized voices.

The resolve, in our opinion, will arise from a renewed
appreciation of the role of moral philosophy (Smith, 1991). The
new philosophical orientation should place epistemology in the
service of moral philosophy. That is, the process of inquiry into
social phenomena should be guided by the potential use of the
inquiry in promoting reciprocal empowerment. The quest for
knowledge should contribute to the affirmation of self-determination for diverse and oppressed groups, to the just allocation
of resources, and to the expression of marginalized voices. In
Canada, this was recently illustrated in constitutional negotia-
tions during which many French Canadians placed their own
interests ahead of those of Native Canadians, a community that
has been oppressed for centuries (Johnson, 1993). An empowerment agenda that seeks primarily to acquire more power for
my group is bound to disempower other oppressed groups, thereby

undermining the principle of distributive justice. This is why we find it necessary to emphasize the notion of *reciprocal* empowerment, so that consideration is given to the welfare of more vulnerable communities.

Conclusion

These are high standards for the discourse on oppression. Our own work only begins to answer some of its requirements. Nevertheless, we think it is necessary to articulate a vision and principles to guide our efforts.

How do we begin to practice these principles? Following a framework for theory development presented by Prilleltensky and Walsh-Bowers (1993), we find it useful to organize principles for practice according to their purpose, process, and content. The *purpose* of theory and action is to remove the internal and external barriers obstructing the full development of all human beings, barriers created by political and material domination and the internalization of self-deprecating views (Taylor, 1992). An example of such an approach is liberation psychology (Martín-Baró, 1986; Montero, 1992). It is explicitly concerned with the physical and spiritual dimensions of domination and is an example of knowledge in the service of moral values.

In order to enact the principle of self-determination and listen to the voices of less powerful groups, theories and interventions would have to incorporate input from stakeholders in the collaboration (Brittan & Maynard, 1984; Morris, 1992). These are important *process* variables. Commitment and shared control should be a hallmark of collaboration. Thus, there needs to be a mechanism for democratic input. This is a radical departure from scholarly practices for deciding what is and is not important in scientific discourse. Many social scientists, ourselves included, may have difficulty in giving up some control over the research agenda. A group of white professionals dedicated to the principles of collaboration and accountability in New Zealand have negotiated an agreement with Maori people whereby the former take the lead from the latter in their research and social actions (Huygens, 1993). This network of professionals gives a voice to the Maori people by letting them take ownership, to a considerable degree, of the agenda for change. The network is called to help the indigenous people depower privileged members of society who restrict their access to resources or diminish their opportunities for self-determination. This may entail making presentations to city councils and professional associations, or staging demonstrations.

In efforts to reduce oppression, the specific *content* of theory and action can be as varied as the settings themselves. The content of a research-and-action plan will vary according to the level of analysis and intervention desired. The subject matter of oppressive international mechanisms (George, 1992; Payer, 1991) will differ from the content of restricted job and educational opportunities for minorities (Mar'i, 1988), which will differ from the oppression of aboriginals in the hands of white colonizers (Johnson, 1993). Although specifics vary from context to context, we claim that an interdisciplinary, grounded-theory approach should be used in every case. We have already discussed the many advantages of an interdisciplinary perspective. Grounded theory (Strauss & Corbin, 1990) seeks particularistic explanations of settings and people based on their unique circumstances. By doing this, it avoids the application of preconceived assumptions that may apply to one culture but not to another. As methodologies, grounded theory and ethnography supplement the process of democratic input.

In our opinion, the realization of interdependent self-determination, distributive justice, and democratic participation will reduce oppression and affirm human diversity. Our own work has just begun. Our efforts to engage members of oppressed groups in social discourse are in their initial stages (Prilleltensky, in press). But for us, the challenge is not only intellectual, but personal as well. Writing is incomparably easier than making moral commitments and personal sacrifices to enhance the welfare of oppressed people. We conclude by humbly paying tribute to the Salvadorean social scientist Ignacio Martín-Baró, who gave his life to end oppression for his people.

References

Abberley, P. (1987). The concept of oppression and the development of a social theory of disability. *Disability, Handicap, and Society, 2*(1), 5–19.

Abramson, J. B. (1984). *Liberation and its limits: The moral and political thought of Freud.* New York: Free Press.

Albee, G. W. (1981). Politics, power, prevention, and social change. In J. M. Joffee & G. W. Albee (Eds.), *Prevention through political action and social change* (pp. 3–24). Hanover, NH: University Press of New England.

Albee, G. W. (1986). Toward a just society: Lessons from observations on the primary prevention of psychopathology. *American Psychologist, 41,* 891–898.

Alpert, H. (1939). *Emile Durkheim and his sociology.* New York: Russell and Russell.

Anderson, B.R.O. (1983). *Imagined communities: Reflections on the origin and spread of nationalism.* London: Verso.

Baran, P., & Sweezy, P. (1966). *Monopoly capital.* New York: Monthly Review Press.

Barrett, M. (1988). *Women's oppression today* (5th ed.). London: Thetford Press.

Bartky, S. L. (1990). *Femininity and domination: Studies in the phenomenology of domination.* New York: Routledge & Kegan Paul.

Berman, M. (1981). *The reenchantment of the world.* New York: Bantam Books.

Bertalanffy, L. V. (1968). *General system theory: Foundations, development, applications.* New York: George Braziller.

Bosmajian, H. (1983). *The language of oppression.* Landham, MD: University Presses of America.

Bottomore, T. (Ed.). (1975). *Crisis and contention in sociology.* London: Sage.

Brittan, A., & Maynard, M. (1984). *Sexism, racism and oppression.* New York: Basil Blackwell.

Bulhan, H. A. (1985). *Franz Fanon and the psychology of oppression.* New York: Plenum.

Burman, E. (1990). Differing with deconstruction: A feminist critique. In I. Parker & J. Shotter (Eds.), *Deconstructing social psychology* (pp. 208–220). New York: Routledge & Kegan Paul.

Burns, S. (1990). *Social movements of the 1960s: Searching for democracy*. Boston: Twayne.

Carmichael, S., & Hamilton, C. V. (1967). *Black power: The politics of liberation in America*. New York: Random House.

Chamberlin, J. (1990). The ex-patients' movement: Where we've been and where we're going. *Journal of Mind and Behavior, 11*(3–4), 323–336.

Collier, B. (1977). Economics, psychology and racism: An analyses of oppression. *Journal of Black Psychology, 3*(2), 50–60.

Conradie, A. L. (1980). Africa. In J. R. Buhr (Ed.), *Handbook of world philosophy* (pp. 389–408). Westport, CT: Greenwood Press.

Danziger, K. (1990). *Constructing the subject: Historical origins of psychological research*. New York: Cambridge University Press.

Etzioni, A. (1991). *A responsive society: Collected essays on guiding deliberate social change*. San Francisco: Jossey-Bass.

Facione, P. A., Scherer, D., & Attig, T. (1978). *Values and society: An introduction to ethics and social philosophy*. Englewood Cliffs, NJ: Prentice-Hall.

Fals Borda, O. (1991). *Knowledge and social movements*. Columbus, OH: Merrill.

Fanon, F. (1963). *The wretched of the earth*. New York: Grove Press.

Femia, J. V. (1981). *Gramsci's political thought: Hegemony, consciousness, and the revolutionary process*. Oxford, England: Clarendon Press.

Fox, D. R. (1993). Psychological jurisprudence and radical social change. *American Psychologist, 48*, 234–241.

Fox-Piven, F., & Cloward, R. A. (1971). *Regulating the poor: The functions of public welfare*. New York: Vintage Books.

Franklin, R. S. (1969). The political economy of black power. *Social Problems, 16*(3), 286–301.

Freire, P. (1972). *Pedagogy of the oppressed*. New York: Herder and Herder.

Freud, S. (1961). *Civilization and its discontents* (J. Stratchey, Trans.). New York: W.W. Norton. (Original work published 1930)

George, S. (1992). *The debt boomerang*. Boulder, CO: Westview Press.

Goldenberg, I. I. (1978). *Oppression and social intervention*. Chicago: Nelson-Hall.

Gonick, L., & Rosh, R. (1988). The structural constraints of the world-economy on national political development. *Comparative Political Studies, 21,* 171–199.

Gramsci, A. (1971). *Selections from the prison notebooks*. London: Lawrence & Wishart.

Gyekye, K. (1987). *An essay on African philosophical thought: The Akan conceptual scheme*. New York: Cambridge University Press.

Hamilton, R., & Barrett, M. (Ed.). (1986). *The politics of diversity: Feminism, Marxism and nationalism*.

Harries-Jones, P. (Ed.). (1991). *Making knowledge count: Advocacy and social science*. Montreal: McGill-Queen's University Press.

Heyworth, E. (1991). "Town"/"Gown" and community relations: Case studies of social empowerment. In P. Harries-Jones (Ed.), *Making knowledge count: Advocacy and social science* (pp. 100–118). Montreal: McGill-Queen's University Press.

Hooks, B. (1984). *Feminist theory from margin to center*. Boston: South End Press.

Horowitz, D. (Ed.). (1971). *Radical sociology*. New York: Canfield Press.

Huberman, L., & Sweezy, P. (1968). *Introduction to socialism*. New York: Monthly Review Press.

Huygens, I. (1993, Oct.). *Depowerment: The new ethic for community psychologists*. Colloquium given at Wilfrid Laurier University, Waterloo, Ont., Canada.

Johnson, P. (1993, June). Oppression and its relationship to the experience of native people. In I. Prilleltensky (Chair), *Understanding and overcoming oppression: The political sphere of primary prevention*. Symposium conducted at the biennial conference of the Society for Community Research and Action, Division 27 of the American Psychological Association, Williamsburg, VA.

Kallen, E. (1989). *Label me human: Minority rights of stigmatized Canadians*. Toronto: University of Toronto Press.

Kiros, T. (1985). *Toward the construction of a theory of political action*.

Antonio Gramsci: Consciousness, participation and hegemony. New York: Lanham.

Kovel, J. (1984). *White racism.* New York: Columbia University Press.

Laclau, E., & Mouffe, C. (1985). *Hegemony and socialist strategy: Towards a radical democratic politics.* London: Verso.

Lerman, H. (1986). From Freud to feminist personality theory: Getting here from there. *Psychology of Women Quarterly, 10,* 1–18.

Lerner, M. (1991). *Surplus powerlessness.* London: Humanities Press International.

Lummis, C. D. (1982). The radicalism of democracy. *Democracy, 3,* 9–17.

Mar'i, S. K. (1988). Challenges to minority counselling: Arabs in Israel. *International Journal of the Advancement of Counselling, 11,* 5–21.

Martín-Baró, I. (1986). Hacia una psicología de la liberación. *Boletín de psicología, 5,* 219–231.

Memmi, A. (1967). *The colonizer and the colonized.* Boston: Beacon Press.

Memmi, A. (1968). *Dominated man: Notes towards a portrait.* New York: Orion Press.

Mermelstein, D. (1975). *Economics: Mainstream readings and radical critiques* (3rd ed.). New York: Random House.

Miller, D. (1978). *Social Justice.* Oxford, England: Clarendon.

Montero, M. (1992). Psicología de la liberación: Propuestra para una teoría psicosociológica. In H. Riquelme (Ed.), *Otras realidades, otras vías de accesso: Psicología y psiquiatría transcultural en América latina* (pp. 133–149). Editorial Nueva Sociedad.

Morris, J. (1992). Personal and political: A feminist perspective on researching physical disability. *Disability, Handicap, and Society, 7*(2), 157–166.

Neisen, J. H. (1990). Heterosexism: Redefining homophobia for the 1990s. *Journal of Gay and Lesbian Psychotherapy, 1*(3), 21–35.

Neumann, S. (1957). Comparative politics: A half-century appraisal. *Journal of Politics, 19*(3), 369–390.

Nobles, W. W. (1976). Extended self: Rethinking the so called Negro self concept. *Journal of Black Psychology, 2*(2), 15–24.

Olson, R. G. (1978). *Ethics.* New York: Random House.

Onyewuenyi, I. (1991). Is there an African philosophy? In T. Serequeberhan (Ed.), *African philosophy: The essential readings* (pp. 29–46). New York: Paragon House.

Ortega y Gasset, J. (1983). *Que es filosofia?* Madrid: Alianza.

Parenti, M. (1977). *Democracy for the few.* New York: St. Martin's Press.

Parker, I. (1992). *Discourse dynamics: Critical analysis for social and individual psychology.* New York: Routledge & Kegan Paul.

Parker, I., & Shotter, J. (Eds.). (1990). *Deconstructing social psychology.* New York: Routledge & Kegal Paul.

Parsons, T. (1947). *The structures of social action.* New York: Free Press.

Payer, C. (1991). *Lent and lost: Foreign credit and Third World development.* London: Zed Press.

Pepitone, A. (1989). Toward a cultural social psychology. *Psychology and Developing Societies, 1* (1), 5–19.

Pettman, R. (1979). *State and class: A sociology of international affairs.* London: Croom Helm.

Pheterson, G. (1986). Alliances between women: Overcoming internalized oppression and internalized domination. *Signs: Journal of Women in Culture and Society, 12*(1), 146–160.

Pottenger, J. R. (1989). *The political theory of liberation theology: Toward a reconvergence of social values and social science.* Albany: State University of New York Press.

Potts, R. (1993, June). Spiritual and political movements of the oppressed: Implications for community psychology. In I. Prilleltensky (Chair), *Understanding and overcoming oppression: The political sphere of primary prevention.* Symposium conducted at the biennial conference of the Society for Community Research and Action, Division 27 of the American Psychological Association, Williamsburg, VA.

Prilleltensky, I. (1993). The immigration experience of Latin American families: Research and action on perceived risk and protective factors. *Canadian Journal of Community Mental Health, 12*(2), 101–116.

Prilleltensky, I. (1994). *The morals and politics of psychology: Psychological discourse and the status quo.* Albany: State University of New York Press.

Prilleltensky, I., & Walsh-Bowers, R. (1993). Psychology and the moral imperative. *Journal of Theoretical and Philosophical Psychology, 13*(2), 90–102.

Rappaport, J. (1977). *Community psychology.* Troy, MO: Holt, Rinehart & Winston.

Rappaport, J. (1981). In praise of paradox: A social policy of empowerment over prevention. *American Journal of Community Psychology, 9*(1), 1–25.

Rappaport, J. (1987). Terms of empowerment/exemplars of prevention: Toward a theory for community psychology. American Journal of Community Psychology, 15, 121–148.

Rappaport, J. (1990). Research methods and the empowerment social agenda. In P. Tolan, C. Keys, F. Chertok, & L. Jason (Eds.), *Researching community psychology* (pp. 51–63). Washington, DC: American Psychological Association.

Rawls, J. (1972). *A theory of justice.* New York: Oxford University Press.

Richardson, B. (Ed.). (1989). *Drumbeat: Anger and renewal in Indian country.* Toronto: Summerhill Press.

Riessman, F. (1986). The new populism and the empowerment ethos. In H. C. Boyte & F. Riessman (Eds.), *The new populism: The politics of empowerment* (pp. 53–63). Philadelphia: Temple University Press.

Riger, S. (1992). Epistemological debates, feminist voices: Science, social values, and the study of women. *American Psychologist, 47,* 730–740.

Riger, S. (1993, Aug.). *What's wrong with empowerment?* Invited address presented at the annual convention of the American Psychological Association, Toronto.

Ross, D. (1991). *The origins of American social science.* New York: Cambridge University Press.

Sampson, E. E. (1993). *Celebrating the other: A dialogic account of human nature.* Boulder, CO: Westview Press.

Serequeberhan, T. (Ed.). (1991). *African philosophy: The essential readings.* New York: Paragon House.

Shreve, A. (1989). *Women together, women alone: The legacy of the consciousness-raising movement.* New York: Viking Penguin.

Sidgwick, H. (1922). *The methods of ethics* (7th ed.). London: Cambridge University Press.

Singer, P. (1993). *Practical ethics* (2nd ed.). New York: Cambridge University Press.

Smith, T. (1991). *The role of ethics in social theory.* Albany: State University of New York Press.

Strauss, A., & Corbin, J. (1990). *Basics of qualitative research: Grounded theory procedure and techniques.* London: Sage.

Taylor, C. (1992). *Multiculturalism and "the politics of recognition."* Princeton, NJ: Princeton University Press.

Turner, J. H., & Singleton, R. (1978). A theory of ethnic oppression: Toward a reintegration of cultural and structural concepts in ethnic relations theory. *Social Forces, 56*(4), 1001–1018.

Unger, R., & Crawford, M. (1992). *Women and gender: A feminist psychology.* Toronto: McGraw-Hill.

Watts, R. J. (1992). Elements of a psychology of human diversity. *Journal of Community Psychology, 20,* 116–131.

Weber, M. (1966). *The theory of social and economic organization.* New York: Free Press.

Weisband, E. (Ed.). (1989). *Poverty amidst plenty: World political economy and distributive justice.* Boulder, CO: Westview Press.

Wolfe, A. (1989). *Whose keeper? Social science and moral obligation.* Berkeley: University of California Press.

Young, I. M. (1991). *Justice and the politics of difference.* Princeton, NJ: Princeton University Press.

Zanardi, C. (Ed.). (1990). *Essential papers on the psychology of women.* New York: New York University Press.

8

Toward an Ethnography of "Voice" and "Silence"

Shulamit Reinharz

The concepts of disenfranchisement and oppression are invoked in various chapters of this book to illuminate the experience of different groups including racial and ethnic minorities, the frail elderly, and women. Although these concepts are useful in clarifying the position of particular groups in relation to others within a macrosociological or political framework (Ramazanoglu, 1989), they do not necessarily reveal how people experience their lives. This problem arises because people tend not to have a single self-definition of their experience. In certain contexts individuals may feel oppressed and in others the same individuals may feel more satisfied or even powerful. In addition, the concepts of oppression and disenfranchisement do not allow room for the experience of ambivalence: in any one situation individuals may feel both powerful and powerless. Perhaps even more significantly, the concepts of oppression and disenfranchisement do not suggest how they might be overcome. Rather, they imply a kind of total helplessness that people can genuinely be expected to avoid acknowledging. Finally, the individual and the observer are likely to have different views of the individual's life if they have different socioeconomic statuses or worldviews.

Although oppression may be an accurate outsider's concept to describe the relative powerlessness of one group vis-à-vis another, it is inappropriate and unjust to label individuals as oppressed when they do not identify themselves as such (Powers, 1986). Feminist sociologist Margaret Andersen (1981) reported on a research project that suffered from this kind of disjuncture between the interviewer's interpretation and the interviewees' experience. Based on her study of twenty women who were wives of corporate executives, Andersen reported that their claim of happiness was false. She discounted their contention that they were fulfilled in their roles of wife, mother, and volunteer. After publication of her study, the women wrote a rebuttal to her interpretation, complete with their interpretation of *her* experience. Specifically, they claimed that she suffered from jealousy of their material resources.

The disjuncture between individual experience and the researcher's redefinition or renaming of the experience poses a dilemma. On the one hand, if we as researchers simply collect and report the views of individuals, we will neither be adding our own thoughts nor producing a procedure for understanding differences among people who are members of the same group. On the other hand, if we do not feel constrained to accept the interviewees' definition of the situation, we may violate it altogether, as in the case reported above.

The concepts of voice and silence may help us out of this dilemma. I have found that members of groups that are frequently labeled oppressed by researchers can better relate to, and prefer, the phrases "having no voice," "losing a voice," "wanting a voice," "not being heard," or "being silenced," rather than defining themselves as oppressed. For this reason, I propose that it is important to understand various groups in terms of these concepts. In her study of female managers, sociologist Judi Marshall describes two relevant literatures: the "reform feminist viewpoint," in which "the male world . . . is tacitly used as a positive model to which women should aspire," and the "radical feminist" viewpoint, which "depicts women as oppressed; with men, as the dominant force in society[,] . . . as their oppressors" (Marshall, 1984, pp. 7–8). Neither view is authentic, in

Marshall's assessment. Rather, she found "a third women's voice[,] . . . the quiet, scarcely verbal voice of what women have been and are. It asks us to remember and value the strengths [women] have developed and lived" (p. 8).

This chapter will analyze the concept of voice and suggest ways by which it can help us to understand the experience of groups and their members whom researchers frequently have labeled oppressed. Beginning with the assumption that voice is a central concept for people interested in empowerment and diversity, I argue that voice is a metaphor that can help oppressed groups gain a stronger position in society. In addition, I illustrate the unusual properties of voice and offer examples of its use in literature concerning powerlessness. I conclude with some of the implications of an understanding of voice.

Voice Defined

Today's dominant metaphors for power relations are voice and silence. Surprisingly, however, these words are rarely defined. For example, Marcia Millman and Rosabeth Kanter edited a widely read book, *Another Voice* (1975), without defining what voice is. This continuous drawing on, and yet not defining, the metaphor of voice is not a shortcoming; rather, it is a clue to its deep cultural acceptance. Poet and writer Tillie Olsen (1978) devoted an entire volume to explicating the ways in which silence operates in culture.

The dictionary suggests why voice serves as a rich metaphor for power relations. The *American Heritage Dictionary of the English Language,* for example, defines *voice* in three different ways, over and above sound-related definitions. These multiple definitions are the ability to produce sounds, a medium or agency of expression, and the right or opportunity to express a choice or opinion. Thus, voice means having the ability, the means, and the right to express oneself, one's mind, and one's will. If an individual does not have these abilities, means, or right, he or she is silent. Many people have neither the ability nor the means to express themselves because these facilities and abilities either were never established in the first place or were taken away after having been provided.

The Power to Silence, The Power to Speak

Whereas in contemporary society, voice is a metaphor for freedom and power, in earlier times it had a more literal meaning. In essence, people without power were not allowed to speak. People with power, by contrast, could speak and could control the right of others to speak. Evidence for this pattern can be found in many dominant texts of our culture. One example is Timothy 2:12 in the New Testament: "I suffer not a woman to teach, nor to usurp authority over the man, but to be in silence." In this example, men have a voice and women have their voice denied, prevented, or removed, leaving them silent. Women are a category, as are men, without regard for individual differences in matters such as virtue.

The power relations between two groups affects the speech of each group—one speaks; the other does not or speaks only by permission. Disregard for individual differences is a fundamental ingredient in the dynamics of oppression. Oppression relies on the ability to subdue diversity. In the passage from Timothy quoted above, the injunction against women's speaking is linked explicitly to teaching and authority, which in turn stand for other injunctions. Conveying this idea in her poetry, Adrienne Rich (1979) wrote that silence reflects violence if language and naming are reflections of power.

The fact that I, a woman, speak and write today, and that you listen to and read my voice, is evidence of the changes in the power relations between women and men that have occurred since the time of Timothy. The history of women's efforts to liberate themselves encompasses the history of women's struggle to seize the right to speak and to be heard.

In 1828, for example, Scottish-born Fanny Wright spoke out in Cincinnati against slavery and religious revivals, thereby also speaking out against the silencing of women (Rossi, 1988). When in 1837, nine years later, two hundred women assembled in New York to form the first Anti-Slavery Convention of American Women, they did so in "fear and trembling" because the norm of the time "required on Biblical authority" that women "be silent and submissive." Never before had there been a public political meeting of U.S. women (Anti-Slavery Convention of American Women, 1987). By gathering to speak, these women were acting both against the enslavement of African Americans and against their own silencing.

In her study of women's study clubs from 1860 to 1910 that were first formed about twenty-five years after the Anti-Slavery Convention, Theodora Penny Martin (1987) writes about the ability of these women to break out of silence by talking to each other: "[My book] is a chronicle of women at once unexceptional and uncommon, ordinary and extraordinary, of women who found individuality in groups, who, unschooled, defined education, women 'working silently as leaven' who dispelled the sounds of silence, selfless women who understood the primacy of self-education. It is the story of women's study clubs in post–Civil War America, a historical study of anonymous women whose distinctive voices call for an audience today" (p. 1). The tradition grew slowly of women who recognized their need to be outspoken, to speak their minds, to create speakouts, and to be speakers in everyday life and in public. There has been a reciprocal relation between women's power and women's speech, each contributing to the other. When women are no longer afraid, they *will* speak up; in order to not be afraid, women *must* speak up.

We know from social psychology that as groups protest their oppression, they try to modify the speech of their oppressors. Thus, women now demand that men (and women) not address them according to their marital status, that they not be harassed verbally, that they not be ignored because of the dominant culture's traditional use of so-called generic language, and that they not be referred to by a physical attribute — for example, as "a blonde." So, too, as minority groups strive to diminish their powerlessness, they choose their names and how they wish to be addressed and remembered. For example, prostitutes are choosing the terms *sex workers* rather than *tricks* or *sexual slaves*. Negro Americans chose the term *blacks* and then *African Americans,* and females have chosen the terms *women* and *Ms.* When people do not name their own experience, others name it for them and obliterate it (Reinharz, 1988b). In her book about female lawyers, Mona Harrington (1994) summarized these issues:

> [The] socially centralized system of power . . . is
> increasingly subject to question and challenge and
> change by outsiders demanding a democratic share
> of effective power over their own lives. They are
> demanding that their voices be heard — in govern-
> ment, in the arts, in the media, in the canon of
> knowledge taught in the schools. . . . As a precon-
> dition for such social rearrangements, outsiders are
> demanding a new respect, forms of public address
> free from demeaning stereotypes, rules of civility
> that preclude insulting or abusive language, and
> fair standards in the media for the depiction of
> women, minorities, and other frequently stigma-
> tized groups [p. 4].

Being Heard and Being Seen

Since the time of Timothy, voice and silence have referred both
to actual speech and to a metaphor for power and powerlessness. Voice, in particular, has become a kind of megametaphor
representing presence, power, participation, protest, and identity. Other metaphors for power have been based on images of
vision and writing, but I believe that these are less potent than
the metaphor of voice.

   Vision or sight is a relatively passive human sense; voice,
by contrast, is active. The metaphor of sight leads to concerns
about "invisible people," and the metaphor of writing leads to
concerns about being "written out of history" (Kelly-Gadol,
1977). When groups complain that they are invisible, they try
to demonstrate that the problem lies not in themselves but rather
in the inability of others to see them. Historians can be considered myopic when they write histories that are inaccurate because their subjects have been made invisible. When women
are "overlooked," it signifies that historians or writers are suffering from "gynopia" — a term I have coined to signify the inability to see women (Reinharz, 1988a). Recognizing that they are
not invisible, but rather are *made* invisible, women and other
overlooked groups attempt to become seen. But being seen is

not enough; being "written into history" is not enough. Being heard is much more active and powerful, even if it is frightening to speak up.

It has never been as threatening to the powerful when powerless people are seen as when they are heard. For example, children may be seen but not heard. In fact, being visible or "looked at" is hardly an achievement for women. Looking at women has been a form of men's privilege. His gaze undresses her; his rapacious gaze has been institutionalized as art. Being seen is a way of losing, not gaining, one's voice. For a woman to "accomplish" being seen by men is thus a dubious victory. Being heard is another matter.

This contrast between being seen and being heard can be applied to understanding affirmative-action policies. If these policies merely support powerless groups' being seen (that is, being physically included) in organizations, and not necessarily being heard, then little change has been accomplished. Affirmative-action policies succeed when formerly excluded people are heard. French feminists Luce Irigaray (1980) and Helen Cixous (1981) remind us how difficult it is to be heard even if one has the chance to speak, because certain things are "unhearable" by certain groups. In particular, they claim that "expressions of female 'voice,' body and sexuality are essentially inaudible when the dominant language and ways of viewing are male." Hearing, they argue, is more difficult than seeing (discussed in Fine, 1988, p. 38).

The metaphor of sound expresses the fact that people are both silent and silenced. A woman is silenced when no one listens, even when she talks. She is silenced when others do all the talking, including speaking for her, especially speaking about her. She is silenced when people cannot understand what she is saying even when she does speak. They cannot "hear" what she is saying.

For example, a study by Michelle Fine (1987) of an urban public high school serving primarily minority students revealed an "insidious push toward silence" among most students. Many of the teachers were also silenced, especially those who encouraged their students by listening to them. She said, "A biology teacher, one of the few black teachers in the school, actually integrated creative writing assignments such as 'My life as an alcoholic' and 'My life as the child of an alcoholic' into her biology class curriculum. Her department chairman reprimanded her severely for introducing 'extraneous materials' into her classroom" (p. 162).

It is not only girls and blacks in high schools who are cut off from speaking their mind or using their voice. The same process occurs in the judge's courtroom. For example, Nancy Marshall produced an *Attorney's Survey Report* for the Gender Bias Committee of the Supreme Judicial Court of Massachusetts. In her survey, 6 percent of the male attorneys, 50 percent of the female attorneys, and 15 percent of all attorneys report having been cut off by judges while speaking. So, too, 11 percent of the male attorneys, 69 percent of the female attorneys, and 22 percent of all attorneys report being cut off by counsel, and 4 percent of the men, 39 percent of the women, and 11 percent of all attorneys report being cut off by court employees (Marshall, 1988, p. 11). These cut-off women are women who are supposed to be defending the rights of others!

Clearly, the power relations between groups affect speech (Ehrenreich, 1981). Language has the function of preserving status relationships and selecting, replacing, or modifying statuses. Language is thus a means of social control (Sotomayor, 1977). Sotomayor writes that language is the fellow of empire; together they wax strong and together they fall. Following conquest is language imposition, so that those who do not have sufficient contact with conquerors will be excluded from power. For the oppressed, language also has the role of providing the group with a feeling of solidarity that helps them to deal with the oppressive majority culture.

When people from different status groups speak with one another, one group feels it has the privilege to interrupt. In the case of men and women, Candace West and Don Zimmerman (1983) found that men exert their power over women in the same way that adults exert power over children: men interrupt women conversationally, just as adults interrupt children.

In another high school study, Michelle Fine (1988) looked

for speech and its absence in courses about teenage sexuality. She examined "the desires, fears, and fantasies which give structure and shape to silences and voices concerning sex education and school-based health clinics in the 1980s" (p. 29). She found that teachers could not discuss female desire, nor could they allow the girls to discuss this topic. The thought itself was repressed because the voices were silenced.

Voice in Texts

Having argued that voice is the metaphor of power because of its multiple meanings, I would like to demonstrate how it is used in texts about oppression and liberation. The illustrative texts I have chosen concern females — working-class women, teenage girls who have anorexia nervosa, women with mastectomies, women elected to Congress, academic women, and women in general. A similar selection of texts could be used to discuss the meaning of voice for other groups.

My first quote is from Nancy Seifer's *Nobody Speaks for Me! Self-Portraits of American Working-Class Women* (1976), which discusses the silence of the silent majority:

> Silence can be as much a sign of disapproval as of approval. It can denote passive acceptance. Or it can simply represent the absence of a voice, or of a means of making one's voice heard. From where I was sitting in the late 1960's, I began to perceive that the Silent Majority was voiceless, but not out of choice. . . . Their anger seemed to stem from two sources, conflicting at times: an inability of most working class people to make their voices heard publicly on major issues and an uneasy feeling that they were not well-informed enough to do so [p. 339].

Nancy Seifer's redefinition of silence as representing a range of issues from compliance to exclusion is informative. Silence masks insecurity and frustration. Silence is subject to misinterpretation.

A second excerpt is from American historian Gerda Lerner, who expresses gratitude to many people at the start of her book, *The Creation of Patriarchy* (1986):

> To the feminist scholars who have wrestled with questions similar to mine and have found other answers; to the students and audiences who helped me test out my ideas over these years and to the anonymous and voiceless women who for millennia have asked questions of origin and justice — my thanks [p. x].

Gerda Lerner recognizes that her voice as a writer is connected to the experience of the women of the past who asked the same questions but who were voiceless because they lacked the means of expression. The voiceless women are those who became anonymous.

My third example is from Joan Jacobs Brumberg's *Fasting Girls: The Emergence of Anorexia Nervosa* (1988). That study examines the relation between adolescent female patients and male adult doctors in the nineteenth century. Brumberg describes how girls' accounts of their bodily experiences were discounted by the very people to whom they turned for help:

> The doctor was more interested in what the body revealed than in anything the patient had to say about her illness. Educated physicians came to regard the process of history taking as secondary to the process of physical examination. Doctors were assured that patient accounts of illness were more often than not prejudiced, ignorant, and unreliable; [they believed that] personal and family narratives were rarely objective and . . . almost always revealed the ignorance of lay people about medical phenomena. In this atmosphere of suspicion about all patient accounts, volatile adolescent girls were considered particularly unreliable informants [p. 167].

Brumberg goes on to write that the silencing of the young girl
insidiously led to her mother's collusion with the physician, further reinforcing the girl's silence. She describes the typical tri-
angle as follows:

> In this scenario, which assumes that doctor, mother
> and patient all played out their expected social roles,
> the examining room reproduced the situation in the
> home. The doctor and the mother were the primary
> conversants; again, two adults, a male and a fe-
> male, were focused on the girl's wasting body and
> her refusal of food. Again, she was told that she
> ought to eat. Her response, shaped by the nature
> of the medical investigation and parental expecta-
> tions, was to say that she could not — eating hurt
> in some vague, nonspecific way. . . .
>
> It is unlikely that the doctor here dismissed
> the mother and tried to see the patient alone in
> order to search out what was troubling the girl and
> causing her to refuse food. Propriety worked against
> such a scenario, as did the conception of the pa-
> tient as a dependent person and the doctor's lack
> of interest in girlish narratives. Adolescent patients
> must have sensed the doctor's disinterest in their
> point of view. A recovered anoretic told her physi-
> cian that, during treatment, "I saw that you wished
> to shut me up" [p. 167].

Silent people cannot be understood, and the constellation of power
that keeps them silent is not challenged when they are silenced.

The inability of girls and women to speak to or be heard
by their male physicians is still a common phenomenon (Andrist, 1993). The following quote from a newspaper article
presents the views of Dr. Oliver Cope, aged eighty-six, professor emeritus of surgery at Harvard Medical School:

> [He was] a man who was never afraid to express
> a controversial medical opinion and who always

took the time to listen to his patients. He laments the fact that many doctors today cannot do the latter. "Sometimes, an hour of listening is worth a dozen x-rays," he maintains. . . .

Cope began to express his iconoclastic views about breast cancer surgery, questioning the validity of mastectomy as the only way to treat it, in the 1940s when a patient told him he had not only removed her breast but her feelings of womanhood. . . . He spoke of his awakening. "As an intern, a resident and junior surgeon, I had done more than 200 radical mastectomies, and nobody had told me how it affected these women psychologically. The surgeons didn't pay attention, and the women didn't dare tell them. It has proved hard to convince the male medical profession that a woman's desires should be considered.

["]As for myself, I had not realized how chauvinistic I had been," he said. In his 1977 book, *The Breast: Its Problems — Benign and Malignant — and How to Deal with Them,* Cope advocated that mastectomies be abandoned entirely. To colleagues who accused him of being "too damn sentimental," Cope would counter by asking them how they would feel "if you had cancer of the penis and knew there were two treatments, equally good. This was usually greeted with silence," Cope said [Negri, 1988, p. 2].

Leaving the realms of high school, courtrooms, and medical practice, we can consider why some people have a voice and others are silenced in politics. The following quote comes from a publication of the National Women's Political Caucus. Entitled *Election Alert — National Women's Political Caucus, 10/88,* it addresses its readers as follows:

You already know the damning statistics. Out of 435 members of the House of Representatives, only 23 are women. When Congress debates issues that

deeply affect our lives, issues like pay equity, child
care, and reproductive rights, less than 5% of the
voices raised in debate are women's voices.

The citizens of this nation are not enjoying representative government, in other words, unless their voices are heard. Those
voices can be heard and expressed, moreover, only if there is
diversity among the representatives, just as there is diversity
within the citizenry. The actual voices of women must be heard
if Congress hopes to address their concerns.

In her study of old people, anthropologist Sharon Kaufman (1986) expresses this idea, implying the need for the entire society to listen to representatives of the older age groups:

Now, as the largest segment of the U.S. population enters middle age, questions of how to cope
with an aging population as well as with one's own
later years arise from people in all age groups and
from many sectors of American life: how to stay
healthy and vital longer; how to provide and pay
for services for those who are ill, disabled, or home-
bound; how to take the nightmarish quality out of
the nursing home; how to maintain a decent standard of living after retirement; how to generate
meaning in the last decades of life; how to best chan-
nel and articulate the voices of older Americans so
that their needs may be understood and met by a
society that has always been youth-oriented [pp.
3–4].

Older people's needs can be understood if their voices are heard.

Yet another realm in which voice has become preeminent
as a metaphor consists of psychological studies concerned with
moral development. In her well-known book, *In a Different Voice:
Psychological Theory and Women's Development* (1982), Carol Gilligan writes about voice as the expression of identity, not necessarily as the assertion of power:

Over the past ten years, I have been listening to
people talking about morality and about themselves. Halfway through that time, I began to hear
a distinction in these voices, two ways of speaking
about problems, two modes of describing the relationship between other and self. . . . Against the
background of the psychological descriptions of
identity and moral development which I had read
and taught for a number of years, the women's
voices sounded distinct. . . . The different voice I
describe is characterized not by gender but theme.
Its association with women is an empirical observation, and it is primarily through women's voices
that I trace its development. But this association
is not absolute, and the contrasts between male and
female voices are presented here to highlight a distinction between two modes of thought and to focus a problem of interpretation rather than to represent a generalization about either sex. . . . My
interest lies in the interaction of experience and
thought, in different voices and in the dialogues to
which they give rise, in the way we listen to ourselves and to others, in the stories we tell about our
lives [pp. 1–2].

Carol Gilligan hears the person speaking his or her true self.
And yet there is a shared property among all those who speak
their true voice — it is the different voice.

The most extensive and thorough analysis to date of the
nature of women's voices is contained in Mary Belenky, Blythe
Clinchy, Nancy Goldberger, and Jill Tarule's *Women's Ways of
Knowing: The Development of Self, Voice, and Mind* (1986). These
psychologists found that "women repeatedly used the metaphor
of voice to depict their intellectual and ethical development."
They also found that "the development of a sense of voice, mind
and self were intricately intertwined" (p. 18). By listening to
the speech of many women, these researchers discovered levels

of development and labeled these levels in terms of types of speech. Their scheme is too elaborate to summarize here. Suffice it to say that women with the most meager sense of self were being silenced and their silence kept their sense of self meager. The researchers report: "The silent women worried that they would be punished just for using words — any words. They said things like, 'I don't like talking to my husband. If I were to say no, he might hit me'" (p. 24). Nevertheless, the women who could speak — even the most articulate "connected" knowers — were still partially silent because they were raised not to speak up if they wanted to remain attractive to men.

Feminist Studies of Women's Voices

The realization that there are many suppressed voices that, if heard, would enable researchers to have a much more accurate picture of the world has led many feminist scholars to seek out voices that have not been heard (Reinharz, 1992). These are the voices of groups of people that are overlooked because they lack power. For example, Nadya Aisenberg and Mona Harrington, authors of *Women of Academe: Outsiders in the Sacred Grove* (1988), interviewed two types of academic women — those who were "deflected" from academic careers and those who had made steady progress up the academic ladder. Surprisingly, they found that similar experiences characterized these two groups.

In their chapter, "The Voice of Authority," Aisenberg and Harrington analyzed the difficulties both types of women have in developing a voice of authority: "A strong, clear voice is necessary to the practice of the profession, both literally in the classroom and figuratively in written research. . . . But to state views boldly in public debate, to challenge the intellectual views of others, still pose problems for professional women" (p. 64). They ask: "Why should this be so? Why do women find persistent difficulty with forms of public assertion? Why do they refer to silence, apology, diffidence, hesitancy, as characteristic of their discourse?" (p. 64).

Listening very carefully to the metaphors and language of the women led to the conclusion that "women . . . struggle, consciously or unconsciously, to resolve contradictory norms, and this struggle unavoidably compromises the development of the voice of authority that normally attends professional empowerment" (p. 64). Women silence their own voice, Aisenberg and Harrington hypothesize, because of contradictory cultural messages or scripts that push them in different directions.

Other scholars who have studied why many women do not develop a voice of their own include sociologist Mirra Komarovsky. Her examination of college women at an elite Seven Sisters college (Komarovsky, 1985) shows how women are conversationally castrated. This phenomenon occurs especially among particularly intelligent women who are cut off by men and who also cut themselves off to please men. She gives several examples of this type of situation:

> A freshman [told me she] was disappointed in the lack of intellectual interchange with male undergraduates. She gave an illustration: Visiting a male acquaintance, she saw a copy of *Ulysses* on his desk, a book she'd just read. She wanted to know what he thought of it but he cut off this conversation by changing the subject [p. 244].

> [A] sophomore called her boyfriend feminist in his attitudes but less so in his behavior. He was raised in a traditional home and expects some traditional behavior from women. For example, he expects her not to talk too much when he's talking to his friends and, certainly, to support his views. He becomes upset if she argues against his views in the presence of his male friends [p. 244].

> [A] student felt that she had gained enough self-confidence over the year to feel freer to argue with the men in her classes. Then she added a qualification: "I would argue less strongly if I were interested in the guy socially. You can't be adamant if you expect to be asked out" [p. 243].

[Another student said,] "There is this guy whom
I find incredibly attractive but I cannot speak to
him. I don't know if it's fear of rejection, or fear
of being perceived as too forward, or, most likely,
a combination of the two. In any case, I feel incredibly stupid" [p. 231].

These disheartening quotations from well-educated women reveal the intrapsychic conflict women face as they attempt to defy
the stereotype that women who want the attention of men must
be silent.

Applications for Diversity Research

There are many ways in which the metaphors of voice and silence can aid us in research, especially research meant to intervene in destructive power relations among groups. In this chapter I have focused on voice in relation to the lives of girls and
women, but the ideas can be applied much more generally.

First, paying attention to voice alerts us to the fact that
listening to people aids in their empowerment. At the same time,
an interest in hearing their voices requires going to them, to
their space, or to a safe space. Research that recognizes diverse
voices will have to take into consideration the desirability of
studying people in ways that enable them to use their native
language, articulate or not. It also means that all texts must be
understood in terms of privileges and suppressed voices. Before researchers can expect to hear suppressed voices, they will
have to examine the power dynamics of the social location they
are studying and their role in it. For example, in a phenomenological study of the concept of caring among different pairs of
people, including students in vocational high schools and their
teachers, sociologist Barbara Tarlow (1994) reported the following:

I had expected that I would have to work hard at
getting in; instead it was easy. I suspect being an
older, married woman, living in one school district

and having grown up in the other lent some kind of a priori credibility to my mission. But I think their eagerness also reflected a desire on their part to be heard. School officials everywhere were under siege, and many were themselves engaged in a kind of institutional self-critique. Change and an aggressive pursuit of better education were prevalent themes in the interviews with both of the school superintendents. Not only the superintendents of the school, but the contact people, informants, student support staff and classroom teachers wanted to tell their story. I felt as though many people, especially teachers working at the schools, were looking for a legitimate place to voice their thoughts and feelings about their work, work that I believe was very meaningful to them. It may have been rewarding if not therapeutic, for teachers to have a chance to describe what they were doing that was right. The interviews demonstrated that many teachers and students were surprised that someone would assume they were doing something right and ask about it [p. 8].

Second, to hear the diverse voices of those whose voices have been suppressed, we have to be able to create a context where the person can speak and we can listen. That means that we must study who we are as well as who we are in relation to those whom we study (Reinharz, 1994). To what extent can a person with a certain set of characteristics study people with other characteristics? Diversity-related research that seeks to hear other people's voices requires understanding the research relationship as one of speaking and listening and therefore requires us to understand who can speak to whom and be heard.

Third, to utilize the concept of voice within diverse groups, we must be willing to hear what others are saying, even when it violates prior expectations or threatens our interests. Denise Connors, a sociologist, gerontologist, and nurse, discovered the necessity of being willing to hear when she was engaged in

research on her dissertation, *I've Always Had Everything I've Wanted . . .
But I Never Wanted Very Much: An Experiential Analysis of Irish-
American Working-Class Women in Their Nineties* (1986). She described how her early interviews were driven by her sense of
what she wanted the women to tell her. As she put it, "I believed that their lives should be recorded — that they should each
have a voice. But I had a vested interest in what their voices
said" (p. 13).

A fourth suggestion for diversity-related research that uti-
lizes the concept of voice is to ensure that sufficient time is allo-
cated, while also recognizing the constraints on interviewees'
time. Belenky, Clinchy, Goldberger, and Tarule (1986) wrote
about this aspect of their study:

> In our study we chose to listen only to women. . . .
> The initial interviews were tape recorded and tran-
> scribed and were from two to five hours in length,
> resulting in over 5000 pages of text. We adopted
> an intensive interview/case study approach because
> we wanted to hear what the women had to say in
> their own terms rather than test our own precon-
> ceived hypotheses, particularly since we included
> a number of disadvantaged and forgotten women
> whose ways of knowing, and learning, identity
> transformations, and moral outlook have seldom
> been examined by academic researchers. We pro-
> ceeded inductively, opening our ears to the voices
> and perspectives of women so that we might begin
> to hear the unheard and unimagined" [p. 15].

The attentiveness of the researchers in this study to the manifestations of voice and silence contributed to the richness and
validity of their data. The difficulty in scheduling enough time
may be overcome by drawing on participant observation techniques that involve the researcher in the ongoing activities of
those who are being studied.

Fifth, those of us who study diverse groups in order to
listen to their voices recognize the potential of harming those

we study when we ask people to "tell it like it is." On the one hand, it seems contradictory to me to have a middle-class researcher "give" a group its voice, as many have claimed they were doing. For example, Oscar Lewis, famous for his studies among the poor in Latin America, wrote, "I have tried to give a voice to a people who are rarely heard" (Lewis, 1965, p. xii). Can anyone give another person or group a voice? I believe not—rather, we can tell the story of our trying to give a voice to another group, presenting the group's speech as contextualized in the process of listening to it. I also believe that it is worthwhile to find ways of helping others to utilize the media to project their own voices, rather than to have it mediated by others.

Similarly we can harm those toward whom we might have noble intentions when we convert individuals into representatives. Sherri Ettinger, an undergraduate with whom I worked, wrote: "It is good to be able to speak, to speak out, and to be outspoken. But it is not good to be spoken for or to be made a 'spokesperson.'"

Writing about men who want to learn about women's experiences, she suggested that they read books in which people define their experience of otherness and go to lectures where people discuss what it is like to be "an other" in this society:

> If they really listen and allow people to define their own experiences, they[,] too, can work toward understanding difference. What all of us who have privilege and power in some area of our life should not do is expect the other to teach us and answer all of our questions about otherness. We have to be willing to read and learn on our own—we cannot expect a person to spend all of her/his time and energy educating us about otherness.
>
> Those of us who have a powerful aspect of our lives need to educate other people who have that same characteristic about otherness. A white person is usually more willing to listen to me explain why something [she/he] said is racist than is a person of color. If a man tells another man that

his sexist joke isn't funny, there is a better chance the man won't repeat the joke than if an "oversensitive" woman is the one who responds. Now, this is not to say that I shouldn't respond to sexist jokes. Rather, it is to say that my primary energy should be toward educating people in the areas [where] I have privilege (e.g. white skin) and toward learning as much as I can about people whose voices are not considered "important" in this society.

Conclusion

My study of the concept of voice suggests that we should study how different groups affect each other with their speech and silence. When does anyone speak? When is anyone heard? When do people listen? What kinds of discourses are available and where? What substitutes for actual voice do people with speech impairments use? What are the speech and listening impairments of able-bodied people like? We need an ethnography and history of speaking and listening — in other words, an ethnography of voice.

References

Aisenberg, N., & Harrington, M. (1988). *Women of academe: Outsiders in the sacred grove.* Amherst, MA: Northeastern University Press.

Andersen, M. (1981). Corporate wives: Longing for liberation or satisfied with the status quo? *Urban Life, 10,* 311–327.

Andrist, L. (1993). *A model of women-centered practice: Shared decision making between breast cancer surgeons and patients.* Unpublished doctoral dissertation. Brandeis University, Waltham, MA.

Anti-Slavery Convention of American Women. (1987). *Turning the world upside down.* New York: Feminist Press.

Belenky, M., Clinchy, B., Goldberger, N., & Tarule, J. (1986). *Women's ways of knowing: The development of self, voice, and mind.* New York: Basic Books.

Brumberg, J. J. (1988). *Fasting girls: The emergence of anorexia nervosa.* Cambridge, MA: Harvard University Press.

Cixous, H. (1981). Castration or decapitation? *Signs: Journal of Women in Culture and Society, 7*(1), 41–55.

Connors, D. (1986). *I've always had everything I've wanted . . . but I never wanted very much: An experiential analysis of Irish-American working-class women in their nineties.* Unpublished doctoral dissertation, Brandeis University, Waltham, MA.

Ehrenreich, B. (1981, May). The politics of talking in couples: Conversus interruptus and other disorders. *Ms.,* pp. 46–48.

Fine, M. (1987). Silencing in public schools. *Language Arts, 64,* 157–174.

Fine, M. (1988). Sexuality, schooling, and adolescent females: The missing discourse of desire. *Harvard Educational Review, 58,* 29–53.

Gilligan, C. (1982). *In a different voice: Psychological theory and women's development.* Cambridge, MA: Harvard University Press.

Harrington, M. (1994). *Women lawyers: Rewriting the rules.* New York: Knopf.

Irigaray, L. (1980). When our lips speak together. *Signs: Journal of Women in Culture and Society, 6*(1), 69.

Kaufman, S. (1986). *The ageless self.* Madison: University of Wisconsin Press.

Kelly-Gadol, J. (1977). Did women have a Renaissance? In R. Bridenthal & C. Koonz (Eds.), *Becoming visible: Women in European history.* Boston: Houghton Mifflin.

Komarovsky, M. (1985). *Women in college.* New York: Basic Books.

Lerner, G. (1986). *The creation of patriarchy.* New York: Oxford University Press.

Lewis, O. (1965). *La vida.* New York: Vintage Books.

Marshall, J. (1984). *Women managers: Travellers in a male world.* Chichester, England: Wiley.

Marshall, N. (1988). *Attorney's survey report for the Gender Bias Committee of the Supreme Judicial Court of Massachusetts.* Wellesley, MA: Wellesley Center for Research on Women.

Martin, T. P. (1987). *The sound of our own voices: Women's study clubs, 1860–1910.* Boston: Beacon Press.

Millman, M., & Kanter, R. M. (Eds.). (1975). *Another voice: Feminist perspectives on social life and social science.* New York: Doubleday Anchor.

Negri, G. (1988, Nov. 4). After 60 years, he's still dedicated. *Boston Globe,* p. 2.

Olsen, T. (1978). *Silences.* New York: Delacorte Press/Seymour Lawrence.

Powers, M. N. (1986). *Oglala women: Myth, ritual, and reality.* Chicago: University of Chicago Press.

Ramazanoglu, C. (1989). *Feminism and the contradictions of oppression.* London: Routledge & Kegan Paul.

Reinharz, S. (1988a). Feminist distrust. In D. Berg & K. Smith (Eds.), *The self in social inquiry* (pp. 152–172). Newbury Park, CA: Sage.

Reinharz, S. (1988b). What's missing in miscarriage? *Journal of Community Psychology, 16,* 84–103.

Reinharz, S. (1992). *Feminist methods in social research.* New York: Oxford University Press.

Reinharz, S. (1994). *Observing the observer.* Newbury Park, CA: Sage.

Rich, A. (1979). *On lies, secrets, and silence: Selected prose 1966–1978.* New York: W.W.Norton.

Rossi, A. (Ed.). (1988). *The feminist papers: From Adams to de Beauvoir.* Boston: Northeastern University Press.

Seifer, N. (1976). *Nobody speaks for me! Self-portraits of American working-class women.* New York: Simon & Schuster.

Sotomayor, M. (1977). Language, culture, and ethnicity in developing self-concept. *Social Casework, 58*(4), 195–203.

Tarlow, B. (1994). *Understanding caring: A process that varies.* Unpublished doctoral dissertation, Brandeis University, Waltham, MA.

West, C., & Zimmerman, D. (1983). Small insults: A study of interruptions in cross-sex conversations between unacquainted persons. In B. Thorne, C. Kramarae, & N. Henley (Eds.), *Language, gender and society.* Rowley, MA: Newbury House.

9

A White Man's Perspective on the Unconscious Processes Within Black-White Relations in the United States

Clayton P. Alderfer

The subject of black-white race relations in the United States can never be far from the consciousness of citizens who do not look away from the information regularly before us. We see effects in our families, churches, neighborhoods, schools, political parties, places of employment, and universities. As the wider culture has adopted the language of dealing with, managing, and valuing diversity, psychology has followed a similar pattern. For some, the focus on diversity is a means of continuing to approach the complex and difficult issues associated with black-white race relations. For others, it is little more than the latest fad in a long pattern of continuing to avoid the phenomena associated with race. That the same word — *diversity* — can result in *both* approach and avoidance is itself a reason for taking account of unconscious processes.

For more than twenty years, I have been involved as a member of race- and gender-balanced research-and-consulting teams dealing with efforts to diagnose and change black-white

Note: I wish to thank Roderick Watts and David Berg for their many helpful comments on the earlier versions of this paper.

race relations within organizations (Alderfer, Tucker, Alderfer, & Tucker, 1988; Alderfer & Thomas, 1988; Alderfer, Alderfer, Bell, & Jones, 1992). This work has proved to be enormously challenging and highly satisfying. It has caused me to rethink many facets of my personal and professional identity as a white, male psychologist and applied behavioral scientist. Perhaps most important of my many learnings is an enriched appreciation of what it means to have a white racial identity and how unconscious components shape my sense of self (Alderfer, 1985; Helms, 1990).

The effects of this work have influenced the theoretical work I do, the methodological approaches I take, and the values I hold. It has reinforced the idea that if we value self-understanding as a key element in the professional equipment of an applied behavioral scientist — as I do — then this knowledge has both individual and group components. We have a more complete awareness of ourselves and of others to the degree that we neither negate the uniqueness of each person, regardless of that person's group memberships, nor deny the ever-present effects of group memberships for each individual (Brewer & Kramer, 1985).

I am one-of-a-kind as a person — as is everyone who reads this chapter. I am also a member of the white racial group — as everyone who reads this chapter is a member of a racial group. I am male — as everyone who reads this chapter has a gender-group membership. In these three psychological conditions, we all participate. Even if I were to try to escape my racial- or gender-group memberships, members of my own and other racial and gender groups would treat me as if I were a member of my groups. Perhaps no document makes this point more powerfully than the account written by John Howard Griffin (1961). A white man, Griffin changed his skin color and lived as a black man in the South for an extended period during the late 1950s. His life was changed irrevocably as a result.

All of us have some choice about how, as individuals, we relate to our own and other racial and gender groups. Increasing our self-understanding at both individual and group levels can be significant in making these choices. Do we accept or deny our group memberships? Under what conditions do we feel proud or ashamed of who we are? How is our way of being group members responded to by our own and other group members? For those of us who are psychologists, how do our group memberships affect how we conduct research and provide service?

The aim of this chapter is to provide my perspective on these and related questions. At its core, the message is about theory and the relations between theory, method, data, and values. According to the theory, psychologists in their roles are also human beings; the laws of human behavior operate on us as we inquire and intervene just as they do on our respondents and clients. How we act when employing methods, what we understand when collecting and interpreting data, and what we affirm when advocating values (including the values of science and of service) in part depend on who we are as people. Therefore, as a statement about method following from theory, taking the several selves of the psychologist seriously is an important part of the work. I shall do so both personally and in relation to others in the pages that follow. Although the predominant pattern is dialogue between data and theory, the beginning has more data and the end has more theory.

Race Relations in the United States: Contemporary and Historical

This initial section examines two concrete examples of the way racial dynamics influence the lives of all U.S. citizens, including psychologists. The first is an example from the news of several years ago, and the second brings a psychological and methodological lens to a controversy that is engaging professional historians.

Black Men and College

On Sunday, February 5, 1989, the front page of the *New York Times* reported the results of a study by the American Council on Education showing that the number of African American males who became college undergraduates reflected a decade-long decline. Over the same period, the number of black women attending college increased. Taken together, the total annual number of black men and black women attending undergraduate institutions decreased by thirty thousand since the high point of 1980 (Daniels, 1989).

The article searched for possible causes of the disturbing college attendance pattern associated with black males. Experts noted that from the time they entered elementary school, black males were more likely to be punished than were white males. The pattern of punishment did not mean that black males broke more rules. Instead, teachers seemed to react with irritation and frustration to the behavior of young black males more than to the behavior of other students (Associated Press, 1988). As reported, the problems confronting black males began early and multiplied rapidly. As a result, school became a bad place for them to learn. Being inattentive and avoiding work became symptoms of stress — not signs of rebellion, as some thought (Daniels, 1989). Joan McCarty, representing the National Coalition of Advocates for Students, interpreted the results to show that schools were not staffed by adults capable of dealing with students who were different (Associated Press, 1988).

These data and others of a similar sort provide powerful evidence of our society's continuing problems in dealing with racial differences. The difficulties with adults that young black males face in elementary and secondary schools provide a partial explanation for their declining enrollment in higher education. Both problems derive from more than three hundred years of white dominance and exploitation of blacks in the United States (Bennett, [1964] 1982). Daily news reports like the stories cited here show that racism remains a strong force in contemporary events. As a country first formed around the Declaration of Independence, the United States has never been free of conflict about the difference between the ideology of freedom and opportunity for all and the reality that black people often have less freedom and fewer opportunities than white people.

The Racial Attitudes and Behavior of Thomas Jefferson

Among the founders of the country, few were as comprehensive and progressive in their thinking as Thomas Jefferson. As author of the Declaration of Independence, Jefferson attempted to strike down the institution of slavery by laying responsibility for it at the feet of the English king—thus implicating neither Southern slaveholders nor Northern slave traders. But his strategy did not work. The Continental Congress voted to remove his words about slavery from the final version (Franklin, 1976). Psychologically, Jefferson's strategy consisted of projecting the blame for slavery onto the English king rather than accepting his own and his compatriots' role in supporting the institutional racism of his time.

In fact, Jefferson's personal and political life showed deep conflicts about the subject of slavery. Raised on a plantation where blacks outnumbered whites, Jefferson had a series of personal slave valets from age fourteen throughout his adult life (Brodie, 1974). His personal records showed that as an adult, he kept a careful account of his more than one hundred slaves. Moreover, the older Jefferson became, the less he was willing to challenge the economic and political establishment of his era on the subject of slavery (Miller, 1977).

The only book that he produced in a lifetime of writing was published in 1781 (Jefferson, 1977, pp. 185–193). It showed a wide range of thoughts and feelings about black people, white people, and the relations between them. He believed that black slaves born after a certain date should be freed on reaching a certain age, provided with resources to care for themselves, and educated according to their abilities at public expense. He also believed that when they achieved adequate strength, they should be moved to a different part of the world. As might be expected, Jefferson stated reasons for separating the races: deeply rooted prejudices by whites, recollections by blacks of the injuries that they sustained at the hands of whites, and real differences between the races that he expected would produce convulsions until one race exterminated the other.

In delineating racial differences, Jefferson began with skin color, body type, and hair but mentioned other biological, temperamental, and intellectual dimensions. On balance, these observations indicated that Jefferson believed that blacks as a group were inferior to whites as a group—for example, they were similar to whites in memory capacity but inferior in reasoning and imagination. He recognized, however, that most blacks were far more confined by their economic conditions and had fewer opportunities for education than whites. In Jefferson's words, we see language and concepts that remain very much alive today among politicians, historians, and psychologists.

The contemporary psychological language for this dispute is the "nature-versus-nurture" controversy. Investigators identified with the testing movement in psychology often emphasize the power of nature (that is, the innate, usually biological, aspects of a person's measurable abilities) in determining a person's life prospects. Those committed to social intervention and change point to the effects of nurture (that is, the effects of changing the environments people face) on the capacities an individual can develop over a lifetime. Though the language has changed somewhat and the field of scientific psychology is now more than a century old, the fundamental vision framed by Jefferson remains with us within psychology today.

Jefferson is a significant figure in the racial history of the United States not only because of the role his ideas played in the founding of the country but also as a consequence of contemporary struggles among historians to understand the great man. Psychologically speaking, historians' interpretations of Jefferson's life at a distance of more than two hundred years are somewhat like the responses of testees to projective tests. How scholars weigh evidence about Jefferson says something about them as individuals as well as about their subject. Similarly, how the scholarly community deals with data about Jefferson's racial attitudes and behavior and with alternative theories and methods to explain these phenomena provides information about our collective capacity to deal effectively with racial dynamics.

Perhaps chief among the controversies is how to assess the evidence that Jefferson, in the years following the death of his wife, had a committed sexual relationship with a black slave woman, Sally Hemings, and fathered several children with her. For some writers, the suggestion of such a relationship cannot be taken seriously (Miller, 1977; Dabney, 1981). For others, such a hypothesis is not only viable but psychologically meaningful (Bennett, 1982; Brodie, 1974).

As a white, male psychologist observing the controversy, I am impressed by the strength of the feelings shown by the researchers. Even though it is probably impossible to settle the question definitively, the relationship scholars form with the hypothesis and with evidence pertaining to it is passionate. One point of view suggests that if the hypothesis were to find unequivocal support, the picture of Jefferson as an ethical leader would be seriously compromised (Miller, 1977; Dabney, 1981). The other argues that Jefferson's humanity is enriched by the possibility of his maintaining such a relationship (Brodie, 1974). The contending scholars, thus, tend to be more critical of one another's opinions than of the pictures of Jefferson they paint.

What is at stake here and what is its relevance to the contemporary psychology of black-white race relations and racism? A significant portion of the Jefferson-Hemings controversy turns on how seriously one takes the report of former slaves, who state without qualification that Jefferson had a sustained intimate relationship with Hemings (see, for example, statements by Madson Hemings and Israel Jefferson given in full in Brodie, 1974, pp. 637–653). The noted historians who said with most certainty that no such intimate relationship existed were white men. The scholars cited here who were most willing to treat the words of the former Jefferson slaves as credible were a black man and a white woman.

Are the racial- and gender-group memberships of scholars relevant to their professional work? Does it matter that much of what white America regards as the historical knowledge of Thomas Jefferson was established by white men? That much of what we believe to be general psychological knowledge was mainly prepared by white people? That the national and regional contexts in which this knowledge was developed included several centuries of white racial dominance over blacks? I have learned to ask questions such as these from my sustained psychological work on race relations with organizations. They follow from the theory of embedded intergroup relations described in the final section of this chapter.

For both historians and psychologists, even to form such questions is problematic. The dominant view is that objective knowledge is available to the properly trained observer regardless of race, gender, or other group memberships. The self of the observer not only can but should be kept out of the inquiry. For others of us, taking account of group memberships and other aspects of the self in research and consultation is a key element in the theory of method. The self cannot be kept out of the inquiry, and a major challenge of sound methodology is to provide a systematic discipline for taking account of our subjectivity.

Social scientists debate the relative merits of native-versus-stranger anthropology and of insider-versus-outsider knowledge (Jones, 1970; Alderfer & Thomas, 1988). One might wonder why only a minority of social scientists argue in favor of including self effects as a part of methodology (Berg & Smith, 1985). Why do so many behavioral scientists act as if they believe that the laws of human behavior do not apply to them in their role of investigator?

In part, the answers to these questions concern how we understand and utilize our knowledge, our methods, and our roles. Comparatively little explicit attention to the nature and use of our own authority is included in the education of psychologists. The less we understand about how the dynamics of authority operate among us, the more unaware we tend to be about our tendency to misuse authority in relation to others — especially those with less power than we have. Until recently, psychology has not been noted for its teachings about oppression.

The Psychological Meaning of Oppression

As a result of slavery, the relationship between blacks and whites in the United States has been characterized from the beginning by oppression of blacks by whites. The development of psychology as a science and profession in this country has occurred in this very same environment and, until recent times, had done comparatively little to deal with its own racial history. Our understanding of race relations is greatly aided by examining the several meanings of oppression.

The Concept of Oppression

Definitions of the noun *oppression* and the verb *to oppress* did not appear in the psychology books and conventional dictionaries I could find easily. *Webster's Third New International Dictionary of the English Language Unabridged* (1981) proved to be most valuable. This source identified three interdependent, yet clearly distinguishable, meanings for the terms. All have the use and misuse of power in relation to human beings as an underlying theme. The first pertains to the use of physical power; its meanings are to crush, to trample, or to overpower. The second involves the misuse of psychological power; its meanings are to burden spiritually or to depress. Finally, the third is a mixture of the political and the psychological; its meanings are to abuse power or authority or to treat with unjust rigor or cruelty.

These three dictionary meanings are more psychological than I had imagined beforehand. The physical connotation implies that the survival of a person or a people is at stake. Being oppressed includes experiencing the psychological fact that one's continued existence may be in question. To burden spiritually or to depress is to assault a person's sense of self, to damage the core of the personality. People who are depressed are less vital and more burdensome to themselves and others than those who are not. The first two meanings focus on the oppression. The third meaning changes the attention to the oppressors, the groups and individuals who threaten the physical or spiritual well-being of others — whether they are authorized to do so or do so simply as a consequence of having raw power to use. The third meaning tells us that oppression is a collective undertaking, the consequence of group forces. Even when relatively few commit oppressive behaviors, larger numbers of people permit oppressive actions to occur by doing nothing, or they encourage the abuse by supporting those who perform the actions.

To these understandings, depth psychology adds yet another. From both clinical and statistical studies, we know that those who have themselves been abused are more likely to abuse others. Anthony Storr (1968) reported on the correlation between homicide and suicide by individuals, and Alice Miller (1983), in her analysis of Adolph Hitler's childhood, showed the unconscious connection between the German dictator's childhood experience of being severely abused and his adult oppression of millions of people — aided by the group psychology of fascist states.

Alice Miller's (1983) analysis of Hitler's personal psychopathology and its relationship to the group psychology of the German people provides important insights into the origins of personal prejudice and institutional racism. While growing up, young Adolph faced constant and severe abuse from his father, who both beat and humiliated him. An episode at age eleven seemed to Miller to be particularly crucial in the development of the Nazi leader. Having been caught running away from home, Hitler endured a particularly harsh assault from his father. At that moment, the preadolescent male vowed to never again allow his father to see him cry as he accepted his beating. Walling off his own physical and psychological pain thus became a way of life.

The anguish and pain, of course, did not go away as Hitler grew older and obtained political power. Instead, according to depth-psychological reasoning, Hitler's hurt and anger were supported by a resonance with the life experiences of many German people who had had similar childhood experiences and by the anti-Semitic ideology of the region and period. These feelings were then projected outward and directed toward Jews and others who were markedly different from the pure Aryan ideal (Miller, 1983). With this interpretation, we have an explanation that ties together in malevolent form the combined effects of both individual and cultural unconscious processes.

Authority and Oppression in Psychology

Psychology's inclination to give little attention to oppression as a concept is paralleled by the profession's tendency to overlook oppression in the conduct of its own activities. In the most basic sense, oppression is the abuse of power and authority. What are some of the more straightforward examples of oppression in psychological research?

Much of psychology treats its findings as if they were independent of the race, ethnicity, gender, and age of investigators and respondents. In fact, a significant proportion of what we consider psychological knowledge is based on work supervised by senior white, Euro-American males studying junior white, Euro-American females and males. During the last two decades, the field has witnessed the growth of population-specific psychologies that take account of race, ethnicity, gender, and age (Boykin, Franklin, & Yates, 1979; Watts, 1992). Yet there remains a tendency within the profession to view findings pertaining to identity groups as outside the mainstream.

In terms of the general use of authority in experiments with humans, the language of the laboratory calls the people who provide data *subjects*. In what other social systems, other than countries headed by royalty, does one find the term *subjects* used to characterize those at the bottom of the social hierarchy? We know that sometimes criticism is directed toward psychology for relying excessively on college sophomores for subjects. But even this critique arises mainly out of concern about restricting the external validity of studies rather than from concerns about the possible abuse of authority in recruiting respondents.

Then there is the widely accepted practice of lying to participants in experiments and other kinds of studies. The need for deception is generally justified on scientific grounds. The practice of deception — and the esteem from colleagues that especially clever experimental treatments generates — reached the point where some authors felt the need to caution against the employment of double deception as a means to combat subjects' suspicions (Carlsmith, Ellsworth, & Aronson, 1976).

A final example is the use of IQ measures to predict performance without taking account of the historical background of the testing movement. In a society that claims to be meritocratic, authorized tests are powerful instruments. They are used to determine who receives certain kinds of education, jobs, and promotions. It is often forgotten that mental-ability tests originally were developed to restrict economic and political power to certain ethnic and racial groups (Sarason, 1981). Forgetting this history increases the likelihood that tests will again be used mainly to protect the status quo rather than to promote fairness for all people.

These examples do not exhaust the ways in which the development and use of psychological knowledge can be oppressive. I do not believe that it is inevitable for abuses of power to take place. Indeed, as a profession, psychology may have the unique ability to develop the kind of collective understandings that will reduce the abuse of power. Many psychologists espouse these goals while conducting research and providing service.

An important question, however, is whether the methods of psychology treat psychologists in professional roles as subject to the laws of individual and collective behavior. In a recent review of the research literature on intergroup attitudes and behavior, Brewer and Kramer (1985, pp. 236–237) conclude, "Group membership influences the attributions we make about our own and others' behavior, intentions, and values." Even though these authors use the pronoun *we*, they remain silent about whether this is merely an editorial convention or meant to imply that the lawfulness they observe from studying others also applies to the investigators in their professional roles.

My own answer is that their conclusion does apply to all of us — both in our roles as psychologists and in the rest of our lives. This apparently simple or obvious conclusion has significant implications for the way we think and act when employing psychological methods. In the case of work on race relations by white people, it means dealing explicitly with the psychologist's individual relationship to the white racial group and with the nature of the white racial group as a collective entity.

Whiteness as an Individual and Group Condition for Psychologists

Viewed from the perspective of the theory of embedded intergroup relations, taking account of group memberships in both their personal and collective meanings is a methodological procedure derived from a conceptual position (Alderfer & Smith, 1982; Alderfer, 1986). The theory, in turn, is based upon empirical results accumulated over decades of research (Brewer & Kramer, 1985). Framed in other terms, this orientation treats the self as an element in the instrumentation employed by psychologists. Understanding the properties of the individual and group selves is thus analogous to knowing the properties of other instruments, whether they are tests, questionnaires, interviews, or experimental treatments (Alderfer, 1985). Therefore, I begin with an account of those aspects of my self that are relevant to conducting research on black-white race relations and consulting with predominantly white organizations.

Personal Meaning of the Work

In what may in part reflect psychology's ambivalence about self-effects in research, I was once the "subject" of research on white investigators who conduct research on black-white race relations. The investigator in this study was a white, female doctoral student who told me that she wanted to study the backgrounds of white people who continued their studies even when research on race was not popular. She collected her data by interviewing me in my office at the Yale School of Organization and Management during the period when Ronald Reagan was president of the United States and Edwin Meese was attorney general. My experience of that encounter was that of being treated with respect by a person who was genuinely interested in learning. I had a different kind of experience when, at a professional conference, I asked a group of senior white, male social scientists to address the question of how they might assist me in designing learning experiences about race relations for groups of white individuals (Alderfer, 1982). From these two experiences and others of a similar nature, I have learned that whites sometimes have certain questions about me as a person and as a professional — and that these questions can be asked in an affirmative spirit of inquiry or from a (perhaps unconscious) desire to demean and discredit (Alderfer, 1982).

What does it mean to be a professional about race relations and racism for someone who is a fifty-three-year-old white, German-Swiss, male professor formerly at Yale University and now at Rutgers? What motives do I have in doing this work? Why do I continue with work that sometimes places me in complex relationships with my own racial, cultural, social-class, and professional groups? After all, I represent many of the groups people think of when they use the term *oppressor* in the context of the United States today. As a result of my work on race relations, I have learned a lot about what it means—to me, to others, and in general—to do this kind of work as a representative of my identity and organizational groups.

What I bring to the work of changing race relations is expertise about white people—particularly white men. Often, when I say this, people are surprised. It is common for white observers of race relations professionals to think of us as experts on black people and on black-white relations—but not on white people. What I have to contribute to the joint undertaking of improving race relations is knowledge about white people and our ways of dealing with race. This knowledge derives both from life experiences and from formal study.

I grew up in Bethlehem, Pennsylvania, a blue-collar community then noted for being the home of a major steel company. In the 1940s and 1950s, the city was diverse ethnically and almost exclusively white racially. At age eighteen, I went to Yale University, after graduating from a large public high school that then sent approximately 33 percent of its graduates to college anywhere. It had been fifteen years since a graduate of that high school had gone to Yale. Counting undergraduate, graduate, and faculty years, I subsequently spent all except two years between September 1958 and June 1992 in the Yale environment.

Although both Bethlehem and Yale were overwhelmingly white settings, they were very different. The people of Bethlehem as I experienced them were close to the earth. They believed that everyone had to work hard to earn a living, and they did. Over the years, despite the demise of the steel company, the community has remained prosperous, although by no means wealthy. It is more racially and ethnically diverse today than when I was living there. In comparison, the people of Yale as I experienced them were elevated, both intellectually and economically. For many, being selected to be there — whether as student or as a faculty member — was a license to look down on others. My intellectual interests often left me feeling apart in the community of my origins, and my difficulty with the elitism (as contrasted with the excellence) of the Yale setting meant that I often was at odds with the Yale way of forming relationships.

From the community of my childhood and adolescence, I developed a sense of what it means to be white in a relatively secure middle- and lower-middle-class sense, and from the university setting of my early and middle adulthood, I learned what it meant for me to be part of an elite, white world. As a result of this combination of sustained experiences, I feel able to be myself and to form empathic relationships across a relatively wide social-class spectrum. For one who does race work in organizations, the direct parallel is being able to develop empathy for both the concerns of members of white bargaining units and the experiences of lower, middle, and senior management — including members of boards of directors.

Yet in each context I often feel somewhat like an outsider. The sense of rarely being a modal member in groups to which I belong probably makes a sustained commitment to work in race relations possible. Similarly, my ability as a white person to form relationships of mutual respect with African Americans may stem in part from common experiences of often feeling like an outsider (although for different reasons) in the dominant white world of the United States.

I am also the adoptive parent of a black son, Benjamin. Ben came into our family when he was six weeks old during the summer of 1972. The experience of being Ben's father — participating in his development through adolescence and contending with the racism he and we have faced in public schools, in the places where I have worked, and in the community where we lived — has been a powerful reason for my sustained involvement in race relations work. My desire to understand race relations and, where possible, to effect change does have this personal component.

It would be a mistake, however, to assume that my personal reasons are the only ones for being involved in this work.

I find the intellectual challenges of studying and changing intergroup relations to be highly rewarding. Even though psychology's history includes labeling race work as "applied," my own view is that nothing is more basic. We all have a race, and little of importance in our society is not influenced by racial dynamics, whether acknowledged or not. Being a professional psychologist doing race work is equivalent to being a medical researcher and physician doing cancer or heart work—although the external rewards are different. I doubt whether there are many topics of greater importance to the continued survival of vital human life. In this and other appropriate contexts, therefore, I describe myself as a nonguilty white male whose professional work concerns intergroup and race relations.

In the course of my adult professional experiences, I have had opportunities to deal with racial dynamics both with and without the special authorization that comes with the role of race relations consultant. Although the authorized professional work is extremely difficult, even more arduous is the task of using what I think I know about racial dynamics in situations that are not specifically identified as pertaining to race. The situation is especially trying when I am in a subordinate role with a group of white men as peers. Without at least one colleague of similar understanding and comparable goals, I have found it virtually impossible to have constructive effects. It is comparatively easy to get myself declared paranoid, crazy, or "our resident black member." Having sensible discussions about racial issues is not something I have been able to achieve as a lone white man with my perspective in a group of white men when none of them share that point of view.

If I am in charge because of holding a role such as journal editor, program director, or committee chair, it is sometimes possible to establish conditions that permit thoughtful discussions about race. But even in these situations, I have to have enough influence to include in the conversations people of color, white women, and white men who are able to discuss racial issues with a significant degree of self-awareness. By itself, even being in charge is not enough. The resistance of most white people to thoughtful discussions of race is high enough so that, alone, I have not been able to engage in such conversations.

Coping Methods of White Racial Groups

White people do not easily discuss race relations. For most whites, the range of feelings goes from uncomfortable to severely uncomfortable. The most common behavioral pattern is avoiding the issue, if at all possible. When that response is not feasible, the next line of defense is to deny the presence of racial dynamics. I imagine that most readers are aware of the Reagan Administration's doctrine of being "color-blind." The problem with that doctrine is that it is both bad physics and bad psychology. It is bad physics because people do see color, unless they are physiologically impaired. It is bad psychology because the effect of pretending to be color-blind is that it robs both whites and others of the racial aspect of their identities. White people have a race, and it shapes our feelings, cognition, and behavior—however uncomfortable this may be for us to accept.

I believe that race relations in the United States can be improved if white people accept that they have a racial identity and that white racism is a psychological reality in most predominantly white institutions. It is important for white people to think about the meaning of racism.

Like many concepts, racism does not have an agreed-upon definition. A set of interdependent meanings for racism include (1) recurrent behavioral patterns with intellectual justifications about why one racial group is superior to another; (2) members of one racial group with more power than another group using that power to demean, subvert, or destroy members of the other group; (3) individuals who are viewed as characterologically bigoted people *and* collective entities that reproduce racist practices regardless of who holds key positions; (4) subtle forms that include racial jokes and unexamined assumptions and heinous actions that involve assaulting and killing people based upon their racial identity; and (5) conscious expression, as when members of the Ku Klux Klan advocate a return of the United

States to the white people to whom it "rightfully" belongs, and unconscious communication, as when public officials deny the meaning of interracial events (Alderfer, Tucker, Alderfer, & Tucker, 1988).

Having advocated using the concept of racism, I also want to say that it is a very bad idea indeed to call individuals racists. Even though characterological racism is an observable concrete phenomenon, it is more important to examine collective racist processes in organizations and in society at large. The number of individuals who are deeply and profoundly racist characterologically is small in comparison to the amount of collective racism most of us participate in a good deal of the time. Moreover, labeling an individual serves mainly as a defensive function for the labeler and, if the expression is made directly to the individual, heightens resistance to learning by that person and by anyone who may observe the event. A more useful alternative is to develop objectives for change framed as "increasing one's competence for dealing with racial matters" or "enhancing one's capacity to speak openly, frankly, and professionally about race relations." This formulation emphasizes greater understanding and improved skill rather than blame.

Lest all of this sound easy, let me assure you that it is not. I have been associated with efforts to change race relations that have achieved measurable benefits for black and white people (Alderfer, 1992; Alderfer, Alderfer, Bell, & Jones, 1992). One project that combined research and consultation has lasted for sixteen years. None of that change has come about without considerable anguish and psychic pain.

The most severe assaults on my personal integrity at Yale University and in client work have come from white people when I have been working to bring about significant change in race relations in predominantly white organizations. I have also learned not to expect black people to have full empathy with the difficulties faced by whites who work actively for real change. Often blacks do understand the difficulties that we encounter with other whites, but sometimes they do not. The theory predicts that as a white person, my understanding of the white group will be different from that of blacks. This is part of what

I bring to race- and gender-balanced consulting teams. It is sometimes a source of significant conflict with black professionals, even when we share common objectives for change.

An especially interesting treatment of blacks and whites in cooperation and in conflict as they struggle to reduce racism is Kaufman's account of the Jewish-black relationship in the United States (1988). Kaufman accepts his Jewish identity clearly and powerfully. He acknowledges that it will influence his reporting and analysis of black-Jewish relations, and he tells how he attempts to discover and correct his potential biases through conversations with a close black colleague. Without using the concepts explicitly, Kaufman demonstrates an understanding of separate individual and group effects on racial identity. His writing is another example of the disciplined subjectivity necessary if social scientists and others are to account for the influence of their own personal histories and group memberships on their work.

Drawing on my experience and the accounts of others, I conclude that whites primarily use four methods to cope with their racial experiences. The first is characterological racism — in which individuals consciously and actively promote racist practices. For example, in one organization where our team worked, we learned of an organization of white managers whose purpose was to prevent the promotion of black managers.

The second is unwitting participation in unconscious processes that serve — not necessarily intentionally — racist ends. These effects occur either because racist episodes take place outside the awareness of white people or because the whites see what is taking place but are unable to speak to counteract racism. Both of these phenomena stem from whites' avoiding the subject of race. One kind of avoidance is unconscious, in that the person is not knowingly aware of what he or she is doing. The other is conscious; the person chooses to remain silent in order to protect her or his standing in the white group.

The third orientation of white people — belonging to a relatively small proportion — is true-believer antiracism — an energetic willingness to call individual white people racists. The belief associated with this orientation, which may be conscious or

unconscious, is that whites as a group or individual white people can cleanse themselves from racism by acting as if the problem is carried by a few atypical white people. The problem of
racism is then solved by declaring these people criminals or patients. In identifying this orientation, I do not wish to suggest
that severely disturbed people who direct hate toward racial
groups do not exist. They exist, they commit destructive acts,
and they should be stopped. Rather, my intention is to identify
the defensive function that name-calling serves for white people who develop a true-believer antiracist perspective.

A newer form of true-believer antiracism is writing in
which white authors portray their whiteness as a "privilege"
(McIntosh, 1986). In these kinds of contexts, the term *privilege*
is used in a manner that demeans white people (often including
the writer) for having white skin. While I think of myself as having had good fortune in many aspects of my life, I also view
myself as working hard, "paying my dues," and not achieving
at others' expense. I do not consider good fortune — mine or anyone else's — to be the equivalent of privilege, when "white privilege" implies not working hard, working unethically, or willfully
benefiting at others' expense. For these reasons I characterize
myself as a nonguilty white male working on race relations. In
comparable fashion, I do not consider myself to be a victim,
even when I am confronted with the abusive behavior, usually
from other whites, that is directed toward white people seeking
to improve black-white race relations. Those difficulties come
with the territory and represent one of the challenges involved
in doing the work well.

The fourth orientation that white people can develop includes a growing acceptance of what it means to be white and
to be a product of one's single or multiple ethnic heritages. It
recognizes both the pride and the shame associated with one's
own group. There is no sense of superiority or inferiority. Individuals with this relationship to their own groups respond in
similar fashion to other groups; they neither elevate nor demean
them. They strive for an appreciation of the richness of racial
and ethnic history, and they demonstrate an acceptance of the
reality that none of us escapes the joy and sorrow of racial- and

ethnic-group conflict. Kaufman's account of black-Jewish relations (1988) shows this fourth pattern.

This analysis of whites' ways of coping with their relationship to their own racial group follows directly from an understanding of the ways in which any intergroup relationship
is embedded in a larger social system. The theory of embedded
intergroup relations presents one framework for understanding
these complex social processes. Of particular importance is the
notion of unconscious parallel processes.

The Perspective of Embedded Intergroup Relations
and the Role of Unconscious Parallel Processes

To take the perspective of the theory of embedded intergroup
relations is to accept as a working hypothesis that neither the
self nor others are ever free of the effects of group and intergroup dynamics on human relationships. Taking the perspective of embedded intergroup relations does not conflict with
recognizing the uniqueness of each person. In fact, the theory
holds both that our intrapsychic condition has a life of its own
shaped by forces other than group and intergroup dynamics and
that each of us develops, over a lifetime, a unique way to come
to terms with our group and intergroup relations. The characteristic patterns we develop for relating to our own and other
groups, in turn, contribute to our way of being ourselves.

In propositional form, the statement is that every transaction between two or more people depends upon (1) the unique
personalities of the individuals, (2) the messages the individuals receive and internalize from their own group, and (3) the
present and historical relationships between the groups that the
individuals represent. Adding items 2 and 3 distinguishes this
intergroup perspective from interpersonal orientations. Whether
they are stated explicitly or implicitly, interpersonal perspectives imply that individuals can escape—either temporarily or
permanently—from their group memberships and intergroup
relations. The theory of embedded intergroup relations assumes
that people cannot leave their web of group affiliations, even
if they should desire to do so (Rice, 1969; Alderfer, 1986).

The idea of understanding human behavior from the perspective of embedded intergroup relations has an important influence on how we conceive of groups as entities. The definition of a group used in this theory reflects the intersection of both internal and external perspectives. It is also consistent with the perspective on understanding individuals described above. A human group is a collection of individuals (1) who have significantly interdependent relations with each other, (2) who perceive themselves to be a group by reliably distinguishing members from nonmembers, (3) whose group identity is recognized by nonmembers, (4) who, as group members acting alone or in concert, have significantly interdependent relations with other groups, and (5) whose roles in groups are therefore a function of expectations from themselves, from other group members, and from nongroup members.

This conception of a group gives the entity a life of its own independently of who its members are at any particular time. It treats the group-as-a-whole as an organic unit worthy of attention on its own terms (Wells, 1980). This understanding of a human group follows from open systems theory and means that we can adequately understand a group only if we are simultaneously attentive to both internal and external conditions.

Thus, the notion of *embedded* intergroup relations means that to understand group dynamics — whether seen through the eyes of an individual representing one or more groups or from the perspective of a group-as-a-whole — is to engage in cross-level analysis (Miller, 1978). A human system is subject to forces not only from its own level of analysis but also from subsystems and suprasystems. Thus, an individual receives messages from her or his intrapsychic processes *and* from groups to which he or she belongs. A group is shaped by the effects of the subgroups of its members and by how that group is located in the larger suprasystems that form its environment. To understand a person or a group, we look both at entities at the same level of analysis and at those from more micro or macro levels (Alderfer, 1986).

To explain the relationship between entities at the same

and different levels of analysis, the theory employs the concept of parallel and unconscious processes (Alderfer, 1986). This refers to the manner in which one entity seems to infect another with its affect, cognitions, and behavior. The infecting entity projects its condition onto the absorbing unit, which takes on the affect, cognitions, and behavior of the infecting unit. For parallel processes to occur, the projecting and absorbing units must have a relationship with each other.

An unusually clear (and nonracial) example of these phenomena occurred at a high school football game. In the stands, the father of a player who was standing on the sidelines began to loudly criticize the officials. Because the father was standing directly behind me, I could hear his voice and observe his son. The son did not turn toward the stands but soon began to echo his father's attack on the officials. As the game moved down the field, an official came to the sidelines and warned the young man that his behavior could result in a penalty being inflicted on his team. At this point, both the son and the father stopped their overt criticism. To my surprise, a number of other people in the stands seemed to notice the connection between the son's and the father's behavior and commented on it. Parallel processes of this kind do not often emerge into consciousness and evoke explicit talk.

Parallel processes occur between systems at the same level of analysis, between suprasystems and systems, and between subsystems and systems. The flow of infection can move from more macro to more micro systems and vice versa. The more common direction, however, is from more powerful to less powerful entities, especially when the phenomena are unrecognized. Learning to observe unconscious parallel processes is a technical skill that is aided by the observer's capacity to entertain the hypothesis that these phenomena do occur. Parallel processes may enhance, damage, or simply change the entities involved.

As a comparison example to the one cited above, which might carry a negative connotation, we may recall the effects that occur when we are engaged in a conversation with another person who conveys an unusual sense of nonpossessive warmth and caring. Before long, we notice ourselves feeling, behaving, and thinking in a similar manner. The sense of positive regard initially carried by one party in the transaction becomes increasingly absorbed by the other. In the realm of bargaining behavior, Kelley and Stahelski (1970) have shown that similar kinds of infectious processes occur in prisoner's dilemma games.

When they are attempting to understand oppression or intervening to reduce it, psychologists can serve their respondents, clients, and themselves if they learn to observe parallel processes and to work effectively with these phenomena. In the area of race relations, white investigators need to be especially attentive to unwitting identification with the aggression of white institutions and other forces that demean black people. Most readers are familiar with the notion of scientific racism, the process whereby the mantle of science is invoked to justify subtle and blatant racism.

Many of us who seriously enter the realm of race relations research raise questions about the assumptions of conventional methodology. This means allowing ourselves to reexamine some of the basic assumptions we were taught at the beginning of our careers. It certainly means rethinking what it means to be objective. The theory of embedded intergroup relations replaces the traditional notion of objectivity (that is, the notion that one can be free from the effects of the phenomena one studies) with the concept of disciplined subjectivity (that is, the idea that one cannot be free of the phenomena but rather can find ways to work with their effects on the investigator and practitioner). In the broadest sense, this kind of questioning of methodological assumptions disrupts top-down parallel processes that perpetuate racism through social science.

Parallel processes can also occur from the less powerful to the more powerful. In a form analogous to identification with the aggressor, we can call these phenomena identification with the victim. White people who act as true-believer antiracists manifest this form of parallel process. They assault other white people who are racists rather than examining the more complicated and subtle racial dynamics in which they themselves participate.

One form of identification with the victim sometimes occurs when white bosses evaluate the performance of black subordinates. Fearful of being labeled racist for criticizing a black person, the white person does not provide the black person with useful feedback about performance. Performance evaluations are perfunctory and uncomfortable. The blacks are aware that they are being denied opportunities to learn. The whites acknowledge that they withhold negative feedback. People in the work area understand that the employee is not performing effectively and that this is seemingly being ignored by the powers that rule. It is possible that someone other than the immediate supervisor will step in and offer constructive criticism. If another black person is aware of the situation, he or she may do it. Often, however, no one does it, and the pattern eventually is broken by a higher-level decision to transfer or terminate the black employee.

At the root of this complicated situation is a white person who feels victimized because he or she has a black subordinate and the two are unable to talk frankly about the complicated emotional dynamics of what is occurring. Too often, the black person becomes the ultimate victim, and the white person asserts that the organization practices reverse discrimination. The concept of reverse discrimination, whether it is stated by an individual employee or converted into legal doctrine, is the outgrowth of a failure to understand and interpret bottom-up parallel processes. White people thus resist changing the balance of power between whites and blacks by asserting that it is not blacks but whites who are being treated unfairly.

When the subject matter is race relations, we cannot avoid taking account of our own racial group and our own race relations. Learning to identify and work with parallel processes is not an easy undertaking. It means thinking of ourselves as members of a racial group who are subject to unconscious parallel processes from our own and other racial groups. It means talking about these effects and listening to people from other groups talk about their analogous experiences. It means accepting that alone, we can never know more than part of the truth and thus we need to be in relationships with others who are different in order to significantly improve the quality of our understanding. This is not easy work! But it can result in fruitful change that serves both black and white people.

Conclusion

The value of working with unconscious processes in race relations has at its core the belief that reducing the projection of unfavorable attributes from members of one group onto another will improve the emotional and intellectual understanding of groups and individual members by one another. Withdrawing our projections and developing a richer appreciation of our own group increases the accuracy of our own perceptions, prepares us more completely to deal with realistic differences, and decreases our tendency to escalate conflict needlessly. These dynamics apply to historians, psychologists, consultants, journalists — to all of us who as members of one racial group have relationships with members of another racial group, regardless of the purpose of the relationship.

The projective and absorptive aspects of parallel processes among individuals and groups emerge from collective history. Thus, to work effectively with these dynamics, we must be prepared to examine the historical roots of sometimes highly disturbing phenomena. Parallel processes take place between entities at the same level of analysis and among subsystems, systems, and suprasystems. We can see their effects in our daily lives and can observe them in the lives of our most distinguished leaders. No one escapes these forces. The challenge is to accept and respect the dynamics — not to deny or avoid them. We cannot overcome the chronic difficulties associated with race relations in the United States if we persist in running away from the phenomena.

References

Alderfer, C. P. (1982). Problems in changing white males' beliefs and behavior concerning race relations. In P. Goodman & Associates (Eds.), *Change in organizations* (pp. 122–165). San Francisco: Jossey-Bass.

Alderfer, C. P. (1985). Taking our selves seriously as researchers. In D. Berg & K. Smith (Eds.), *The self in social inquiry* (pp. 35–70). Newbury Park, CA: Sage.

Alderfer, C. P. (1986). An intergroup perspective on group dynamics. In J. Lorsch (Ed.), *Handbook of organizational behavior* (pp. 190–222). Englewood Cliffs, NJ: Prentice-Hall.

Alderfer, C. P. (1992). Changing race relations embedded in organizations: Report on a long-term project with the XYZ Corporation. In S. Jackson (Ed.), *Diversity in the workplace* (pp. 138–166). New York: Guilford Press.

Alderfer, C. P., Alderfer, C. J., Bell, E. L., & Jones, J. (1992). The Race Relations Competence Workshop. *Human Relations, 45,* 1259–1291.

Alderfer, C. P., & Smith, K. K. (1982). Studying intergroup relations embedded in organizations. *Administrative Science Quarterly, 27,* 35–65.

Alderfer, C. P., & Thomas, D. A. (1988). The significance of race and ethnicity for organizational behavior. In G. Cooper & I. Robertson (Eds.), *International Review of Industrial and Organizational Psychology* (pp. 1–42). New York: Wiley.

Alderfer, C. P., Tucker, R. C., Alderfer, C. J., & Tucker, L. (1988). The Race Relations Advisory Group: An intergroup intervention. In W. A. Pasmore & R. W. Woodman (Eds.), *Research in organizational change and development* (Vol. 2, pp. 269–321). Greenwich, CT: JAI Press.

Associated Press. (1988, Dec. 12). Blacks twice as likely as whites to be punished, labeled at school. *New Haven Register,* p. 14.

Bennett, L., Jr. (1982). *Before the Mayflower.* New York: Penguin Books. (Original work published 1964)

Berg, D., & Smith, K. K. (1985). *The self in social inquiry.* Newbury Park, CA: Sage.

Boykin, A. W., Franklin, A. J., & Yates, J. F. (1979). *Research directions for black psychologists.* New York: Russell Sage Foundation.

Brewer, M., & Kramer, R. M. (1985). The psychology of intergroup attitudes and behavior. *Annual Review of Psychology, 36,* 219–244.

Brodie, F. M. (1974). *Thomas Jefferson: An intimate history.* New York: Bantam Books.

Carlsmith, J. M., Ellsworth, P. C., & Aronson, E. (1976). *Methods of research in social psychology.* Reading, MA: Addison-Wesley.

Dabney, V. (1981). *The Jefferson scandals: A rebuttal.* New York: Madison.

Daniels, L. A. (1989, Feb. 5). Ranks of black men shrink on U.S. campuses. *New York Times,* p. 1.

Franklin, J. H. (1976). *Racial equality in America.* Chicago: University of Chicago Press.

Griffin, J. H. (1961). *Black like me.* New York: New American Library.

Helms, J. E. (1990). *Black and white racial identity: Theory, research, and practice.* Westport, CT: Greenwood Press.

Jefferson, T. (1977). *Notes on the State of Virginia.* In M. D. Peterson (Ed.), *The portable Thomas Jefferson* (pp. 23–205). New York: Penguin Books.

Jones, D. J. (1970). Towards a native anthropology. *Human Organization, 29,* 251–259.

Kaufman, J. (1988). *The turbulent times between blacks and Jews in America.* New York: Charles Scribner's Sons.

Kelley, H. H., & Stahelski, A. J. (1970). Social interaction basis of cooperators' and competitors' beliefs about others. *Journal of Personality and Social Psychology, 16,* 66–91.

McIntosh, P. (1986, Apr.). *White privilege and male privilege: A personal account of coming to see correspondences through work in women's studies.* Paper presented at the Virginia Women's Studies Association Conference in Richmond, VA.

Miller, A. (1983). Adolf Hitler's childhood: From hidden to manifest horror. In A. Miller, *For your own good: Hidden cruelty in child-rearing and the roots of violence* (pp. 142–197). New York: Farrar, Straus & Giroux.

Miller, J. C. (1977). *The Wolfe by the ears: Thomas Jefferson slavery.* Charlottesville: University of Virginia Press.

Miller, J. G. (1978). *Living systems.* New York: McGraw-Hill.

Rice, A. K. (1969). Individual, group, and intergroup processes. *Human Relations, 22,* 565–584.

Sarason, S. B. (1981). *Psychology misdirected.* New York: Free Press.

Storr, A. (1968). *Human aggression.* New York: Atheneum.

Watts, R. (1992). Elements of a psychology of human diversity. *Journal of Community Psychology, 20,* 116–131.

Webster's third new international dictionary of the English language unabridged (1981). Springfield, MA: Merriam-Webster.

Wells, L., Jr. (1980). The group-as-a-whole: A systemic socioanalytic perspective on interpersonal and group relations. In C. P. Alderfer & C. L. Cooper (Eds.), *Advances in experiential social processes* (Vol. 2, pp. 165–199). New York: Wiley.

10

Culture and
Human Diversity

Walter J. Lonner

We humans belong to a remarkably diverse species. One prominent way to account for our diversity is to look at culture as a powerful *contributing* factor if not a decisive *causal* factor in shaping most aspects of variability in human behavior. This chapter is organized around four interrelated perspectives on culture: (1) culture as a concept to be defined, (2) culture as a way to organize ideas regarding how human societies vary (3) culture as a component in research design and sample selection, and (4) culture as something to avoid or ignore.

Culture as a Concept to Be Defined

Social scientists of various persuasions have been intrigued with the concept of culture for many years. In an oft-cited document, Kroeber and Kluckhohn (1952) told how they searched the literature and found 164 different definitions of culture, none of which was adopted by everyone either up to that time or since. However, they said that the essential core of culture consists of traditional ideas and especially their attached values. They also said that cultural systems may be considered both as products of action and as conditioning elements of further action. Another common anthropological definition of culture conceives of it as the mass of behavior that human beings in any society learn from their elders and pass on to the younger generation. Melville Herskovits (1948) was briefer than most when he said that culture is the human-made part of the environment, a definition endorsed by the authors of a recent text concerned with social psychology across cultures (Moghaddam, Taylor, & Wright, 1993). Anthropologists, who were probably responsible for the development of the concept of culture in the first place, for various reasons continue to debate and otherwise come to grips with the term.

Marshall Segall (1984), a cross-cultural psychologist, noted that if anthropologists had not invented culture, social psychologists probably would have. He said that the concept of culture enables the psychologist to account for the fact that social stimuli do not impinge on individuals with equal probability in different places and at different times. For example, in my life some social stimuli are more probable than others. My children are extremely unlikely to greet me by prostrating themselves and kissing my feet, especially now that they are in their twenties. If they did, I would suspect that something was radically amiss, because such behavior is inconsistent with expectations in my specific culture. On the other hand, a Ganda householder in his East African grass-thatched house is not likely to eat a bowl of cornflakes for breakfast while studying last night's hockey scores.

These improbable scenarios carry the important implication that culture and society are roughly coterminous. Because every human group has a culture, behavioral patterns tend to be different from society to society and group to group. This fact is central to the culture-and-personality school in anthropology (Keesing, 1974) as well as to all other academic disciplines in which culture plays a role in explaining human diversity and variability. It is also central to the idea that every culture creates in its members a characteristic pattern of behavior that is distinctly different from the way in which other cultures program their members to exhibit *their* patterns of behavior. Here, then, is perhaps the best reason for focusing on the concept of culture: it helps to categorize and explain many important differences in human behavior that in the past were erroneously attributed to ill-defined biological differences or to the all-but-abandoned idea of instinct.

Because the field of anthropology traditionally has the strongest interest in understanding the role played by culture in influencing behavior, perhaps it is appropriate to make special note of a lengthy definition of culture contained in a recent book written by Donald E. Brown (1991), an influential anthropologist:

> Culture consists of the conventional patterns of thought, activity, and artifact that are passed on from generation to generation in a manner that is generally assumed to involve learning rather than specific genetic programming. Besides being transmitted "vertically" from generation to generation, culture may also be transmitted "horizontally" between individuals and collectivities. Examples of culture are tools, kinship terminologies, and world-views — which in each case may take distinct forms among peoples who are genetically indistinguishable. Culture is divisible into "traits" (single terms) and "complexes" (more or less integrated collections of traits) and typically thought of as though it were attached to collectivities rather than isolated individuals. This deemphasis of the individual stems not from an anthropological belief that individuals do not create culture but from the observation that any given individual receives more culture than he or she creates. Because so much culture is imposed upon rather than created by any particular individual, anthropologists (and others) often think of culture as a sort of supraindividual entity called "society" [p. 40].

Another approach to defining a culture is described by Boesch (1991), who characterizes culture as a "field of action," a construct that "defines possibilities and conditions for action." But he also says that a culture does not simply make people uniform or homogenize them: "It rather sets trends from which in some cases it allows, and in other cases even encourages, deviation: be it by attributing differentiating roles, or simply by encouraging individual differences in fashion, imagination, or style. In other words, a culture seems to need both uniformity and individuality, as it were, albeit to varying extents" (p. 36).

If we accept that action potentials differ from culture to culture, we are still left with the problem of boundary definition. Action potentials and the resulting behavioral patterns between strongly contrasted cultures or societies (for example, Japanese versus Brazilians) will almost certainly be very clearly different. However, can we expect similar clarity between, for instance, African American culture and the culture of Asian Americans? Between Haitians and Puerto Ricans? Between Protestants and Catholics? Between members of the Elks Club and members of the Masonic Order? Is there an Elks "culture" and a Masonic "culture"?

Consider a generalized test: Does being a member of (insert the name of a group, society, or culture) create in an individual a potential for action that influences her or his behavior in some strong and predictable way, so that an observant onlooker would be able to discern how this behavior differs significantly from the behavior of a member of (insert the name of another group, society, or culture)? At what point does a group of people become like-minded enough to be noticeably different from all other people who are like-minded, so that behavioral differences can be attributed to action potentials that membership in their specific group, society, or culture create? When does a difference in culture actually *make* a difference in behavior?

The above array of definitions of culture has several ingredients in common:

1. Culture is not a God-given term. It is an abstract idea, a hypothetical construct, that is created by humans and is useful primarily for scientific reasons.
2. Culture is *not* behavior. It simply provides complex settings

in which various behaviors may occur. To say that Astrid behaves in a certain way because she is Swedish is like saying that a man limps because he is lame. Culture creates for individuals certain potentials for reaction. These potentials differ from time to time and place to place. Culture shapes and bends behavior by interacting with individuals. Not even the most sophisticated and enlightened definition of culture can *explain* behavior, because definitions are themselves static and undynamic. A good definition, however, may help us to organize the various ways in which we might formulate explanations of differences in behavior.

3. Any culture contains values, beliefs, attitudes, and languages that have emerged as adaptations to the peculiar geographic and temporal circumstances that have impinged on the lives of a group of people who agree on what to call themselves.

4. The values, beliefs, attitudes, and languages that have proved to be adaptive are considered important enough to pass on to the next generation. Such generational transmission either can be done explicitly, by using formal instruction and rules (the *socialization* process), or can be implicitly and subtly taught to succeeding generations in the course of everyday life (the *enculturation* process).

Culture as a Way to Organize Ideas Regarding How Human Societies Vary

Assorted academic disciplines, primarily anthropology, have developed different ways to explain how human societies vary. The best example of such organizational attempts is the Human Relations Area Files (HRAF). Started in the 1930s, HRAF was given an alphanumeric system to categorize all known cultures of the world. Based on detailed ethnographic reports that are coded and then catalogued, it is an archival collection of both societies (cultures) and substantive topics. The reports can be scanned and retrieved for many purposes, ranging from research to simple descriptions of many known cultures.

Two major sources of information-guided and HRAF-related inquiries are the *Outline of World Cultures* (Murdock, 1975) and the *Outline of Cultural Materials* (Murdock, Ford, & Hudson, 1971), often referred to as *OWC* and *OCM*. OWC lists and describes many of the world's cultures. A companion listing of cultures is the *Ethnographic Atlas* (Murdock, 1967). It includes nearly nine hundred societies, and it is organized around six culture areas: Sub-Saharan African, Circum-Mediterranean, East Eurasia, Oceania, North America, and South America.

HRAF materials are usually used for a special kind of research called holocultural or hologeistic (Naroll & Cohen, 1970); these research strategies are discussed in several books on cross-cultural research and methodology (Lonner & Berry, 1986; Berry, Poortinga, Segall, & Dasen, 1992). Combining the universe of cultures (although not all cultures are covered in HRAF) and an assortment of cultural characteristics, the researcher can seek answers to many questions without the need for a valid passport, health shots, or a large grant. This has been called "armchair safari research." For instance, one can search HRAF in the library (the complete files can be found in only about twenty libraries around the world, although many libraries have a good portion of them) and try to determine if type of religion is correlated with female circumcision, or if laws concerning property ownership are correlated with beliefs about the nature of the known universe. Hypotheses that can be generated from holocultural approaches are limited only by the researcher's creativity and imagination.

Culture as a Component in Research Design and Sample Selection

The concept of culture plays the greatest role in the development of designs for research that either explicitly or implicitly involve comparisons between cultures. It is impossible to include, in one study, all the world's cultures. Because of this, cultures have to be sampled from the known universe of cultures. Some sort of logical strategy typically governs the selection of samples at four levels:

1. Which cultures or societies should be selected, and why?
2. Which communities or groups within each culture should be selected, and why?
3. Which individuals within the groups should be selected, and why?
4. Which behaviors of the individuals should be sampled, and why?

In addition to addressing the above questions, cross-cultural researchers are guided by two general types of strategies with respect to selecting cultures. One strategy requires the use of some sort of representative sampling plan (usually called probability sampling) so that generalizations can be made to all cultures. For example, if a researcher wants to make a generalizable statement about the nature of human aggression, in designing the study he or she should attempt to systematically include the possibility that each culture has an equal chance of being included. If such provisions are not made and the research is carried out by using convenient samples of cultures, such biased sampling could contribute to a misleading, untrue, or incomplete statement about human aggression.

The second and most common strategy for sampling cultures is to examine systematic interactions between culture and behavioral variables. In this strategy, "'culture' *per se* is *not* important. What *is* important is the 'independent variable'—and specifically to find a sufficient range of variation of the independent variable—so that statements about causation can be made. Because this type of strategy constitutes 'quasi-manipulation by selection' of the independent variable, the importance of probability samples decreases. Rather, nonrandom samples . . . are required" (Lonner & Berry, 1986, p. 89).

These two strategies underscore the fact that anthropologists tend to study culture "writ large," for example, by using HRAF. Cross-cultural psychologists, on the other hand, more often seek a more specific or parsimonious approach in their research by viewing culture as a quasi-manipulated independent, or predictor, variable. As such, it would have somewhat the same conceptual status as age, sex, or years of schooling as an antecedent of specific behavior.

In fact, authors of cross-cultural psychological experiments are generally not concerned with *definitions* of culture. Rather, they are interested in the effects that some social, linguistic, or ecological factors might have on certain dependent variables. For example, Berry (1966) contrasts two groups with markedly different subsistence economies, child-rearing practices, languages, and ecologies — the Temne of Africa and certain Canadian Eskimo groups — and clearly shows that the variables that differ between the groups are related to perceptual skills.

Similarly, the strategy used by Segall, Campbell, and Herskovits (1966) to study the relationship of culture and visual illusions is not driven by a concern about culture and its definitional boundaries but by a concern about explaining variations in susceptibility to illusions against a background of environmental and experiential factors. For this they relied on Campbell's evolutionary epistemology. This involves the key ideas of adaptiveness and systematic fit. To begin theorizing, they consider what features of the environment could select specific behaviors and how, or through what process, these behaviors become adaptive. Empirical research then involves a series of studies where competing hypotheses that do not survive the winnowing process are abandoned in favor of those that better explain the fit between theory and fact.

The term *culture* in research of this kind is synonymous with a sample of subjects from a certain population (an ethnic or cultural group) who the researcher believes have something in common. With culture thus operationalized, the samples of individuals within each group are usually given some test or subjected to some experimental procedure. In line with the research traditions of orthodox psychological methodology, the average score of the samples (which by definition allow for some variation) are consequently compared with one another to determine if the null hypothesis of no differences between groups can be accepted.

Valsiner (1988) has criticized this approach. He says,

By positing that "culture" (as a substantive entity — irrespective of whether it is meant in behavioral or mental terms —) is something that is, in its essence, shared in a qualitatively similar manner by all (or almost all) members of the given "culture" (as a population, society, or ethnic group), research in cross-cultural psychology sometimes arrives at a state of perfect tautology in casual explanations. . . . The inferential route taken by the investigators in making the shift from "culture-as-population" to "culture-as-casual-entity" use of the term is based on the same cognitive manipulation that is used in "mainstream" psychology — inductive homogenization of heterogeneous classes, followed by deductive application of the generalized unitary abstractions to the particular cases.

Rather, Valsiner says, "culture becomes a unique kind of 'dependent variable' — it becomes re-constructed when the ways of life of human beings are challenged by novel demands."

This lack of definition or clear focus has occasionally troubled scholars who have reviewed manuscripts for the *Journal of Cross-Cultural Psychology* (*JCCP*) since its inauguration in 1970. For nearly twenty-five years, *JCCP* has published the results of comparative cultural studies, yet it has often been unclear what authors of submitted manuscripts have meant by the term *culture*. If we analyzed the samples used in *all* cross-cultural psychological research during the past fifty years, we would find that "samples of convenience" have been much more prevalent than any other sampling strategy. Because the samples differ at least on the important dimension of "living elsewhere" (someplace other than where the subjects in comparison groups live) and usually speak a language different from that spoken by subjects in other samples, we assume that cultures are being contrasted. What is really being contrasted, however, is behavior that we assume is somehow influenced by culture.

The problems discussed in this chapter tend to cause culture-comparativists to worry about what they are doing when they make cross-cultural contrasts in some domain of human behavior. In 1984, a special section of *JCCP* was devoted to differing views on culture. In that special section, Ronald Rohner, an anthropologist, chided cross-cultural psychologists doing culture-comparative research for treating culture as a "packaged variable" without ever giving serious consideration to what culture really is. Rohner (1984) defined culture as "the totality of equivalent and complementary learned meanings maintained by a human population, or by identifiable segments of population, and transmitted from one generation to the next" (1984, pp. 119–120). He advocated the development of a better conception of culture for cross-cultural psychology. Two prominent cross-cultural psychologists, Gustav Jahoda and Marshall Segall, were invited to respond to Rohner. Segall (1984) noted that both Rohner and Jahoda (1984) apparently believed two things: (1) that efforts to try and define culture are needed and can succeed and (2) that when this success is attained, empirical cross-cultural research and theory building will be advanced. Segall, by contrast, said (1) that efforts to define culture are unnecessary and are bound to fail and (2) that theoretical advances in cross-cultural psychology depend on abandoning the struggle to conceptualize culture definitively and instead depend on intensifying the search for whatever ecological, sociological, and cultural variables might be systematically associated with established variations in human behavior. "Whatever these variables are (and we surely have identified a large number of them already)," he says, "they are all less abstract and far more measurable than 'culture' in any or all of its many insubstantial shapes" (Segall, 1984, p. 154). It is tempting to endorse such a utilitarian approach.

Culture as Something to Avoid or Ignore

Culture as a concept and as a predictor of behavior has generally been ignored or avoided by most mainstream psychologists. A mainstreamer might be defined as one who focuses only on scientific issues, as if the problem or research question at hand naturally impinges on *all* humans in roughly the same way. To many of these people, culture either is not important enough or is too abstract to influence their research efforts. This is why cross-cultural psychologists have occasionally been described as miscreant stepchildren—researchers who either should not be taken very seriously or are chasing rainbows in exotic places. This sentiment is captured well in a quote from Epicurus that Bond (1988) used in the front matter of one of his texts: "Hoist sail, my dear boy, and steer clear of culture."

In the text *The Cross-Cultural Challenge to Social Psychology* (Bond, 1988), Wheeler and Reis (1988), two mainstream social psychologists, express some strong reservations about cross-cultural psychology, and hence the concept of culture. They express little interest in trying to understand any culture other than their own and write: "It takes more intellectual resources than we have just to understand our own current culture. . . . We just don't have time to read about [other cultures]" (p. 36). Because of this, they say they will not read articles dealing with other cultures, even if the studies are theoretically interesting and methodologically sophisticated.

These are rather unsettling statements, coming as they do from influential social psychologists. Such sentiments, however, seem rather widespread among the European American psychologists who represent the dominant white majority. An analysis of the cultural and cross-cultural content of thirty-five current introductory psychology tests (Lonner, 1990) found that such content was rather narrow, shallow, and predictable. In short, most students taking introductory psychology courses in the United States are not being exposed very much to the concept of culture and its implications for understanding human behavior. Several reasons why the authors of introductory texts give such spotty coverage of cultural material were identified:

1. The authors may believe in the essential validity and generalizability of most of the psychological theories and principles that have been based on experiments with college sophomores in the United States. This is somewhat shortsighted and ethnocentric.
2. Similar to the sentiments expressed by Wheeler and Reis, they may believe that it is difficult enough to explain behavior in the dominant culture in their limited space, let alone trying to explain behavior in other cultures. Culture complicates things.

3. The authors may feel that they only have room for the basics, and culture simply may not be considered basic enough to be included.
4. The authors of most of the texts, like so many other American psychologists, may not be familiar enough with other cultures to attempt to explain differences in behavior that may be attributed to membership in a different culture.
5. Students, particularly most students in the United States, may lack the experience and hence the constructs necessary to accommodate cross-cultural material. It is difficult to explain culture-related concepts to students who have limited exposure to relevant experiences.

Beyond the somewhat simplistic coverage of a few obligatory topics that are found in almost all basic texts, coverage of cultural matters and topics is generally rather bland and uninformative in most texts. The situation does, however, seem to be improving. An increasing number of basic texts are paying significant attention to the cultural, ethnic, and ecological factors that influence human behavior.

Conclusion

This chapter has reviewed four different ways in which the concept of culture has been used (and, in one case, ignored) as a way to help explain human diversity. The concept of culture is human-made, abstract, and complex, and it seemingly defies precise and certain definition. However, we cannot understand human diversity without understanding how culture contributes to the substantial variations we observe every day. Thus, while I believe that it will not be fruitful to attempt yet another definition of culture, it does seem important to find where the boundaries between cultures may be, and in which specific ways culture contributes to variation within and among societies.

I believe that advances in understanding the sources of human diversity that are attributable to culture can be, and indeed probably always have been, made without reliance on a precise definition of culture. Culture as a *general* concept, despite wide definitional variations and the inherent abstractness of the term, has proved to be useful as a way to orient our research interests and efforts. Even if a definitive conception of culture were now available, however, it might have little effect on how research on human diversity is conducted. Perhaps it would be sufficient to know that cultures are dynamic entities that are constantly shaping our thoughts, attitudes, and beliefs, as well as all other aspects of our behavior that cannot be attributed to factors other than human culture as it is currently understood.

References

Berry, J. W. (1966). Temne and Eskimo perceptual skills. *International Journal of Psychology, 1,* 207–229.

Berry, J. W., Poortinga, Y. H., Segall, M. H., & Dasen, P. R. (1992). *Cross-cultural psychology: Research and application.* Cambridge, England: Cambridge University Press.

Boesch, E. E. (1991). *Symbolic action theory and cultural psychology.* Berlin: Springer-Verlag.

Bond, M. H. (Ed.). (1988). *The cross-cultural challenge to social psychology.* Newbury Park, CA: Sage.

Brown, D. E. (1991). *Human universals.* Philadelphia: Temple University Press.

Herskovits, M. J. (1948). *Man and his works: The science of cultural anthropology.* New York: Knopf.

Jahoda, G. (1984). Do we need a concept of culture? *Journal of Cross-Cultural Psychology, 15,* 139–151.

Keesing, R. M. (1974). Theories of culture. *Annual Review of Anthropology, 3,* 73–97.

Kroeber, A., & Kluckhohn, C. (1952). Culture. *Papers of the Peabody Museum, 47,*(1).

Lonner, W. J. (1990). The introductory psychology text and cross-cultural psychology: Beyond Ekman, Whorf, and biased I.Q. tests. In D. Keats, D. Munro, & L. Mann (Eds.), *Ninth International Conference of the International Association for Cross-Cultural Psychology.* Lisse, The Netherlands: Swets and Zeitlinger.

Lonner, W. J., & Berry, J. W. (1986). *Field methods in cross-cultural research.* Newbury Park, CA: Sage.

Moghaddam, F. M., Taylor, D. M., & Wright, S. C. (1993). *Social psychology in cross-cultural perspective*. New York: Freeman.

Murdock, G. P. (1967). *Ethnographic atlas*. Pittsburgh, PA: University of Pittsburgh Press.

Murdock, G. P. (1975). *Outline of world cultures* (5th ed.). New Haven, CT: Human Relations Area Files.

Murdock, G. P., Ford, C. S., & Hudson, A. E. (1971). *Outline of cultural materials* (4th ed.). New Haven, CT: Human Relations Area Files.

Naroll, R., & Cohen, R. (Eds.). (1970). *Handbook of method in cultural anthropology*. New York: Natural History Press.

Rohner, R. P. (1984). Toward a conception of culture for cross-cultural psychology. *Journal of Cross-Cultural Psychology, 15,* 111–138.

Segall, M. H. (1984). More than we need to know about culture, but are afraid not to ask. *Journal of Cross-Cultural Psychology, 15,* 153–162.

Segall, M. H., Campbell, D. T., & Herskovits, M. (1966). *The influence of culture on visual perception*. New York: Bobbs-Merrill.

Valsiner, J. (1988, Sept.). *Culture is not an independent variable: A lesson from cross-cultural research for "mainstream" psychology*. Paper presented at the symposium "The Contributions of Cross-Cultural Psychology to Mainstream Psychological Theory," Twenty-Fourth International Congress of Psychology, Sydney, Australia.

Wheeler, L., & Reis, H. (1988). On titles, citations, and outlets: What do mainstreamers want? In M. H. Bond (Eds.), *The cross-cultural challenge to social psychology* (pp. 36–47). Newbury Park, CA: Sage.

11

Culture and Disability: An Anthropological Point of View

Jessica Scheer

In recent years, a segment of the American disability community — primarily individuals who have seen themselves as part of the Independent Living and Disability Rights movement — have come to identify themselves as sharing a distinct "disability culture." As one unidentified disability rights activist said at the National Independent Living Conference in Washington, D.C., in May 1989, "We believe that there is a 'Disability Culture' based on the life experiences shared by all people who have disabilities." Defined by believers as a set of secret, shared knowledge known only to those who have disabilities, disability culture is described as being based on common life experiences that people with all disabilities share only with each other. It is generally agreed, by social scientists and activists alike, that one of the significant outcomes of the Independent Living and Disability Rights movement has been an awakening of kinship among people with a variety of disabilities who have previously been painfully isolated from each other. However, whether or not a broadly shared disability culture exists remains in question.

Culture has not been a central concept in the study of people with disabilities. Anthropologists, however, have identified a series of cultural patterns that are present in contemporary American society, such as the formation of subcultures among certain groups of people with disabilities like the deaf (Becker, 1980) and long-term institutionalized psychiatric patients (Estroff, 1981). Another American cultural pattern that has been recently identified is the social liminality shared by most people with disabilities in American society (Murphy, Scheer, Murphy, & Mack, 1988; Murphy, 1987). Murphy and his colleagues argue that in addition to the social devaluation shared by most people with disabilities, they also share a liminal social identity. In social liminality, individuals are defined by others as being "betwixt and between" cultural categories, in this case, the cultural categories of health and illness. People with disabilities are not fully accepted as complete; they are viewed as being neither sick nor fully well. This indeterminacy and ambiguity of the liminal cultural pattern has important consequences for personal identity and social integration.

Although the concept of culture has not been used to analyze the disability experience in American society, the identification of cultural patterns such as disability subcultures and social liminality has provided useful insights about the social consequences of having a disability that have been accepted by most social scientists (Albrecht, 1992). In addition, it is generally agreed that studies of groups within a society have much to inform us about the society-at-large, specifically the characteristics of its broadly shared culture. Thus, all disability studies, in the United States and in other times and places, are contributions to understanding aspects of a particular society's broadly shared culture (Scheer, 1988).

Stigma, a cultural pattern of "undesired difference" which was first identified by the sociologist Erving Goffman (1963), has been the most common concept used by social scientists to analyze the devaluation and marginality of people with disabilities in contemporary American society. The concept of stigma is used to explain why one of the unintended results of devaluation and marginalization of people with disabilities has been the formation of kinship bonds among certain groups of people with disabilities. Kinship is created among those who have lived together in long-term residential institutions and in other segregated contexts, such as summer camps for children with disabilities. However, people with disabilities who do not have shared institutional experiences often do not come into contact with many other people with disabilities, and when they do, they often tend to avoid each other as a way to minimize their shared stigma. The Independent Living and Disability Rights movement has been instrumental in providing social contexts and opportunities that allow a new group of people with disabilities to interact and discover a kinship among themselves.

The question raised is whether this newfound kinship is based on an emerging awareness of a shared disability culture or, instead, whether disability culture stands as an idiom for the newly discovered sense of mutual relatedness and identity found among a segment of the American disability community. The notion of disability culture may provide a concept that some people with disabilities can use to describe a major shift in their personal identities, from internalized devaluation to positive evaluation of disability-related experiences. In some situations, belief in a disability culture serves as the basis for political-group empowerment. From the point of view of an anthropologist trained to examine broad cultural patterns, the differences between how the concept of culture is defined technically by anthropologists in general and how it is used in the vernacular by a group of people with disabilities is worth further examination.

This chapter provides the reader with some anthropological reflections on the questions raised by the new interest in a disability culture. It will first review how anthropologists in general have technically defined culture. Second, it will describe broad parameters of the American disability experience in terms of the technical definition of culture. Third, it will consider how the concept of culture has been used in the vernacular form by some disability activists to define a disability culture. Finally, the chapter will conclude with a case study of community life among a small group of people with disabilities who share (1) long-term residential proximity in both institutional and community settings, (2) a kinship based on long-term shared personal histories, and (3) common knowledge about the personal, social, and physical consequences of living with spinal cord injuries and diseases. The case study will allow preliminary conclusions to be made about the usefulness of the technical definition of culture in understanding the recent emergence of a disability culture.

The Technical Concept of Culture

Most anthropologists believe that the concept of culture is their unique contribution to the social science tool kit. In anthropological circles, the concept of culture is the unifying analytic framework that connects the diverse range of research and analysis pursued by anthropologists—from kinship organization in the rural Philippines to concepts of mental health in urban Mexico or the study of exchange networks in precapitalist societies. Although anthropologists continually debate among themselves about the analytic usefulness of several competing theories of culture and cultural change, when they enter the applied research arena, they generally return to the basic and traditional definitions of culture that most of them share.

Technically, one of the defining features of culture is that it is *learned* in dense social contexts, among our elders and our peers—initially in the emotionally rich context of the family, with knowledge transmitted through the generations, and later in our social institutions. Though cultural knowledge is not innate in itself, the ability of humans to learn language and culture lies within the structure of the human brain.

Culture can be defined technically as all of tradition and its expression in behavior (Alland, 1980). In the vernacular, *culture, traditions, ways of life,* and *customs* are used interchangeably to describe the kind of knowledge that is transmitted across the generations. In the analytic sense, *culture is the total body of broadly shared tradition transmitted from generation to generation,* specifically "the norms, values, and standards by which people act, and it includes the ways distinctive in each society of ordering the world and rendering it intelligible. . . . It provides us with a definition of reality" (Murphy, 1986, p. 29).

One of the best examples of what anthropologists mean

by the term *culture* and its totality is the way the late Morton
Fried, a cultural anthropologist who conducted fieldwork in a
mainland Chinese peasant village in 1946, was perceived by his
Chinese neighbors. At the time, Fried was not the only American living in the village. A geologist lived up the road, a tall
man with red hair and a long, red beard. Fried was a short,
stocky man with dark brown hair and no beard, who wore horn-
rimmed glasses. Fried was surprised that even after he and the
geologist had been living in the village for over six months,
the local postman continued to deliver the geologist's mail to the
anthropologist and vice versa. One day, he asked the postman
directly, "Why do you regularly deliver my mail to the geologist who lives up the road?" The postman responded quite simply, "Why, you Americans look so much alike I can't tell you
apart." This is culture — it runs deep and embodies perceptions
that appear "natural" only to the insider.

However, according to Murphy (1986), "The elements
of culture are not natural, but are artificial and changeable, enduring though they may seem" (pp. 25–26). The arbitrariness
of cultural elements does not mean that they are without rhyme
or reason, only that the meanings are humanly imposed, vary
from society to society, and are not absolute or natural. In fact,
a method for identifying cultural elements taught to anthropolo-
gists-in-training is that whatever in a culture is stated as if it
were *natural* is precisely what is *cultural*.

The American Disability Experience

In American society in general, it is "natural" to view people
with disabilities as being different from people without disabilities. This difference is culturally constructed, based on beliefs
about individuals who depart from the norms in their physical
appearance and function. The sense of difference has profound
consequences for people both with and without disabilities. One
of the major contributions of anthropology to disability studies
has been to confirm that disability is a cultural category, rather
than a biomedical "fact" grounded in functional characteristics.
American culture beliefs about physical appearance and func-

tion operate to make it appear that people with disabilities are naturally different from others.

For example, many Americans consider the social marginality experienced by many people with disabilities to be a natural consequence of their physical impairments, rather than the reflection of a set of sociocultural beliefs about people with disabilities. Cross-cultural research has demonstrated that the marginal status of people with disabilities is a variable cultural pattern, not a natural occurrence present in all societies. The diverse range of social responses to physical and mental disabilities has only recently begun to be appreciated (Scheer & Groce, 1988; Groce, 1985).

The lack of appreciation for cultural variability is in part structured by Western cultural blinders. A hallmark of Western industrialized nations is that the general population has lost the traditional familiarity with disability found in many preindustrial societies. In these societies, physical and mental disabilities were accepted as one of the consequences, for some, of being alive and human, and people with disabilities were well integrated into their communities. For example, in the early twentieth century, between 2 and 10 percent of the Cuna Indian population on the San Blas Islands of Panama inherited a dominant gene for albinism (Wafer, 1934). Sensitive to direct sunlight, the affected men adapted the traditional role of fisherman, which was common to all adult males, by becoming night fisherman. In Cuna culture, albinism was not a disability; instead, it was identified as simply one of the many characteristics of an individual.

The institutionalization of people with disabilities is a relatively recent custom, having emerged in Western and Central Europe during the late seventeenth century and later in the United States (Stone, 1984). Yet the negative stigma of having a visible disability in American society has historically been quite strong, based in part on our European heritage of social welfare, charity, and concepts of morality (Goffman, 1963; Rothman, 1971; Zola, 1982; Murphy, 1987). Beginning with the late eighteenth century, Americans with disabilities who were not sheltered within the traditional community-based web of family and neighbors were sent to municipal almshouses, where they received custodial care and confinement (Berkowitz, 1987; Stone,

1984; Rothman, 1971). Nineteenth-century almshouse reform led to the practice of giving shelter to people with disabilities whose families could not provide for them, in disability-specific institutions and hospitals for long-term care. In some cases, the institutions provided education for children and young adults with disabilities, such as the specialized schools and residential facilities that were developed for people with deafness, blindness, and developmental disabilities. It was in these settings that subcultures of disability emerged.

People with disabilities who remained in community settings generally lived with their families, were not well integrated into community life, and were isolated from other people with disabilities. Given this tradition of isolation, the recent emergence of people with disabilities in community settings has sometimes allowed a powerful bond to form. Beginning with the educational mainstreaming of children who had polio, blindness, and developmental disabilities in the 1950s and 1960s, continuing with the community involvement of people with spinal cord injuries and polio in the late 1960s, and culminating in the birth of the Independent Living and Disability Rights movement in the late 1960s and early 1970s, people with all types of disabilities earned political empowerment by working together for the passage of the Americans with Disabilities Act in 1990.

It is useful at this juncture to discuss how the broadly shared experiences of Americans with disabilities fit the technical criterion of the concepts of culture and cultural knowledge — that is, they are learned in residential proximity to a variably defined family with individuals who are connected by generations. First, people with disabilities generally have not grown up in families where knowledge about the realities of living with a disability was based on personal experience; instead, they generally have grown up in families that did not include other members with disabilities. Second, disabilities do not always develop at birth, and they occur throughout the life span. In these cases, individuals have already acquired a nonpersonalized form of deeply embedded cultural knowledge about living with a disability. Third, because of the isolation most people with disabilities have lived with, until recently, they have had limited contact with other people with disabilities who could have served as peers or mentors.

Because disabilities have been culturally defined as medical problems, and services and resources have often been made available to the individual based on his or her type of disability, people with disabilities have generally identified themselves as members of a type of disability group, such as those with spinal cord injury, polio, or cerebral palsy, and not as members of the umbrella group "people with disabilities." Not only have individuals been isolated from each other, but until the Independent Living and Disability Rights movement, disability-specific groups were separated from other disability-specific groups in competition for services and resources, thus losing the potential for finding common ground.

In contrast to its medical definition, the sociopolitical definition of disability connects people with the broadest range of disabilities to each other by locating disability in the interaction of the person within her or his environment, rather than solely within the individual (Hahn, 1988). As a member of a minority group that shares a similar environment, the individual becomes connected to everyone defined by society as having a disability. The minority-group concept has provided much-needed support for the social integration of all people with disabilities and has been a useful legal tool in seeking civil rights and reasonable accommodation in American society.

In the process of identifying themselves as members of a minority group, people with disabilities have followed the path of other groups in American society. In terms of the technical concept of culture outlined in this chapter, Table 11.1 summarizes some similarities and differences with other groups in American society who identify themselves as members of devalued, marginalized cultural minority groups: ethnic groups (African Americans, Latinos, Asian Americans, and others), women, lesbians and gay men, and people with disabilities.

People with disabilities share the experiences lived by lesbians and gay men, who also do not grow up in families with other group members and who learn about being a group member later in life, sometimes in proximity with other peers and

Table 11.1. Characteristics of Cultural Minority Groups.

Cultural Minority Group	Shared Knowledge	Knowledge Transmitted Within the Family Across Generations	Residential Proximity with Other Group Members	Lifetime Identification as Group Member
Ethnic groups	Yes	Yes	Varies	No
Women	Yes	Yes	No	No
Lesbians and gay men	Yes	No	Varies	Varies
People with disabilities	Yes	No	Varies	Varies

mentors, but sometimes not. This form of isolation has specific social consequences and may be the driving force behind the recent search for a disability culture.

Using the Concept of Culture in the Vernacular

In the January-February 1987 issue of the *Disability Rag,* a national newsletter and forum for the Independent Living and Disability Rights movement, clinical psychologist Carol Gill observes that many people with disabilities are "in search of a Disability Culture" (Johnson, 1987, p. 4). Gill describes these seekers as using counter-mainstream American cultural symbols and attributes to change the widely shared images of marginality, tragedy, and dependence associated with disabilities to pride, strength, power, and style. "Crip Power," "Disabled and Proud," "Disability Cool," and "Disabled People Do It Creatively" are the slogans of the new awareness. Being disability-cool involves acquisition of a new set of personality attributes, attitudes, and behaviors. It means being competent, assertive, and proud of oneself as an individual, independent in decision making, and able to transcend the definitions held by others about the correct way to participate in the activities of daily living, such as dancing, eating, or making love. Gill invites people with disabilities to invent new cultural forms of pride and celebration.

From an academic point of view, the sociologist Harlan Hahn, who was mobility-impaired by polio before he left his parents' home, describes a unique kind of knowledge that emerges from being disabled in American society (Hahn, 1988). He recommends that this shared knowledge be acknowledged and celebrated by people with disabilities, rather than being framed as unfortunate. Hahn explains that the insiders' knowledge of disability is an experiential knowledge about the lived experience of adversity in a society that devalues vulnerability. It is a kind of knowledge that cannot be truly known by people who have not had a disability. He also raises the point discussed earlier, that in the majority of cases, parents of children with disabilities do not have disabilities themselves and cannot transmit knowledge across the generations in the deeply emotional way that cultural knowledge is transmitted.

This process of understanding shared life experiences and learning to identify oneself as being like others is not what anthropologists technically define as culture, but it is what disability activists mean when they use the term *culture* in the vernacular. Culture serves as the idiom through which a common bond and kinship with others is forged. Carol Gill also mentions the difficulties disability culture advocates have had in creating the groundswell for a collective acknowledgment of a disability culture (Johnson, 1987). First, many adults with disabilities have a difficult time meeting with other disabled adults, for reasons of physical inaccessibility, obviously, but also because deeply ingrained avoidance strategies have been used for years to minimize stigma and shame. Second, Gill describes the severe problem experienced by most people with disabilities of having not grown up in households with disabled parents or siblings and of never having had contact with a significant number of disabled adults who could serve as role models. This isolation and alienation is precisely what seekers of a disability culture hope to transcend.

Island Town: A Case Study

The case of a small group of people with disabilities who lived almost a lifetime in close proximity to each other, in both institutional and community settings, provides an interesting case study with which to think about the questions raised by our discussion of a disability culture. From 1980 to 1982, I conducted an eighteen-month participant-observation study among fifty-five adults with highly visible mobility impairments who lived in a wheelchair-accessible apartment-house community known as Island Town, on Roosevelt Island, New York (Scheer, 1988).

From the late 1970s until the mid 1980s, 1 percent of the total number of Island Town residents were people who used wheelchairs. About a third of these residents had been disabled by polio during the epidemic years and had a unique shared history, having lived from the 1950s until 1976 in Goldwater Hospital, a municipal chronic care and rehabilitation hospital also located on Roosevelt Island. Most of the people who had polio used portable respirators attached to their wheelchairs during the day and to their bedsides at night. The other two-thirds of the residents with disabilities had been disabled by a variety of spinal cord injuries and diseases and had received rehabilitation and residential care for one to ten years in either Goldwater Hospital or Coler Hospital on Roosevelt Island. Most of them did not use portable respirators.

Prior to moving to the Island Town wheelchair-accessible apartments, most of the people who had polio had known each other as fellow patients since the 1950s, when they had been children, adolescents, or young adults, and others had known each other for about a decade, beginning as adolescents or young adults. In addition, the residents with disabilities had a range of ethnic and social-class backgrounds (Scheer, 1988). At the time of the study, two-thirds were unemployed, although a third of the unemployed were engaged in voluntary community activities. Among those considered employed, one-third worked full-time, one-third worked part-time, and one-third were in school or vocational training programs. Fewer than one-third were involved in Independent Living and Disability Rights activities.

Island Town was not a typical urban neighborhood in the metropolitan New York area. It was built in the mid 1970s as a planned community on Manhattan's Welfare Island, using a variety of federal and state community development funds. It has several unique design features: (1) its singular location, 800 yards off the shore of Manhattan's Upper East Side; (2) its small scale—the island is two miles long, 800 feet wide at its broadest point, and 147 acres in total size; (3) a wheelchair-accessible aerial commuter cable car that transports residents to Manhattan; (4) a relatively automobile-free residential design; (5) a relatively wheelchair-accessible local environment; and (6) fifty wheelchair-adapted studio apartments. The presence of a group of people with disabilities living in a relatively wheelchair-accessible local environment, half of them having known each other as patients in rehabilitation hospitals for as long as thirty years, created a unique research setting. It was very attractive to an anthropologist-in-training who had cut her intellectual teeth on stories of anthropologists who studied remote populations on exotic islands. Islands contain the small-scale human setting necessary for the labor-intensive methods characteristic of participant-observation ethnographic research.

Roosevelt Island was also a unique research setting in which to investigate, over time, the changing social consequences of being mobility impaired in a Western industrial state. During the nineteenth and early twentieth centuries, Roosevelt Island was referred to in the popular press as New York City's "island of exile" (Buckley, 1973). Beginning with the purchase of the island in 1827 from the Blackwell family, the city used the island to locate almshouses (where people with disabilities who were not cared for by family or neighbors were sheltered), workhouses, asylums, prisons, fever hospitals in the 1880s, and two municipal chronic care rehabilitation hospitals in the 1930s and 1950s; finally, it was used as an apartment-house neighborhood for 5,500 people, including 55 residents with mobility impairments. Thus, Roosevelt Island had a unique and haunting heritage of the presence of people with disabilities—first in almshouses, then in chronic care and rehabilitation hospitals, and finally when a small group was integrated into the apartment-house community.

The shift from kin- and community-centered care of people with disabilities to institutional isolation and seclusion and then back to community-centered care is graphically represented on Roosevelt Island. Archeological remains of the former institutions stand on the island, away from the neighborhood boundaries but within view. The Gothic remains of eighteenth- and nineteenth-century almshouses and fever hospitals, as well as the current operation of the two chronic care and rehabilitation hospitals in which the Island Town residents with disabilities had lived a substantial portion of their lives, stand as testimony to the tradition of isolation lived by people with disabilities.

Despite the best intentions of the planners, architects, and developers, the tradition of isolation was replicated in the so-called accessible design. The wheelchair-adapted apartments are all one-room studio apartments, suitable only for one person. Implied is the notion that people with disabilities do not marry or have roommates, families, or even large social gatherings. Although the accessible kitchens and bathrooms are generally appreciated by residents, many complain about cramped living quarters. The residents with disabilities who need personal assistants (those who do not have upper-body strength) do not require adapted kitchens or bathrooms, so they live in non-adapted two-bedroom apartment units. These residents do not complain about the lack of space and have more freedom to easily have roommates and marry. A small number of them have had children since moving there.

Another way in which the tradition of isolation was frozen in the community's design was that one-quarter of all Island Town apartment units have a steep flight of stairs leading up to the living room from the entrance vestibule. It is impossible for a person who uses a wheelchair to visit a neighbor who lives in one of these apartments. The stereotype that people with disabilities do not interact much with nondisabled residents is reflected in this aspect of the design.

When Island Town was being planned and built during the late 1960s and early 1970s, the primary goal of advocates for wheelchair accessibility was to build barrier-free homes and communities. However, reducing the architectural barriers for the *people* who use the wheelchairs was not a specific goal until the late 1970s. In the adapted studio apartments, the electrical outlets are too low for most wheelchair users to use comfortably, and the design of the kitchen cabinets is not optimum for use. The design focus was on the wheelchair, not the wheelchair user.

Table 11.2 contrasts characteristics of the lives of people with disabilities in general and the Island Town group. The distinguishing feature of the Island Town group was that they were not isolated from each other and other people with disabilities for at least a decade. In fact, those who had polio had lived together in extremely close proximity in an institutional setting for as long as thirty years prior to moving into the community and becoming neighbors with each other. This raises a question: Did this feature about the Island Town group of people with disabilities lead to formation of a disability culture or a disability subculture?

Table 11.2. Characteristics of Island Town Group.

Cultural Minority Group	Shared Knowledge	Knowledge Transmitted Within the Family Across Generations	Residential Proximity with Other Group Members	Lifetime Identification as Group Member
People with disabilities	Yes	No	Varies	Varies
Island Town group	Yes	No	Yes	Varies

I believe that it did not. There was great variation in beliefs among the group about what it meant to be disabled in American society. There was no consensus about whether being disabled should be considered a tragedy, a circumstance, a life experience, or an opportunity. There also was no consensus about what the proper and fair social position of people with disabilities should be; in other words, is segregation easier and safer or is integration better for everyone? What did exist was a profound kinship among the residents, especially those who had polio, that transcended race, gender, social class, and educational level.

It is a bond based on a uniquely shared set of personal histories rooted in long-term residential proximity. Together, the disabled residents' lives moved along a common stream. In bodies transformed by spinal cord injuries and/or disease, they learned how to conduct life from a wheelchair, how to deal with family and old friends, how to make new families and friends, how to negotiate with employers and medical and social agencies, and how to live with the fear of leaving an institution and making the difficult transition from the institution to the community. Decades of birthdays and holidays, a series of marriages and divorces, and the birth of children tied them together. This is one way to create kinship and, indeed, Island Town's disabled residents experienced themselves as being related for life in spite of the usual range of personality differences and moral disputes. It is possible, however, that if more of the residents with disabilities had been Independent Living and Disability Rights activists and identified as members of a minority group (see Table 11.2), even more beliefs about the nature of being disabled might have been shared.

Conclusion

Among a segment of the American disability community, the emerging consciousness and sense of mutual identification known as disability culture has functioned to shatter traditional cultural patterns of isolation. Broadly shared understandings of common life experiences have served as a basis for uniting people with a variety of disabilities who were perhaps disabled at different chronological ages and who currently live with a variety of physical limitations and possibilities. It is not clear whether other potentially divisive social characteristics, such as race, gender, and social class, have been muted by a common identification in disability culture. However, in technical terms, what is understood as disability culture is not a culture per se, but a kinship based on identification of shared understandings of common life experiences.

For these reasons, I would caution social scientists against allowing the concept of disability culture to become part of the scientific discourse (Johnson, 1987). I also sound an alert to social scientists and activists to look carefully at using concepts that are thought to promote empowerment, but that may have unintended consequences. We have learned from the experiences of other cultural minorities that self-awareness and consciousness raising are important and necessary steps toward empowerment. But there have been political costs to emphasizing the differences that some believe separate cultural minority group members from the larger society. The cost of promoting a disability culture is that it reinforces the broadly shared cultural belief that people with disabilities are different from others. At this time, when the Independent Living and Disability Rights movement is fighting for fair and just implementation of the Americans with Disabilities Act, people with disabilities cannot afford to be perceived as different. Should they then have different civil rights, different health benefits, a different quality of life? The term *disability culture* implicitly raises these questions. It's worth thinking about.

References

Albrecht, G. (1992). *The disability business: Rehabilitation in America* (Sage Library of Social Research no. 190). Newbury Park, CA: Sage.

Alland, A., Jr. (1980). *To be human: An introduction to anthropology.* New York: Wiley.

Becker, G. (1980). *Growing old in silence.* Berkeley: University of California Press.

Berkowitz, E. (1987). *Disabled policy: America's programs for the handicapped.* New York: Cambridge University Press.

Buckley, T. (1973, Aug. 22). Roosevelt Island: Town in the making. *New York Times Magazine,* p. 46.

Estroff, S. (1981). *Making it crazy: An ethnography of psychiatric clients in an American community.* Berkeley: University of California Press.

Goffman, E. (1963). *Stigma: Notes on the management of a spoiled identity.* Englewood Cliffs, NJ: Prentice-Hall.

Groce, N. (1985). *Everyone here spoke sign: Hereditary deafness on Martha's Vineyard.* Cambridge, MA: Harvard University Press.

Hahn, H. (1988). The politics of physical differences: Disability and discrimination. *Journal of Social Issues, 44*(3), 39–47.

Johnson, M. (1987, Jan.-Feb.). Emotion and pride: In search for a disability culture. *Disability Rag.*

Murphy, R. (1986). *Cultural and social anthropology: An overture* (2nd ed.). Englewood Cliffs, NJ: Prentice-Hall.

Murphy, R. (1987). *The body silent.* Troy, MO: Holt, Rinehart & Winston.

Murphy, R., Scheer, J., Murphy, Y., & Mack, R. (1988). Physical disability and social liminality: A study in the rituals of adversity. *Social Science and Medicine, 26*(2).

Rothman, D. (1971). *The discovery of the asylum: Social order and disorder in the new republic.* Boston: Little, Brown.

Scheer, J. (1988). *The social consequences of mobility impairment in a New York City neighborhood.* (Doctoral dissertation, Columbia University, 1987). *Dissertation Abstracts International, 4903,* 539.

Scheer, J., & Groce, N. (1988). Impairment as a human constant: Cross-cultural and historical perspectives on variation. *Journal of Social Issues, 44*(1), 24–26.

Stone, D. (1984). *The disabled state.* Philadelphia: Temple University Press.

Zola, I. (1982). *Missing pieces: A chronicle of living with a disability.* Philadelphia: Temple University Press.

12

Acculturation and Human Diversity in a Multicultural Society

Dina Birman

The term *acculturation* has been defined in anthropology as "those phenomena which result when groups of individuals having different cultures come into continuous first-hand contact with subsequent changes in the original pattern of either or both groups" (Redfield, Linton, & Herskovits, 1936, p. 149). At the group, or cultural, level, acculturation is the process by which the collective culture of a group is changed through contact with another culture (Berry, Trimble, & Olmedo, 1986). Psychological acculturation, on the other hand, refers to the changes in behavior of individual members of such a group, who may differ with respect to the extent and type of their acculturation. Psychological acculturation is contrasted with *enculturation*, which describes the influences on behavior exerted by the culture in which one develops, and which does not involve cultural change.

This chapter will address issues of acculturation, or cultural change, among members of ethnic groups in multicultural societies. The term *ethnic group* is used here to refer to a group "which is defined or set off by race, religion, or national origin, or some combination of these categories" (Gordon, 1964, p. 27). The assumption in ethnic psychology (Berry, Chapter Six of this volume) is that an ethnic group is characterized by its own, not necessarily autonomous, culture. While the thicket of the meaning of culture has been discussed elsewhere in this volume (Berry, Chapter Six; Helms, Chapter Thirteen; Lonner, Chapter Ten; Scheer, Chapter Eleven; and Watts, Chapter Three), it deserves some attention here, particularly because as Helms (Chapter Thirteen of this volume) points out, the terms *culture, ethnicity,* and *race* have all been used differently in writings on acculturation. Further, different models of acculturation have attended differentially to these related concepts, some focusing on behavioral cultural change, others on ethnic identity, and still others on the development of racial identity.

The difficulties in defining the boundaries and distinctions between culture, race, and ethnicity reflect the different ways these concepts are constructed in different parts of the world. For example, though race is generally treated as an immutable and obvious descriptor of an individual, racial categories vary tremendously in different societies. While a world history book printed in the United States (Stavrianos, 1966) refers to the existence of three races — Caucasoid, Negroid, and Mongoloid — the U.S. government most frequently uses four racial categories (Asian, Black, Caucasian, and Native American/Pacific Islander). In Latin America, further distinctions are made between those of mixed racial origin, such as mestizos and mulattos. Similarly, ethnic origin is tracked in the United States only for Hispanics, while other societies note other ethnic, cultural, linguistic, or religious differences.

The salience of the different concepts also varies across cultures. In the United States, race has emerged as perhaps the most important dimension defining power, privilege, social category, and class. In the European context, the constructs of ethnicity and nationality have been important as sources of classification and identity for members of distinct populations.

Confusion of the term *ethnicity* with the constructs of culture and race stems from the fact that ethnicity is generally used to represent at least three conceptually distinct constructs: (1) *ethnicity,* or the collective culture of a minority cultural group with some distinctive cultural characteristics within a larger society (Berry, Chapter Six of this volume); (2) *ethnic origin,* or a classification system based on one's biological ancestors; and (3) *ethnic identity,* or the extent to which individuals choose to incorporate a particular ethnic classification into their sense of self. Thus, *ethnicity* conceptually resembles the concept of culture in that it is collectively created over the course of generations out of the shared experience of a group of people who come to identify themselves as a group with a unique history and origins. On the other hand, individuals born into an ethnic group, such as Croats, Polish Americans, Ukrainians, and African Americans, cannot change their ethnic origin, though they differ with respect to their ethnic identity, or sense of belonging to the group.

The European emphasis on ethnicity and ethnic origin as salient dimensions has its roots in a particular historical moment—the rise of nationalism in late eighteenth-century Europe—which helped to sharpen the differences between ethnic and national groups on the European continent. In the United States, efforts were made to depart from the notion of European nationalism and ensure that national and ethnic origins should not stand in the way of attaining the American Dream. As John Dewey noted in 1918, "the American contribution is radical. We have solved the problem by a complete separation of nationality from citizenship. Not only have we separated the church from the state, but we have separated language, cultural traditions, all that is called race, from the state— that is, from problems of political organization and power. To us language, literature, creed, group ways, national culture, are social rather than political, human rather than national, interests" (cited in Eisele, 1983, p. 153).

The persistence of ethnicity as an important distinguishing characteristic of some groups in U.S. society speaks to the failure of the American experiment. Though some White ethnic groups have assimilated into the Anglo-American majority, in the United States, political power and resources have yet to be distributed independent of race and ethnic origin.

The difficulties in disentangling these concepts of race, culture, and ethnicity are well illustrated by the experience of

Jews, who at different historical moments and in different societies have been described as belonging to a race, an ethnicity, a culture, a nationality, and a religion. The experience of Soviet Jewish immigrants in the United States during the last two decades highlights the extent to which these notions are constructed in a given society. In the Soviet Union, citizens were classified according to their "nationalities," a concept resembling ethnic origin. The designation of an individual's nationality was inherited from his or her parents, regardless of the geographic location of her or his birth. Because Soviet society was secular, being Jewish was considered a nationality rather than a religion, in the same way that Soviet citizens could be born Russian, Ukrainian, or Armenian. The nationalities of Soviet citizens appeared in all official documents, including registration in schools and places of employment.

In the case of Jews, this notion of nationality included an implicit understanding that Jews had distinctive physical characteristics that distinguished them from Slavic peoples, making the concept of nationality similar to the idea of race. This official designation had many negative consequences for Jews in Soviet society, denying them access to many of its institutions. However, it was also an important source of their sense of identity as ethnically non-Russian Soviet citizens, though culturally, most were assimilated into the Russian culture.

Given this already-complex background, immigration to the United States has involved a profound redefinition of the cultural, ethnic, religious, and national identity of Soviet Jews (Birman, in press). In the United States, being Jewish is generally defined through participation in the Jewish religion and, to a lesser extent, by ethnicity. Thus, to their bewilderment, for the first time in their lives, Soviet Jews find themselves being referred to as "Russians," because Americans assume that they are ethnically Russian people who practice the Jewish religion. Moreover, American Jews wrongly assume that being Jewish in the USSR was only a negative experience, ignoring the fact that it was also a positive source of Jews' identity. In the United States, the Jewish religion, which is quite foreign to most of the Soviet Jewish refugees, thus becomes the primary link to the American Jewish community and a primary source of identity as a Jew. Finally, because of the salience of racial categories in the United States, resettlement for Soviet Jews also involves being defined as White, which offers the possibility of assimilating into the dominant culture. It is not surprising that, in this vortex of varied meanings, Soviet Jewish refugees have chosen a variety of labels to describe their cultural identity in immigration (Simon & Simon, 1982), suggesting a confusion in the way they define themselves in their new cultural context.

While the issue for Soviet Jews of whether being Jewish represents a culture, an ethnicity, a race, or a religion seems unusually complex, similar issues arise for other immigrant groups. For example, the culture, ethnicity, and race of immigrants from Latin American countries is redefined in the United States through the U.S. government's category of Hispanic, which is applied to all Latin Americans regardless of the wide variety of races, ethnicities, and cultures of their ancestors. Birman (1992), for example, found that Latin American immigrant adolescents did not know how to answer the question of what race they were, frequently writing in "Hispanic" rather than choosing one of the many possible designations of race listed on the questionnaire, including "Black," "White," "mestizo," and "mulatto." Their confusion reflects the dynamic process by which the Latino community as a whole and its individual members are defining and redefining the boundaries and characteristics of their group identity in their new cultural context.

The implication of this complexity is that the cultural change referred to in the definition of acculturation needs to be understood as integrally related to a myriad of factors that shape the distinctive characteristics of acculturating groups, including the racial and ethnic characteristics of a group as well as the attitudes and policies of the larger society. Thus, models that examine acculturation, ethnic identity, and racial identity are all relevant to the field of acculturation, as each explores a different facet of this process. It is with this image of culture in mind that the remainder of this chapter will address the field of acculturation.

The Study of Acculturation

While early research on acculturation addressed the impact of modernization on indigenous peoples and traditional societies (Olmedo, 1979), the field has focused more recently on the experience of immigrants and ethnic minority groups (Rogler, Cortes, & Malgady, 1991), thus broadening its application to a wider range of situations involving cultural contact. Moreover, the concept has been embraced by those studying the adjustment of nonethnic minority groups to mainstream society — for example, that of lesbians and gay men (Brown, 1989).

Although the initial definition of *acculturation* made no explicit assumptions about the direction of cultural change, when it is operationalized in research, the term has come to denote assimilation of an acculturating group into the culture of the dominant group (Berry, Trimble, & Olmedo, 1986), "whereby immigrants change their behavior and attitudes toward those of the host society" (Rogler, Cortes, & Malgady, 1991, p. 585). This phenomenon seems to reflect an erroneous assumption that the culture of the majority is not affected by such smaller groups. The recent work of Helms (1984) and Phinney (1990) on aspects of the racial and ethnic identity of Whites represents a rare exception to the rule of attending to acculturation of the minority and not the majority and suggests that acculturation must involve some mutual accommodation between the groups involved.

In studying psychological acculturation to a dominant or majority culture, the fundamental research question has addressed the ways in which acculturating individuals respond to pressure to give up their unique ethnic, racial, and religious characteristics and assimilate to the culture of the larger society. In psychology, two distinct influential frameworks have been developed to describe such acculturation experiences. One emphasizes culture and has been incorporated into the biculturalism model (Szapocznik, Kurtines, & Fernandez, 1980) and the biculturalism-multiculturalism model (Ramirez, 1984). These models suggest that culturally distinct groups benefit by maintaining an allegiance to their culture of origin as well as by participating in the host culture. The other framework is focused more on racial and ethnic origin, and has been called the cultural identification model (Helms, 1985), the ethnic identity model (Phinney, 1989), and the racial identity model (Helms, 1984; Chapter Thirteen of this volume). The identity models argue that for racial and ethnic minorities, the best resolution of acculturative conflicts involves the primacy of establishing a positive sense of identity as a member of one's own cultural, ethnic, and racial group, while retaining some degree of competence in the larger society.

This chapter will argue that while both the biculturalism and identity frameworks offer unique insights about the acculturation experience, they were developed to address very specific acculturation experiences, thus limiting their generalizability across varied groups. One such limitation of models of biculturalism, and of the cross-cultural perspective from which they are derived (Watts, Chapter Three of this volume), is an emphasis on cultural competence without attention to the constraints of oppression on the possibility of attaining biculturalism. On the other hand, the identity models have been limited in their focus on the psychological, intrapsychic experience of identification with a cultural, ethnic, and racial group and have not examined the behavioral dimensions of this process that are addressed by the biculturalism models.

Implicit in the present argument is the notion that acculturation theories are themselves a function of the cultural context within which they were developed. Thus, the range of specific acculturative styles outlined by these models reflects the particular circumstances of cultural contact of the group in question. It is thus argued that acculturation at the individual level cannot be understood without examining the acculturation of the group to which an individual belongs. The collective experience of an ethnic community, including oppression and other factors, creates a backdrop against which individual acculturation takes place by shaping the options available to individuals who make choices about the cultural spaces in which to locate their lives.

This chapter will propose an expanded framework of acculturation that integrates aspects of both the biculturalism and

identity frameworks. This expanded framework can be applied
to a variety of cultural, ethnic, and racial groups coexisting in
a multicultural society. First, the theories of psychological acculturation will be examined, and the biculturalism and identity
frameworks will be described in the context of the distinctive
population whose acculturation they were designed to address.
Then the proposed differentiated model of acculturation will be
presented.

Acculturative Styles

Earlier in this century, social scientists (Stonequist, 1937) believed that two alternatives were possible for acculturating individuals: they could give up their culture of origin and assimilate to the majority culture, or they could retain their cultural
affiliation and remain on the margins of the larger society.
Although in recent years assimilation has come to be seen in
a negative light (Buriel, 1984; Ramirez, 1984), it once represented both a desirable and a positive alternative to marginality for white Europeans. Around the turn of the twentieth century, Eastern and Southern Europeans were entering the country
in large numbers to escape poverty and oppression in Europe,
and the country welcomed them as long as they were willing
to adopt its culture and obey its laws. In this context, assimilation was the only option considered possible or desirable by these
immigrants, who were approaching their new life with both op-
timism and idealism. Ironically, many did not assimilate despite
their desire to do so, and many neighborhoods in the boroughs
of New York City give testimony to the persistence of ethnic
enclaves despite positive attitudes of the newcomers toward assimilation.

Alternatives to Marginality and Assimilation

In psychology, the assumption that assimilation was the most
adaptive acculturative style remained largely unchallenged until the 1970s, when alternatives to the assimilation model were
introduced in the context of the civil rights movement. These
newer theories were based on the contention that acculturation

to the Anglo-American culture at the expense of giving up identification with the culture of origin causes distress (Cross, 1971),
low self-esteem (Franco, 1983), and poor achievement (Buriel,
1984) for the acculturating groups.

The context within which this challenge to the assimilationist perspective emerged deserves some attention. Assimilation did not prove to be a viable option in racist U.S. society
for anyone who was not White. Moreover, even if assimilation
could be achieved, it implied buying into society's racist attitudes toward one's own group, leading to self-deprecation and
psychological maladjustment. Thus, alternative models sought
different paths of acculturation for those who were visible ethnic or racial minorities. These newer models, including models
of racial identity and biculturalism, emphasized the idea that
identification with the culture of origin of the minority groups
needed to be reestablished for positive psychological adaptation.

The identity and biculturalism models, while related,
arose in different populations. Identity models were developed
to address the experience of African Americans in particular
(Cross, 1971; Helms, 1984) and ethnic minority groups more
generally (Atkinson, Morten, & Sue, 1979; Phinney, 1989),
while biculturalism models emphasized the immigrant-refugee
experience (Szapocznik, Kurtines, & Fernandez, 1980; Ramirez, 1984) and not the consequences of minority status per se.
Both types of models stress that the most psychologically adaptive outcome for the acculturating individual is to develop the
ability to participate in both the "old," or minority, and "new,"
or majority, cultures. In this sense, as Helms (1985) has pointed
out, both types of models are implicitly bicultural.

The biculturalism models have redefined acculturation as
a two-dimensional process, in which the acculturating individual undergoes two independent processes of acculturation—
one to the culture of origin and one to the new host culture
(Berry, Trimble, & Olmedo, 1986; Mendoza, 1984; Szapocznik, Kurtines, & Fernandez, 1980). Thus, it is possible for an
acculturating individual to be highly acculturated to either both,
or neither culture, resulting in four possible acculturative styles
of assimilation, separation, marginalization, and biculturalism-
integration (see Figure 12.1).

Figure 12.1. Biculturalism: A Two-Factor Model.

Acculturation to
the Culture of Origin

		HIGH	LOW
Acculturation to the Dominant or Host Culture	**HIGH**	Biculturalism	Assimilation
	LOW	Separation/ Traditionalism	Marginality

Note: Based on the model described elsewhere by Berry, 1980; Berry, Trimble, & Olmedo, 1986; Mendoza, 1984; and Szapocznik, Kurtines, & Fernandez, 1980.

Since its introduction in the literature, biculturalism has been increasingly touted as the most adaptive acculturative style; currently, however, only a handful of published studies test the biculturalism hypothesis (Fernandez-Barillas & Morrison, 1984; Szapocznik, Kurtines, & Fernandez, 1980; Garza, Romero, Cox, & Ramirez, 1982). Further, interpretation of the results of these studies is problematic, because all of them have assessed biculturalism in ways that have confounded biculturalism with marginality.

Moreover, most researchers on biculturalism have not sufficiently articulated a precise operational definition of biculturalism. For example, LaFromboise, Coleman, and Gerton (1993) distinguish between an *alternation* and a *fusion* model of biculturalism. The alternation model implies alternate participation in distinct cultural contexts, while fusion suggests a blended cultural identity, consisting of a synthesis of aspects of both cultures.

Biculturalism as Alternation. The notion of biculturalism as articulated by Szapocznik, Kurtines, and Fernandez (1980) resembles the alternation model. They hypothesize that for Cuban

Americans in Miami, successful adaptation would require competence in and comfort with both the Cuban and the American
cultures. The experience of Cuban Americans in Miami is, however, very different from that of Europeans, who came through
Ellis Island with the expectation of severing all ties with the countries they were fleeing and who longed to assimilate to American culture. The population of Miami is predominantly Cuban
American, settled largely by those who fled Castro's regime in
1959, with other waves arriving in subsequent years. The tremendous concentration of members of one ethnic group in one
city, the resources the exiles brought with them, and the dedi-
cation of the community to help other Cubans escape and resettle
there have created a truly unique cultural enclave, where Cuban
culture has continued to thrive. Thus, the thrust of the argument of this approach to biculturalism rests on the assumption
that the environment to which the Cuban refugee families must
adapt is not monocultural, but consists of two distinct cultural
contexts: Cuban and American.

However, the study of biculturalism among Cuban American adolescents (Szapocznik, Kurtines, & Fernandez, 1980),
while supporting the notion that biculturalism is adaptive, failed
to explicitly test the alternation model. Successful adaptation
of students was assessed by their bicultural Cuban American
teachers, not across a range of monocultural situations that
would require alternation to occur. Thus, it is not clear that
the alternation style of biculturalism is advantageous for these
adolescents. However, in a study with Latino immigrant adolescents in an urban Latino community, Birman (1992) did find
support for the alternation model of biculturalism; high involvement in American and Hispanic culture predicted perceived
competence in relationships with American peers and Latino
peers, respectively, while biculturalism predicted an overall sense
of self-worth.

Biculturalism as Fusion. The biculturalism-multiculturalism
model described by Ramirez (1984), developed in the context
of Mexican Americans in the Southwest, more closely resembles a fusion image of biculturalism than an alternation image:

"the personality-building elements, which the person acquires from different cultures, have the potential for uniting to develop multicultural patterns of behavior, multicultural perspectives, transcendence, and a multicultural orientation to life" (p. 92).

Thus, Ramirez describes successful individuals as having developed a synthetic, blended multicultural pattern. Rather than having distinct cultural repertoires that can be brought out in different cultural circumstances, the multicultural individuals described by Ramirez belong to neither culture and have transcended both. This model is perhaps also a function of the specific cultural circumstances of Chicanos in the Southwest, a region where the influence of Mexico and Latin America is strong. As Ramirez notes elsewhere (1983), although segregation of races and cultures has occurred in many regions of the United States, Latin American history is characterized by a mixing of various races and cultures, resulting in "genetic mestizos" who "could play the roles of cultural 'ambassadors' and 'brokers' because they spoke two or more languages [and] were familiar with the two sociocultural systems which were being amalgamated" (pp. 25–26). In such a historical context, a fused bicultural model may seem more desirable and adaptive for Mexican Americans.

Biculturalism as Expressed in Identity Models. The context of the African American experience raised distinctive issues in the search for alternative models to assimilation. While the Latino and Asian communities are defining their experience in the context of continued migration to the United States from Latin America and Asia, the migration of Africans to the United States is negligible, representing 2 percent of the total for the years 1955–1990 (U.S. Immigration and Naturalization Service, 1991, p. 39). Thus, the experience of African Americans in the United States is defined primarily against the background of the forced migration of Africans to this country in the context of slavery. This history, followed by segregation and today's more subtle forms of racism, has made assimilation into Euro-American society problematic for African Americans. Retaining positive affiliations to African culture was also made difficult by the systematic destruction of African culture in North America. As a result, as Watts, Machabanski, and Karber (1993) point out, "[as] a group, African Americans provide an example of marginalization" (p. 231).

To form a model of the development of racial and ethnic identity for African Americans, Helms (1984) built a developmental model of racial identity based on models by Cross (1971) and others. Helms's model takes the acculturating individual from a marginalized state through a separatist stage to internalization of her or his racial identity (see Helms, Chapter Thirteen of this volume). An analogous model has been described by Atkinson, Morten, and Sue (1979) in the more general context of the ethnic minority experience. The last and healthiest stage of acculturation in these models represents the establishment of positive cultural identification with the minority culture without rejection of the majority society, where a person "is confident with his or her racial identity and proud of his or her cultural heritage" (Helms, 1984, p. 155).

Similarly, Phinney (1989) suggests that the development of ethnic identity is an integral part of the development of personal identity for minority youths. As with other aspects of identity, ethnic identity involves a sequential process, with the last stage reflecting a commitment to an ethnic identity (Phinney, 1989). Phinney emphasizes achievement of ethnic identity as a developmental milestone, similar to the way Erikson (1968) describes the resolution of the identity crisis in adolescence. Support for these identity models is offered by several studies (Phinney & Alipuria, 1990; Parham & Helms, 1985) that have found a relationship between positive psychological adjustment and the last stage of the models.

Differences Between Biculturalism Models

The last stages of identity models seem to endorse an alternation style of biculturalism with respect to competence in the two cultures, but a monocultural style with respect to a psychological sense of identification with one's own culture. In this way, these models highlight a further distinction between the types

of biculturalism — the difference between psychological identification with a culture and behavioral participation in it. While
Szapocznik, Kurtines, and Fernandez (1980) and Ramirez
(1984) attend to competence and behavioral participation in the
two cultures, Helms (Chapter Thirteen, this volume) and Phinney (1989) focus on identification.

   This difference stems in part from the fact that the models
were developed to address the experiences of different groups
in different circumstances of cultural contact. Biculturalism
models have largely been articulated in the context of refugee
and immigrant communities and have focused on the need to
acquire the cultural skills and knowledge required to function
in a new cultural environment. The question of identity is not
as pressing for most immigrants and refugees as it is for members of oppressed ethnic and racial groups who were born in
the United States, because their separation from their culture
of origin is recent, and a firm sense of belonging to the culture
they come from is more easily maintained. Instead, the most
pressing problem for immigrants to a country is survival in their
new environment. Thus, for immigrants and refugees, the extent to which they are able to behave in ways that maximize
their participation in their surrounding community has become
the focus of investigation and intervention.

   On the other hand, the identity models were developed
to address the experience of ethnic and racial minority groups
and have emphasized the consequences of oppression on the
minority experience. For members of racial and ethnic minority
groups, the language and knowledge of the majority culture
generally does not pose a problem in adapting to the surroundings. Rather, the experience of oppression has led to marginalization, making it difficult for minorities to have a positive sense
of their cultural identity, which is linked to self-esteem and other
psychological variables. Thus, in studying the acculturation of
ethnic and racial minority groups, attention has focused on understanding such identity development.

   The distinction between identity, or attitudinal, acculturation and behavioral acculturation has been addressed in the
literature and has been incorporated within the same model (Bir-

man & Tyler, 1994; Clark, Kaufman, & Pierce, 1976; Szapocznik, Scopetta, Kurtines, & Aranalde, 1978), suggesting that an individual may identify with one culture, but exhibit behavioral characteristics typical of another. Some support for the notion that attitudes and behavior may represent related but distinct processes is offered by a study of intergroup relations (Lambert, Mermigis, & Taylor, 1986). The authors examined how Greek Canadians rated other ethnic groups on a variety of dimensions that would suggest positive attitudes toward these groups, such as intelligence, honesty and trustworthiness, and kindness. Then the same subjects were asked how they would feel if members of these other ethnic groups were close to them, as co-workers, friends, neighbors, or spouses of their children. The results were startlingly different, suggesting that having positive attitudes toward other ethnic groups is not related to a willingness to interact with them. It is quite possible that the same distinction would hold for one's own ethnic group as well: liking and preferences for aspects of a culture or its members do not have to correspond to engaging in behaviors characteristic of that culture.

Acculturation: A Differentiated Model

It has been argued thus far that each of the different models of biculturalism and ethnic and racial identity has been developed in the context of the experience of specific groups in U.S. society. However, the phenomenon of acculturation is everpresent in a multicultural society such as the United States and is applicable to a variety of groups. Thus, a model is needed that might capture this diversity of experiences of acculturation. Such a model is outlined in this section.

An Expanded Typology

The acculturation models described thus far have varied with respect to whether they describe an alternation or a fusion image of biculturalism. Further, some models focus on behavioral participation in a culture, while others emphasize a psychological sense of identification with it. All of these distinctions can be captured by a revision of the four-square typology of acculturative styles, presented in Figure 12.1, by adding the dimension of whether the identity or behavioral aspects of acculturation are considered (see Figure 12.2). With this addition, each acculturating individual can be characterized by two distinct cultural orientations: one related to behavior and the other to identity. Many acculturative styles are possible in this model, resulting in up to sixteen different combinations of identity and behavior. Figure 12.2 outlines some of the more frequently encountered styles of acculturation.

    This expanded typology includes the three acculturative

Figure 12.2. Acculturation: A Differentiated Model.

Acculturative Styles	Identity Acculturation		Behavioral Acculturation	
Assimilation	Biculturalism	**Assimilation**	Biculturalism	**Assimilation**
	Separation	Marginality	Separation	Marginality
Separation	Biculturalism	Assimilation	Biculturalism	Assimilation
	Separation	Marginality	**Separation**	Marginality
Marginality	Biculturalism	Assimilation	Biculturalism	Assimilation
	Separation	**Marginality**	Separation	**Marginality**
Blended Biculturalism	**Biculturalism**	Assimilation	**Biculturalism**	Assimilation
	Separation	Marginality	Separation	Marginality
Instrumental Biculturalism	Biculturalism	Assimilation	**Biculturalism**	Assimilation
	Separation	**Marginality**	Separation	Marginality
Integrated Biculturalism	Biculturalism	Assimilation	**Biculturalism**	Assimilation
	Separation	Marginality	Separation	Marginality
Identity Exploration	Biculturalism	Assimilation	Biculturalism	**Assimilation**
	Separation	Marginality	Separation	Marginality

styles described in the earlier two-dimensional typology (Figure 12.1). Separation, or traditionalism, is characterized by high involvement in both identity and behavior in one's own culture and low involvement with respect to both in the majority culture. Assimilation is characterized by the opposite: high involvement in both identity and behavior in the majority culture and low involvement in one's culture of origin. Low involvement in both cultures with respect to both identity and behavior would represent marginalization. The remainder of all of the possible combinations represent many different types of biculturalism — as many as thirteen different types in this three-dimensional model. While many forms of biculturalism are possible, the following section describes the ones most frequently adopted by acculturating people: blended biculturalism, instrumental biculturalism, integrated biculturalism, and identity exploration.

Types of Biculturalism

Acculturation of bicultural individuals is complex and varied, and it is somewhat misleading to characterize any one individual as a "type," because few individuals exclusively adopt either alternation or fusion. As Agar (1991) points out, the extent to which bicultural individuals balance and incorporate aspects of the cultures they are in contact with can be likened to the processes by which they acquire, maintain, and incorporate language: "So, with culture we come to the same result as we did in the review of lexical issues. Two languages may be organized into overlapping or separate cultural frames — just as bilinguals have both one and two lexicons, recover their two languages after aphasia together and separately, free associate in ways that both do and do not show the influence of their other language, experience anomie but compensate with balance, feel that their identity in different languages in some ways is different and in some ways stays the same" (p. 174).

With this in mind, the typology presented below is not absolute. Further, the specific cultural, community, family, and other circumstances in which individuals live may interact with individual styles to create an even greater diversity of patterns.

Still, the typology presented can serve as a framework for understanding the myriad of ways acculturating individuals acquire, discard, blend, and transform their cultural realities.

Blended Biculturalism. The individual who is highly identified with both cultures and participates behaviorally in both is likely to have synthesized, or "fused," the two, like the multicultural person described by Ramirez (1984), and can be described as a blended bicultural. Agar (1991) describes the experience of an Arab American who has adopted a blended bicultural style: "At home in the Middle East I am seen as the Americanized Arab . . . and in America, I am seen as an Americanized Arab by people that have come to realize that they are Americanized Arabs also. Therefore, almost anywhere I go I make sure my world is full of Americanized Arabs" (p. 272). On one hand, the Arab American described here has come to terms with not feeling at home in either the American or Arab culture. On the other hand, in acknowledging that his own culture represents a blend of the two, he has transcended the limitations of both and seeks the companionship of others who have also synthesized the two into a new hyphenated identity. This experience is not alienating for him but gives him a sense of belonging to a community of other blended biculturals.

The blended bicultural style may be impossible to attain for members of some ethnic and racial groups, because for groups that experience oppression, identification with the culture of the dominant majority may include endorsing the society's racist attitudes. Thus, the two cultures involved may be in conflict for these individuals, making psychological affiliation to both impossible to attain.

Instrumental Biculturalism. Individuals adopting the instrumental bicultural style are like the blended biculturals in that they are involved in both cultures, but this involvement is limited to behavioral participation and does not include a psychological sense of identity. Thus, instrumental biculturals are likely to be torn about their sense of identity. They may be able to pass as members of either culture in a chameleonlike fashion, without the accompanying sense of identity as belonging to either or both cultures. The result is a sense of psychological marginality, though behaviorally, the individual is competent in both cultures. The instrumental bicultural is most likely to live outside a bicultural immigrant or minority community, feeling like an outsider in both worlds.

Integrated Biculturalism. Integrated biculturals are highly behaviorally involved in both cultures but do not have a blended identity; rather, they have a firm sense of identity as a member of their culture of origin. The last stages of theories of racial and ethnic identity describe such an integrated bicultural style, which is generally seen as most adaptive for members of oppressed groups. This style allows a strong identification with (or commitment to) one's own ethnicity, culture, and race; this sense of identity may be accompanied by pride and a positive sense of belonging to one's own people. At the same time, integrated biculturals are comfortable in the majority culture because they have the skills needed to survive in it. Among immigrants, integrated biculturals may speak English with an accent but without embarrassment. Such people are frequently called upon to represent the interests of their own communities, because they have the competence to converse with the dominant majority, yet maintain the integrity of their own cultural affiliation.

Identity Exploration. Individuals who are highly involved behaviorally in the majority culture and not their culture of origin, but who have a high identification with their culture of origin and not the majority culture, can be described as exploring their culture identity and wishing for a reconnection with their cultural roots. Such people may have grown up in the majority, or new, culture and may feel fairly comfortable in it. However, either because of a negative "encounter" experience, or out of interest, individuals in these circumstances may engage in a process of discovering their cultural roots. In this process, they may become strongly identified with the culture of their ancestors though unable to participate behaviorally, perhaps because no cultural community is around to provide such opportunities. To some extent, both the attempts of many members of the African American community to reconnect to their African heritage and the third stage in Phinney's theory (1989), which describes exploration of ethnic identity, are examples of this type of biculturalism.

Conclusion

The different types of biculturalism described above are not exhaustive, and many more combinations of identity and behavioral acculturation are possible. They may be conceptualized as stages, as in the ethnic identity models, or as distinct styles of acculturation that differ wih the demands of the particular context of resettlement or acculturation. The identity dimension of acculturation may be more critical for native-born members of ethnic and racial minority groups, while behavioral acculturation may be more important for immigrants; however, attending to both identity and behavior creates a richer picture of a bicultural acculturation process. Thus, each of the bicultural styles described above may be adaptive, depending on the individual; the circumstances of the ethnic, racial, and cultural groups to which the individual belongs; and the attitudes and constructions of ethnicity, race, and culture in a given society. Moreover, in some circumstances, assimilation may be a positive option, while in others separatism may be a useful strategy to ensure individual and group survival.

For example, a blended bicultural may feel alienated without a community of other blended biculturals around. Blended bicultural individuals may also be at a disadvantage when the two cultures involved are in conflict, because they have to experience this conflict within themselves. Instrumental biculturals can avoid such inner conflict, but they suffer from alienation from both cultures. Integrated biculturals may lack the flexibility to be able to truly participate in the majority culture and can become alienated from their children, who may grow up assimilated into it. Those who are exploring their identity may feel unable to bridge the gap between themselves and the culture they wish to claim for their own. Finally, though much modern writing in psychology argues against Stonequist's assumption (1937) that the acculturating individual will be a "marginal man" unless assimilation is achieved, it is important to remember that in some situations this may indeed be true. Living outside an ethnic community, a person who is able to "pass" as a member of the dominant group may see assimilation as a viable, adaptive, and psychologically healthy option, while under other circumstances, such as colonization, a separatist stance makes sense. Acculturation theorists need to make sure that by suggesting the "best" modes of acculturation, they do not blame people for adapting to their particular circumstances of cultural contact, particularly when those circumstances are coercive and oppressive. Instead, the theories must appreciate and explain individual choices within the demands of different cultural and sociopolitical contexts.

As a final comment, a return to the experience of acculturation for Jews can help caution against an overenchantment with the now-popular stance that biculturalism is advantageous for acculturating individuals. Acculturation has been a consistent theme in the history of the Jews in the Diaspora and, ironically, in the history of those who have "returned" to modern Israel, and have had to acculturate to the specific version of Jewish culture constructed there by its modern founders. The biblical heroes Moses and Joseph represent different attitudes toward acculturation. Joseph's assimilationist attitudes in Egypt allowed him to rise to a high position in Pharaoh's court and to help his family when they came there to survive the famine. Moses, however, was a separatist, leading the Jewish people out of Egypt to escape slavery. Both are heroes in Jewish history, for unless each of them did what he did, the Jewish people would not have survived either the famine in Canaan or slavery in Egypt. These examples serve as reminders that there are times, situations, and contexts when assimilation and separatism, and not biculturalism, are viable, understandable, and preferable acculturative options.

References

Agar, M. (1991). The biculture in bilingual. *Language in Society, 20,* 167–181.

Atkinson, D. R., Morten, G., & Sue, D. W. (1979). *Counseling American minorities: A cross cultural perspective.* Dubuque, IA: Brown.

Berry, J. W. (1980). Acculturation as varieties of adaptation. In A. Padilla (Ed.), *Acculturation: Theory, models and some new findings.* Boulder, CO: Westview Press.

Berry, J. W., Trimble, J., & Olmedo, E. (1986). Assessment of acculturation. In W. J. Lonner & J. W. Berry (Eds.), *Field methods in cross-cultural psychology.* Newbury Park, CA: Sage.

Birman, D. (1992). Biculturalism, sex role attitudes, and adjustment of Latino immigrant adolescents in the U.S. (Doctoral dissertation, University of Maryland, College Park, 1991). *Dissertation Abstracts International, 5304,* 2051.

Birman, D. (in press). Towards understanding the interactions between Soviet Jewish refugees and U.S. service providers: A cross-cultural perspective. In D. Birman, T. Bornemann, J. Carp, R. B. Cravens, B. Goldberg, P. Handelman, J. Schulhoff, & P. Seubert (Eds.), *National Conference on Soviet Refugee Health and Mental Health Conference Proceedings.* Kansas City, MO: Marion Merrell Dow/Spangler.

Birman, D., & Tyler, F. (1994). Acculturation and alienation of Soviet Jewish refugees in the United States. *Genetic, Social, and General Psychology Monographs, 120*(1), 101–115.

Brown, L. S. (1989). New voices, new visions: Toward a lesbian/gay paradigm for psychology. *Psychology of Women Quarterly, 13*(4), 445–458.

Buriel, R. (1984). Integration with traditional Mexican-American culture and sociocultural adjustment. In J. Martinez & R. Mendoza (Eds.), *Chicano psychology.* San Diego, CA: Academic Press.

Clark, M., Kaufman, S., & Pierce, R. C. (1976). Explorations of acculturation: Toward a model of ethnic identity. *Human Organization, 35*(3), 231–238.

Cross, W. E. (1971). The Negro to black conversion experience: Toward a psychology of black liberation. *Black World,* *20*(9), 13–27.

Eisele, J. C. (1983). Dewey's concept of cultural pluralism. *Educational Theory, 33*(3–4), 149–156.

Erikson, E. (1968). *Identity: Youth and crisis.* New York: W.W. Norton.

Fernandez-Barillas, H. J., & Morrison, T. L. (1984). Cultural affiliation and adjustment among male Mexican-American college students. *Psychological Reports, 55,* 855–860.

Franco, J. N. (1983). A developmental analysis of self-concept in Mexican American and Anglo school children. *Hispanic Journal of Behavioral Sciences, 5*(2), 207–218.

Garza, R. T., Romero, G. J., Cox, B. G., & Ramirez, M. (1982). Biculturalism, locus of control, and leader behavior in ethnically mixed small groups. *Journal of Applied Social Psychology, 12*(3), 237–253.

Gordon, M. (1964). *Assimilation in American life.* New York: Oxford University Press.

Helms, J. E. (1984). Towards a theoretical explanation of effects of race on counseling: A black and white model. *Counseling Psychologist, 12*(4), 153–165.

Helms, J. E. (1985). Cultural identity in the treatment process. In P. Pedersen (Ed.), *Handbook of cross-cultural counseling and psychotherapy.* Westport, CT: Greenwood Press.

LaFromboise, T., Coleman, H.L.K., & Gerton, J. (1993). Psychological impact of biculturalism: Evidence and theory. *Psychological Bulletin, 114*(3), 395–412.

Lambert, W. E., Mermigis, L., & Taylor, D. M. (1986). Greek Canadians' attitudes toward own group and other Canadian ethnic groups: A test of the multiculturalism hypothesis. *Canadian Journal of Behavioral Science, 18*(1), 35–51.

Mendoza, R. H. (1984). Acculturation and sociocultural variability. In J. R. Martinez, Jr., & R. H. Mendoza (Eds.), *Chicano psychology.* San Diego, CA: Academic Press.

Olmedo, E. L. (1979). Acculturation: A psychometric perspective. *American Psychologist, 34,* 1061–1070.

Parham, T. A., & Helms, J. E. (1985). The relationship of racial identity attitudes of self-actualization and affective states of black students. *Journal of Counseling Psychology, 32*(3), 431–440.

Phinney, J. S. (1989). Stages of ethnic identity development in minority group adolescents. *Journal of Early Adolescence, 9*(1–2), 34–49.

Phinney, J. S. (1990). Ethnic identity in adolescents and adults: Review of research. *Psychological Bulletin, 108*(3), 499–514.

Phinney, J. S., & Alipuria, L. L. (1990). Ethnic identity in college students from four ethnic groups. *Journal of Adolescence, 13,* 171–183.

Ramirez, M. (1983). *Psychology of the Americas: Mestizo perspectives on personality and mental health.* Elmsford, NY: Pergamon Press.

Ramirez, M. (1984). Assessing and understanding biculturalism and multiculturalism in Mexican-American adults. In J. L. Martinez, Jr., & R. H. Mendoza (Eds.), *Chicano psychology.* San Diego, CA: Academic Press.

Redfield, R., Linton, R., & Herskovits, M. J. (1936). Memorandum on the study of acculturation. *American Anthropologist, 38,* 149–152.

Rogler, L. H., Cortes, D. E., & Malgady, R. G. (1991). Acculturation and mental health status among Hispanics: Convergence and new directions for research. *American Psychologist, 46*(6), 585–597.

Simon, R. J., & Simon, J. L. (1982). The Jewish dimension among recent Soviet immigrants to the United States. *Jewish Social Studies, 44*(3–4), 283–290.

Stavrianos, L. S. (1966). *The world since 1500: A global history.* Englewood Cliffs, NJ: Prentice-Hall.

Stonequist, E. V. (1937). *The marginal man: A study in personality and culture conflict.* New York: Russell & Russell.

Szapocznik, J., Kurtines, W. M. & Fernandez, T. (1980). Bicultural involvement and adjustment in Hispanic-American youths. *International Journal of Intercultural Relations, 4,* 353–365.

Szapocznik, J., Scopetta, M., Kurtines, W., & Aranald, M. A. (1978). Theory and measurement of acculturation. *Interamerican Journal of Psychology, 12,* 113–130.

U.S. Immigration and Naturalization Service. (1991). *Statistical yearbook of the Immigration and Naturalization Service, 1990.* Washington, DC: U.S. Government Printing Office.

Watts, R., Machabanski, H., & Karber, B. (1993). Adolescence and diversity. In P. H. Tolan & B. J. Cohler (Eds.), *Handbook of clinical research and practice with adolescents.* New York: Wiley.

13

The Conceptualization of Racial Identity and Other "Racial" Constructs

Janet E. Helms

Social and behavioral scientists are becoming increasingly aware of the significance of social or collective identities as factors contributing to interpersonal and intrapersonal functioning and adjustment. In Western-oriented cultures, for instance, Taylor and Dube (1986) have discussed the vagaries involved in determining under what circumstances a person reacts to any given situation as a "we" rather than an "I." Social, or collective, identities can be defined as those social groups to which a person belongs; from which the person acquires a sense of self; by which society socializes, appraises, or makes sense of the person; and by which the person makes sense of herself or himself.

For psychologists, considerable confusion seems to surround the issue of specifying which of each person's many social groups can reasonably be assumed to form the core components of that person's identity during his or her lifetime. In

Note: In this chapter names of racial groups (such as Blacks and Whites) are capitalized, in accordance with the standard style of the American Psychological Association, third edition. Capitalizing these terms acknowledges that these labels are proper nouns referring to sociopolitically defined groups of people rather than adjectives describing skin color.

psychology in the United States, race has been the collective identity least acknowledged, valued, and investigated. Several reviewers of the literature have noted the virtual invisibility of race as a construct in psychological theory and research (Casas, 1984; Cox & Nkomo, 1990). For example, Cox and Nkomo reported that only 1.7 percent of 11,804 published articles in industrial organizational psychology from 1964 to 1989 concerned race, whereas 11 percent and 3.9 percent concerned the potential collective identity groups of gender and age, respectively.

In this chapter, I will argue that although race has been a neglected area of inquiry, racial-group membership is a core aspect of identity development in the United States regardless of a person's racial classification, because of the country's emphasis on racial markers as preliminary credentials for access to reward or punishment. Furthermore, I will suggest that the process by which identity development occurs is similar across racial groups, although the content within groups may differ depending on whether or not the person's group (rather than the person per se) is sociopolitically powerful.

Prior to making the argument for racial identity, it will be necessary to comment on the ways in which the construct of race has been investigated and defined in psychology. Although we would generally expect conceptualization and definition of a construct to precede operationalization, in fact, such has not been the case in psychology. Thus, at best, race in psychology is an ambiguous construct; at worst, it is an ever-changing specter.

Notwithstanding social scientists' difficulty in construing the term, I will argue that race is a salient collective identity in this society. I will use Black Americans (who have minority sociopolitical status) and White Americans (who have majority political status) as my illustrative groups, although I intend my points to be relevant to other racial groups of similar statuses as well.

How Has Race Been Studied?

Erikson (1968), usually considered to be the original social identity theorist in personality theory, suggested that successful human development requires resolution of intrapsychic conflict involving membership in the following groups: (1) gender, (2) religion, (3) age, (4) occupation, (5) political ideology, and (6) sexual orientation. Missing from Erikson's list as a salient aspect of identity was racial-group membership.

Although Erikson did view racial-group membership as a significant aspect of negative identity development in African Americans, he had no notion of racial-group membership as a significant aspect of White people's identities. Nor did he have a postulate by which identification with one's racial group could have positive implications for personality adjustment for members of any racial group.

Yet in the United States, of the many collective identity groups to which a person might belong, race is the most salient, enduring, recognizable, and inflammatory. Although Erikson might be excused for not portending the major societal implications of racial-group membership in today's society, contemporary theorists also have tended to shy away from the study of racial-group identity as an aspect of human development.

Efforts to avoid the topic of race as a psychological construct have taken one or more of four general forms: (1) treatment of race as a nominal or classificatory variable, (2) use of laboratory-defined constructs assumed to be analogous to race, (3) use of euphemisms for race, and (4) multiculturalism.

Nominal Race

Most of psychology uses the nominal approach when race is an area of inquiry. When race is treated as a nominal variable, individuals are classified into one of several supposedly mutually exclusive "racial" categories. Occasionally, the classification is based on observable physical characteristics (usually observed skin color), but more often it is based on self-designation, geographic location (for example, census track), or unspecified research criteria.

In the nominal approach, race is sometimes considered to be a status condition analogous to gender or religious affiliation and is frequently treated as a "nuisance" variable to be ignored rather than a viable construct in its own right. At other times, racial-group classification and biogenetic endowment or psychosocial endowment are used virtually synonymously, with different groups assumed to be differently endowed. Such racial classifications are then used to infer intrapsychic characteristics such as self-esteem, self-concept, and intelligence.

One example is a long-enduring methodology used to study the self-esteem of Black children. In this approach, Black and White children are shown Black and White dolls (or other facsimiles of people such as line drawings) and are asked to state which they prefer, which is prettier, and so on (Powell-Hopson & Hopson, 1988). Between-group differences in own-group preferences are used to infer levels of self-esteem and quality of racial socialization of Black (but not White) children.

The Doll Study methodology has been criticized by various authors (for example, Abdullah, 1988; Banks, 1976) because of its underlying assumption that group and individual identity characteristics can be inferred from a behavioral sample without measuring either aspect of identity. Knowledge of a person's racial-group classification reveals nothing about the person's self-esteem and probably nothing about her or his identity, and doll preferences reveal nothing about racial collective identity.

The problems inherent in the Doll Study approach to investigating collective racial identity in psychology can be generalized. The nominal approach reduces potentially complex psychological dimensions to mere demographic or group-level classifications from which information about individual behavior within groups is inferred rather than observed or measured.

Simulated Race

In the second approach by which race in psychology has been overlooked, "minority" and "majority" groups are created or simulated in a laboratory setting (Chaiken & Stangor, 1987). Such groups rarely are formed by using race as a dimension, they rarely include race as a factor in the hypothetical interactions that occur in the simulations, and the races of participants are rarely specified. Nevertheless, the minimal-group paradigm is occasionally used to speculate about how race (or rather majority-minority status) becomes a significant source of friction within society.

In the matter of collective racial identity, studies of illusory correlation and social stereotyping seem particularly relevant (Schaller & Maass, 1989). Illusory correlation refers to the hypothesis that people associate infrequently occurring concurrent events in their memory so that when one is recalled, so is the other. In the words of Schaller and Maass, "Because interactions with minority members are generally rare and because undesirable behaviors occur frequently, people are likely to overestimate the association between minority membership and negative behaviors [and underestimate the association between undesirable behaviors and majority membership]" (p. 709). In Schaller and Maass's study, as is typical of studies in this genre, minorities and majorities were produced by presenting subjects with more (majority) or less (minority) descriptive statements about hypothetical stimulus persons alleged to be members of Group A or Group B. Stereotyping was inferred from reactions (that is, illusory correlations) under varying conditions of attribution presentation.

Minimal-group researchers' use of quasi-racial language does not parallel its usage in society more generally. In society, *minority* typically refers to racial or ethnic groups of color, and *stereotyping* frequently refers to the attribution of negative characteristics to people of color. In society, these terms are emotionally laden. Thus, the minimal-group strategy trivializes the complex psychological history as well as the sociopolitical history of racial dynamics in this country by implying that twenty minutes or so in a laboratory can duplicate these dynamics.

Euphemistic Race

The third approach used to study race in psychology avoids consideration of race per se by substituting euphemisms such as *ethnicity* or *culture* for the construct of race. In their analysis of the terminology used to describe nontraditional students in the educational literature from 1950 through 1989, Westbrook and

Sedlacek (1991) point out that usage of derivatives of culture (for example, multicultural, culturally deprived, and cross-cultural) became prevalent. They note: "If non-White ethnic minority groups cooperate in having themselves labeled with any of the current terms that include 'cultural,' they have a choice between being put-down with 'culturally deprived' or of being put-out (of the national citizenship network) with 'cross-cultural'" (p. 25).

A basic premise underlying the euphemistic perspective is that if the word *race* is not used, it does not exist as a meaningful societal construct and as an element of a person's identity formation. The unintended consequences of this approach are that (1) it encourages the use of deficit models to investigate the psychology of members of groups of color and (2) it consigns racial collective identity to groups other than Whites while ignoring the implications of the construct of racial identity for White people.

Race Subsumed by Multiculturalism

In the multiculturalism approach, other aspects of diversity or types of collective identity such as gender, religious affiliation, or sexual orientation are held to be equivalent to race in terms of sociopolitical implications and psychological consequences. Thus, it is assumed that whatever is true of race as a psychological characteristic is also true of these other diversities to the same extent and in the same ways.

This assumption of the equivalence of collective identity is apparent in the phrase "women and racial or ethnic minorities." "Women" should include women members of racial or ethnic minority groups but apparently does not; "racial or ethnic minority groups" ought to include women as well as men, but apparently does not. In psychology, theorists' and researchers' unwillingness to discriminate between the various identity groups has contributed to imprecise specification of the types of oppression experienced by each. Consider, for example, how much more interpretable the following quote would be if the author had acknowledged the multiple classifications of the population being discussed: "White workers and management [White men?) may believe that minorities [women and men?] and [White?] women are less suitable for management roles or positions in the company than are nonminorities [White men and White women?] and [White and minority?] men" (Sue, 1991, p. 102). Be that as it may, the combining of potential collective identity groups is usually intended to communicate an experience of shared oppression.

Although applications of multiculturalism have proliferated since the 1960s (Axelson, 1993; Pedersen, 1991), it is virtually impossible to find a conceptual or operational definition of the term. According to Pedersen, "The multicultural perspective combines the extremes of universalism and relativism by explaining behavior both in terms of those culturally learned perspectives that are unique to a particular culture [for example, phenomena of racism, sexism, ageism, and other exclusionary perspectives] and in the search for common-ground universals [an overexaggeration of which was the melting pot metaphor] that are shared across cultures" (p. 6). He further adds that multiculturalism is no longer limited to the analysis of "exotic groups," but can also be used to understand ourselves (whoever that might be).

The multicultural perspective's major strength and major deficit is that it intends to be all-inclusive. Too pluralistic an approach communicates the message that the construct of race holds no different psychological significance than do any of the variety of dimensions on which humans may vary or the social groups to which they might be assigned; therefore, it requires no special theoretical consideration or investigation. Consequently, it has the potential to move the field even further away from the issue of how or whether racial-group commitment is a meaningful aspect of people's collective identity.

What Is Race?

Considerable confusion exists with respect to the definition of race. In addition to the previously discussed alternatives, such as multicultural and minority or majority status, the terms *culture, ethnicity,* and *race* are often used interchangeably. Neither culture nor ethnicity necessarily has anything to do with race as the term is typically used in U.S. society or psychology. Therefore, it is useful to suggest a definition for each of these terms and propose a definition for race as used by racial identity theorists.

Culture

Culture might be thought of as at least two constructs, a macroculture (symbolized here as CULTURE) and a variety of subsidiary cultures identified with particular collective identity groups (symbolized here as "culture"). Thus, culture pertains to the customs, values, traditions, products, and sociopolitical histories of the social groups that exist within a CULTURE, whereas CULTURE refers to the dominant society or group's epistemology or worldview. It is the not necessarily conscious guiding principles of life to which all members of a society (regardless of social-group memberships) are expected to conform. Tensions occur between the person and other members of the CULTURE when his or her observable actions or ascribed personality traits are assumed to be incongruent with the rules of the CULTURE.

Various authors (Kluckhohn & Strodtbeck, 1961; Katz, 1976; Boykin, 1983) have attempted to delineate the central dimensions of CULTURE. Although groups within CULTURES may differ in the extent to which they conform to its principles, in general, social groups (for instance, gender groups) within a CULTURE adopt characteristics sufficient to make themselves distinguishable to themselves and others from members of other CULTURES, even if they are of the same race. Stewart (1972), for example, has delineated an American macroculture valuing "rugged individualism" as opposed to the collective orientations said to characterize many Asian countries, such as Japan or China. In the United States, great personal success in spite of societal obstacles is considered heroic, whereas in Japan, a smoothly functioning society is considered heroic.

In other words, CULTURE is that intangible aspect of identity that often allows Americans of different races to recognize and accept each other when they are in another country better than they do when they are at home. CULTURE is also what causes sojourners to another CULTURE to approach their experience with impatience, anxiety, or trepidation, that is, with "culture shock," and perhaps occasionally with appreciation. People can form commitments to a CULTURE (that is, a CULTURAL identification) that differ markedly from their racial-group identifications. CULTURAL identifications, then, represent macro-level or global aspects of identity and might appropriately be measured and otherwise studied by macro-level constructs such as worldview or value orientation inventories (Carter & Helms, 1990; Ibrahim & Kahn, 1987).

Ethnicity

Although ethnicity is often used as a euphemism for race as well as for other sociocultural affiliations (such as religious and linguistic groups, it might better be defined as a social identity based on the culture of one's ancestors' national or tribal groups as modified by the demands of the CULTURE in which one's group currently resides. Quoting Van den Berghe (1977), Jones (1991) contends that ethnicity "[refers to] a group that is *socially defined on the basis of cultural criteria*" (p. 454; emphasis in original). Thus, customs, traditions, and values rather than physical appearance per se define ethnicity. People who consider ethnicity to be one of their collective identities not only identify with a particular ethnic group, but also are linked by their willingness to share or at least pretend to share aspects of a common ethnic-group culture.

Casas (1984) has pointed out that the same ethnic group can consist of individuals of various races and that any single racial group is made up of many ethnicities. From Kelman's perspective (1961), an individual's ethnic identity is defined by a group whose values, beliefs, and customs the individual adopts or internalizes because the group is important to her or his sense of self in a manner that might not be obvious to observers. Thus, although ethnic classification may be inferred from external criteria such as physical characteristics or symbolic behaviors (for example, ethnic dress), ethnicity is self-defined and maintained because it "feels good" rather than because it is necessarily imposed by powerful others. Consequently, although the individual may form a collective identity based on dimensions of ethnicity that are visible and/or meaningful to him or her and other members of the ethnic group, it is unlikely that societal rewards and punishments will be associated with ethnicity unless its membership dimensions are made salient and easily recognizable by nongroup members with reinforcement or punishment powers.

Phinney's discovery (1989) that the term *ethnicity* meant nationality to White Americans, but race, ethnicity, or cultural group to Black, Asian, and Latino adolescents, probably means that members of the respective groups initially internalize different social identities. It also suggests that in the absence of consistent societal messages regarding ethnicity, the construct may have few, if any, implications for intergroup interactions independent of CULTURE, culture, or race.

Nevertheless, theorists and researchers in the United States who have speculated about the effects of ethnicity on identity development have not operationally defined the concept in a manner that distinguishes it from other similar collective identity constructs. Moreover, they have often confused the terms *ethnic identity* and *ethnic classification*. Identity is defined from the inside (of the person) out (to the world), whereas classification is defined from the outside in.

Race

Although race and ethnicity have been confounded in psychological literature, in practice they have had different sociopolitical consequences, and therefore they may have different implications for an individual's collective identity development. Presumably, members of groups whose experiences of oppression or domination were based on racial rather than ethnic classification must resolve the tensions associated with that aspect of themselves more than those for whom the converse was true.

In the United States, race is a reified, socially defined

categorization system that has become the basis of one form of social identity. Various authors (Zuckerman, 1990; King, 1981) have observed that the necessary biological characteristics required to unequivocally differentiate one so-called racial group from another do not exist, perhaps because of centuries of cross-racial mating or because all peoples have evolved from the same original African ancestors.

Racial demarcations in psychology and, more generally, in contemporary society are even more obscure, because we usually do not have to search through antiquity for evidence of racial mixing. Nevertheless, in the United States, the national societal consensus is that there are four distinguishable racial groups — Asians, Blacks, Whites, and Native Americans. While often treated as a fifth racial group, Latinos may exhibit the "racial" characteristics or phenotypes of the other groups (Casas, 1984).

The irrationality of the racial classification system becomes quite evident when we consider Native Americans. The original Native Americans are assumed to have had Asian ancestors who migrated to the Americas from Asia, but as a result of sexual exploitation, oppression, and interracial liaisons and marriages, present-day Native Americans are mixtures of Asian, African, and White ancestry (LaDue, 1990). To distinguish them from members of other "racial" groups, the federal government uses "blood quantum," or the amount of "Indian blood" a person possesses. LaDue reports that originally 25 percent Native American ancestry was required to be considered a member of a tribe, but because this excludes so many who identify themselves as Native Americans, several tribes have revised this standard to include any person who can verify that a parent or grandparent was an enrolled member of the tribe in which the person intends to enroll. Moreover, for Native Americans, it is adherence to cultural norms that identifies an individual as a member of the group (LaFromboise, 1988).

To further illustrate the confusion, according to Samuda (1975), who uses several sources, including Pettigrew (1964), of the group commonly known as "black" (descendants at least in part of the Africans who were in the United States during the slavery era), the majority (72 to 83 percent) have at least one known White ancestor, 25 percent have equal numbers of Black and White ancestors, 27 percent have at least one known Native American ancestor, and the average Black person has a minimum of from 25 to 31 percent "white genes." Consequently, Samuda argues, "The average American black [sic] is about as far removed from the pure Negroid type as he is from the pure Caucasian type" (p. 53).

Various legal and governmental procedures have been used to differentiate Blacks from members of other racial groups, including last names and percentages of African ancestry. In many Southern states, registries of "black" last names were kept to identify Black people even if they did not look Black. Moreover, in what has been referred to as the "one-drop rule," as little as one-thirty-second of known African ancestry was considered sufficient to classify a person as Black (Spickard, 1992). For members of the group itself, however, perceptions of a shared history of sociopolitical oppression is usually enough to define a person as Black regardless of physical appearance.

As a means of escaping racial oppression, many Blacks whose physical characteristics permitted "passed" into White or Asian racial groups, whereas others chose to identify with their Native American or Latino cultural heritage. Passing, or clandestinely entering into another racial group, may occur among Asians and Native Americans as well, although this issue does not frequently appear in the relevant literature. Since Whites are the dominant racial group, they can choose to expel from their ranks individuals who do not look White, making it difficult to assess the purity of the White group. Thus, the group may appear more racially homogeneous than it actually is.

In spite of the ambiguity of racial classifications, in this country, people "know" to which group they belong by the time they are three years old, although they may not understand the social implications of such group membership (Katz, 1976). Even individuals who describe themselves as "biracial" or "multicultural" generally know which groups define them (Root, 1992).

Elsewhere, Helms (1992) and Gotunda (1991) have argued that race as used in the United States has three types of definitions: (1) quasi-biological, (2) sociopolitical-historical, and (3) cultural. Each type may have relevance for how race becomes one of an individual's collective identities.

Quasi-Biological Race. Quasi-biological definitions of race are based on visible aspects of a person that are assumed to be racial in nature, such as skin color, hair texture, or physiognomy. These characteristics are assumed to be present in each racial group in some form but to differ in type sufficiently to distinguish members of one group from another. Thus, Native Americans and Asian Americans are assumed to have some skin color that supposedly differs from that of White Americans, who, in turn, supposedly differ from Black Americans.

Group-defining racial characteristics generally are selected by the dominant or sociopolitically powerful group. Thus, in the United States, White people specify the relevant racial traits and use themselves as the standard or comparison group. Native Americans are considered "red" as compared to Whites; Blacks are black in contrast to Whites. The selected racial-group defining traits are assumed to be stable, enduring, and mutually exclusive; to have a genetic or biological basis; and to influence a person's psychological aspects such as intelligence and personality.

However, racial characteristics so defined are quasi-biological, because the phenotype (physical appearance) reveals virtually nothing about the genotype (genetic makeup). As Zuckerman (1990) points out: "For features like skin color, which can be ranged on a metric, there is great variation within, as well as between, so-called races. In Africa, skin color of groups called *Negroid* ranges from black or dark brown to yellowish tan. There are groups classified as *Caucasoid* who are darker than certain African groups classified as Negroid. The same diversity in various features exists in European groups" (p. 1298).

Moreover, observable racial markers are social constructs or fictions rather than biological realities because the varieties of racial groups in the United States change even though the physical markers on which they are based apparently do not. Thus, according to Spickard (1992), "In 1870, the U.S. Bureau

of the Census divided up the American population into *races:*
White, Colored (Blacks), Colored (Mulattoes), Chinese, and
Indian. . . . In 1950, [the races were] White, Black, and Other.
By 1980, the census categories reflected the *ethnic* blossoming
of the previous decades: White, Black, Hispanic, Japanese,
Chinese, Filipino, Korean, Vietnamese, American Indian, [and
seven other mostly Asian categories]" (p. 18; emphasis added).

The "blossoming" to which Spickard (1992) alludes perhaps reveals the differential salience of Spanish CULTURE for
Latinos and ethnic cultures for Asians as sources of collective
identity. It may also symbolize the group boundaries that were
the basis for these groups' sociopolitical oppression. Thus, different laws and regulations have pertained to the various Asian
ethnic groups in spite of the fact that non-Asians and sometimes
Asian ethnics themselves have difficulty differentiating between
the groups (Helms, 1989; Sue & Sue, 1990).

With the exception of two groups, White and Black, the
census categories do not represent different racial groups even
if they are defined by imprecise physical criteria. However, they
do suggest that racial-group membership may be an important
source of identity for Blacks and Whites, if an individual's collective identity depends on society's recognition of his or her
group status. The imprecision of racial-group categories perhaps
accounts for theorists' attempts to find euphemisms for race
(Westbrook & Sedlacek, 1991). Yet calling race by any other
name does not change its sociopolitical implications within mac-
rocultures or the smaller cultural groups existing within those
cultures. Nor does it change the significance of race to people
who must survive in environments that differentially value or
devalue their ascribed racial characteristics.

Sociopolitical Race. Race can also refer to a quasi-biologically
defined racial group's sociopolitical history and experiences of
domination and/or subjugation. According to Spickard (1992),
efforts to differentiate groups by means of mutually exclusive
racial categories also imply a hierachy with respect to psychological characteristics, such as intelligence and morality, with
gradations in skin color or other relevant racial-group markers

determining the group's location along the hierarchy. On virtually every socially desirable dimension, the descending order
of superiority has been Whites, Asians, Native Americans, and
Africans. Contemporary racial sociobiologists tend to use the
same hierarchy, except that the order of Asians and Whites is
sometimes reversed (Rushton, 1988).

According to Franklin (1991), Thomas Jefferson made
"the classic early American statement on the innate inferiority
of blacks [sic] and Native Americans" when he observed: "Comparing them by their faculties of memory, reason, and imagination it appears to me, that in memory they are equal to whites
[sic], in reason much inferior; as I think one could scarcely be
found tracing and comprehending the investigations of Euclid;
and that in imagination they are dull, tasteless, and anomalous"
(p. 208).

The racial-superiority hierarchy historically was used to
justify the enslavement and racial oppression of people of color
in this country as well as to justify the advantaged status of
Whites. It can be argued that each new group that migrated
to the country was fitted with one of the preexisting sets of racial stereotypes. Thus, for example, like Native Americans and
Black Americans before them, Asian Americans were originally
stereotyped as "immoral," "oversexed," "unclean," and with "low
standards of living" (Takaki, 1989).

Native Americans, followed by African Americans, have
had the longest and most consistently negative sociopolitical histories of oppression under a White-dominant "racial" group. It
seems evident that when intergroup contact occurs between these
groups, perceived similarities and dissimilarities of sociopolitical experience will be one dimension by which each defines its
own social (racial) identity as well as the social identity of the
other groups. The shared sociopolitical history then becomes
an aspect of each group's culture.

However, because Asian and Latino Americans' experiences of discrimination in this country have varied according
to ethnicity and perhaps CULTURE and perceived race, the construct of race may not have as much meaning to them or consistent meaning to their potential oppressors. Therefore, whether

or in what manner racial groups act as a source of social identity for these groups is not clear.

Cultural Race. As previously mentioned, "culture" refers to the customs, traditions, products, and values of (in this instance) a racial group. Many theorists locate the origins of racial-group cultures in ancient or classic CULTUREs such as those of Greece or Africa. For instance, Myers's version of Afrocentric transpersonal psychology (1985) is drawn from "the teachings of ancient Africans (i.e., Egyptians over 5,000 years ago)" (p. 34). However these CULTUREs have become cultures in order to survive in the larger sociopolitical system. That is, to the extent that groups exist in close proximity, certain of their CULTURAL principles are likely to be modified by diffusion across groups, oppression, and other forms of social influence. Moreover, natural changes in CULTUREs caused by evolution over time also serve to change CULTUREs to cultures within groups.

Thus, in the case of Whites and Blacks in the United States, we may expect some similarities in culture resulting from periods during which the groups have existed in close proximity. However, we may also expect dissimilarities because Whites, as the sociopolitically dominant group, could (and can) (1) determine the distance between groups through policies of racial segregation and (2) determine which aspects of CULTURE are socially desirable. Thus, the current debates over multiculturalism in the educational system reflect attempts by White Americans to maintain their CULTURAL dominance while people of color are attempting to redefine CULTURE to include their own cultures.

One consequence of either self-selected or imposed racial-group separation is that the dimensions that define cultures survive through intracultural group breeding. These cultures may have dimensions that are traceable back to ancient CULTUREs; they may also have dimensions resulting from the different sociopolitical experiences of racial groups within this country. Thus, we would expect the cultures of groups of color to share some cultural similarities to the extent that the groups have experienced similar forms and amounts of racial oppression. The assumption of homogeneity resulting from similar oppression underlies general models of oppression and identity development (Atkinson, Morten, & Sue, 1989; Ossana, Helms, & Leonard, 1992). However, to the extent that groups' experiences of racial oppression or CULTURAL origins differ, the content of their identity development (though not necessarily the process) should also differ. Therefore, the content of the racial identity of African and European Americans is different because both the CULTURAL origins and the sociopolitical histories of the two groups in this country have differed markedly.

Development of Racial Identity

For all racial groups in the United States, a primary identity issue concerns the development of a positive sense of oneself as a member of a racial group in a racist society. For African Americans and other groups of color, the central themes in development are the effort required to overcome society's generally negative evaluation of their group and the development of an identity with its roots in the culture and sociopolitical experiences of their socially ascribed racial group. For Whites (that is, European Americans and those Whites who are commonly assumed to share such origins), central developmental issues are the recognition and abandonment of internalized White privilege and the creation of a nonracist, self-defining White identity.

Theoretical Models

Helms (1993) proposes that for all groups, the process is characterized by successive differentiations of the ego, called ego statuses. The statuses are not assumed to be mutually exclusive or discontinuous. Rather, we might think of them as arranging themselves within a circumplex (symbolizing the ego), with the statuses that occupy the greatest percentage of the ego having the most influence over an individual's racial identity or self-expression. The statuses that develop later in the process are more cognitively complex and permit the person to cope with and negotiate increasingly more complex racial information about herself or himself as well as others. Nevertheless, once a status "appears" within the ego, it is always potentially available to influence the quality of the person's functioning to some extent. Dominant statuses are those that are reinforced most consistently in the environments in which the person interacts, that help to maintain the individual's own personal esteem, and that require the least amount of personal suffering.

In earlier versions of racial identity theory, Helms (1990, 1992) as well as other identity theorists (see Atkinson, Morten, & Sue, 1989) used the concept of stages rather than ego statuses to define the developmental process. However, because people tend to think of stages as being located external to the person and of transitions between stages as being fixed or relatively stable, such usage encourages minimization of the dynamic aspects of the developmental process. Substitution of the construct of ego status or differentiation of the ego means that once an ego status has manifested itself, it is always potentially present, although the ego as a whole is always potentially changing in response to new (racial) societal messages. Thus, earlier modes of coping can influence people even after they think that they have resolved their racial identity issues.

The characteristics of the various ego statuses are summarized in Table 13.1 for people of color and Table 13.2 for Whites (see Helms, 1990). For African Americans, the model I have used most often has been the adaptations of Cross's Negro-to-Black conversion model (1971). For other groups of color, I have recommended Atkinson, Morten, & Sue's model (1989) with slight modifications. Table 13.1 presents side-by-side comparisons of the two perspectives to illustrate that their content is similar even though the names of developmental constructs within each perspective differ. With respect to White identity, although other models of White identity exist (see Hardiman, 1982; Sabnani, Ponterotto, & Borodovsky, 1991), Helms's model (1984, 1990) is the only one to date to have received any empirical substantiation (Helms, 1990).

For each group, the statuses are listed in ascending order of complexity. Thus, for African Americans and other groups of color, Pre-encounter or Conformity are the first statuses to evolve and the least cognitively complex, whereas Contact is the analogous status for Whites. For the groups of color, be-

Table 13.1. Summary of Analogous Racial Identity Ego Statuses
Adapted from Conversion and MID Racial Identity Models.

Model and Statuses		
Negro-to-Black	*MID*	*Composite Description*
Pre-encounter	Conformity	Minimization of membership or denigration of one's own as well as other VREGs;[a] idealization of Whites and White culture
Encounter	Dissonance	Disorientation and confusion regarding own-group and majority-group affiliations and appreciation
Immersion and emersion	Resistance and immersion	Idealization of one's own VREG and physical and psychological withdrawal into one's own group; rejection and denigration of "Whiteness"
	Introspection	Search for a more rational group self-definition and more balanced intergroup relations
Internalization	Integrative awareness	Positive sense of VREG self, capacity to value and respect other racial and ethnic groups
Internalization and commitment		Recognition of shared oppressions with broad range of societal groups and the will to promote change

[a]The term *visible racial and ethnic groups* (VREGs) is used to refer collectively to Asian, Black, Native, and Hispanic Americans of color.

Source: Status descriptions are Helms's condensations and adaptations (1992) of Cross's Negro-to-Black conversion model (1971) and Atkinson, Morten, & Sue's minority (racial/ethnic) identity development model (MID) (1989, 1990).

cause society professes assimilation as a universal ideal while making it impossible for members of these groups without abandoning respect for their own racial groups, the first ego status impels people of color toward assimilation and, therefore, to nonconscious internalized racism or own-group deprecation. Later statuses involve attempts to overcome the negative personal effects of disparaging one's own racial group as well as of society's deprecation of the group, to become aware of the effects of racism on the group, and to evolve a racial identity based on greater (racial) self-actualization and definition.

On the other hand, the assimilation norm requires Whites

Table 13.2. Summary of Some Characteristics
of White Racial Identity Ego Statuses.

Type of Ego Status	General Description	Behavioral-Cognitive Dimensions
Contact	Naïveté, obliviousness to sociopolitical implications of race	Has difficulty consciously thinking of self as White; claims to be color-blind and thinks it a positive attribute
Disintegration	Disorientation and confusion	First conscious acknowledgment of the value of being White; awareness of racial moral dilemmas is salient
Reintegration	Endorsement of White superiority and supremacy is guiding theme	Displaced anger and hostility toward people of color is in the forefront; identity is maintained by increasing White privilege
Pseudoindependence	Intellectualized acknowledgment of implications of racial-group membership; feels responsible for "helping" the less fortunate groups become more like Whites	Attempts to resolve racial tensions by feeling guilty; believes that racism is not personally relevant if one has a friend of color; contends that racism is engaged in only by bad Whites
Immersion and emersion	A search to define and abandon personal racism and to define a nonracist White identity	Attempts to help Whites understand their role in perpetuating racism; tries to build a network of nonracist Whites
Autonomy	Racial humanism; internally defined nonracist identity; valuing of racial diversity	Seeks opportunities to increase the diversity in his or her life; does not force White culture on others

Source: Adapted from J. E. Helms, 1992.

to push from their awareness the benefits of White privilege that accrue from belonging to the White group. Whites who can camouflage those cultural circumstances (for example, traditions) or sociopolitical circumstances (for example, ethnicity) that distinguish them from other Whites can assimilate into the White group and compete with in-group members for societal resources without feeling guilty about the suffering of groups of color.

Disavowal of the existence of White privilege takes the form of denying that a White *racial* group exists that benefits from White privilege. For instance, in criticizing a White identity development model attributed to Sue and Sue (1990), Axelson (1993) argues that White identity does not exist because (1) there are no pure races, (2) various White ethnic groups as well as groups of color worldwide could be racist if the conditions were right, and (3) even if light-skinned Europeans think that they are superior to others, theorists should not address the implications of White racial-group membership on White people's identity development in the United States because "[to do so] seems to be a throwback to the rhetoric of Black-White encounter groups during the late 1960s and early 1970s wherein the participants would verbally attack each other and, feeling satisfied, go their separate ways" (p. 397).

From Axelson's perspective, a true multicultural orientation requires that theorists and practitioners ignore the differential implications of race on individual development as well as on intergroup relations in society. Though Axelson's observation concerning racial purity is true, it does not negate the historical and sociological evidence that in the United States, the White group has proceeded as though it were not only pure, but superior. Whether or not White people or people of color in other countries do or could practice racism is irrelevant to the matter of how White people in this country develop racial identity. Moreover, if White people better understood the processes by which their own racial identity issues aggravate racial tensions, there would be fewer of the types of confrontations that so distress Axelson (Helms, 1992).

Be that as it may, the dialectic between the statuses is that earlier statuses and later evolving statuses may pull an individual in contradictory directions. Recognition of the existence of these contradictory forces makes it possible to explain how the same individual can engage in contradictory racial behavior even within a short span of time. So, for instance, Hacker (1992) can ask of his racemates, "[Is] it right to impose on members of an entire [Black] race a lesser start in life, and then to expect from them a degree of resolution that has never been demanded from your [our?] own [White] race?" (p. 218).

Within that single question, the operation of at least two ego statuses is apparent. The first and more psychologically advanced (immersion and emersion) motivates him to educate Whites about their role in promoting racism, whereas the second (pseudoindependence) allows him to distance himself from his own racial group and, consequently, from his portion of personal responsibility for maintaining racism. The first status is evidenced by his capacity to raise the question at all and the second is reflected in his use of the second-person possessive, ("your") rather than the first-person possessive ("our") with respect to race.

Implications

Racial identity models may be used to examine the manner in which racial group becomes at least one of a person's collective identities. However, if the developmental process is as complex as Helms (1990, 1992) hypothesizes, then it may involve more than a dichotomous commitment to one group rather than another. Moreover, the consequences or outcomes of the developmental process may have implications for the individual's level of adjustment as well as for the quality of the interactions in which she or he engages and for the environment more generally.

From my perspective, race is defined primarily as a sociopolitical construct rather than a quasi-biological or cultural construct. Increasing maturity signifies increasing awareness of the conditions of oppression associated with race and the manner in which they have been internalized. Thus, whereas it is possible that individuals may not appear to be members of the racial group to which their ancestors belonged, as long as they are aware of that ancestry, then they must find a way of resolving the sociopolitical issues associated with that status. Also, whereas it is possible that as people mature with respect to racial identity, they will become more cognizant of the cultural dimensions of their relevant racial group and engage in those cultural practices themselves, it is also possible that they will not. Similarly, it is possible that people who lack maturity with respect to racial identity development will consistently engage in the cultural practices of their racial group. Racial identity and cultural identity are not necessarily congruent.

Conclusion

The foregoing discussion suggests that in psychology, theorists, researchers, and practitioners have relied too heavily on sterile conceptualizations of race and simplistic explanations of human race-related behavior (for example, nominal strategies). It also suggests that resolution of societal conflict concerning race requires social scientists to become more adventurous in their consideration of race as a psychological construct.

For psychologists in particular, it seems important that we move from merely treating race, culture, and related constructs as nominal categories whose complexities can be understood by locating people in one category rather than another. Moreover, as long as the variety of "racial" constructs are treated as synonyms, their differential impact on human existence must surely remain hidden. Consensual use of the various race-related constructs may require the development of different theoretical approaches as well as innovative research methodologies in which each entity is treated as a potentially independent force in collective identity development. Some recommendations follow from conceptualizing race as a social identity dimension to viewing it from a racial identity perspective. They also pertain more generally to the investigation of race in psychology.

First, in theorizing about or investigating racial identity as an individual variable, it may be important to develop and make use of idiographic or emic methodologies. We may need to make use of constructs that reflect the unique racial history of the individual we are attempting to assess.

Second, if the notion of successively more complex ego differentiations has merit, it may be important to devise more complex and diverse strategies for assessing racial identity development. For the most part, psychology has been constrained by its virtually exclusive emphasis on linear approaches to personality assessment as reflected in classical test theory (Nunnally, 1978). Moreover, ease of quantification often has been the basis by which a construct's existence is determined. The search for strategies to validly represent the complexity of racial identity development may force psychologists to search for alternative and more flexible methodologies for representing an individual's reality.

Third, existing evidence suggests that it may not be appropriate to generalize across racial groups in this country. Premature acceptance of a universalistic or multicultural perspective may aggravate rather than resolve societal tensions. Thus, it may be important to conceptualize universal processes that potentially operate across groups (such as racial identity development) and then develop group-specific definitions or descriptions and methods for operationalizing them.

A final implication is that psychologists should actually begin investigating the psychological dimensions of race for all racial groups within the society rather than merely proceeding as though they have done so. Racial identity models offer one approach by which this complex task can be begun.

References

Abdullah, S. B. (1988). The media and the Doll Studies. *Journal of Black Psychology, 14*(2), 75–77.

Atkinson, D. R., Morten, G., & Sue, D. W. (1989). *Counseling American minorities: A cross-cultural perspective.* Dubuque, IA: Brown.

Axelson, J. A. (1993). *Counseling and development in a multicultural society* (2nd ed.). Pacific Grove, CA: Brooks/Cole.

Banks, W. C. (1976). White preference in blacks: A paradigm in search of a phenomenon. *Psychological Bulletin, 83*, 1179–1186.

Boykin, A. W. (1983). The academic performance of Afro-American children. In J. T. Spence (Ed.), *Achievement and achievement motives* (pp. 322–371). New York: W. H. Freeman.

Carter, R. T., & Helms, J. E. (1990). Intercultural Values Inventory. *Tests in microfiche test collection.* Princeton, NJ: Educational Testing Service.

Casas, J. M. (1984). Policy, training and research in counseling psychology: The racial/ethnic perspective. In S. D. Brown & R. W. Lent (Eds.), *Handbook of counseling psychology* (pp. 785–831). New York: Wiley.

Chaiken, S., & Stangor, C. (1987). Attitudes and attitude change. *Annual Review of Psychology, 38,* 575–630.

Cox, T., Jr., & Nkomo, S. (1990). Invisible men and women: A status report on race as a variable in organization behavior research. *Journal of Organizational Behavior, 11,* 419–431.

Cross, W. E. (1971). The Negro to Black conversion experience: Toward a psychology of Black liberation. *Black World, 20*(9), 13–27.

Erikson, E. (1968). *Identity: Youth and crisis.* New York: W.W. Norton.

Franklin, V. P. (1991). Black social scientists and the mental testing movement, 1920–1940. In R. L. Jones (Ed.), *Black psychology* (pp. 207–224). Berkeley, CA: Cobb & Henry.

Gotunda, N. (1991). A critique of "Our constitution is color-blind." *Stanford Law Review, 44,* 1–69.

Hacker, A. (1992). *Two nations.* New York: Charles Scribner's Sons.

Hardiman, R. (1982). *White identity development: A process oriented model for describing the racial consciousness of White Americans.* Unpublished doctoral dissertation, University of Massachusetts, Amherst.

Helms, J. E. (1984). Towards a theoretical explanation of effects of race on counseling: A Black and White model. *Counseling Psychologist, 12*(4), 153–165.

Helms, J. E. (1989). At long last—paradigms for cultural psychology research. *Counseling Psychologist, 17*(1), 98–101.

Helms, J. E. (1990). *Black and white racial identity: Theory, research, and practice.* Westport, CT: Greenwood Press.

Helms, J. E. (1992). *A race is a nice thing to have: A guide to being a white person or understanding the white persons in your life.* Topeka, KS: Content Communications.

Helms, J. E. (1993). I also said, "White racial identity influences white researchers." *Counseling Psychologist, 21,* 240–243.

Ibrahim, F. A., & Kahn, H. (1987). Assessment of world views. *Psychological Reports, 64,* 349–352.

Jones, J. M. (1991). The concept of race in social psychology: From color to culture. In R. L. Jones (Ed.), *Black psychology* (pp. 441–467). Berkeley, CA: Cobb & Henry.

Katz, P. A. (1976). The acquisition of racial attitudes in children. In P. A. Katz (Eds.), *Toward the elimination of racism* (pp. 125–150). Elmsford, NY: Pergamon Press.

Kelman, H. C. (1961). Processes of opinion change. *Public Opinion Quarterly, 25,* 57–78.

King, J. C. (1981). *The biology of race.* Berkeley: University of California Press.

Kluckhohn, F. R., & Strodtbeck, F. L. (1961). *Variations in value orientations.* Evanston, IL: Row & Peterson.

LaDue, R. (1990). An Indian by any other name or don't "Kemo Sabe" me, Tonto. *Focus, 4*(2), 10–11.

LaFromboise, T. D. (1988). American Indian mental health policy. *American Psychologist, 43,* 388–397.

Myers, L. J. (1985). Transpersonal psychology: The role of the Afrocentric paradigm. *Journal of Black Psychology, 12*(1), 31–42.

Nunnally, J. (1978). *Psychometric theory.* New York: McGraw-Hill.

Ossana, S., Helms, J. E., & Leonard, M. (1992). Do "womanist" identity attitudes influence college women's self-esteem and perceptions of environmental bias? *Journal of Counseling and Development, 70,* 402–408.

Pedersen, P. B. (1991). Multiculturalism as a generic approach to counseling. *Journal of Counseling and Development, 70*(1), 6–12.

Pettigrew, T. F. (1964). *A profile of the Negro American.* N.J.: Van Nostrand.

Phinney, J. S. (1989). Stages of ethnic identity development in minority group adolescents. *Journal of Early Adolescence, 9*(1–2), 34–49.

Powell-Hopson, D., & Hopson, D. S. (1988). Implications of doll color preferences among black preschool children and white preschool children. *Journal of Black Psychology, 14*(2), 57–63.

Root, M.P.P. (1992). *Racially mixed people in America.* Newbury Park, CA: Sage.

Rushton, J. P. (1988). Race differences in behavior: A review and evolutionary analysis. *Personality and Individual Differences, 9,* 1009–1024.

Sabnani, H. B., Ponterotto, J. G., & Borodovsky, L. G. (1991). White racial identity development and cross-cultural counselor training: A stage model. *Counseling Psychologist, 19,* 76–102.

Samuda, R. J. (1975). Nature and nurture. In R. J. Samuda (Ed.), *Psychological testing of American minorities* (pp. 35–62). New York: HarperCollins.

Schaller, M., & Maass, A. (1989). Illusory correlation and social categorization: Toward an integration of motivational and cognitive factors in stereotype formation. *Journal of Personality and Social Psychology, 56,* 709–721.

Spickard, P. R. (1992). The illogic of American racial categories. In M.P.P. Root (Ed.), *Racially mixed people in America* (pp. 12–23). Newbury Park, CA: Sage.

Stewart, E. C. (1972). *American cultural patterns: A cross-cultural perspective.* LaGrange Park, IL: Intercultural Network.

Sue, D. W. (1991). A model for cultural diversity training. *Journal of Counseling and Development, 70*(1), 99–105.

Sue, D. W., & Sue, D. (1990). *Counseling the culturally different: Theory and practice.* New York: Wiley.

Takaki, R. (1989). *Strangers from a different shore.* New York: Penguin Books.

Taylor, D. M., & Dube, L. (1986). Two faces of identity: The "I" and the "we." *Journal of Social Issues, 42,* 81–98.

Westbrook, F. D., & Sedlacek, W. E. (1991). Forty years of labels to communicate about nontraditional students: Does it help or hurt? *Journal of Counseling and Development, 70*(1), 20–28.

Zuckerman, M. (1990). Some dubious premises in research and theory on racial differences. *American Psychologist, 45*(12), 1297–1303.

14

Identity Development and Sexual Orientation: Toward a Model of Lesbian, Gay, and Bisexual Development

Anthony R. D'Augelli

Traditional notions of psychological identity stress the ontogenesis of personal coherence, with individuals moving slowly, if not always surely, toward a particular developmental end-state. Conventional wisdom holds that identity is normatively achieved at a certain point in chronological time, usually during late adolescence or early adulthood, and then endures. Such an essentialist position has dominated psychological models of development, reflecting a philosophical position that privileges certain kinds of individual action, reflection, and accomplishment while marginalizing others.

In contrast is the view that identity is a social construction. In this view, notions of personal consistency are no more fundamental than any other social reflection, custom, or script. Our awareness of the degree to which we are shaped by social circumstances varies over time as well; our images of identity are transient and malleable. Such a view is deeply suspicious of essentialist views of identity, seeing such constructions as disguised efforts at social moralism. Exemplifying the essentialist view, Erikson wrote of our "accrued confidence to maintain inner sameness and continuity" (Erikson, 1959, p. 89). Nearly twenty years later, Zurcher (1977) proposed an alternative, a "mutable self," an identity that is (and should be) fundamentally plastic. More recently, Gergen (1991) described the "saturated self" of contemporary postmodern society, an identity subject to perpetual scrutiny and redefinition. The self as multiple identities is well demonstrated in an analysis of lesbians, gay men, and bisexual people.

Being lesbian, gay, or bisexual in our culture requires living a life of multiple psychological identities. At the very least, lesbians, gay men, and bisexually identified people live in a predominantly heterosexual society that demands adherence to certain personal, relational, and social norms. On the other hand, difference becomes expressed in its own lesbian, gay, or bisexual coherence or identity, its own set of relational norms, its own communities, and its own culture (Herdt & Boxer, 1992). "Becoming" lesbian, gay, or bisexual requires two processes. On the one hand, it involves a conscious distancing from heterosexist essentialism — the person must become "ex-heterosexual" and cast off the mandated identity of mainstream culture. She or he must also create a new identity oriented around homosocial and homosexual dimensions. Constructing a complex "essence" is the task.

Living as a lesbian, gay, or bisexual person in our society demands identity diffusion in the traditional Eriksonian sense; at the same time, a lesbian, gay, or bisexual life exemplifies the functionality of identity differentiation and plasticity. In their analysis of sexual scripts, Simon & Gagnon (1986) state it well: "Recent considerations of the Eriksonian model have required increasing emphasis to dimensions of personality 'off the diagonal' of his epigenetic chart: the emphasis shifts from the linear developmental line to the maintenance of the self process with multiple sources of uncertainty. . . . What was once understandably perceived as a failure of socialization, a failure of identity crystallization, increasingly comes to be seen as the flexibility whose dialectical partner is cohesiveness" (p. 114).

In this chapter, I will use the example of sexual orientation and the development of lesbian, gay, and bisexual identities to point out how psychological views of identity function to reinforce heterosexist privilege. Heterosexism is the belief that "normal" development is heterosexual and that deviations from this identity are "unnatural," "disordered," or "dysfunctional." The general concepts underlying my analysis are these: (1) concepts of identity are rooted in a sociopolitical context, although this is seldom articulated; (2) this dynamic is demonstrated in historical views of lesbian and gay sexual orientation; (3) a model of lesbian,. gay, and bisexual identity development based on a human development metatheory overcomes the fundamentally oppressive structure of earlier identity development views; and (4) such a model provides generative power for research and thinking about the development of sexual orientation and may be useful as well for other analyses of identity. A review of theoretical and metatheoretical issues related to sexual orientation is beyond the scope of this chapter. For such analyses, the reader is referred to McWhirter, Sanders, and Reinisch (1990), Sedgwick (1990), Stein (1992), and Weeks (1989).

Development of Sexual Orientation

Women and men who come to define themselves as lesbian, gay or bisexual must create their own consistencies in the face of two powerful barriers — the *social invisibility of the defining characteristic* and the *social and legal penalties* attached to its overt expression. Many writers on cultural diversity stress the process of self-acknowledgment — the proclamation of existence as the first critical step in personal and, later, social change. This simple proclamation is a revolutionary act in its repudiation of a socially imposed, majority identity and its silencing of difference. Lesbian, gay, and bisexual people are unique in that their defining difference — their sexual orientation — is invisible. Since they can literally hide their difference from others' gaze, the affirmation of their existence is delayed. To the degree that identity is a socially mediated subjectivity, lesbians and gay men develop their identities in a uniquely private way. Consolidation of identity is driven by internal processes, with few positive and many negative social facilitators. The universal "coming-out" story is nearly always one of difficult *personal* discovery, of slowly and painfully appreciating a personal consistency that cannot be explored through routine socialization mechanisms.

Not only is lesbian and gay identity development intensely personal and private, but it is also conditioned by fear and shame. Even in early childhood, individuals learn that such an identity is problematic. Homophobic comments are routine in elementary schools, and exploration of same-sex physical and emotional closeness is severely punished by parents and others as soon as it appears. (More extreme sanctioning is applied to affection between boys.) The "hidden curriculum" of heterosexism is taught to all, even those children who as adults will self-identify as lesbian, gay, or bisexual. In contrast to other groups, lesbians, gay men, and bisexual people have grown up absorbing a destructive mythology before they appreciate that it is meant for them.

Homophobia at such an early age is unusually resistant to change. Lesbian, gay, and bisexual people have been socialized from birth in the normalcy of heterosexual identity and have been trained to reject any homosocial characteristics, especially those involving serious emotional or sexual expression. Becoming conscious of the pervasiveness of heterosexual socialization is difficult, since it demands an awareness of the historical nature of personal identity and an appreciation of the arbitrariness of identity concepts. Ultimately, as lesbians, gay men, and bisexual people acknowledge their difference, the introjected stereotypes that have silently directed their lives for many years become clearer. The disentangling of introjected identity concepts from personal history and individual characteristics is an enormously difficult task.

For this reason, the process of creating a lesbian-gay-bisexual identity is a prolonged one. Exiting from the heterosexual identity that has been etched into consciousness since birth is profoundly unsettling and is greatly complicated by the many real societal barriers. The task is so difficult because heterosexual identity is not considered socially constructed but is rather viewed as natural. No self-consciousness exists about sexual orientation — unless one deviates from the unstated natural order. Our cultural script is that we must (painfully) create a non-heterosexual identity; heterosexuality exempts us from this kind of identity struggle, though surely contemporary heterosexual women and men confront some complex issues of sex-role articulation. Heterosexuality, in fact, has its own social history (Katz, 1990). Heterosexual men and women, however, do not need to create a sexual identity by *resistance* — by rejection of a cultural heritage that renders them suspect, deprives them of intimacy, and deracinates them from society. The other task of lesbian-gay-bisexual identity — the creation of a life that affirms one's nonheterosexual identity — is also profoundly difficult, yet it is less complex than exiting heterosexual identity.

The need for lesbians, gay men, and bisexual people to struggle to proclaim their identity — first internally and privately in early adolescence, and then more and more publicly in early adulthood — contrasts with the degree to which core sexual identity remains unquestioned in most heterosexual women and men. This contrast highlights the power of achieved identity as a cultural concept that is to be developed by late adolescence — with emotional, vocational, and spiritual pieces all in place. But for lesbian, gay, and bisexual people, a critical piece — sexual identity — has resisted the heterosexist imperative and remains discordant, rendering other identity dimensions unstable.

This distinction forms the conceptual basis for heterosexism — the privileging and normalizing of one set of socioaffectional characteristics. The entire dynamic is possible only because sexual identity is removed from its historical and political context. As a result, lesbian, gay, and bisexual lives are assumed to be unrelated and unresponsive to social circumstances, history, or culture, allowing for the image of an "essential homosexual" with mythic identity characteristics. This construction of an "essential" sexual identity prevents the fluidity of lesbian, gay, and bisexual sexual development from disturbing the achieved heterosexual statuses of the majority. Monolithic concepts of sexual identity, which assume that achieved psychological coherence is accomplished before adulthood, perpetuate heterosexist hegemony and fuel the many layers of very real victimization that nonheterosexual people must tolerate.

Scholars, theorists, and researchers have historically colluded in promoting an essentialist, unidimensional, and ahistorical perspective on lesbian-gay identity. For example, the view that homosexuality is a psychiatric disorder, which has dominated cultural concepts for most of this century, dismisses the historical, community, or social factors that shape the expression, repression, suppression, or denial of same-sex attractions. When the context is assumed to be irrelevant, homosexuality becomes a treatable reification, a dysfunctional *individual* identity detached from common experience. Presumed difference is transformed into distinct deviance. Such analyses readily lead to therapeutic methods to alter the deviant identity and to social policies and laws that institutionalize the stigma. The entire oppressive sequence is driven by a normative heterosexual pattern of identity development that constructs homosexuality as deviant, pathological, and illegal. The social opprobrium and criminalization attached to the deviant identity is consistent with the metatheoretical model that underlies these analyses.

The Human Development View

Lesbian and gay identity processes must be described using a conceptual model that explicates the complex factors influencing the development of people in context over historical time. The most powerful metatheoretical model for these processes is a life-span human development perspective (Baltes, 1987; Lerner, 1991). This general view, which has many individual variants, involves the explication of patterns of dynamic interaction of multiple factors over time in the development of an individual person. The developing woman or man must be understood in context; simultaneous descriptions of the person's social network, neighborhood and community, institutional settings, and culture are complemented by descriptions of individual physical and psychological change and stability. In contrast with earlier developmental views, the human development model stresses the impact of historical time on processes of development, whether the processes are observed during an individual's life, over the lives of family members, within a community, or in a culture. The human development perspective is an effort to discover variations among individuals as they move in time through social situations, the community, culture, and history. Moreover, they are not passive recipients of social history but shape circumstances and contexts as well.

A model for analyzing the development of sexual orientation must account for several broad sets of factors: individual changes from birth through adulthood to death, patterns of social intimacy across the life span, and linkages between the person, his or her significant others, and his or her proximal and distal environments. The first set of variables helps describe *personal subjectivities and actions,* the second set involves *interactive intimacies,* and the third set concerns *sociohistorical connections.* In contrast to either essentialist or constructivist models in which one set of explanatory constructs is deemed sufficient, a more appropriate framework must link the following three sets of factors:

1. How individuals feel about their sexual identities over their lives, how they engage in diverse sexual activities with different meanings, and how they construct their sexual lives and feel about them (*subjectivities and actions*). This element is influenced by and influences the second set of factors.
2. How sexuality is developed by parental and familial factors, how age-peer interactions shape and modify the impact of early parental and familial socialization, and how this learning affects and is affected by intimate partnerships of different kinds (*interactive intimacies*). All of this results from and affects the third set of factors.
3. Social norms and expectations of various geographic and subcultural communities; local and national social customs, policies, and laws; and major cultural and historical continuities and discontinuities (*sociohistorical connections*).

The goal is to locate an individual's life within a dynamic matrix of these three sets of factors. The life-span human development view is sufficiently comprehensive to meet the challenge of organizing these factors into a coherent system. This model, shown in Figure 14.1, presents the six identity processes that will be described later in this chapter.

Figure 14.1. Model of Lesbian-Gay-Bisexual Development.

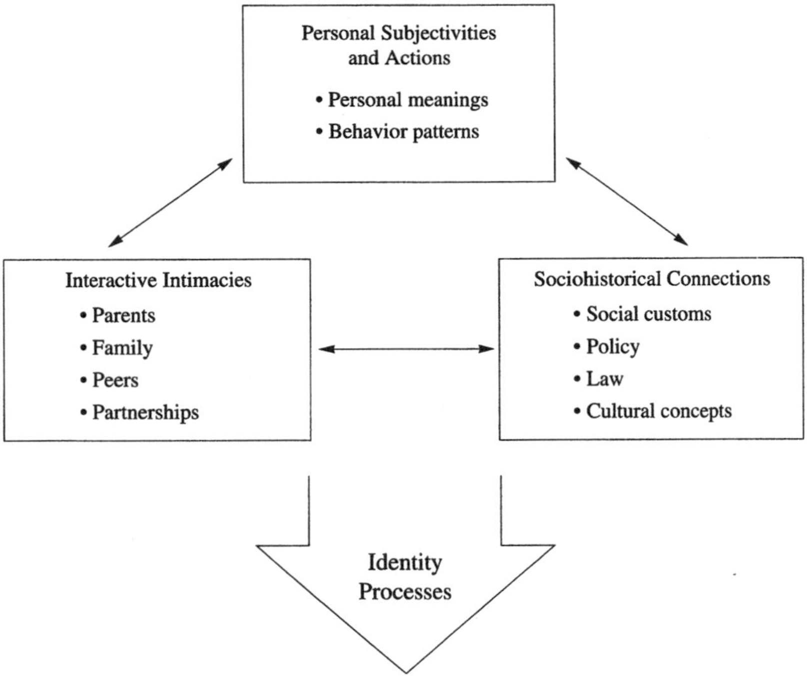

```
                    ┌─────────────────────────┐
                    │  Personal Subjectivities │
                    │       and Actions        │
                    │                          │
                    │   • Personal meanings    │
                    │   • Behavior patterns    │
                    └─────────────────────────┘
          ↗                                        ↘
┌───────────────────────┐          ┌───────────────────────────┐
│ Interactive Intimacies │          │ Sociohistorical Connections│
│   • Parents            │ ←──────→ │   • Social customs         │
│   • Family             │          │   • Policy                 │
│   • Peers              │          │   • Law                    │
│   • Partnerships       │          │   • Cultural concepts      │
└───────────────────────┘          └───────────────────────────┘
                  ↓ Identity ↓
                    Processes
```

1. Exiting heterosexual identity
2. Developing a personal lesbian-gay-bisexual identity status
3. Developing a lesbian-gay-bisexual social identity
4. Becoming a lesbian-gay-bisexual offspring
5. Developing a lesbian-gay-bisexual intimacy status
6. Entering a lesbian-gay-bisexual community

The major characteristics of a human development model are described below, with brief descriptions of their relevance to lesbian, gay, and bisexual identity development.

The first perspective is that *individuals develop and change over the entire course of their life spans.* This means that psychological, cognitive, behavioral, emotional, and physical change does not stop after the achievement of socially defined "adulthood" (usually heterosexual marriage and occupational stability). The development of sexual orientation is a lifelong process. This concept strikes at the heart of a view of sexual orientation as fixed early in life. Such a view is a historical anachronism, although it may be currently consistent with women's and men's phenomenological perceptions of their sexual identity. That sexual and affectional feelings can change in varying degrees over the course of one's life must be assumed; efforts to suggest otherwise are disguised social constructions. For instance, for an older man or woman to focus his or her emotional life on someone of the same gender late in life does not necessarily imply repression of *earlier* homosexual feelings. Feelings of physical and emotional closeness for an individual of the same gender can evolve throughout life; they are highly conditioned by social, family, and personal normative expectations.

The labels *lesbian* and *gay* and their negative connotations for older adults create a powerful barrier to the expression of intense closeness to same-sex others. Likewise, individuals who define themselves as lesbian or gay may experience affectional and sexual interest in people of the opposite sex across the span of their lives, though the plasticity of this process is limited by the current scripts about how to become lesbian or gay in contemporary society.

The human development model also embodies the importance of *developmental plasticity*. Plasticity suggests that human functioning is highly responsive to environmental circumstances and to changes induced by physical and other biological factors. The human development model makes few assumptions about the fixed nature of human functioning, but it suggests that plasticity is a prime characteristic of human behavioral development. Plasticity may change over chronological time: at different ages, certain components of human behavioral functioning are resistant to or responsive to differing circumstances. The implication for the development of sexual orientation is that sexual identity may be very fluid at certain times in the life span and more crystallized at others.

Given the role of hormonal development in sexual identity development, for instance, the likelihood is that the years in which changes in hormonal development in men and women occur are periods in which cognitive concepts of sexual orientation become especially salient. Sexual cues may be heightened and may have a greater impact on the individual because of her or his cognitive development. Yet this is not an inevitable, "natural" process. Adolescent peer culture in our society forces a social definition of sexual interests so that "expected" dating behavior can occur. This dating behavior happens with increasing distance from family monitoring and thus becomes increasingly subject to peer and distal sociocultural influences.

Self-awareness of lesbian-gay identity occurs for many during early adolescence (Herdt, 1989; Hetrick & Martin, 1987). However, the negative consequences of any homosocial-homosexual feelings are heightened because peer relationships would likely be threatened by the expression of these feelings. For many young people, the combination of cues, expectancies, and social circumstances are such that their sociosexual feelings remain diffuse, consciousness of their meaning is not well developed, and social circumstances, including pervasive homophobia, make the emergence of same-gendered affect or behavior improbable. The consequences of early disclosure for those teens whose feelings crystallize, however, are risky (Remafedi, Farrow, & Deisher, 1991).

The human development model emphasizes *interindividual differences in the development of intraindividual behavior.* In other words, the perspective focuses on behavioral variation; individual women and men are unique in their own development over the life span. The nature of interindividual differences in intraindividual functioning varies at different points in life, in different settings, and in different historical periods. The issue of variability is essential to the development of sexual orientation. Indeed, the concept strikes directly at the trichotomization of sexual life, in which individuals are assumed to be heterosexual, gay or lesbian, or bisexual. The human development perspective suggests a continuum of sexual feelings and experience, but it would predict less variance in individual sexual self-definitions at certain phases of life (for example, in later adulthood), in certain kinds of families (for instance, those that do not value difference), in certain communities (such as those with strongly traditional values and those that are highly homogeneous in nature), and at certain historical times (like the 1950s). That sexual diversity increases during adulthood is the result not only of postadolescent experiential factors, but also of exposure to less restrictive expectations and of the availability of an increased range of behavioral models for diversity.

Finally, the human development perspective suggests that the deterministic views of behavior that often are seen in traditional models of development underestimate *the impact that individuals have on their own development.* The actions of an individual shape his or her development. Individuals and their families are not passive respondents to social circumstances; behavioral development also results from conscious choice and directed action. Individual acts and the acts of family members (in consort or in varying degrees of coordination) have an impact on the developmental process of the individual person and on the family unit. If we assume that development involves differentiation, then individuals who are likely to be more highly "developed" are those who possess refined abilities to behave in diverse ways, whose psychoemotional responsiveness allows for behavioral complexity, and whose social skills allow for competent performance in a wide range of social settings. These abilities to act in differentiated ways and to manipulate one's own development are at the core of lesbian, gay, and bisexual life.

But this power to self-create is also rooted in context. Lesbians and gay men shape their own development out of necessity in a heterosexist culture that provides no routine socialization practices for them. Because of this historical need, lesbians and gay men have created social institutions that provide socialization experiences. For example, the primary structure for urban gay men has been the gay bar, while earlier cohorts of gay men were socialized in urban bathhouses designed for multiple, anonymous sexual partnerings. (These have nearly disappeared as a result of the human immunodeficiency virus (HIV) epidemic.) In the past, lesbian socialization occurred more often in small, nonpublic informal groups or in women's "communities."

The increasing number of nonsexual opportunities for gay men and the greater number of expressive options for lesbians today will have a tremendous impact on their distinctive, "normative" development. Surely contemporary lesbian and gay youths face far more opportunities to share their adult identities than did their predecessors. These opportunities will counteract the prior identities shaped by the gay bar and women's communities: that gay men are sexual machines unable to form lasting attachments, lesbians are relationship-bound and disinterested in sexual pleasure, and bisexuals are ambivalent (for histories, see Faderman, 1991; Herdt, 1992; Hutchins & Kaahumanu, 1991).

Thus, the tenet that individuals help to direct their own development is extraordinarily powerful for understanding lesbian and gay development at different historical times. For an adult in 1954 to decide that she or he had strong lesbian or gay feelings and to publicly say this was an extremely different event than it would be today, although the actions may seem similar. One area where such changes are vivid involves disclosure to family.

In earlier days families could fear their offspring's arrest, loss of employment, social censure, and isolation. By definition, disclosure of lesbian or gay status was admission of criminal status and mental illness. The typical familial response was shame, and many lesbians and gay men chose to relocate to supportive urban communities without telling their families about their sexual orientation. In pursuing self-definition under the conditions of the time, they were forced into dual identities — the emerging lesbian-gay identity of their new context and the ongoing heterosexual identity presumed by their families. For many lesbian and gay adults, their self-development thus yielded two nonoverlapping "families" — their family of origin and their family of creation (Weston, 1991).

Though disclosure to family remains a highly stressful part of lesbian and gay development, it is now facilitated by increased cultural acceptance, more positive imagery in media, and many more affirmative resources, including parental support networks. These changes have moderated the intense familial rejection of earlier generations by increasing social acceptance and by the erosion of prevalent myths about parental responsibility for sexual orientation. Families have fewer realistic fears of horrific negative consequences for their offspring, with the exception that parents of gay men report considerable worry about HIV infection (Robinson, Walters, & Skeen, 1989).

Yet powerful barriers to self-development remain. Because of the lack of legal protection that lesbians and gay men experience in asserting their rights in housing, adoption of children, military service, and so on, self-development remains compromised. Identity development and integration must be influenced if it jeopardizes employment and careers, family relationships, and personal safety. Historical, institutional, and cultural practices still negatively influence the self-development of lesbians, gay men, and bisexual people with multiple levels of victimization (Herek, 1992; Berrill & Herek, 1992).

The human development model serves as a powerful alternative to the pathologizing influences of the past and to approaches emphasizing one set of influencing factors to the exclusion of others. It suggests a very different psychological model from the traditional identity development view. In the next section, I will show one use of the human development model to explicate the processes of lesbian, gay, and bisexual identities.

Steps Toward a Model of Lesbian and Gay Male Development

The preceding section suggests that many current models of lesbian and gay male identity formation suffer from an excessive emphasis on the internal processes of personal development, usually conceived of in stage-model terms. In contrast, from a human development perspective, identity is conceived of as the dynamic processes by which an individual emerges from many social exchanges experienced in different contexts over an extended historical period — the years of his or her life. Several processes must be considered in studying lesbian and gay lives, using a human development metatheory as a guide. These processes are mediated by the cultural and sociopolitical contexts in which they occur.

Exiting Heterosexual Identity

This set of concerns involves personal and social recognition that one's sexual orientation is not heterosexual. Generally, this includes understanding the nature of one's attractions and labeling them. Initially, the breadth of meaning for the new label is uncertain: Does this mean a new life or no change at all? Historically, the label connoted a new identity, but this surely has changed. Exiting from heterosexuality also means telling *others* that one is lesbian, gay, or bisexual. This "coming out" begins with the very first person to whom an individual discloses and continues throughout life, decreasing only to the extent that the person is consistently and publicly identified with a non-heterosexual label. The pervasiveness of heterosexist assumptions makes the development of a continuing method for asserting nonheterosexuality a necessity.

Developing a Personal Lesbian-Gay-Bisexual Identity Status

An individual must develop a sense of personal socioaffectional stability that effectively summarizes thoughts, feelings, and desires. Surely, such an initial status may be subject to revision as more experience is accumulated. This personal status functions as a mobilizing force, bringing along with it directives for action. Given that sexual orientation is fundamentally social in character, a lesbian, gay, or bisexual label propels people toward social interaction. To a large degree, they cannot confirm their sexual-orientation status without contact with others. Thus, they must learn how to be gay, lesbian, or bisexual, with these constructs defined by their proximal community of lesbians, gay men, or bisexual people.

In addition, a critical part of personal identity status is coming to an appreciation of internalized myths about nonheterosexuality. Some of these myths are the obvious stereotypes about inversion and dysfunctional development. Others are less well articulated, maintaining that lesbians and gay men do not have long-lasting relationships, that their families reject them, that they can never be engaged in child-rearing, and that they cannot have positions of power in society. To the degree that these views have been consciously incorporated, they are easy to challenge, but they must be challenged by demythologizing personal contact. Such occurrences as recognizing long-term lesbian and gay couples, talking to parents who warmly accept their children, and interacting with gay men and lesbians with children slowly modify the more deeply entrenched myths.

Developing a Lesbian-Gay-Bisexual Social Identity

This involves creating a large and varied set of people who know of the person's sexual orientation and are available to provide social support. This, too, is a lifelong process that has a profound effect on personal development. Ideally, one's social network is *affirmative;* that is, the people in it actively, continually, and predictably treat the person as lesbian, gay, or bisexual. A network composed of people who would prefer the person to hide his or her sexual orientation or who do not discuss it at all is not an affirming one. Tolerance is indeed harmful in this regard, in that it subtly reinforces societal interest in lesbian, gay, and bisexual invisibility. The process of creating a support network is long-lasting for this very reason. It takes time for a person to truly know the nature of others' reactions. These reactions are not uniform and may change over time. Also, many reactions are hypothetical: the reality of the person's orientation has not been translated into a real difference. For example, some may not find the person's orientation problematic until a dating partner emerges. The reality of sexual orientation in others' eyes is a complex process too: members of the individual's social network must also "come out" in their acknowledgment to others about her or his orientation.

Becoming a Lesbian-Gay-Bisexual Offspring

Parental relationships are often temporarily disrupted with the disclosure of sexual orientation. All available research suggests a return to the predisclosure state, though possibly only after the passage of some time (Cramer & Roach, 1988; Robinson, Walters, & Skeen, 1989; Strommen, 1989). Reintegration into the family of origin is the preferred outcome of the process, and the family (as a support network) must also be affirmative. Generally, families show complex patterns of adaptation, with parents, siblings, and members of the extended family coming to overlapping, but not identical, approaches. Much of the responsibility for movement from tolerance falls to the lesbian, gay, or bisexual person; families generally prefer to "contain" the deviance as much as possible (Boxer, Cook, & Herdt, 1991). This maneuver reinforces stigmas and myths and keeps the person in a distinct (nonheterosexual) category. While it is surely still the case that the burden will fall on the individual, more and more parents are taking active steps to reintegrate the person and to understand and affirm his or her life.

Developing a Lesbian-Gay-Bisexual Intimacy Status

The psychological complexities of same-sex dyadic relationships are made much more problematic by the invisibility of lesbian and gay couples in our cultural imagery. The view that gay men are solitary and cannot form relationships of any duration because of sexual excesses has surely dominated our views, even of lesbians. It is the case that our social and cultural apparatuses for heterosexual bonding are not available to lesbians and gay men (thus producing fewer examples of committed relationships and/or "marriages," for instance); this is a good example of how social structure reinforces heterosexism. The lack of cultural scripts directly applicable to lesbian, gay, and bisexual people leads to ambiguity and uncertainty, but it also forces the emergence of personal, couple-specific, and community norms, which should be more personally adaptive. (Note how the norms have radically changed in urban, gay male communities in the wake of the HIV epidemic.)

Entering a Lesbian-Gay-Bisexual Community

This set of identity processes involves the development of commitments to political and social action. For some who believe their sexual orientation to be a purely private matter, this never

happens. For others, public engagement in social or political
action is literally risky, in that jobs or housing may be jeo-
pardized. However, an understanding of one's own identity development as a lesbian, gay, or bisexual person generally involves confrontation with current social and political barriers
to development. The inequities become clearer as the person
becomes more and more open or learns how much hiding is
needed and why. To be empowered as a lesbian, gay, or bisexual person involves awareness of the structure of heterosexism,
the nature of relevant laws and policies, and the limits to freedom and exploration. To be lesbian, gay, or bisexual in the
fullest sense—to have a meaningful identity—leads to a consciousness of the history of one's own oppression. It also, generally, leads to an appreciation of how the oppression continues,
and a commitment to resisting it.

Conclusion

The processes of lesbian, gay, or bisexual identity formation
are very different for a 20-year-old in 1994 than they were for
a person aged twenty in 1974. In the twenty years spanning
the two lives, major events have occurred in lesbian-gay history, events that *fundamentally* restructure the processes of identity development. The changes have been dramatic—from mental illness to alternative life-style to sexual variation to diverse
minority. In 1974, a young man who felt attracted to other men
would label himself homosexual; the label was equivalent to self-
diagnosis of mental illness. Management of this mental illness
in a positive way—asserting it at all—involved entering into the
marginal world of the gay ghettos of large metropolitan areas.
If disclosure of sexual orientation occurred, the probability of
familial rejection was exceedingly high. Out-migration to certain metropolitan areas often occurred without disclosure to the
family, so that the new urban dwellers created a local gay identity while maintaining their former heterosexual identity for their
family, many friends, and most co-workers.

Many people, of course, unconsciously repressed their
feelings, entering heterosexual marriage; many consciously sup-

pressed their feelings as well. The societal concept of gay identity was sufficiently repellent to thwart the formation of a positive identity. The sociological reality of the times directed men into highly secretive and highly sexualized settings for their socializations. Despite twenty years' progress, our culture is hardly lesbian- and gay-affirming. Explicit discrimination is legal in most places, and severe penalties for lesbian (and gay male) sex can be imposed in nearly half of the states (Rivera, 1991). All evidence points to the general acceptance in our culture of antilesbian and antigay views, feelings, and action (Berrill & Herek, 1992; Comstock, 1991).

Lesbian identity development was even more invisible in our culture twenty years ago, though considered no less pathological in nature. Within the gay urban neighborhoods, women were less visible — there were fewer bars and no female version of gay baths, and cultural stereotypes of lesbian behavior never evolved to the precision of gay male stereotypes. Because of these factors and others related to their status as women, lesbians had a much harder time exiting heterosexual identities. The time to awareness of their sexual orientation was prolonged because their sexual feelings were generally devalued. Same-gendered feelings between women could be readily assimilated as emotional, not sexual. Without the cultural salience of the lesbian label and without a meshing of internal feelings and social anchors, women's identity formation was considerably more complex. Fortunately, lesbians could find some support within the women's movement, although this support was never entirely unambiguous.

For a woman aged twenty who is coming out in 1994, some aspects of creating a lesbian identity may seem similar, but much is different. As of May 1987, "ego-dystonic homosexuality" has been deleted from the *Diagnostic and Statistical Manual of Mental Disorders* (DSM-III-R) (American Psychiatric Association, 1987); professional groups have stressed the normality of diverse sexual identities, and a rich lesbian culture of literature and music is relatively accessible. Yet context remains crucial. A young woman in Berkeley, California, comes out very differently from one in rural central Pennsylvania, so much so that one might consider these women as inhabiting different psychological worlds. Thus, the young woman in central Pennsylvania who tells her mother that she is dating her female college friend may unleash a psychological storm that nongay people will never experience, though its consequences will probably be less traumatic than her 1974 counterpart's would have been. Many will not tell their fathers or mothers, but those that do may be told not to tell the extended family and to keep it to themselves.

Women can still create an identity for themselves more easily than in the past, since more helping resources exist, even in geographical areas formerly without such resources (D'Augelli, 1989). The process of "becoming lesbian" is far more psychologically manageable, yet it is still compromised by pervasive social and institutional stigmatization that cannot be simply relegated to the background. The risk of loss of employment, housing, family relations, and so on is still fundamental to the *psychological* processes of identity, and these realities cannot be left out. How can someone achieve identity when to do so may lead to job loss, eviction from housing, and even arrest?

In the future, research on lesbian, gay, and bisexual life must start with the assumption that identity is mutable. Although individuals' views of their identity status are perceived as fixed, they are flexible; this should become the focus of study in itself (see Kitzinger, 1987, for an excellent example of this). Identity is heuristically conceived as a dynamic process of interaction and exchange between the individual and the many levels of social collectives during the historical period of her or his life. For many (including lesbian, gay, and bisexual researchers), the achievement of a sense of integrated affectional identity may *seem* to be the end-point of affectional development. This view is surely fueled by the emotional strains of heterosexual exiting and the heterosexist barriers that must be faced daily. Our concepts and research may unintentionally replace conceptual heterocentrism with homocentrism and may preclude the analysis and study of continued evolution and process in identity in lesbian and gay populations. The elimination of the concept of identity as a predetermined, implicitly heterosexual developmental goal would help us explore how humans continue to develop.

A revision of our operational definition of sexual orientation must occur, allowing for study of the continuities and discontinuities, the flexibilities and cohesiveness, of sexual and affectional feelings across the life span, in diverse contexts, and in relationship to culture and history. Any model of sexual orientation that does not address the influence of heterosexism, homophobia, and disenfranchisement will provide unintended corroboration for oppression. A life-span human development model can, in principle, mitigate this by its simultaneous analysis of exogenous and endogenous variables over time. This approach reflects complexities of lesbian, gay, and bisexual lives and allows analysis of how these lives will change in the future. It is also a model that insists on addressing diversity — so that crucial dimensions that were once "off the diagonal," such as gender, race, ethnicity, and class, are considered fundamental to an analysis of sexual orientation as well as other aspects of human development. How these dimensions affect the many processes of personal development, however, cannot be assumed, but must be studied. Much of this is fundamentally uncharted territory. As Fuss (1991) comments, "Interrogating the position of 'outsiderness' is where much recent lesbian and gay theory begins, implicitly if not always directly raising the questions of the complicated processes by which sexual borders are constructed, sexual identities assigned, and sexual politics formulated. Where exactly . . . does one identity leave off and the other begin?" (p. 2).

References

American Psychiatric Association. (1987). *Diagnostic and Statistical Manual of Mental Disorders* (3rd ed.). Washington, DC: Author.

Baltes, P. B. (1987). Theoretical perspectives on life-span developmental psychology: On the dynamics between growth and decline. *Developmental Psychology, 23,* 611–626.

Berrill, K. T., & Herek, G. M. (1992). Primary and secondary victimization in anti-gay hate crimes: Official response and public policy. In G. M. Herek & K. T. Berrill (Eds.), *Hate crimes: Confronting violence against lesbians and gay men* (pp. 289–305). Newbury Park, CA: Sage.

Boxer, A. M., Cook, J. A., & Herdt, G. (1991). Double jeopardy: Identity transitions and parent-child relations among
  gay and lesbian youth. In K. Pillemer & K. McCartney
  (Eds.), *Parent-child relations throughout life* (pp. 59–92). Hillsdale, NJ: Erlbaum.
Comstock, G. D. (1991). *Violence against lesbians and gay men.* New
  York: Columbia University Press.
Cramer, D. W., & Roach, A. J. (1988). Coming out to mom
  and dad: A study of gay males and their relationships with
  their parents. *Journal of Homosexuality, 15,* 79–92.
D'Augelli, A. R. (1989). The development of a helping community for lesbians and gay men: A case study in commu-
  nity psychology. *Journal of Community Psychology, 17,* 18–29.
Erikson, E. H. (1959). *Identity and the life cycle.* New York: In-
  ternational Universities Press.
Faderman, L. (1991). *Odd girls and twilight lovers: A history of lesbian life in twentieth-century America.* New York: Columbia
  University Press.
Fuss, D. (1991). Inside/out. In D. Fuss (Ed.), *Inside/out: Lesbian theories, gay theories* (pp. 1–10). New York: Routledge & Kegan Paul.
Gergen, K. J. (1991). *The saturated self: Dilemmas of identity in
  contemporary life.* New York: Basic Books.
Herdt, G. (1989). Gay and lesbian youth: Emergent identities
  and cultural scenes at home and abroad. *Journal of Homosexuality, 17,* 1–42.
Herdt, G. (Ed.). (1992). *Gay culture in America: Essays from the
  field.* Boston: Beacon Press.
Herdt, G., & Boxer, A. (1992). Culture, history, and life course
  of gay men. In G. Herdt (Ed.), *Gay culture in America: Essays
  from the field* (pp. 1–28). Boston: Beacon Press.
Herek, G. M. (1992). The social context of hate crimes: Notes
  on cultural heterosexism. In G. M. Herek & K. T. Berrill
  (Eds.), *Hate crimes: Confronting violence against lesbians and gay
  men* (pp. 89–104). Newbury Park, CA: Sage.
Hetrick, E. S., & Martin, A. D. (1987). Developmental issues
  and their resolution for gay and lesbian adolescents. *Journal
  of Homosexuality, 14,* 25–43.
Hutchins, L., & Kaahumanu, L. (Eds.). (1991). *Bi any other
  name.* Boston: Alyson.

Katz, J. N. (1990). The invention of heterosexuality. *Socialist Review, 21,* 7–34.

Kitzinger, C. (1987). *The social construction of lesbianism.* London: Sage.

Lerner, R. M. (1991). Changing organism-context relations as the basic process of development: A developmental contextual perspective. *Developmental Psychology, 27,* 27–32.

McWhirter, D. P., Sanders, S. A., & Reinisch, J. M. (1990). *Homosexuality/heterosexuality: Concepts of sexual orientation.* New York: Oxford University Press.

Remafedi, G., Farrow, J. A., & Deisher, R. W. (1991). Risk factors for attempted suicide in gay and bisexual youth. *Pediatrics, 87,* 869–875.

Rivera, R. R. (1991). Sexual orientation and the law. In J. C. Gonsiorek & J. D. Weinrich (Eds.), *Homosexuality: Research implications of public policy* (pp. 81–100). Newbury Park, CA: Sage.

Robinson, B. E., Walters, L. H., & Skeen, P. (1989). Response of parents to learning that their child is homosexual and concern over AIDS: A natural survey. *Journal of Homosexuality, 18*(1–2), 59–80.

Sedgwick, E. K. (1990). *Epistemology of the closet.* Berkeley: University of California Press.

Simon, W., & Gagnon, J. H. (1986). Sexual scripts: Permanence and change. *Archives of Sexual Behavior, 15*(2), 97–120.

Stein, E. (1992). (Ed.). *Forms of desire: Sexual orientation and the social constructionist controversy.* New York: Routledge & Kegan Paul.

Strommen, E. F. (1989). "You're a what?": Family members' reactions to the disclosure of homosexuality. *Journal of Homosexuality, 18,* 37–58.

Weeks, J. (1989). *Sexuality.* New York: Routledge & Kegan Paul.

Weston, K. (1991). *Families we choose: Lesbians, gays, kinship.* New York: Columbia University Press.

Zurcher, L. A. (1977). *The mutable self: A self-concept for social change.* Newbury Park, CA: Sage.

15

Age as a Dimension of Diversity: The Experience of Being Old

Margaret Gatz
Brian Cotton

"The aged" defines a group that every person is eligible to join by virtue of living long enough. When we consider the aged as a category of people who receive differential treatment in society, we are talking about our future selves.

Recognition of the disenfranchisement of individuals on the basis of age was brought to broad public attention with Robert Butler's Pulitzer prize–winning book, *Why Survive? Being Old in America* (1975). Ageism is portrayed as similar to racism and sexism, insofar as stereotyping based purely on age is used to discriminate systematically against individuals. Butler suggests that ageism operates at an institutional or societal level as well as at an individual level, among both young and old. According to his analysis, for younger people, ageism offers a way to both (1) insulate themselves from the prospect of becoming old and (2) establish the aged as a separate and different group, for whom it is unnecessary to feel personally responsible.

Note: The authors thank the computing support center of the State University of New York College at Plattsburgh for electronic mailing services and April Smith for her assistance and input.

Moreover, Butler submits that older adults collude with these processes by concealing their age or refusing to identify themselves as elderly. He says, "Ageism, like all prejudices, influences the self view and behavior of its victims. The aged tend to adopt negative definitions of themselves and to perpetuate the very stereotypes directed at them" (p. 13).

In literature concerning human diversity, age has not been consistently included in the discussion. Yet, along with gender and race, age may be one of the most fundamental cues by which individuals are rapidly placed into social categories (Fiske & Neuberg, 1990; Milord, 1978; Zebrowitz, 1990). In turn, consideration of age as a dimension of human diversity and as a component of a person's identity suggests new ways of looking at the experience of aging and helps to point to some of its unique aspects.

As a minority (or nondominant) category, the aged are different from other minorities in at least three respects. First, whereas some social identities are primarily ascribed (for example, ethnicity or gender) and others are expressly acquired (for example, profession or political party), membership in the group "the aged" is both. Being old is an ascribed identity achieved by attaining a certain age that is considered old by others in society. A person can also be considered aged by joining an organized group of older people such as the American Association of Retired Persons (AARP) or a local Senior Citizens club or by moving to a retirement community. Here, the individual actively chooses an identification as aged.

The second respect in which the aged are different is in the degree of permeability of the boundaries of group membership and the fact that this permeability is defined developmentally. Whereas some social categories are permeable to new members (for example, the physically disabled and gays and lesbians), most minority groups have a membership that is largely fixed by gender, ethnicity, or other factors. Moreover, the influx of new members into the aged category is virtually assured, with the numbers increasing much more rapidly than those of other minority groups with permeable boundaries (Manton, 1990). Further, the definition of "aged" is more dynamic than that of other minority groups. Neugarten and Neugarten (1989) hold that although age sixty-five is commonly used to define the age of eligibility for entitlement programs such as Medicare, arguments can be made for moving the marker to age seventy-five, when people become more likely to suffer major physical, mental, or social losses. Moreover, as a result of increases in longevity, the fastest-growing population segment is the oldest old—those aged eighty-five and older (Suzman & Riley, 1985).

Third, the identity of "aged" is added to the repertoire of social identities a person already holds. Because everyone becomes old, the aged are likely to be much more varied than other minority groups. Women, racial and ethnic minorities, and gays and lesbians all become old, creating multiple group memberships for such individuals. Moreover, there are vast differences between subgroups of the aged, only some of whom are disadvantaged by being poor or physically frail.

These three fashions in which the aged differ from other minority groups add to the challenge of describing and understanding identity in older adults. A framework is required that takes into account the sociocultural stereotypes about age, individuals' perceptions of themselves in the second half of life, institutionalized processes that discriminate on the basis of age, and the way these factors shape one another. Consequently, this chapter is divided into three topical areas: (1) stereotypes of old age, (2) the self-perception processes of self-stereotyping and social comparison, and (3) the use of advocacy groups to counter age-based discrimination through identity. First, we briefly review social identity theory (Tajfel & Turner, 1986) and a derivative called self-categorization theory (Turner, 1987) as theoretical tools for considering how people perceive themselves, and how intergroup relations shape and are shaped by self-perception processes.

Identity and Identification in the Elderly

Social identity theory explains how individuals derive their sense of self from membership in social groups and how different social groups relate to each other. The central tenet of social identity theory is that individuals define their identities along two dimensions. The first is social: an individual is defined by membership in various social groups, both ascribed and acquired. Group memberships give individuals a sense of belonging (Tajfel, 1982) and a standard against which to evaluate others when the group membership is made salient by situational cues (Doise & Sinclair, 1973). Furthermore, individuals may consider themselves members of many different groups at any given time but would not hold two mutually exclusive memberships simultaneously (for example, a person could not be an elderly adolescent).

The second dimension of identity is personal; that is, it includes the idiosyncratic attributes that distinguish an individual from all other individuals. These attributes can be physical (a chronic illness or ears that stick out), psychological (a particular life experience or a personality trait), or relational (being a daughter or a spouse). Social and personal identity are thought to lie at opposite ends of a continuum (Tajfel & Turner, 1986). That is, there is a temporal trade-off, with one dimension of identity becoming more salient than the other depending on the context (Turner, 1987). Deaux (1993) argues that there is a fundamental interplay between the two dimensions: "Personal identity is defined, at least in part, by group memberships, and social categories are infused with personal meaning" (p. 5). Thus, personal and social identities are not neatly separable. Following this conception, age represents both social and personal identity, because it encompasses both categorical membership and personal meaning.

Social identity theory also speaks to the interrelation between groups in a social context. Groups exist only in relation to other groups; they cannot stand alone but must serve as definitional contrasts to each other (Brown, 1988). Thus, the social group "the deaf" has no meaning unless it is at least implicitly contrasted with "the hearing"; "the aged" must be contrasted with "the young." Social identities serve the functions of providing status, enhancing self-esteem, and supplying coherence to an individual's self-description (Deaux, 1993; Hogg & Abrams, 1988). Individuals who identify with a given social group have a sense of their social power and status derived from the status held by that group.

Group identification serves a major function in defining self-esteem. According to the theory, because people are motivated to evaluate themselves positively, they will tend to evaluate positively any group of which they are a member (Tajfel & Turner, 1986). Moreover, a positive social identity requires people to have a positive bias in evaluating their own group as a way to keep that group distinct from others. The result of successfully gaining positive distinctiveness is a raised sense of self-esteem (Lemyre & Smith, 1985; Oakes & Turner, 1980). Conversely, people will discriminate against groups that are perceived to pose a threat to their own social identity, generating intergroup discrimination (Turner, 1975).

This is not to say that people always have a positive social identity, nor that discrimination against the outgroup is the only way to ensure a positive social identity. Deaux (1993) suggests that whether group identification correlates positively with self-esteem depends on contextual factors, such as the involvement of people around the individual with the culture of the group. In situations where low-power in-groups find it impossible or extremely difficult to discriminate successfully against a higher-power out-group, some members may attempt to maintain self-esteem by leaving the group for another in which they can reestablish a positive social identity (Tajfel & Turner, 1986).

Another mechanism for maintaining self-esteem is "the denial of personal disadvantage," in which individuals see other members of their group as discriminated against, while they believe themselves to have escaped (Crosby, 1993). For instance, findings from the Harris survey of a representative U.S. sample (Harris & Associates, 1981) showed that both younger and older adults rated the generic aged as more lonely, in poorer health, and more useless than the same older adults rated themselves.

A derivative of social identity theory is self-categorization theory (Turner, 1987). One aspect of that theory, self-stereotyping, describes how individuals come to perceive themselves as members of a specific social group. A three-step sequence of perceptual and cognitive actions is posited. First, individuals learn the stereotypical attributes and behaviors that define the group they wish to join or anticipate joining. Second, the individuals assign these stereotypical attributes and behaviors to themselves and incorporate them into their self-concept. And third, the individuals act according to these attributes and behaviors whenever the social identity tied to that group membership is salient. Thus, individuals learn the characteristic attributes of a group before incorporating that membership into their repertoire of identities.

The mechanisms described by social identity theory provide a conceptual basis for examining the processes suggested by the term *ageism*. We begin by considering what is known about the social identity of the aged through images and stereotypes of older age available in the culture.

Stereotypes of Old Age

Stereotypes are generalizations of primarily negative attributes and behaviors to an entire group of individuals. They may motivate discriminatory behavior toward the stereotyped group and may enhance self-esteem for the group practicing it (Crocker & Luhtanen, 1990), presumably through permitting them to distance themselves from the stereotyped group.

Are older adults viewed negatively by people in this society? In a comprehensive meta-analytic review of the literature, Kite and Johnson (1988) found that overall, older people tended to be evaluated more negatively than younger people. However, this finding was qualified on several counts. First, the difference between older and younger people was strongest when older people were rated on dimensions of attractiveness and competence rather than on other dimensions such as personality traits, where the difference was small or not significant. Second, age differences were most apparent when the target was a generic old person, but did not obtain when individuating information was provided. Third, differences were stronger for within-subject design (that is, when the same judge rated both younger and older targets) than for between-subject design (when different judges rated old and young targets). Finally, age was found to be less important than other types of information in determining the valence of attitudes toward older people. For example, judgments of severity of psychopathology have been shown to be more related to the type of disorder than to the age of the individuals (Hochman, Storandt, & Rosenberg, 1986). These conclusions suggest that negative attitudes are elicited only when conditions are established under which the judge will draw upon stereotypes of aging (for example, when an "old" social identity is made salient), not by advanced age per se. Thus, data supporting a negative generalized perception of the aged as an out-group are equivocal.

From a social identity perspective, however, comparisons between the out-group and the in-group *by* the in-group should show the out-group rated more negatively and the in-group rated more positively. Indeed, when younger subjects were asked to describe both young and old people, they supplied more positive attributes for younger people than for older people (Kite, Deaux, & Miele, 1991). In addition, the dominant culture provides ample evidence of being youth-oriented. Advertisements either celebrate youth or provide products for maintaining a youthful appearance, such as creams to eliminate wrinkles.

Several reviews (Kite & Johnson, 1988; Kite, Deaux, & Miele, 1991) have suggested that negative views of the old (they are irritable, have wrinkles, are in mental decline) represent a threat of what the self will become when old age is achieved. Thus, as social identity theory suggests, holding discriminatory views of the aged may represent an effort to distance oneself from a seemingly inevitable decline in cognitive and physical capabilities and physical appearance. Extrapolating from this point, the threat may increase with the approach of old age. Consistent with such a prediction, Seccombe and Ishii-Kuntz (1991) found that the most negative perceptions of old age were held by respondents aged fifty-five to sixty-four. It is also evident that—as adults observe age-related changes in themselves and in their parents—they find the prospect of aging less agreeable. With either interpretation, the most negative views were found among those for whom the matter had become more personally salient.

Hendricks and Leedham (1989) shift attention from the cosmetic; they suggest that the most dominant and destructive stereotype of the elderly is that they are dependent, with the stigma attached by this society to becoming dependent. These authors point out how, paradoxically, value decisions in society about the meaning of dependency, and about social policy choices, actually foster dependency in old age. One example is when retirement is forced or encouraged though society promulgates the value of productivity. Another is when Medicare coverage is offered for acute conditions but not for limited supportive care that would enable a chronically ill person to continue to remain relatively independent (Hendricks & Leedham, 1989).

Many of the stereotypical attributes associated with old age are factually correct, albeit undesirable, at least for some proportion of older individuals. To defuse stereotypes and foster more positive attitudes and policies toward the aged, it seems essential to separate attitude items according to accuracy. Some attributes of old age are correct but undesirable (gray hair, a less sharp memory). Other negative attributes may be true for some older adults, but probably are not statistically more common in old age than at any other age (for instance, nosiness). As Cook (1992) points out, literature on attitudes toward older adults fails to distinguish between lack of knowledge (believing that most older adults live in nursing homes) and frankly discriminatory attitudes (believing that older adults are undeserving of governmental support). Though the issue of stereotyping is not unique to the elderly, this issue is particularly nettlesome when such assessment devices as attitude scales combine these different sorts of items to draw inferences about how older adults actually behave.

It would also be a mistake to assume that all stereotypes of the elderly are negative. Kite, Deaux, and Miele (1991) found positive as well as negative characteristics listed by subjects asked to describe an older person. However, the effects of positive stereotypes can be more insidious than negative stereotypes if they set unrealistic standards against which older adults must compare themselves. For example, in *Avoid the Aging Trap*, gerontologist and clinical psychologist Muriel Oberleder (1982) tries to counteract what she refers to as "the myth of senility," opining that conditions labeled as senility are often preventable and reversible. She says, "There is one major brain disease that results in senility. It is called Alzheimer's disease and possibly is a congenital disease like Down syndrome, or Mongolism. But it affects less than 2 percent of elderly people and usually shows up in middle rather than old age. Ninety-eight percent of us need not worry about it" (pp. 36–37).

This statement represents an overly positive summary of the evidence. Dementia is generally thought to affect some 6 percent of those aged sixty-five and older (Mortimer & Hutton, 1985). Dementia of the Alzheimer's type is the most frequent of the dementias, accounting for some 70 percent of cases. Rates escalate with age, with the prevalence of mild to severe dementia in those aged eighty-five and older ranging from 23.8 percent to 41.5 percent (George & others, 1988). While it is true that many overestimate the risk of dementia, believing that far more older adults become senile than is actually the case (see Gatz & Pearson, 1988), it could also be destructive to suggest that Alzheimer's disease is a myth, especially for individuals and their relatives who are actively facing this disorder.

Social identity theory recognizes that people have multiple group memberships (Allen, Wilder, & Atkinson, 1983; Deaux, 1993). Numerous writers have suggested that stereotypes associated with each group membership can have a multiplicative effect. For instance, it has been suggested that there is a double devaluation associated with being both old and gay or with being both old and a member of a racial or ethnic minority, and a "triple jeopardy" associated with being old, female, and a member of a racial or ethnic minority (Quam & Whitford, 1992). Older gays and lesbians face special difficulties with health care financing and medical care systems, and older African Americans, especially women, are among the most impoverished older adults. People who are discriminated against by multiple "-isms" may be unable to distinguish which social category is more salient in the way they are being perceived and treated by others.

There is some evidence, however, that facing old age is actually made easier by having endured discrimination in the past. Quam and Whitford (1992) report that some older lesbians felt stronger from having managed the stress of ostracism for their sexual orientation. Life expectancy for African Americans is notably lower than for Anglos, by five to six years. Yet, African Americans who live to age eighty have a longer life expectancy than their Anglo counterparts, as if having survived the earlier discrimination led to a strength not enjoyed by others (Padgett, 1988).

In summary, stereotyping of the aged can be located in all age groups. Negative stereotyping of older people, however, is not as pervasive as it is sometimes portrayed. In the next section, we review how negative stereotypes can become incorporated into older adults' self-image, thereby setting the stage for problems such as depression and low self-esteem. We reserve for the final section a discussion of how group empowerment processes and structures can counteract the negative effects of social stereotypes of the aged and the perception that their problems are their own fault, rather than a result of societal forces (Cooper & Goethals, 1981).

Self-Perception Processes

Gerontological research has long been concerned with older people's self-image and sense of well-being. The research literature is filled with studies measuring self-conceptions, from self-rated health status to happiness (Bengtson, Reedy, & Gordon, 1985), and urging the importance of self-concept for understanding individual aging (see the review by Markus & Herzog, 1991). One way to look at self-perception in later life is to relate it to the social and personal aspects of an individual's identity. We begin with self-categorization theory, which deals with the way stereotypes become incorporated into the elder's self-image, and then turn to mechanisms by which individuals compare themselves with others in order to locate themselves relative to other individuals.

Identification and Self-Stereotyping

Both the social breakdown syndrome (Kuypers & Bengtson, 1973) and self-categorization theory (Turner, 1987) represent somewhat similar processes through which younger people's negative and stereotypic perceptions of older people may influence the older people's sense of self. In social breakdown syndrome, the elderly individual is posited to become more susceptible to external sources of evaluation as familiar sources of feedback are lost — for example, through retirement or loss of family members or friends to death. The remaining external sources of feedback are more likely to systematically label the older adult negatively, based on standards of self-worth held by the younger majority members of society (for example, standards based on socioeconomic contributions). The negative label is internalized, resulting in a negative self-concept.

Are older adults viewed negatively by older individuals? Kite, Deaux, and Miele (1991) found that older subjects supplied more negative attributes for older people than for younger people, and Troll (1984) is clear in declaring that from the point of view of a member of the oldest generation, "being an old woman is not generally considered a desirable state" (p. 2).

One obvious strategy to combat the vicious cycle and to maintain a positive self-image is simply not to identify oneself as old, thereby invalidating the aged stereotype as an appropriate source of self-evaluation. Self-report inventories often inquire about subjective age or age identity. In one large survey, the proportion of people indicating that they felt younger than their chronological age increased monotonically from 54 percent in the forties to 86 percent in the eighties (Goldsmith & Heiens, 1992). In another large probability sample of adults, the proportion of men and women identifying themselves as old was obtained (Logan, Ward, & Spitze, 1992). In their sixties, 18 percent of both men and women identified with being old; in their seventies, 49 percent of men and 35 percent of women identified with being old; and even in their eighties, only 63 percent of men and 66 percent of women identified with being old. Previously, Bultena and Powers (1978) found that fully 32 percent of respondents aged seventy and older continued to describe themselves as middle-aged. Additionally, Montepare and Lachman (1989) found that at age sixty-five, on the average, men felt themselves to be forty-nine, while women felt themselves to be forty-two. Finally, health problems were related to whether people thought of themselves as old or as middle-aged (Bultena & Powers, 1978; Logan, Ward, & Spitze, 1992).

Another approach is to ask respondents to define old age. Logan, Ward, and Spitze (1992) observed that, as people grew older, their definition of the age at which old age begins became older and older. Similarly, Seccombe and Ishii-Kuntz (1991) found that those aged eighty-five and older defined old age as beginning about ten years later than did fifty-five- to sixty-four-year-olds. Gender differences were observed, with men, on average, thought to become old between the ages of sixty and sixty-four and women between the ages of fifty-five and fifty-nine. This difference may reflect society's emphasis on women's needing to look youthful in order to be labeled attractive (Troll, 1984).

Based on their responses to questions about age identification, we suspect that a substantial proportion of older adults escape the social breakdown syndrome by identifying themselves as members of a younger age group. A prediction consistent with this line of thinking is that older individuals who identify themselves as younger will have correspondingly higher self-esteem. Indeed, most gerontological literature has implied or assumed that subjective age is associated with morale, with greater morale related to feeling younger at heart. (Intriguingly, the fact that this assumption is at variance with using the language of *denial* to refer to older adults' identifying themselves as middle-aged is not mentioned.)

Tests of this notion have been somewhat inconsistent. Logan, Ward, and Spitze (1992) found that life satisfaction was lower and stress was higher for those who thought of themselves as old. In contrast, Montepare and Lachman (1989) found that in older women, but not in older men, having an older subjective age was significantly related to greater life satisfaction. This effect for older women is contrary to what the literature on denial of aging would have suggested, but it is consistent with the idea that congruency between subjective and actual age would lead to greater satisfaction. Additionally, fear about aging—operationalized in terms of dreading gray hair, being afraid of outliving friends, and feeling apprehensive about widowhood — was not a significant predictor of life satisfaction in older adults.

Whether or not individuals decide to identify themselves as old may depend on whether or not they subscribe to negative stereotypes about aging. Ward (1977) hypothesized that believing that old age was stigmatizing would make a person more reluctant to accept the label "old." He found that self-esteem had no overall relationship to age identification. However, for those who believed that older people are looked down on by others, viewing themselves as old was related to lower self-esteem.

Reconciling these findings may require a more differentiated view of the meaning of subjective age. One's social identity as aged as defined by a variety of biological, sociological, and psychological attributes (Birren & Cunningham, 1985). How people identify themselves, how old they feel, the age that corresponds to their interests and activities, and what age they believe that they look could be quite different response domains. Moreover, as is true for any attributional process, each of these dimensions may vary according to the context in which the responses are given.

Social identity theory would suggest that evolving more positive conceptions of the aged in society should lead more older people to identify themselves as old and to have more positive self-evaluations. Yet part of the uniqueness of the aged as a social group is that the boundaries are fluid and defined developmentally, and that subjective age may differ from chronological age. Accordingly, a more complex understanding of identity and group identification is required in order to explain self-esteem in older adults.

Social Comparison in the Elderly

Social comparison provides an individual with information to locate the self relative to someone else on some identity dimension. The most useful information on social comparison is obtained from others similar to the self (Festinger, 1954); such comparisons can provide a more positive picture of one's own social group than comparisons to social stereotypes, which may give a negative and inaccurate impression. Upward comparison with similar others who are doing slightly better on a given dimension can serve as a source of aspiration ("If Andy can keep up with the younger members of the hiking club at age eighty, then I should be able to too"). Downward comparison to those who are doing slightly worse can protect the individual and serve to boost self-esteem ("I must be doing pretty well for my age, because I don't have the kind of health problems that poor Mary does, between her blood pressure and her arthritis") (Cooper & Goethals, 1981; Suls, Marco, & Tobin, 1991).

Social comparison processes may explain some apparently contradictory findings concerning older people's attitudes and evaluations of aging. Health is one arena where self-evaluations are typically positive, with most older adults rating their own health as better than average, yet older adults generally hold the stereotype that the aged are physically frail. Supporting the hypothesis of downward comparison, Suls, Marco, and Tobin (1991) found more positive self-rated health among those older individuals who reported comparing their health to people who were worse off.

Another comparison target is the self as a younger individual, or temporal comparison (Albert, 1977). On several dimensions of psychological well-being — for example, purpose in life, self-acceptance, and autonomy — Ryff (1991) found that young and middle-aged adults saw the present as an improvement over the past and anticipated still more gain in the future. On other dimensions, older adults had more similar evaluations of their past and present and of expected declines in the future. These negative expectations were offset through adjusting their ideal selves to be more in line with their real selves. Comparison of the present self with the past self can also have adverse effects on present ratings. Suls, Marco, and Tobin (1991) asked older subjects, with a mean age of nearly eighty, to rate their physical health and, for one group, to compare their present health with their past and anticipated health. Subjects tended to rate their present health as poorer under conditions of temporal comparison to prior health than if they were not asked to engage in temporal comparison, independent of their actual physical health status.

Thus, the role of social comparison in self-evaluation depends on the comparison target and the context in which the comparison takes place. Self-evaluative processes can have negative psychological consequences if older people internalize society's stereotypic definitions, as suggested by social breakdown theory (Kuypers & Bengtson, 1973). Alternatively, self-evaluative processes, particularly if they are used selectively, may function to preserve self-esteem and a sense of well-being (Markus & Herzog, 1991; Ryff, 1991). Looking at other members of the aged may help older adults to identify with a more differentiated picture of old age. Additionally, this sort of positive vision may enable the aged to combat disenfranchisement at the societal level that is associated with the stereotypical vision of the elderly.

Advocacy Groups That Counter Age Discrimination

Thus far, we have discussed two main social psychological processes that contribute to disempowering older people: stereotyping and self-perception. Elderly individuals can counter the effects of negative stereotypes either by not identifying with these stereotypes during self-categorization or by dispelling the stereotypes during social comparison. These efforts take place at the personal level. A much wider range of counteracting strategies is available when efforts are made at the group and societal levels. As a social minority, the aged can effectively influence the younger majority insofar as they have a consistent platform and a distinct identity (Nemeth, 1986). When the aged are identified as a cohesive constituency, they form an important political force.

Identifying the aged as a constituency has been achieved through such well-known organizations as the AARP, the National Council of Senior Citizens, and the Gray Panthers (see Huddy & Goodchilds, 1985). AARP, founded in 1955 by Ethel Percy Andrus, is one of the largest organizations and advocates pragmatic agendas. Members have access to insurance policies that supplement Medicare, low-cost generic prescription drugs, and hotel and rental-car discounts. One of the most heavily activist groups is the Gray Panthers, founded in 1970 by Maggie

Kuhn as a grass-roots organization to counteract ageism. Their agenda recognized that (1) poverty and poor health care for the aged were linked to other social issues and (2) most social service programs were premised on the dependency of the recipients, in effect increasing the latter's lack of power. Following this philosophy, the Gray Panthers take "Youth and Age" as their motto and aspire to be an interest group working to improve the lot of all disadvantaged individuals, not the elderly alone.

Organizations of and for the aged resemble those of other minority groups and sometimes deliberately adopt language and concepts from racism and sexism, although there has been little actual linkage. There are advocacy groups specific to older African Americans (the National Caucus on the Black Aged), older Latinos (Asociación Nacional pro Personas Mayores), and women (the Older Women's League). While representing distinct subgroups, all are concerned with issues that primarily affect older people.

Although thus far we have focused on the aged as a disenfranchised social minority, the extent of disadvantage experienced by older people is quite variable. While an unacceptably high proportion of older people who are also women, blacks, or Hispanics remain in the ranks of the poor or near poor, they form a sharp contrast to more economically successful retirees. The fact that many older adults are not economically destitute, in combination with the pressing economic concerns of the country, has led to allegations that federal programs for older adults, especially entitlement programs (Medicare, Medicaid, and Social Security), are depriving future generations. These charges have been emphasized in recent years by groups such as Americans for Generational Equity (AGE). Founded in 1985 by Senator David Durenburger and Representative James R. Jones, AGE views benefits provided to older adults on the basis of age, such as Social Security and health care entitlements, as discriminatory against younger people, and calls for ending unfairness to the younger generations. These issues are again being widely discussed as part of current proposals for economic reform.

Of conceptual importance is the perspective underlying

the debate, which is amenable to a social identity analysis —
namely, that the aged are a group in competition with other
groups for material and political goods. Both the disenfranchisement and competition images of the aged may ultimately be
related to the dependency of the minority on the majority for
self-definitional information and material resources. To combat this divisiveness, it is necessary to reframe the debate, making the point that both the aged and children who live in poverty
present shared evidence of the failure of broader economic and
social policies affecting these groups (Neugarten & Neugarten,
1989). Thus, Hendricks and Leedham (1989) suggest that advocacy groups make a deliberate effort to speak of "equity of
access to resources to forestall dependency at all ages" (p. 385).
Such a stance would make the aged a more powerful group by
dispelling destructive views of the aged in society and by identifying common concerns shared by both young and old.

In summary, advocacy groups can contribute to countering the negative effects of stereotyping and potential disenfranchisement of older individuals. The visible organization of
the elderly presents in-group members with a distinctive identity and out-group members with a salient group seeking to better
their position in society. These groups provide a number of concrete benefits for the aged, such as health insurance and a strong
voice in political affairs. They also provide a number of psychological benefits, such as a sense of cohesiveness stemming
from categorizing themselves as similar to other older persons
and different from younger persons (Hogg & Abrams, 1988),
and a sense of perceived control over their fate as a group (Rodin
& Langer, 1980). Identification with a powerful group is a constructive alternative to identification with a negative stereotype
and may prove to be more personally beneficial than not identifying oneself as old.

Conclusion

In this chapter, we have used social identity theory to examine
the manner in which stereotypes influence the social and personal aspects of older individuals' identities. We have suggested

a variety of processes through which a positive self-image may be maintained and have emphasized the complexity of social identity. Lillian Troll (1984) has put forth the view that the opposite of stereotyping is the recognition of diversity, while Maggie Kuhn (1991) has declared that the biggest myth challenged by Robert Butler's *Why Survive?* was the myth that all older people are alike.

Among other dimensions of human diversity, age is perhaps unique as a social category, because essentially everyone moves from not being in this group to being in it. We have tried to show that age as a dimension of human diversity is complex, cutting across personal, social, and societal levels of analysis. Moreover, self-definition according to age can serve as a complement to other varieties of self-definition such as gender, ethnicity, and sexual orientation, making it a particularly rich source of information for understanding prejudice and discrimination in our society. Therefore, including the aged in a discussion of nondominant groups in society enriches our appreciation of the complexity of creating an interdependent psychology of human diversity.

References

Albert, S. (1977). Temporal comparison theory. *Psychological Review, 84,* 485–503.

Allen, V. L., Wilder, D. A., & Atkinson, M. L. (1983). Multiple group membership and social identity. In T. R. Sarbin & K. E. Scheibe (Eds.), *Studies in social identity* (pp. 92–115). New York: Praeger.

Bengtson, V. L., Reedy, M. N., & Gordon, C. (1985). Aging and self-perceptions: Personality processes and social contexts. In J. E. Birren & K. W. Schaie (Eds.), *Handbook of the psychology of aging* (2nd ed., pp. 544–593). New York: Van Nostrand Reinhold.

Birren, J. E., & Cunningham, W. (1985). Research on the psychology of aging: Principles, concepts, and theory. In J. E. Birren & K. W. Schaie (Eds.), *Handbook of the psychology of aging* (2nd ed., pp. 3–34). New York: Van Nostrand Reinhold.

Brown, R. (1988). *Group processes within and between groups.* New York: Blackstone.

Bultena, G. L., & Powers, E. A. (1978). Denial of aging: Age identification and reference group orientations. *Journal of Gerontology, 33,* 748–754.

Butler, R. N. (1975). *Why survive? Being old in America.* New York: HarperCollins.

Cook, F. L. (1992). Ageism: Rhetoric and reality. *The Gerontologist, 32,* 292–293.

Cooper, J., & Goethals, G. R. (1981). The self-concept and old age. In S. B. Kiesler, J. N. Morgan, & V. K. Oppenheimer (Eds.), *Aging: Social change* (pp. 431–452). San Diego, CA: Academic Press.

Crocker, J., & Luhtanen, R. (1990). Collective self-esteem and ingroup bias. *Journal of Personality and Social Psychology, 58,* 60–67.

Crosby, F. J., (1993). Why complain? *Journal of Social Issues, 49,* 169–184.

Deaux, K. (1993). Reconstructing social identity. *Personality and Social Psychology Bulletin, 19,* 4–12.

Doise, W., & Sinclair, A. (1973). The categorization process in intergroup relations. *European Journal of Social Psychology, 3,* 145–157.

Festinger, L. A. (1954). A theory of social comparison processes. *Human Relations, 7,* 117–140.

Fiske, S. T., & Neuberg, S. L. (1990). A continuum of impression formation, from category-based to individuating processes: Influences of information and motivation on attention and interpretation. In M. P. Zanna (Ed.), *Advances in experimental social psychology* (Vol. 23, pp. 1–74). San Diego, CA: Academic Press.

Gatz, M., & Pearson, C. G. (1988). Ageism revised and the provision of psychological services. *American Psychologist, 43,* 184–188.

George, L. K., & others. (1988). Psychiatric disorders and mental health service use in later life: Evidence from the Epidemiologic Catchment Area program. In J. Brody & G. Maddox (Eds.), *Epidemiology and aging* (pp. 189–219). New York: Springer-Verlag.

Goldsmith, R. E., & Heiens, R. A. (1992). Subjective age: A test of five hypotheses. *The Gerontologist, 32,* 312–317.

Harris, L., & Associates. (1981). *Aging in the eighties: America in transition.* Washington, DC: National Council on Aging.

Hendricks, J., & Leedham, C. A. (1989). Creating psychological and societal dependency in old age. In P. S. Fry (Ed.), *Psychological perspectives on helplessness and control in the elderly* (pp. 369–394). North-Holland: Elsevier.

Hochman, L. O'B., Storandt, M., & Rosenberg, A. M. (1986). Age and its effect on perceptions of psychopathology. *Psychology and Aging, 1,* 337–338.

Hogg, M. A., & Abrams, D. (1988). *Social identifications: A social psychology of intergroup relations and group processes.* London: Routledge & Kegan Paul.

Huddy, L., & Goodchilds, J. D. (1985, Feb. 11). *SPSSI Task Force on Aging as a Social Issue: Summary report.* Unpublished manuscript, University of California, Los Angeles.

Kite, M. E., Deaux, K., & Miele, M. (1991). Stereotypes of young and old: Does age outweigh gender? *Psychology and Aging, 6,* 19–27.

Kite, M. E., & Johnson, B. T. (1988). Attitudes toward older and younger adults: A meta-analysis. *Psychology and Aging, 3,* 233–244.

Kuhn, M. (1991). *No stone unturned.* New York: Ballantine Books.

Kuypers, J. A., & Bengtson, V. L. (1973). Social breakdown and competence. *Human Development, 16,* 181–201.

Lemyre, L., & Smith, P. M. (1985). Intergroup discrimination and prejudice in the minimal group paradigm. *Journal of Personality and Social Psychology, 49,* 660–670.

Logan, J. R., Ward, R., & Spitze, G. (1992). As old as you feel: Age identity in middle and later life. *Social Forces, 71,* 451–467.

Manton, K. G. (1990). Mortality and morbidity. In R. H. Binstock & L. K. George (Eds.), *Handbook of aging and the social sciences* (3rd ed., pp. 64–90). San Diego, CA: Academic Press.

Markus, H. R., & Herzog, A. R. (1991). The role of the self-concept in aging. In K. W. Schaie & M. P. Lawton (Eds.), *Annual review of gerontology and geriatrics* (Vol. 11, pp. 110–143). New York: Springer-Verlag.

Milord, J. T. (1978). Aesthetic aspects of faces: A (somewhat) phenomenological analysis using multidimensional scaling methods. *Psychological Review, 92,* 289–316.

Montepare, J. M., & Lachman, M. E. (1989). "You're only as old as you feel": Self-perceptions of age, fears of aging, and life satisfaction from adolescnece to old age. *Psychology and Aging, 4,* 73–78.

Mortimer, J. A., & Hutton, J. T. (1985). Epidemiology and etiology of Alzheimer's disease. In J. T. Hutton & A. D. Kenny (Eds.), *Senile dementia of the Alzheimer's type.* New York: Alan R. Liss.

Nemeth, C. J. (1986). Differential contributions of majority and minority influence. *Psychological Review, 93,* 23–32.

Neugarten, B. L., & Neugarten, D. A. (1989). Policy issues in an aging society. In M. Storandt & G. R. VandenBos (Eds.), *The adult years: Continuity and change* (pp. 147–167). Washington, DC: American Psychological Association.

Oakes, P. J., & Turner, J. C. (1980). Social categorization and intergroup behavior: Does minimal intergroup discrimination make social identity more positive? *European Journal of Social Psychology, 16,* 295–301.

Oberleder, M. (1982). *Avoid the aging trap.* Washington, DC: Acropolis Books.

Padgett, D. (1988). Aging minority women: Issues in research and health policy. *Women and Health, 14,* 213–225.

Quam, J. K., & Whitford, G. S. (1992). Adaptation and age-related expectations of older gay and lesbian adults. *The Gerontologist, 32,* 367–374.

Rodin, J., & Langer, E. (1980). Aging labels: The decline of control and fall of self-esteem. *Journal of Social Issues, 36,* 12–29.

Ryff, C. D. (1991). Possible selves in adulthood and old age: A tale of shifting horizons. *Psychology and Aging, 6,* 286–295.

Seccombe, K., & Ishii-Kuntz, M. (1991). Perceptions of problems associated with aging: Comparisons among four older age cohorts. *The Gerontologist, 31,* 527–533.

Suls, J., Marco, C. A., & Tobin, S. (1991). The role of temporal comparison, social comparison, and direct appraisal in the elderly's self-evaluations of health. *Journal of Applied Social Psychology, 21,* 1125–1144.

Suzman, R., & Riley, M. W. (1985). Introducing the "oldest old." *Milbank Quarterly, 63,* 177–186.

Tajfel, H. (1982). Social identity and intergroup relations. *Annual Review of Psychology, 33,* 1–39.

Tajfel, H., & Turner, J. C. (1986). The social identity theory of intergroup relations. In S. Worchel & W. G. Austin (Eds.), *The social psychology of intergroup relations* (2nd ed., pp. 7–24). Chicago: Nelson-Hall.

Troll, L. E. (1984, Aug.). *Old women: "Poor, dumb, and ugly."* Invited address at the annual convention of the American Psychological Association, Toronto.

Turner, J. C. (1975). Social comparison and social identity: Some prospects for intergroup behavior. *European Journal of Social Psychology, 5,* 5–34.

Turner, J. C. (1987). *Rediscovering the social group: A self-categorization theory.* Oxford, England: Blackwell.

Ward, R. A. (1977). The impact of subjective age and stigma on older persons. *Journal of Gerontology, 32,* 227–232.

Zebrowitz, L. A. (1990). *Social perception.* Pacific Grove, CA: Brooks/Cole.

PART IV

Applying Paradigms and Concepts of Human Diversity

Conducting
Diversity-Conscious
Research and Creating
Settings Supportive
of Diversity

16

Empowerment as a Guide to Doing Research: Diversity as a Positive Value

Julian Rappaport

Unfortunately, most people who have had the occasion either to be research subjects or to make use of human services tend to be seen as deviant if they do not conform to a presumed common standard. In part, this attitude is reinforced by the traditional worldview of psychology as both a science and a profession. If social scientists are to foster an appreciation and an understanding of human diversity, we must have a coherent worldview that actively claims diversity as a positive value. The empowerment social agenda is one such worldview.

Psychologists have most often viewed difference as deviance. Once the idea of an agreed-upon single standard is conceded, the conceptual game is lost. It requires the labeling of people as deviants, and the very word conjures up images of degraded people. The concept of diversity expects people to be different in a positive sense; therefore, it requires us to look for

Note: Portions of this chapter were presented in a somewhat different context at the National Institute of Mental Health Workshop on Conceptual Research Models for Preventing Mental Disorders (DHHS Publication No. (ADM) 90-1713, Alcohol, Drug Abuse and Mental Health Administration) and at the Biennial Meeting of the Society for Community Research and Action, June 1993.

a variety of strengths in individuals and communities and to
search for a variety of standards to capture those strengths. This
is exactly the sort of search that the empowerment worldview
encourages.

Although psychology has a long tradition in the study of
individual differences, the way this has typically been approached
is to compare or rank-order individuals on one or more standard measures that are presumed to be important to all people.
Because the intention of psychology has been dominated by a
search for universals, the desire to foster genuine diversity in
social contexts requires an act of will and an attempt to overcome this tradition and replace it with the intention to understand different groups and individuals on their own terms, rather
than as deviants who are defined by their problems in living.
To accomplish this requires a worldview that makes more room
for people to speak for themselves, more room for policies that
help people to arrive at their own goals, and more room to find
strengths rather than deficits.

As researchers, we will always represent our own voices,
and it would be naive to assume that we can ever simply present
the voices of others. Nevertheless, it is possible to adopt a worldview that not only values diversity, but also requires researchers, scholars, interventionists, and policy makers to continuously
ask, "Whose interests are being served?" In this chapter, the empowerment social agenda is offered as one such worldview with
direct implications for the practice of social science research and
action. Examples from research, conducted with a number of
colleagues and students who have tried to keep an empowerment worldview in mind, are referred to in the last section. Before detailing the empowerment viewpoint in particular, the politics of viewpoints that honor diversity are briefly considered.

The Politics of Diversity

For those who want social science and social policy to honor
diversity, claims to be an objective or neutral social scientist
whose private values can be separated from scientific method
are no longer believable. Sampson (1993) puts it this way: "To

maintain a point of viewlessness about what both historically and currently has been associated with one group's particular point of view is to operate politically while denying that any politics is involved. It is to deny voice to those whose experiences are rooted in a different culture or to grant them voice but only if they speak in ways that undo their own particularities" (p. 1226).

This chapter is about research questions and social values, ideas and action, conception and method, research and policy. I take the position that these are not polarities, but aspects of an interdependent whole. The scholar necessarily finds some questions to be more interesting than others because of the values the scholar holds rather than because of something inherent in the problem itself. Stated otherwise, the questions the researcher asks reveal what he or she thinks is worth asking. In this view the researcher is a claims-maker (Spector & Kitsuse, 1987) who is competing with other claims-makers for public attention and resources (Humphreys & Rappaport, 1993). Research methods are free neither of values nor of the conceptual framework the researcher holds. If this is the case, then the researcher who claims to understand or make statements about others is faced with the task of representing the experience of others. To do so in an intellectually honest way will require a means to hear the voices of the people themselves. Often the voices of those outside the mainstream, or those whose identity has been historically degraded, will be difficult to hear. To amplify their voices (and to avoid providing them with our own scripts) a way of doing research is required that consciously attends to this goal.

Do we really believe that differences between the powerless and the powerful are not necessarily signs of individual deficits among the powerless; that all children can learn; that there are many people who are economically poor but who know quite a bit about how to raise children, live life, and create community? Do we believe that alternative forms of family structure can raise children who function well? Do we believe that many homeless or so-called chronically mentally ill people actually know a good deal about what they need in order to live well, often lacking only resources? Do we believe that it is possible to have a fair share of the wealth of our society without becoming a cultural convert to Western European mercantile values? Is it necessary to sit still in a classroom in order to learn? Does a child who has spent six years learning about her neighborhood by exploring rather than by sitting need to sit still and be quiet in order to learn how to read and count once she enters school? Could we design learning environments suitable to children's needs rather than to the convenience of schools as they are currently organized? Can people who score poorly on multiple-choice college entrance exams do well in college? Can we design environments for people, with people, rather than forcing people into environments that are likely only to defeat and frustrate them? Asking such questions implies that human diversity is a positive value. Answering yes to these questions implies a worldview that is different from the one behind the traditional practices of social science, which are largely designed to represent the values of a mainstream social reality that seeks conformity and consensus rather than self-defined identity and maximization of a diversity of strengths.

It is time for research psychologists who believe in the value of human diversity to act in our professional lives as if what we do matters. We live in a time when logical-positivist claims are challenged by many who espouse alternative philosophy (Manicas, 1987) and research (Denzin & Lincoln, 1993) and when many have laid the groundwork for a politics of identity that calls for a different kind of psychological research as both needed and sensible (Sampson, 1993). No longer can we claim to separate our views as citizens from our views as professionals, researchers, or scholars. We know too much to hide. We know that the social world is constructed. We know that social scientists are among those who do the constructing. We teach, write, counsel, encourage policy, and claim knowledge before both our colleagues and the young people who attend our colleges and universities. We are among the legitimated agents permitted to say for public consumption what is real and what is myth. We decide to pay attention to the voices of some and not to others as we seek to explore and explain the social world. We know that unidirectional causality in the social world is a false idea, and that there are no defensible single standards of competence in the absence of strongly held, preconceived values.

At least two implications follow from this knowledge. One pertains to the ethics of social responsibility and the other to the methods. First, all researchers have an obligation to acknowledge whose interests are served by the research they conduct. Second, methods for conducting research should be consistent with the claims made about whose interests are served. It is this second point that this chapter pursues: What kind of research methods are consistent with an empowerment worldview that claims to assert human diversity as a positive, rather than merely a passive, value? To begin requires an explication of the empowerment worldview, its epistemology, and its presuppositions.

The Epistemology of Empowerment

In an illustration attributed to Hadley Cantril (Stacey, 1989), we find a simple summary of some basic issues with respect to epistemology and research in the social and behavioral sciences. Cantril describes a conversation between three baseball umpires that goes something like this. The first umpire says, "There's balls and there's strikes and I calls 'em as they is." The second umpire replies, "I calls 'em as I sees 'em." The third umpire takes a different stance. She says, "There ain't no such thing as balls or strikes until I says so."

Those who ascribe to an empowerment framework for research and intervention concerned with problems in living take the position that the first umpire is both arrogant and wrong. She may have the power to act as she pleases, but given human fallibility, including attitudinal, cognitive, and perceptual biases, her power to define reality is best understood to be derived from social convention—the rules of the game, so to speak—rather than from the accuracy of her calls. In our view this is one of the difficulties with an approach to psychology driven by the application of a single standard for what constitutes mental health, social adjustment, or other prosocial behavior, despite its conventional acceptability and familiarity. The argument is not that there are no standards, but rather that there are many problems for which alternative constructions are needed that take into account local context, history, and symbols. For example, the child who enters school having spoken black dialect and communicated well with his neighbors and friends must be afforded the respect of teachers who value his current language skills rather than those who treat it as wrong. How to teach such a child to read and to speak in Standard English is a legitimate educational task, but it cannot be done fairly by people who do not accept the child's current language as legitimate.

Our attitude about the second umpire is that admitting she calls them as she sees them is at least a fair way to describe her role in the game. Indeed, given the now widely acknowledged influence of training, values, presuppositions, and worldviews on the content and interpretation of data, most psychologists would probably agree that the second umpire is closer than the first to a fair description of how she conducts her business. We take for granted all the individual as well as shared cultural fallibilities, biases, values, and preferences held by the umpire. If we wish to play the game with a minimum of disruption, we will at least not dispute the good intentions of this umpire. To the extent that we are playing well, see ourselves as being treated fairly, and so on, a certain amount of leeway and good faith is granted for the sake of a smoothly operating game. We all can remember the chaos of our childhood games when there were no umpires to whom we could grant authority.

But what if you are Jackie Robinson? What if you are the first woman who wants to play in the league? What if the umpire knows you are gay? What if you play from a wheelchair? What if you have a shabby uniform, or none at all? Acknowledging the second umpire's view has different implications. Perhaps you are more likely to argue with her; perhaps you are less likely to be willing to go along with the umpire's judgment for the sake of keeping the game running smoothly. Perhaps you are more willing to be unreasonable, to understand that a certain amount of disruption in the game is necessary to keep everyone honest. Thus, those interested in diversity might agree with Feyerabend's argument (1978) that today we should be less worried about the separation of church and state than about the separation of science and state. We must break the alliance that, through government-funded research, tends to homogenize research methodology.

The empowerment perspective is most congruent with the third umpire's view of her role. It is what in a political context might be called a critical consciousness. In philosophical terms, this view is consistent with the view of those who argue that reality is socially constructed, and perhaps it is also consistent with the emerging deconstructionist views. One could call on a variety of both mainstream and feminist literature (Berg & Smith, 1988; Fine, 1989; MacKinnon, 1987; Manicas, 1987; Miller, 1987) to make such arguments, and other chapters in this volume do so. Here all I want to point out is that a fondness for the views of the third umpire is not something invented by those of us who are concerned with empowerment in the struggle to capture a place on the sociopolitical agenda for the last decade of the twentieth century. And, make no mistake about it, concern with human diversity is part of the sociopolitical agenda. The empowerment perspective on the one hand, and the single-standard point of view in which individual differences equal deviance on the other, have quite different social agendas and therefore quite different research agendas.

Many social scientists feel a certain uneasiness about the third umpire's statement. She seems to imply that there is no reality until it is interpreted. But in the world of history that is written by the winners of wars, as in psychology and social theory, such ideas do not seem to be quite so outrageous. Common examples of ideas previously justified by "scientific analysis" include explanations for the limited intelligence of both voluntary immigrants and African Americans, constructions concerning "women's nature," and the belief that homosexuality is a disease, all popular in psychology and psychiatry only a few decades ago. Yet let us not fool ourselves; those who held such scientifically respectable beliefs were no more foolish or illogical than we are. Being comfortable with knowing that we (that is, the umpire) get to decide who strikes out and who does not is difficult for those of us who pride ourselves on a rational-scientific-humanistic attitude. For those who favor an empowerment framework, it is impossible.

In the empowerment worldview, the concern becomes how to collaborate with people to create, encourage, or assist them to become aware of, obtain, or create the resources they may need to make use of their competencies. However, empowerment is not limited to individual competencies. It also involves contextual or setting variables as well as social and political processes. Working with different people may lead to different outcomes in different settings, under various social realities, at different times, and under different historical, political, and economic conditions; the same behaviors may not be construed as problems or as assets in all contexts or by alternate conceptual schemas.

The Empowerment Construct:
Some Presuppositions and Implications

Empowerment is a multilevel construct applicable to individual citizens as well as to organizations and neighborhoods; it suggests the study of people in context (Altman, 1993; Altman & Rogoff, 1987; Felner & Felner, 1989; Florin & Wandersman, 1990; Seidman, 1988; Trickett, 1984; Zimmerman, 1990). The concept suggests both individual determination over one's own life and democratic participation in the life of one's community, often through the mediating structures of society, which include the family, the school, the neighborhood, the church, and voluntary associations, as well as self- and mutual-help groups and organizations.

In a recent statement from the Cornell University Empowerment Group (1989), a project funded by the Ford Foundation and concerned with application of empowerment concepts to the challenges faced by low-income families in both the United States and other countries, the following is offered as a definition: "Empowerment is an intentional, ongoing process centered in the local community, involving mutual respect, critical reflection, caring, and group participation, through which people lacking an equal share of valued resources gain greater access to and control over those resources" (p. 2).

Since processes (means) are as important as products (ends), and since many different end-products may be beneficial to people, those of us who hold an empowerment viewpoint have difficulty with a public policy that limits us to programs we design, operate, or package for social agencies to use on people. We want the form and the metacommunication as well as the content of our work to be consistent with empowerment. In this view of empowerment as a *process,* or as a *mechanism* by which people gain mastery over their affairs, we assume that it will look different for different people, organizations, and settings. Diversity is to be expected.

Social science language is metaphoric and symbolic. The language of empowerment creates images that are different from those created by the more familiar language of medicine and the helping professions. We speak of citizens rather than patients, resources rather than cures, and collaboration rather than treatment. A concern with empowerment may lead us to question the metacommunication and assumptions hidden in the language of professions that are steeped in a history of white, male prerogative, the myth of the rugged individual, capitalist myths of a classless society, competitive rather than cooperative ideals, and historical goals more consistent with adjustment to the status quo than with social justice. Iatrogenic effects resulting from the "medicalization" of almost everything are also questioned (Seidman & Rappaport, 1986).

Those who are concerned with empowerment will confront the paradox that even people who appear to be the most incompetent, in need, and apparently unable to function require more rather than less control over their lives. Nor does control mean that individuals must be entirely self-sufficient. Being part of a group, an organization, or a community in which one is both helper and helpee is one way to expand on our typically individualistic views of control. It is one way to concretize what Sampson (1988) has called "ensembled individualism." Here one can find both meaning and identity as well as material resources through shared connections based on something other than power over others or control over scarce resources (Katz, 1984; Sampson, 1988). Indeed, consistent with many of the feminist writers, power may be thought of as the power to empower others, rather than to control others (Miller, 1987).

Empowerment implies that many competencies are already present or at least possible, given niches and opportunities. It is consistent with a focus on strengths rather than weaknesses (Saleebey, 1992) and rejects an analysis of social problems that includes blaming the victim or applying a single standard of competence. Thus, empowerment lends itself to a variety of locally rather than centrally controlled solutions based on different assumptions in different places, settings, and neighborhoods. Cultural and local diversity is seen as a positive value. Empowerment demands that we look to diverse local settings where people are already handling their own problems of living, in order to learn more about how they do it. It also demands that we find ways to make what we learn from them more public and accessible to others who are shut out from such settings. One way to do this is to use our research to give voice to the people of concern by authenticating their experiences (Lincoln & Guba, 1985, 1986; Rappaport, 1990). As a consequence, an empowerment worldview requires knowing (not just knowing about) the particular people we claim to understand because we have provided an opportunity for them to speak for themselves. Learning how to provide opportunities for researchers to actually know the people they hope to understand is one of the tasks of the empowerment social agenda and its program of research.

Empowerment, Research, and Authentication

At the heart of the problem for research on human diversity within psychology is the received view that the best research that can be done is necessarily an experimental, replicable test of a theoretically derived hypothesis. The test is measured by operationalizing standard constructs and linking them to the unidirectional causal and linear thinking of logical positivism as interpreted by standard textbook methodology, in order to make universal statements about people. In such a view the researcher, for the sake of objectivity, becomes separated from the people he or she is trying to understand. Empowerment thinking implies interdependence, contextual meaning, and the understanding that what "works" in terms of concrete actions in one setting may not be transportable by means of manuals or measures. It implies a different epistemology and ultimately a different methodology. One such approach is naturalistic or qualitative research that seeks to be both trustworthy and authentic. This does not necessarily prohibit quantification, or counting and comparing, but it does not assume that this will always be the best way to know the people we are trying to understand. Through the search for authenticity in our research, it is possible to enhance access to resources for the people of concern. How this can be done has been the subject of study for some researchers in the naturalistic tradition, especially those who have emphasized qualitative evaluative research.

Writers such as Lincoln & Guba (1985, 1986), who have emphasized research in educational settings, provide a set of ideas and methods that may be applicable to other settings as well. They believe that the research act itself should be empowering, rather than disempowering. In a previous paper (Rappaport, 1990), I summarized some of these ideas with respect to conducting research. The conceptual framework offered here has methodological implications, many of which are consistent with the naturalistic research paradigm as explicated by Lincoln and Guba (1985, 1986) and applied to the empowerment social agenda in Rappaport (1990).

Lincoln and Guba address themselves to the ways by which naturalistic research may handle the traditional problems of internal and external validity, reliability, and objectivity. Their answers require the researcher to establish credibility by prolonged engagement and observation, by thick (detailed) observation that permits other researchers to determine the potential transferability of findings to new contexts, and by internal and external audits. Such methods tend to require the researcher to establish role relationships with the people of concern that are both long-term and based on mutual respect — relationships that challenge many of the ideas of "objective" social science.

In developing these ideas, they also suggest that naturalistic research must concern itself with what they call authenticity. The notion of authenticity as a criterion for adequacy of research demands that the research process itself be empowering rather than disempowering. There are many implications of that demand, the most overarching of which is that the research be what they call "fair" — that it represent the social reality of the people researched, that involvement be informed, and that feedback and collaboration be continuous. Such research, which seeks to give voice to the voiceless, is one means of increasing access to resources among the people of concern. It is consistent with the epistemology of empowerment.

The final sections of this chapter refer to a series of projects that take the above concerns seriously while for the most part remaining within the mainstream traditions of psychological research methodology. They range from projects where data collection was the most important goal through those in which the creation of empowering contexts was the raison d'être. Most of these projects are not examples of the most radical methodological implications that follow from the ideas expressed above. Rather, they are examples drawn from my own experience as a researcher who takes empowerment seriously and as a supervisor of research for students who have wanted to become research psychologists and who take empowerment seriously, but who also take the research traditions of the discipline seriously. It is my hope that we can learn how to do a better job of representing the diversity of human experiences in our future work, and it is my expectation that to do so will require us to learn more about how to do qualitative research than we heretofore have. Nevertheless, these projects are serious attempts to honor diversity in the ways discussed above.

In psychology, there are few traditions of qualitative research that represents the voice of the people studied. One difficult task before us is to develop standards for evaluating our own work when we try to develop a psychology of diversity rather than deviance. It is far more difficult to do good research when the methods for doing it are vague and unspecified. Although efforts at specification of qualitative methods in social science are being made (Denzin & Lincoln, 1993), these efforts tend to come from those who are outside the traditions of psychological science. On the other hand, while they tend to think of their work as program evaluation, some serious methodologists within psychology, such as Cook and Shadish (1986), are willing to speak of "worldly evaluation." They do recognize that "because evaluators are paid to improve social programs they must interact with the programs on the latter's terms. They have to embrace the whole messy world of social programming, knowing that its boundaries do not respect those of the disciplines in which they were trained, while also realizing that they will have to learn practical lessons they could not have been taught, or would not have appreciated during their training" (p. 194).

It is precisely this attitude that must be held by those who want to apply the empowerment social agenda to research that fosters diversity. However, one point of departure from the above quote concerns whose voice is represented. Many in program evaluation are "paid to improve social programs" that are developed by governmental or social agencies from the top down. These are the people who usually control the resources to hire evaluators and researchers. For those of us who are concerned with amplifying the voices of the powerless with fairness and authenticity and with serving as a catalyst for the development of bottom-up social policies, the task becomes finding ways to do "worldly evaluation" from a different point of view — that is, from the viewpoint of the people we are trying to understand, rather than from the viewpoint of social programmers.

Below I refer to several such efforts that have emerged from my own work with both colleagues and students. It is worth noticing that the word *empowerment* is not always acknowledged in this work. Frankly, there are now so many people who use the word in so many contexts that I am more concerned when the word is used loosely — when it serves as a cover for old ways of doing things, or as a political strategy for excusing government from the responsibility of providing adequate resources for people, or as a trait that is reified — than I am when new ways of doing things do not use the word (see Zimmerman, 1993). What matters is that the research should be designed and carried out in a way that reflects the worldview described above. Finally, it is also worth noting that to conduct such research does not necessarily require a large expenditure of financial resources, and that projects concerned with empowerment and the fostering of diversity are feasible for graduate students as well as for more senior researchers.

Research from an Empowerment Perspective

Much of the development of my own ideas about empowerment and diversity, described above, was formulated in the context of a twenty-year history of involvement in the Our Gang Day Care Center and the Oasis Graphics information and communication center located in the African American community of Champaign-Urbana, Illinois (Rappaport, Davidson, Wilson, & Mitchell, 1975). These settings were designed for training and service, rather than as research projects, and it was there that I learned about collaborating without controlling people. Because the projects were arranged in a way that enabled local community leaders to set their own agendas and allowed students to help them accomplish their aims, they took on a shape and format that reflected the voice of the participants, rather than my own. This meant that the setting provided me less with a place to do research than with a place to hear a viewpoint different from the one I typically encountered at the university. Here the idea of empowerment came to life for me.

For those who value genuine diversity, engagement in such settings is quite valuable. The function this particular setting served for me and my students was as a place in which we could comfortably encounter local people for whom the university provided resources in exchange for allowing us to learn from listening to them talk about their experiences. Many research projects developed out of this sort of engagement. The projects were not direct results of the setting, but rather the result of exchanging ideas with the people we were able to meet there. It was there that I began to understand the value of long-term engagement with nonuniversity people and how unusual it is for academic researchers.

My own lengthy association with the GROW mutual-help organization, organized by people who consider themselves to be former mental patients, is one example of long-term engagement (Rappaport and others, 1985). We have conducted longitudinal, collaborative research describing the history and development of the organization, its impact over time on members, the nature of their small groups, and the ways in which the organization has empowered its members (Luke, Rappaport, & Seidman, 1991; Luke, Roberts, & Rappaport, 1993; Rappaport and others, 1985; Rappaport, Reischl, & Zimmerman, 1992; Roberts and others, 1991; Toro, Rappaport, & Seidman, 1987; Toro and others, 1988; Zimmerman and others, 1991).

This work has utilized multiple methods of both data collection and analysis. What has been consistent, however, has been a willingness to describe the organization from the viewpoint of the members themselves. It began with collaboration in the design of the study and the measures and was carried out with a team of researchers who consistently sought feedback from the members themselves. Most recently, I have come to see that in order to understand the experience of the members, we need to find better ways to hear them tell their own stories in their own words. The understanding of the organization as a *narrative community* is one that is consistent with the intention to take diversity seriously; some of the thinking behind this approach has been described in a recent paper (Rappaport, 1993). In the more general context of research methodology, I suspect that those who care to represent diversity in other settings may also find it useful to consider ways to record and amplify the stories of the people they care to represent. A number of other projects adopting this approach are mentioned below, along with the work of past and present graduate-student colleagues who conducted their own research in community settings, while they were students, in ways that I consider to be consistent with the empowerment agenda.

I mention these projects because they were all spearheaded by graduate students who conducted their own research by pursuing an understanding of some group of people with whom they were willing to engage in long-term relationships. They did this in a way that both was concerned with the development of empowering role relationships and was feasible for a graduate student. My focus here is not on the results (although there are many interesting findings — at least as many as we typically find in more usual studies) as much as on the ways in which the projects were conducted. I did not supply financial support for any of the research, although I hope that I supplied intellectual and personal support. These are all projects in which the then graduate students took their own intellectual and action initiatives. I find them all to be consistent with the empowerment social agenda and the desire to foster diversity as a positive value. One important similarity is that they all were conducted in settings where the researcher had already developed mutually beneficial relationships. That is, the researcher had spent considerable time in the setting, often helping people to accomplish their own aims, before deciding to conduct research.

Project 1

Several years ago, Kenneth Maton conducted a dissertation in a nondenominational Christian church community (Maton, 1985). He spent two years getting to know people and letting them get to know him. He did this in a way that was quite genuine — attending both religious services and small-group Bible-study meetings in which he sought to see the world from the perspective of the community of interest. One reason they were of interest was because the members appeared to have a sense of empowerment, expressed in both their private lives and their involvement with social issues. This led to a series of interviews with members about their own lives and aspirations. It also led to a questionnaire study of empowerment and the sense of community as they were defined by the members themselves.

As a result of the relationships that developed between Maton and the community members, he discovered the community's expressed desire to share both their material and nonmaterial goods and services with each other. This later led to his setting up an intervention — a bartering system. The system grew directly out of the members' own interests and was organic to the organization. Although Maton made a number of empirical discoveries about the impact of material and nonmaterial giving and receiving, some of which led him to later studies of social support, none of this could have come from a researcher who did not know the setting in the deep way that he had come to know it. Details of this work may be found in Maton (1987) and Maton and Rappaport (1984).

Project 2

A second researcher, Bruce Ambuel (1989) was interested in the problems experienced by young women who sought pregnancy counseling. He and his wife began to volunteer at Planned Parenthood, where they worked for several years. Because he was also interested in both legal issues and developmental psychology, Ambuel followed the legal arguments of the U.S. Supreme Court that suggested that teenagers were less competent to make decisions concerning abortion, child-rearing, or adoption than legal adults. His observations of young women in the medical setting did not match the court's arguments, nor did they match what he knew about cognitive development. However, no studies of adolescents who made pregnancy decisions had been conducted in the actual context of a real decision following a pregnancy test. Previous work had posed only hypothetical questions.

Ambuel was in an ideal setting to conduct a study of actual decision making because he already understood the setting and had developed a keen sense of mutual trust with its members. He worked closely for two years with Planned Parenthood counselors to enable them to conduct interviews that permitted us to answer questions about decision making in an ecologically valid context. We were permitted to tape-record the interviews and therefore could develop content analysis methods for assessing competence in real decision-making sessions. Again, the data, which have been used in Supreme Court briefs submitted by the American Psychological Association (*Hodgson v. Minnesota,* 1989) as well as in journal articles (Ambuel & Rappaport,

1992), speak to empowerment partly because of how they were collected. But this study also led us to propose a social policy of empowerment that is based on the legal concept of informed consent and on linking clients to sources of information and participation (Ambuel & Rappaport, 1992).

Project 3

A third dissertation was conducted by Karla Fischer (1992). She spent three years, while studying as both a graduate student and a law student, as a volunteer and advocate at a local women's shelter. Again, this was a long-term commitment, one in which she worked hard at being useful to both the clients and the staff at the shelter over a period of years. In the process, she came to understand, from the ground up, the experiences of women seeking an order of protection from their male partners who had been physically and emotionally abusive to them. Because of both her direct experience and her genuine assistance to this community, Fischer was able to frame interesting and contextually sensible research questions. She later collected data from and interviewed many women who shared their stories with her as part of their desire to deal with their life circumstances. Her dissertation, which explored the practical and psychological experiences of women who seek such legal assistance, was the basis for her communication of the stories told by the women in ways that authentically represented them.

Project 4

A study recently completed by Keith Humphreys (1993) is an intensive qualitative analysis of the experiences of twenty members of a local chapter of Adult Children of Alcoholics. Humphreys provides a thick description of their meetings and a content analysis of the organization's reading material. Like the other researchers, Humphreys engaged the members in close contacts over a period of years, at first because of his own personal interest in them, their stories, and their organization. He did not approach the members as subjects, but rather as informed critics of their own lives. He listened to them for a long time and developed a framework that seemed to explain their worldview and how it changed when one of their members experienced recovery. He then treated this worldview as a set of hypotheses about the group meetings, the reading material, and the life stories he later listened to.

Project 5

A fifth study, for which the data have just been collected, is in some ways more traditional (in that it is based on questionnaire data) and in other ways more directly concerned with the conditions of empowerment. Brad Heil spent over a year working with both school administrators and teacher's union organizers and officers in order to obtain joint sponsorship for a study of participative decision making among teachers in a public school district. He spent many days listening and learning to understand the language and the very real concerns of teachers and the fears of administrators. He did this under conditions of mutual mistrust between the union and the administration, yet he was able to obtain data from all sixteen schools and some 67 percent of the teachers. What is remarkable is that by treating both sides of this adversarial context with respect, he earned respect for his own work; in turn, he helped teachers and administrators to develop respect for each other. The study, informed by many hours of before-the-beginning discussion, conceptualizes decision making in the classroom, the school building, and the district. When completed, it will speak to the relative contributions of various kinds of decision making to teacher satisfaction and to differential student success across the sixteen schools.

Project 6

We have established a small research group composed of people interested in studying the relationship between individual life stories and the narratives of their communities. This has led to several projects with certain features in common—including the effort to apply methods such as interviews, focus groups, and multiple contacts over time—to settings in which the researcher becomes both known and knowledgeable. Such work has led to descriptions of life in a religious community among a group of nuns, in a student religious foundation, among members of Alcoholics Anonymous, and in a public housing project (Rappaport, 1992).

It is worth noting that one of these projects has fostered yet another dissertation. This one, by Mark Salzer, is now in the data analysis stage. Many of its ideas grew from Salzer's experiences working over a period of years with Mark Aber, another Illinois faculty member, and local organizers of a resident management group in a public housing project. The experience of listening, over a long period of time, to the local residents' stories about their lives, told in context, and discovering how different these stories were from the stereotypes about housing project residents heard on television and in other media presentations that are taken out of context, led to a study of stereotyping among college students through an analysis of their narratives about hypothetical housing project residents.

Conclusion

In summary, work done by those who take diversity as a positive value, and who are guided by an empowerment perspective, is both feasible and satisfying if they are willing to engage in long-term relationships with the people of concern. These relationships are feasible for graduate students as well as for more senior researchers. Research guided by the empowerment social agenda and methods will reflect:

1. Explicit social values that favor bottom-up rather than top-down development of social policies concerned with increased access to resources, and with authenticity and fairness as well as with trustworthiness
2. A worldview that sees people in context and respects that context, often by amplifying the voices of the people of concern

3. A methodology that makes use of interviews, stories, and focus groups designed to provide the people of concern with ways to express their own perspective
4. Attention to the development of role relationships between the researcher and researched that are mutual rather than exploitative, and that engage the people of concern as genuine collaborators over time.

References

Altman, I. (1993). Challenges and opportunities of a transactional world view: Case study of contemporary Mormon polygynous families. *American Journal of Community Psychology, 21,* 135–163.

Altman, I., & Rogoff, B. (1987). World view in psychology: Trait, interactional, organismic, and transactional perspectives. In D. Stokols & I. Altman (Eds.), *Handbook of environmental psychology.* New York: Wiley.

Ambuel, B. (1989). *Developmental change in adolescents' psychological and legal competence to consent to abortion: An empirical study and quantitative model of social policy.* Unpublished doctoral dissertation, University of Illinois at Urbana-Champaign.

Ambuel, B., & Rappaport, J. (1992). Developmental trends in adolescents' psychological and legal competence to consent to abortion. *Law and Human Behavior, 16,* 129–154.

Berg, D. N., & Smith, K. K. (Eds.). (1988). *The self in social inquiry.* Newbury Park, CA: Sage.

Cook, T. D., & Shadish, W. R. (1986). Program evaluation: The worldly science. *Annual Review of Psychology, 37,* 193–232.

Cornell University Empowerment Group. (1989, Oct.). *Networking bulletin, 1*(2) [Special issue].

Denzin, N. K., & Lincoln, Y. S. (Eds.). (1993). *Handbook of qualitative research.* Newbury Park, CA: Sage.

Felner, R. D., & Felner, T. Y. (1989). Prevention programs in the educational context: A transactional-ecological framework for program models. In L. Bond & B. Compas (Eds.), *Primary prevention in the schools.* Newbury Park, CA: Sage.

Feyerabend, P. (1978). *Science in a free society* (pp. 73–107). London: NLB.

Fine, M. (1989). Coping with rape: Critical perspectives on consciousness. In K. K. Unger (Ed.), *Representations: Social constructions of gender.* Amityville, NY: Baywood.

Fischer, K. (1992). *The psychological impact and meaning of court orders of protection for battered women.* Unpublished doctoral dissertation, University of Illinois at Urbana-Champaign.

Florin, P., & Wandersman, A. (1990). An introduction to citizen participation, voluntary organizations, and community development: Insights for empowerment through research. *American Journal of Community Psychology, 18,* 41–54.

Hodgson v. *Minnesota* (1989). U.S. Supreme Court. APA brief for amici curiae. Washington, DC: American Psychological Association.

Humphreys, K. (1993). *World view transformations in Adult Children of Alcoholics mutual help group.* Unpublished doctoral dissertation, University of Illinois at Urbana-Champaign.

Humphreys, K., & Rappaport, J. (1993). From the community mental health movement to the war on drugs: A study in the definition of social problems. *American Psychologist, 48*(8), 892–901.

Katz, R. F. (1984). Empowerment and synergy: Expanding the community's healing resources. *Prevention in Human Services, 3,* 201–226.

Lincoln, Y. S., & Guba, E. G. (1985). *Naturalistic inquiry.* Newbury Park, CA: Sage.

Lincoln, Y. S., & Guba, E. G. (1986). But is it rigorous? Trustworthiness and authenticity in naturalistic evaluation. In D. D. Williams (Eds.), *Naturalistic evaluation.* New Directions for Program Evaluation, No. 30. San Francisco: Jossey-Bass.

Luke, D., Rappaport, J., & Seidman, E. (1991). Setting phenotypes in a mutual help organization. *American Journal of Community Psychology, 19,* 147–167.

Luke, D. A., Roberts, L., & Rappaport, J. (1993). Individual, group context, and individual-group fit predictors of self-help group attendance. *Journal of Applied Behavioral Science, 29,* 214–236.

MacKinnon, C. A. (1987). *Feminism unmodified: Discourses on life and law.* Cambridge, MA: Harvard University Press.

Manicas, P. T. (1987). *A history and philosophy of the social sciences.* New York: Basil Blackwell.

Maton, K. (1985). *Economic sharing among church members: Psychological correlates and evaluation of an economic barter-sharing service.* Unpublished doctoral dissertation, University of Illinois at Urbana-Champaign.

Maton, K. I. (1987). Patterns and psychological correlates of material support within a religious setting: The bidirectional support hypothesis. *American Journal of Community Psychology, 15,* 185–208.

Maton, K., & Rappaport, J. (1984). Empowerment in a religious setting: A multivariate investigation. *Prevention in Human Services, 3,* 37–70.

Miller, J. B. (1987). Women and power. *Women and Therapy, 6,* 1–10.

Rappaport, J., (1990). Research methods and the empowerment social agenda. In P. Tolan, C. Keys, F. Chertok, & L. Jason (Eds.), *Researching community psychology: Integrating theories and methodologies.* Washington, DC: American Psychological Association.

Rappaport, J. (1992, May). Chair. *Community narratives and personal stories.* Symposium presented at the annual meeting of the Midwestern Psychological Association, Chicago.

Rappaport, J. (1993). Narrative studies, personal stories, and identity transformation in the mutual help context. *Journal of Applied Behavioral Science, 29*(2), 237–254.

Rappaport, J., Davidson, W. S., Wilson, M. N., & Mitchell, A. (1975). Alternatives to blaming the victim: Our places to stand have not moved the earth. *American Psychologist, 40,* 525–538.

Rappaport, J., Reischl, T., & Zimmerman, M. (1992). Mutual help mechanisms in the empowerment of former mental patients. In D. Saleebey (Ed.), *The strengths perspective in social work practice: Power in the people.* White Plains, NY: Longman.

Rappaport, J., and others. (1985). Collaborative research with a mutual help organization. *Social Policy, 15,* 12–24.

Roberts, L. J., and others. (1991). Charting uncharted terrain: A behavioral observation system for mutual help groups. *American Journal of Community Psychology, 19,* 715–737.

Saleebey, D. (Ed.). (1992). *The strengths perspective in social work practice: Power in the people.* White Plains, NY: Longman.

Sampson, E. E. (1988). The debate on individualism: Indigenous psychologies of the individual and their role in personal and societal functioning. *American Psychologist, 43,* 15–22.

Sampson, E. E. (1993). Identity politics: Challenges to psychology's understanding. *American Psychologist, 48,* 1219–1230.

Seidman, E. (1988). Back to the future, community psychology: Unfolding a theory of social intervention. *American Journal of Community Psychology, 16,* 3–24.

Seidman, E., & Rappaport, J. (Eds.). (1986). *Redefining social problems.* New York: Plenum.

Spector, M., & Kitsuse, J. I. (1987). *Constructing social problems.* Hawthorne, NY: Aldine.

Stacey, M. (1989, Sept. 4). Profiles (Allen Walker Read). *New Yorker,* pp. 51–74.

Toro, P., Rappaport, J., & Seidman, E. (1987). The social climate of mutual help and psychotherapy groups. *Journal of Consulting and Clinical Psychology, 55,* 430–431.

Toro, P. A., and others. (1988). Professionals in mutual help groups: Impact on social climate and members' behavior. *Journal of Consulting and Clinical Psychology, 56,* 631–632.

Trickett, E. J. (1984). Toward a distinctive community psychology: An ecological metaphor for the conduct of community research and the nature of training. *American Journal of Community Psychology, 12,* 261–280.

Zimmerman, M. (1990). Taking aim on empowerment research: On the distinction between individual and psychological conceptions. *American Journal of Community Psychology, 18,* 169–177.

Zimmerman, M. (1993, May). *Empowerment theory: Where do we go from here?* Paper presented at the Annual Meeting of the Midwestern Psychological Association, Chicago.

Zimmerman, M., and others. (1991). Expansion strategies of a mutual help organization. *American Journal of Community Psychology, 19,* 251–279.

17

"It Ain't What You Do, It's the Way That You Do It; That's What Gets Results": Another Look

Forrest B. Tyler

My title, "It Ain't What You Do, It's the Way That You Do It; That's What Get Results" constitutes "another look" because Jim Kelly used almost the same title a few years ago (1979). I remember it as a line in a song that was popular at a time in my life when I was sure of neither what I wanted to do nor how to do it. As is usually the case for most of us, I had some peers who were certain they knew what to do, and others who were sure they knew how to do it. Those who knew what to do were convinced that how to do it would come naturally. Those who knew how to do it were convinced that the results of applying their method would define and yield what they wanted.

Writing this chapter many years later, I continue to be struck with the extent to which psychologists continue to choose one or the other side of that dichotomy. This chapter has as its focus the "how to do it" side; that is, it is about methodology. Nevertheless, I do not feel comfortable viewing the choice between a focus on issues and a focus on methods as an Aristotelian dichotomy. It is not that I reject method as important; I think it is very important. However, science, society, and the quality of individual lives do not advance by a commitment to method alone. Nor do they advance by a commitment to goals alone. Rather, our collective efforts will be optimally effective if each of us, whether we are focusing on what to do (goals) or how to do it (methods), attempts to integrate our question asking, question answering, and problem solving in complementary ways.

I will illustrate how to resolve this dilemma of integrating goals with method by citing examples from my own life and career as a psychologist. In retrospect, it seems to me that I have led a hyphenated life. My graduate education prepared me to be a scientist-professional. I sought a university position as a scholar-teacher-clinician. I became involved in community psychology as a participant-conceptualizer. I spent several years as a scientist-administrator. Then I sought to develop a graduate program at the University of Maryland that had a community-clinical focus.

My perspective in psychology rests on the argument that we humans are shaped by our natures and our lives and, in turn, shape our natures and lives by our discretionary involvement. This view is an integration of two perspectives: first, that we are influenced by our histories, which to some extent can be used to predict our (known) experiences, and second, that we are also knowers who create our futures by using our acquired knowledge in discretionary ways to influence our future. We make choices. We are neither totally constrained by our nature and our past nor totally free from those factors. Rather, we reflect a hyphenated reality: we are knowers-known or known-knowers.

Elsewhere, I have emphasized the self-reflexive nature of our education as well as of our scholarship and our professional and personal engagements with society and our own lives. That is, I have argued that we should apply our principles to ourselves, since we will defeat our endeavors unless we do. If we educate our students and ourselves about constructive principles of community development (our end-goal), but do not embody those principles in our own educational community (our means), then we will end up at war with our own efforts. Margy Gatz and I wrote an article about that idea as it was embodied in the Maryland Clinical/Community program. We called it,

"If Community Psychology Is So Great, Why Don't We Try It?" (Tyler & Gatz, 1976).

Further, she and I and several others (Gatz and others, 1982) created a *facilitator-activator role* as an approach for getting elderly natural leaders in communities to work effectively to help less capable elderly residents in those communities. We focused on teaching the leaders to *facilitate* the solving of the current problems of those they were working with and also to *activate* the problem-solving skills and capabilities that those less capable elders had given up on. Out of that and other projects, my collaborators and I put together the outlines of a *resource-collaborator* model (Tyler, Pargament, & Gatz, 1983) for psychologists to utilize in interacting with others. This approach attempted to integrate several types of hyphens, including those of known-knower (facilitator-activator), means-end (collaboration-independence), and individual-community (psychological-social) differentiations and integrations. Now my work focuses on cross-ethnic, cross-racial, and cross-cultural concerns. This listing of hyphenated roles and patterns underscores the interconnectednesses among the myriad aspects of our lives, our activities, and our milieus, which must be included in our conceptualization of both means and ends.

The Life of a Hyphen

In the remainder of the chapter I will discuss methodology from the perspective of a *hyphen-person*. That is, I will focus on the necessity of incorporating consideration of these interfaces and their contradictions in our approaches to our research and change activities. By methodology, I mean both a methodology for answering questions about finding problems and a methodology for answering questions about solving problems. Both activities have a methodology, and the questions, methodologies, and answers they yield are inextricably tied together.

For example, if our task is to use methodologies to incorporate attention to diversity into our activities, we need to attend to the diversity of participants in all our interactions, including those between an investigator and a respondent. To

ignore these differences or to consider them to be variable error is to accept that our chosen methodology cannot be used
to formulate or answer questions about the impact of diversity.
It cannot answer questions about the nature of people who are
different from the investigator or from his or her chosen model,
nor can it answer questions about how each person copes with
her or his uniqueness and the uniqueness of others. For example, as long as we view gender-related differences between men
and women as variable error rather than phenomena in their
own right, we will never understand men or women. Blacks and
whites, upper and lower classes, Anglos and Latinos, or any
other such categorical distinctions can be substituted in the above
sentence. The point is the same. Both the investigator and the
respondent interact out of the entirety of their natures, which
our methodology needs to include and understand. Until we
acknowledge that reality, our efforts to understand either their
similarities or their differences will necessarily fail.

My basic framework for incorporating these considerations into methodology are contained in two essays written over
the last few years. One of them was called "Psychosocial Leaps
and Spirals" (Tyler, 1987). In it I argued and cited supporting
evidence for the following:

1.   We can never eliminate the personal element from our ob-
     servations and judgments.
2.   Any assertion of fact or other statement about reality rests
     on a leap of faith. Reality does not compel our account of it.
3.   Any leap of faith — that is, any belief about what to do or
     how to proceed or what is good — rests in turn on assump-
     tions about the nature of reality, about facts.

We proceed by making leaps of faith, then studying what the
world and our lives are like. We can use those new findings to
study and evaluate the leaps of faith on which they rest. Then
we can make new leaps and start over again. In short, we proceed through cycles of creation, development, and dissolution,
only to start over again at a new point with different questions.

In another and more recent essay, "A Psychosocial Perspective on Cross-Cultural Unit in Psychology" (Tyler, 1989), I built in the earlier position I have just described. I referred to evidence, for instance, that human socialization begins before birth and argued that psychosocial differentiation begins in utero. Even newborns have already incorporated some of their society's culture. Putting all of these considerations together, I come to the conclusion (leap of faith, if you prefer) that the questions we psychologists ask, the ways we answer them, the answers we draw from them, and what we do with those facts contain ineradicable personal and cultural components. In the researcher-respondent relationship, ineradicable personal and cultural components also enter the interaction and must be understood as part of our method. They include the processes by which our respondents form their understanding of our questions, the ways they answer them, the answers they give, and the inferences they draw and incorporate in their lives from participating in our research enterprises.

Basically, I have taken the position that people are actively involved in constructing, organizing, living, and enjoying or suffering their lives. To the extent that they are, we need to focus on their individual latitude to choose between options and create other options. We also need to focus on them not just in terms of etics (universals) and emics (particulars). Rather, we need to focus on the idea that they operate within a framework of diversity that embodies some convergence with, some divergence from, and some conflict with themselves, their environment, and others within their worlds (Tyler, Susswell, & Williams-McCoy, 1985).

How do we embody all of these considerations in our methodologies? We do it an interface at a time. We focus on one hyphen and the factors it links—for example, the relationship between investigators and their respondents. We develop the possibilities there, then focus on another one, such as the relationship between the cultural backgrounds and the research approach biases of different investigators. It is only after we have focused on a number of such hyphens that we can begin to flesh out a picture of human identity, human diversity, and the way people interrelate to build human communities. I can best

illustrate this point by providing some examples from the hyphenated work of my colleagues and myself.

The Resource-Collaborator Hyphen

The hyphen in the *resource-collaborator* notion (Tyler, Pargament,
& Gatz, 1983) concerns the perspective that everybody involved
in a research or intervention project has something to offer as
well as something to learn, and that includes us, the psychologists. We invoked the resource-collaborator notion in the facilitator-activator study with community-dwelling elderly (Gatz and
others, 1982) by asking the community to identify the community's elderly natural leaders and including them in our research
project as contributors, subjects, and workers. We had workshops and lectures for them about our concepts, our hypotheses, our methods, and our findings as they became available.
These people developed a high level of involvement in the research. They grew in competence during the study, and so did
the community-dwelling elderly with whom they worked. We
did not investigate what contributed to those changes and we
did not check whether we had changed, so we did not get a complete picture. Nevertheless, what we did find illustrates that the
leaders and those they helped both gave to each other and gained
from each other.

In another study, in which we worked with high school
counselors, we did try to sort out some of those effects (Tyler,
Pargament, & Gatz, 1983). We constructed a scale to measure
how well we had implemented the resource-collaborator concept, how we had applied it to ourselves, and how we had
changed as a result of the project. We asked the counselors to
fill out the scale and found out how they viewed our implementation of the concept and the changes in us. We found that they
saw us as collaborators, too. They did *not* see themselves as face-
less objects to be manipulated. They saw themselves as active
agents participating in this project, who were working with us
to accomplish their objectives. Their objectives including having an impact on us and judging whether we practiced what
we preached. Although we do not know, it seems likely that the

substantive results of the project would have been different if they had seen us differently or if we had not changed as we all interacted. While psychologists usually ignore such considerations, they need to be as much a part of our methodologies as any other considerations.

In another, more recent, collaborative project, Sandy Tyler and I organized a project with two outreach organizations working with street children in Bogotá, Colombia (Tyler, Tyler, Echeverry, & Zea, 1986). They asked us to help them document and publicize the lives, situations, and strengths as well as the problems, of street youth and we agreed, on the condition that we would all work together collaboratively. After spending three years working with them to decide what information to seek, we built collaboratively a structured interview. We trained them to collect data; then we analyzed it. Finally, we agreed together on the uses to which we could put that information. They included, at their request, our applying the findings of our collaborative research to writing (with their assistance as editors) a training guide and resource manual for nonprofessional outreach workers. The uses of the results also included, at our request, our presenting the findings from the project to professional audiences.

In sum, we built the notion of resource collaboration out of previous experience and tested it out in several other contexts. In working with the elderly, we applied a resource-collaborator approach in our relationship to the leaders and taught them to apply it in their interactions with those they helped in the community. In the school project, we asked the high school counselors to judge whether we had been collaborators. Finally, in the street youth project we asked street workers, several of whom were ex–street youths, to help us design the focus of the study. In all of those instances, we found evidence of resourcefulness by all of the parties involved and support for the value of collaboration.

The Knower-Known Hyphen

The *knower-known* distinction refers to the perspective that people are both active in their own lives and products of their histories.

For example, over twenty years ago, Bill Simmons and I (Simmons & Tyler, 1964; Tyler & Simmons, 1964) hypothesized that hospitalized mental patients construct a functionally useful picture of their situation. Using George Kelly's personal-construct theory and his repertory scale, we asked patients on a milieu therapy ward how they constructed their reality — that is, we asked them to report as knowers of their own reality. We also asked the staff how they thought the patients constructed that reality — that is, we asked them to report on the patients' reality as it was known from an external perspective. We found that the staff believed that the patients saw them in terms of their explicitly described therapeutic roles. In other words, the staff believed that the patients' reality simply reflected what they had been told and was not actively constructed by the patients. We discovered that patients who did (actively or passively) reflect the staff view stayed in the hospital longer. Other patients, who saw the staff simply as people doing a job and controlling the patients' options, got out of the hospital sooner. These patients actively constructed a perception of the staff; they assumed their right to be knowers. The methodological point, however, is that by treating both staff and patients as potential knowers, we discovered that at least some of the patients were actively constructing their reality by not accepting what the staff told them. We also found out that the staff were not sensitive to the patients' roles as people exercising self-direction (as self-knowers) but responded to them as designated patients (as known objects).

Another research area related to the knower-known distinction involves one of the most focused research topics of the last two decades: locus of control. This concept was originally conceptualized by Rotter (1966) as a generalized expectancy that a class of behaviors will, in a class of situations, lead to a class of reinforcers. More recently, a variety of alternative scales have been developed and efforts have been made to develop locus-of-control scales that measure control in specific areas, such as health behavior. The original scale has been used to assess whether specified minority or deviant groups are less internal than the predominantly Anglo U.S. norm groups and to assign both predictive significance and evaluative status to that differential. Efforts have also been addressed to the question of whether locus of control is an etic or an emic characteristic.

From the hyphenated perspective of the present chapter, it seems limiting to focus exclusively on questions such as who is more internal, whether it is always good to be more internal, and whether locus of control is the same for everyone. Alternatively, the concept of locus of control can serve as the centerpiece in explorations of the role individuals have, or choose to have, in defining and shaping their own realities and relationships to the world around them. If there is a personal equation and people are involved in constructing their own realities, then there *is* no universally patterned locus of control. Rather, we need to ask with regard to what external and internal circumstances a person is being internal or external. Further, if people live in different cultures or social systems, it is not possible to judge that being more (or less) internal is always better.

Does this mean that we cannot or should not make comparisons about how people construct their control relations to their realities and how those approaches would work in other realities? Of course not! It only means that we need to frame these issues differently.

I will cite a few examples from some of the research with which I have been associated. Our research group collected a substantial number of Rotter I-E protocols (Rotter, 1966) on black and white senior high school students in Prince George's County, Maryland. As others have, we found that internal locus-of-control scores were related to such characteristics as relatively high levels of constructive problem solving, self and counselors' ratings of improvement in counseling, and overall level of adjustment—that is, constructive control of their lives (Tyler & Pargament, 1981).

We were also interested in how black and white, male and female, and exemplary and marginal students constructed their sense of control. To answer those questions, we needed to know what the scale items asked people to make decisions about. We did a structural analysis of the domain the items tap, by taking each item alternative and analyzing what assumptions the students needed to make to agree with it. We then built a structural matrix of the resulting dimensions. We found that the scale does not provide a representative stimulus sampling of the dimensions it spans; it differentiates people's responses into an active-agent stance (creating events and controlling outcomes), passive-agent stance (waiting for events and controlling outcomes), and victim status (controlling neither events nor outcomes). We then factor-analyzed the protocols and found striking differences between the way males and females construct their sense of control (Tyler, Gatz, & Keenan, 1979). We found that males' responses reflected "asserting active control over tasks but attributing control to external sources with regard both to personal issues and to more abstract systems-related issues. Females organized their senses of self-efficacy with a central theme being that of a passive agent stance, plus an expectation that circumstances would provide equality of opportunities to which they could respond" (p. 11). In other words, we found that within the dimension of control, there seem to be complex matrices in diverse areas of people's lives.

Other colleagues and I have also identified distinctive, culturally relevant, intracultural and cross-cultural patterns among Puerto Rican college students (Tyler, Labarta, & Otero, 1986) and college students in India (Tyler, Dhawan, & Sinha, 1988). Among entering college students in India, we found that men tended to be active agents, women passive agents. However, the active-agent orientation of Indian males pervaded their lives, not just their task activities. Unlike American females, Indian females did not expect an equality of opportunities in their lives. This difference between the control orientations of the American and Indian males evidently stemmed from the different normative expectations about equality of opportunity for males and females in their respective cultures.

Among Puerto Rican college students, the distinctive sex differences previously found among U.S. and Indian students did not appear. What did appear was a distinctive structure-factor pattern. In the American and Indian samples, three internally coherent major factors emerged, which consistently reflected either an internal or an external orientation. Among the Puerto Rican students, nine small factors emerged. Further, seven of these contained contradictory factor loadings. For example, factor 1 included four items about control of political and world affairs. Three of them loaded positively and one negatively. It seemed that these respondents were consistently endorsing the belief that they did and did not control each identified aspect of their lives. Evidently, culturally based diversity even exists among individuals' patterns of intrapersonal organization of knower-known orientations.

Later, using the same scales and working with the elderly, we encountered a fourth structural pattern that does not appear on the Rotter protocols at all. We began differentiating control of the occurrence of events from control of the outcomes. I have come to call this fourth pattern the salvation, or redemption, pattern. Some people see themselves as creating (controlling) the production of events (more specifically, problems) but expect that positive solutions will come from outside of them (they will be saved or redeemed) (Gatz, Sigler, George, & Tyler, 1986).

These studies illustrate that people are both products and creators of their situation, their past, and their possibilities. Some aspects of their reality govern them and they govern some aspects of their lives and reality. Further, they do so in ways that are in part individually constructed and in part shaped by factors of individual circumstance such as culture, gender, race, or patient status. It is only as we acknowledge this diversity and its embeddedness in the context of people's cultures and lives that we will be able to collaborate with them to study, understand, and benefit mutually from continuing our locus-of-control explorations and the knower-known distinctions embodied in them.

More recently, there has been a provocative cross-cultural contribution to this kind of analysis. Specifically, some Japanese and American investigators (Azuma, 1984; Kojima, 1984; Weisz, Rothbaum, & Blackburn, 1984a, 1984b) have pointed out that the meaning of control is different in the two cultures. In the United States, primary control means adapting the world to your wishes, secondary means adapting to the external reality. For Japanese, primary control involves adapting to external reality. Which meaning of control is correct? The question makes no sense. From the present perspective, it seems more justifiable to extend this exploration in other structural directions. For example, is there any specific orientation that is better for all people in all circumstances? Are there identifiable orientations that are better for identifiable specific circumstances? To what extent do our particular biases about what is a "good" locus-of-control orientation shape our expectations or demands that others structure and adapt to the world the way we do? Are there possibly a variety of patterns of locus of control that are useful life strategies but that offer different strengths and limitations for negotiating life's events?

The following is an example of another attempt to answer questions about locus of control, conducted in the sphere of religion. In his dissertation, Kenneth Pargament (1977) wanted to explore the relationship between locus of control and religious involvement. He designed and conducted a study involving Jewish, Protestant, and Catholic congregations, using the Levenson locus-of-control scale and adding Kopplin's God control scale. Thus control was conceptualized as including the structures of personal control, control by powerful others, chance control, and God control. Those structures yielded differences between the religious groups, all of whom see God as an important source of control.

Five distinct statistical clusters emerged that appeared to be conceptually meaningful. One cluster seemed to be a prototypical internally controlled group. People in that category were high in personal control, moderate in control by powerful others and God control, and low in chance control. Another group seemed to look to God for support and guidance. They were high in God control, moderate in chance control and control by powerful others, and low in personal control. A third group seemed to see themselves as largely externally controlled, since they were high in God control, chance control, and control by powerful others and low in personal control. Further, these clusters had different psychosocial competence correlates, some of which were more benign than others when judged by adaptation and life satisfaction criteria. For example, the first group, who were high in personal control, and the second group, who were low in personal control but high only in God control, yielded relatively high psychosocial-competence correlates. The third group, who were high in all aspects of external control and low in personal control, were lowest in psychosocial competence. Another point seems worth adding. Most people, including me, think of God control as external. Pargament decided to ask. He found that for some people God is an external controller, for some he is an internal controller, and for some he is a partner in control (Pargament and others, 1988).

I subsequently took the scales Pargament used to India, worked with colleagues there to adapt them to the Hindu reality, and used them to study locus-of-control patterns among Hindu religious pilgrims (Tyler & Sinha, 1988). Those findings were complex; they reflect how individuals organize their lives in diverse ways, yet reflect their social milieu. For example, men were higher on personal control and lower on chance control than women. Further, factor analyses indicated that among men, one factor involved control by powerful others and chance control, the other personal control and active planfulness. Among women, the first factor involved control by powerful others and God control plus trust of others. Their second factor included chance control and lack of trust. Overall, men organized their lives around autonomy and duty; women organized theirs in a prosocially oriented way around both individual concerns and collective concerns such as social community support and social gain.

The richness of these studies extends far beyond what can be covered in this chapter. However, they do serve to support its general thesis. People and their circumstances are diverse, and people organize their lives in distinctive ways that reflect those circumstances. For example, in retrospect, it does not seem surprising that we might more clearly identify the distinct differentiation of control of events and outcomes among the elderly. As life expectancy grows short, resources diminish, and problems mount, circumstances predispose us all to look to others, including our deities, for solutions. Our findings indicate that each set of circumstances permits a range of ways of responding to it.

Religious congregants in the United States and Hindu pilgrims revealed differing adaptation patterns among themselves. They also showed commonalities across cultures. Males in both cultures were more oriented toward personal control and control by powerful others as well as toward obligation in their religious practices. Women were more concerned about control by external factors and God control as well as being more oriented toward personal salvation and community in religion. The Hindu pilgrims, perhaps reflecting their harsher reality and lesser control of it, did rate themselves as more involved in religion than did religious congregants in the United States (Tyler, 1992).

Finally, in each environment some ways of negotiating life events work better than others. Across environments, there are some commonalities among effective life-styles and some among less effective styles. Yet there seems to be no single way that is better for everybody. In short, diversity makes sense in light of the diversity of circumstances.

With respect to our methodology, in none of these studies have we met all of the often-suggested criteria in cross-cultural psychology of conceptual equivalence, functional equivalence, and metric equivalence (Berry, 1969). This cross-cultural methodology has been characterized as the emic-etic approach. In all of our studies, we have found some generalities (so-called etics, perhaps) and some specific patterns (emics, perhaps). For example, I am convinced that in many ways the Western concept of chance and the Eastern concept of fate are not conceptually equivalent, yet we have some indications that they yield metric similarities and function in similar ways.

But my goal is not that of seeking universals and particulars. Rather, it is to explore how people converge in the ways they construct their sense of control of their worlds and their lives (through active-agent commonalities), how they diverge (through active versus passive agentry), and how they conflict (for example, the United States' view that active manipulation of circumstances is primary control differs from the Japanese view that active adaptation to circumstances is primary control). With that information I am better able to ask and answer how people from such vastly different realities relate to and interact with themselves and each other. I do not believe my approach of incorporating contextual and constructionist considerations is methodologically inferior, nor that the etic-emic approach of controlling them is. However, the questions my line of research asks are different from those asked by researchers working from the emic-etic perspective, and therefore we need different methodologies. I also believe that research, understanding, and efforts to enrich the human condition will continue to be seriously handicapped until we incorporate diversity in the methodologies we endorse, the questions we consider appropriate, the diversity among the people we study and work with, and the diversity in the ways we interact with them to ask as well as answer questions and contribute to solving problems.

The Fact-Value Hyphen

Now let me turn to another area, which concerns the distinction between facts and values. My earlier argument was that they necessarily influence each other. In that argument I identified facts as the knowledge or information whose truth status we consider to be subject to empirical verification or refutation and that we act on accordingly. Values, on the other hand, are preferences that may be held irrespective of empirical status or may not be subject to empirical verification, as is the case with certain religious beliefs. To illustrate the importance of this hyphen, let me refer again to Ken Pargament's work (1977). Findings from that study indicated that people's ways of relating to religious creeds and organizations are related to how they organize themselves psychosocially, and both in turn relate to how they live their lives. That is, their religious beliefs are related to their views about the factual nature of human life and to how they live.

One of Pargament's students extended some of that work to develop a scale of religious functions (Echemendia & Pargament, 1982). Initially, it was composed of the dimensions of personal salvation and satisfaction, sense of community, social gain, and obligation. Correlations were found between religious beliefs, the functions religion served, and the nature and effectiveness of psychosocial functioning. In our use of those scales in India, we found that beliefs about control, the functions of religion, and patterns of negotiating life's events were intertwined (Tyler & Sinha, 1988). We also found that there was substantial diversity in the way people intertwined religious and secular considerations in their lives. Some people were more value- or belief-oriented in that they relied less on active, empirically oriented approaches to manage their lives and more on nontested or nontestable preferences and judgments. Some people were more fact-oriented than others in that they relied more on seeking and utilizing empirical information in their lives. M. Brewster Smith (1985) would say that the latter group had more freedom, because they relied more on actively shaping their own futures. The ways in which Hindu pilgrims or other religious congregants manage their lives on the basis of values or of facts are related to their religiously based values.

Of course, even those who espouse no formal religious belief system incorporate untested and untestable preferences and values (beliefs) in their ways of managing their lives and in deciding what they can control and what they must accept. I think that we have opened a potentially rich and important arena for research and for personal and social change by formulating questions about the interrelation (hyphen) of facts and values and by trying to answer them using a resource-collaborator approach.

The Convergence-Divergence-Conflict Hyphen

Finally, let me focus briefly on the field of acculturation, which considers how people integrate the various cultures around them into their lives. There is a veritable thicket of contention about acculturation as it relates to adaptation or adjustment or biculturality or other concepts. Questions range from those that focus on the relationships between acculturation, adaptation, and adjustment to those that focus on whether acculturation is a unilevel or multilevel phenomenon and those that ask whether acculturation is a unidirectional or multidirectional process.

Dina Birman (1988) completed a master's thesis in which she explored the acculturation and adjustment of Russian Jewish émigrés living in the United States (Birman & Tyler, 1994). She found differences between men and women in how they have adapted to their new environment. For men, she found that length of time lived in the United States was positively correlated with retaining an affiliation to Russian culture. Yet affiliation to Russian culture did not predict alienation. The expected conflict between the American and Russian cultures did not occur; the men apparently managed to see the two cultures as simply divergent, but compatible. For women, the longer they had lived in the United States, the more they became acculturated to American culture, and for them, affiliation to Russian culture did predict alienation; the two cultures appeared to be in conflict, and they chose the new American pattern. As Birman and Tyler (1993) note, the women's pattern seems particularly puzzling, because they are generally thought to be the ones who maintain ties to traditional culture in the family.

I find these results comforting in that they suggest that people find a variety of ways to negotiate new circumstances. Overall, these findings seem akin to some of the more recent findings in the androgyny literature. People are now exploring different styles within androgyny, such as blending sex roles rather than alternating between them. That is, people are asking and finding affirmative answers to the question of whether there are a variety of ways of combining prototypical masculine and feminine ways of negotiating life. It would seem that we can also ask similar kinds of questions about uprooting oneself and settling in another culture; the results we see show that people do find a variety of ways of combining their past and future cultures.

Conclusion

Let me cite a vignette to make my final point. In the summer of 1988, my wife and I visited the Fiji Islands. During their history, the Fijians have been intruded on by people from the Anglo world and people from India. We could ask what they are acculturated to and what dominant force has shaped them. But I would like to suggest that we look at them a little differently. So let me tell you my story. We were told that the Fijian all-purpose greeting and farewell is "Bula." It means hello, good-bye, good wishes, and so on.

One morning, I was walking down the beach and was approached by a Fijian. Here is our conversation:

Fijian: Bula.

FT: Bula.

Fijian: How are you?

FT: Fine, it's a beautiful day.

Fijian: Ah cha!

Now *Ah cha!* is the all-purpose Hindi word for "I agree" or "That's fine with me."

So what was this Fijian acculturated to? I think to himself as much as anything. He was Isaac Newton's apple. He was pulling the world to him in the same way that the world was pulling him to it. He was using a Fiji-Anglo-Hindi language and, most probably, way of being and living.

That is the missing element in our methodologies. We do not see others as having their own internal as well as external pulls, their own histories, destinies, continuities, and autonomies. If we can put in the hyphens (the interrelatedness), we can begin to see that we are all actively involved in our own lives as well as each other's. Then we can begin to seek out convergences and build from them. We can identify divergences and try to understand them and control them in nondestructive ways.

We need to incorporate these considerations into our methodologies of question asking as well as question answering. The questions we ask, the results we obtain, and the meaning of both can be understood as a function of the nature of the investigator as well as of the tests and approaches used.

So I close with Bula! Namaste! ¡Adiós! and hope that we can construct new and differently integrated lives in the future.

We do not have to choose between holding on to the past and building a future. We do not have to fight about means versus ends. We do not have to fear difference, or be frightened by individuality. We can cherish and respect who we are, who others are, and the diversity we represent. We can also cherish our similarities and our interrelatedness. And we, as psychologists, can contribute to that endeavor.

References

Azuma, H. (1984). Secondary control as a heterogeneous category. *American Psychologist, 39,* 970–971.

Berry, J. W. (1969). On cross-cultural comparability. *International Journal of Psychology, 4,* 119–128.

Birman, D. (1988). *Acculturation and adjustment among Soviet Jewish refugees in the United States.* Unpublished master's thesis, University of Maryland, College Park, MD.

Birman, D., & Tyler, F. (1994). Acculturation and alienation of Soviet Jewish refugees in the United States. *Genetic, Social, and General Psychology Monographs, 120*(1): 101–115.

Echemendia, R. J., & Pargament, K. I. (1982, Aug.). *The psychosocial functions of religion.* Paper presented at the meeting of the American Psychological Association, Washington, DC.

Gatz, M., Sigler, I., George, L., & Tyler, F. B. (1986). Attributional components of locus of control. In M. M. Baltes & P. B. Baltes (Eds.), *Aging and the psychology of control.* Hillsdale, NJ: Erlbaum.

Gatz, M., and others. (1982). Enhancement of individual and community competence: The older adult as community worker. *American Journal of Community Psychology, 10,* 291–303.

Kelly, J. (1979). Tain't what you do, it's the way that you do it. *American Journal of Community Psychology, 7,* 244–261.

Kojima, H. (1984). A significant stride toward the comparative study of control. *American Psychologist, 39,* 972–973.

Pargament, K. I. (1977). *The relationship between the church/synagogue as an organization, the fit of the members with the church/synagogue, and the psychosocial effectiveness of the member.* Unpublished doctoral dissertation, University of Maryland, College Park, MD.

Pargament, K. I., and others. (1988). Religion and problem solving: Three styles of coping. *Journal for the Scientific Study of Religion.*

Rotter, J. B. (1966). Generalized expectancies for internal versus external control of reinforcement. *Psychological Monographs, 80*(609), 633–645.

Simmons, W. L., & Tyler, F. B. (1964). A comparison of patient and staff conceptions of therapists. *Journal of Clinical Psychology, 20,* 508–512.

Smith, M. B. (1985). Toward a secular humanistic psychology. *Journal of Humanistic Psychology, 26,* 7–26.

Tyler, F. B. (1987). Psychosocial leaps and spirals. In J. Pandey (Ed.), *Perception and social reality* (pp. 61–79). New Delhi, India: Concept.

Tyler, F. B. (1989). A psychosocial perspective on cross-cultural unity in psychology. In D. M. Keats, D. Munro, & L. Mann (Eds.), *Heterogeneity in cross-cultural psychology.* Lisse, The Netherlands: Swets & Zeitlinger.

Tyler, F. B. (1992). Psychosocial competence in developing countries. *Psychology and Developing Societies, 3,* 171–192.

Tyler, F. B., Dhawan, N., & Sinha, Y. (1988). Adaptation patterns of Indian and American adolescents. *Journal of Social Psychology, 128,* 633–645.

Tyler, F. B., & Gatz, M. A. (1976). If community psychology is so great, why don't we try it? *Professional Psychology, 7,* 185–194.

Tyler, F. B., Gatz, M., & Keenan, K. (1979). A constructivist analysis of the Rotter I-E Scale. *Journal of Personality, 47,* 11–35.

Tyler, F. B., Labarta, M., & Otero, R. (1986). Attributions of locus of control in a Puerto Rican sample. *Interamerican Journal of Psychology, 20,* 23–44.

Tyler, F. B., & Pargament, K. I. (1981). Racial and personal factor and the complexities of competence oriented changes in a high school group counseling program. *American Journal of Community Psychology, 9,* 697–714.

Tyler, F. B., Pargament, K. I., & Gatz, J. (1983). The resource collaborator role: A model for interaction between change agents and community members. *American Psychologist, 38,* 388–398.

Tyler, F. B., & Simmons, W. L. (1964). Patients' conceptions of therapists. *Journal of Clinical Psychology, 20,* 122–133.

Tyler, F. B., & Sinha, Y. (1988). Psychosocial competence and belief systems among the Hindus. *Genetic, Social, and General Psychology Monographs, 114,* 33–49.

Tyler, F. B., Susswell, D., & Williams-McCoy, J. (1985). Ethnic validity in psychotherapy. *Psychotherapy, 22*(2 S), 311–320.

Tyler, F. B., Tyler, S. L., Echeverry, J. J., & Zea, M. C. (1986, Aug.). *A preventive psychosocial approach for working with street children.* Poster presented at the meeting of the American Psychological Association, Washington, DC.

Weisz, J. R., Rothbaum, F. M., & Blackburn, T. C. (1984a). Standing out and standing in: The psychology of control in America and Japan. *American Psychologist, 39,* 955–970.

Weisz, J. R., Rothbaum, F. M., & Blackburn, T. C. (1984b). Swapping recipes for control. *American Psychologist, 39,* 974–987.

18

Integration of Ethnic Minorities into Academic Psychology: How It Has Been and What It Could Be

Martha E. Bernal

Tokenism, racism, sexism, organizational resistance to change and diversity, and creation of parallel structures of participation but not power are some of the processes that produce barriers to the full participation of minority academicians within colleges and universities. This chapter deals with these issues because they can have profound effects upon ethnic-minority psychologists working in academic settings. The issues have implications for the field of psychology as it tries to deal with the rapidly changing demographics of this country by increasing faculty and student diversity. These processes, activated by dominant-culture institutions and individuals, are active in all aspects of academia: faculty hiring, student admissions, teaching, conducting research, serving on committees, mentoring, and so on. A description of these issues, with examples of the ways in which they affect ethnic-minority faculty, will be followed

Note: I am grateful to Ed Trickett, Dina Birman, and Roderick Watts, who read earlier versions of this manuscript and provided invaluable feedback that led to its present form. I am also grateful to the people who administer Arizona State University for providing me with the opportunity to experience a setting that strives for cultural diversity.

by recommendations for a series of changes that foster cultural diversity in training. Descriptions and examples will be drawn from the literature and my own experience.

Because my personal experience is relevant to this discussion, some background is in order. I am a Mexican American, born and raised by immigrant Mexican parents in Texas, where a strict social dividing line exists between Anglos and Mexicans. I was trained as a clinical psychologist at Indiana University at Bloomington, where I received my doctorate in 1962. Although I am not among the earliest Mexican American psychologist pioneers of this century, I am the first woman of my ethnic group to receive a doctorate in psychology in this country. I have spent my entire career, spanning thirty-one years, in academic psychology in four different universities. Beginning in the early 1970s, I became involved in numerous activities within the American Psychological Association (APA), the National Institute of Mental Health, and the National Hispanic Psychological Association, with the goal of access to opportunity and equality for ethnic minorities generally and within psychology. As a minority training consultant, I have visited several departments in this country to advise them on issues relevant to the topic of this chapter. Thus, I have been in academic psychology longer than most of my colleagues of Mexican American descent and have had broad experience as a social activist, and as a token minority, in a variety of professional settings.

My life as a Mexican American woman in academic psychology has not been a completely comfortable one, and at times it has been acutely painful. The issues that I will write about here still face me and continue to pose dilemmas, so I will not pretend to have dealt with—or dealt well with—all of them. In sharing my experiences, I hope to cast them in a conceptual framework that will articulate the sociopsychological processes that affect others like myself in professional settings. An understanding of these processes and issues provides a framework for the creation of training contexts in which ethnic minorities, and cultural diversity, can thrive. It also may be useful to ethnic-minority faculty seeking to cope with oppressive environments.

As a member of an ethnic minority and a woman, I have experienced the combined effects of racism and sexism in academic life. Separation of the source of these effects is impossible, however. In any given situation, I cannot tell whether my gender or my ethnicity elicits prejudice and discrimination, although I feel their dual effects. Other women also can be racist and sexist, and I have experienced comparable oppression from female and male colleagues. So while I believe that the process of sexism is oppressive and destructive to minority women in academia, and that it exacerbates the effects of the other processes about which I will write, I will not treat it separately. When I refer to cultural diversity, the culture of women is included.

The Context of Ethnic-Minority Faculty Issues

Faculty in psychology, as well as in other disciplines, have an immense and varied workload, and in all of their activities, they interact with university administrators, other faculty, undergraduate and graduate students, university staff, the community, funding agency staff, colleagues across the country, and many others. It is in this interactive context, and primarily in the conduct of departmental and specialty-area business, that the ethnic-minority professor's painful encounters occur. Furthermore, the tough times are frequent in contexts where departmental resources are at stake, such as the filling of an open faculty position, the admission of graduate students into programs that have large numbers of applicants and few openings, additions to the graduate curriculum, and the allocation of financial support to students. It is important to recognize that there often is competition among faculty for these resources; different faculty members have different reasons for wanting to control them. In the following section, these interactive contexts will be analyzed in terms of the issues they raise for the ethnic-minority professor.

Hiring of Ethnic-Minority Faculty

Announcements of openings for psychology faculty in colleges and universities commonly encourage applications from women and minorities. The people who write these ads have a variety of rationales for wanting to bring ethnic minorities into a department. Strong political rationales prevail as the major motivating force behind this move: the hiring of minorities meets administrative or institutional guidelines, and/or satisfies criteria set by the APA's accreditation committee and by federal agencies administering training and research grants and contracts.

Other less cynical secondary rationales exist among some administrators and faculty, however; they concern the values of affirmative action and cultural diversity. Some people seek to add faculty who have been underrepresented in psychology. In other cases, minority faculty are sought who can contribute in a substantive way to the training mission of either a specialty area or the entire department by introducing content in courses, research supervision, and practica that is relevant to ethnic minorities. Of critical importance, however, is recognition of the fact that the minority faculty person will enter an institutional setting that resists change, especially ideological change, and that preordains the perceptions and attitudes of members of the setting. These oppressive processes and attitudes create isolation and alienation, as well as severe professional discomfort, for minority faculty.

My personal experiences with faculty recruitment have shattered my hopes of having a minority colleague. I have seen academics pay lip service to affirmative-action principles but behave in ways that contradict their words. After the candidate visits, such faculty quickly bring up his or her shortcomings, and in the ensuing discussions they gain the support of colleagues for their biased views. While I have seen both minority- and majority-culture applicants who I would agree were not likely to contribute to a teaching and research program in an exciting, competent way, I have also seen minority applicants with promising careers be turned down, and I was unable to understand or agree with the basis for the negative evaluations that were made of them. Some of these "false negative" applicants later became outstanding professors and investigators of minority-related areas of research. One of the best examples was an applicant who had the support of the majority of the faculty, but who was evaluated by one of my colleagues as someone who would never be able to survive in academia.

Role Expectations

It is doubtful that, in hiring their first ethnic-minority faculty member, others in the department can foresee how they will perceive the new member's role in the department and their attitudes toward and expectations of the person resulting from her or his minority status. Neither is the new minority faculty member likely to anticipate the negative processes that he or she will activate. One form that these processes take is the communication of expectations and the assignment of roles. One common expectation is that minority faculty will take charge of doing the ethnic-minority "things" that need to be done: teaching minority courses, recruiting and mentoring minority students, preparing minority training applications, giving guest lectures on minority topics, serving on search committees that require minority representation, representing the department at meetings about minority issues, and so on. The minority faculty member is charged with the realization of cultural diversity in the department. Underlying these expectations are the unspoken messages: "Minority things are your responsibility, not those of white faculty," and "White faculty don't want to be bothered with minorities."

The faculty member who tries to meet these expectations will suffer several negative consequences, in addition to possible loss of self-esteem. Since doing so will take time away from other faculty responsibilities, she or he will have less time for research, teaching, and students, the work whose products are the currency that academics trade for tenure, promotion, salary increases, and the recognition of colleagues. Young minority faculty sometimes fare poorly in the tenure-and-promotion review process because by doing this extra work, they had insufficient time to develop their research program. This observation is supported by data from Hills and Strozier (1992), who conducted a survey of minority training in counseling psychology and reported that assistant professors carry much of the burden for multicultural activities. But more senior minority faculty also get caught in this trap, especially if there are no junior minority faculty, and become burdened with work that should be the responsibility of the entire faculty.

Resistance to Ideological Diversity

A related issue is the expectation that minority faculty will bring phenotypical and cultural diversity into a department, but not ideological diversity. Because of their life experiences and backgrounds, minority faculty bring new perspectives to a department, and they may want to integrate them into their work as scholars and researchers. For example, they are likely to get excited about introducing multicultural content into the training program. Many faculty will resist such changes, because of their racist belief that members of ethnic-minority groups, and their perspectives, are inferior. The rationale for resistance will be disguised, however. Some arguments that I have heard against the introduction of multicultural perspectives into the curriculum are that it is undesirable to add another course to an already large set of course offerings, that minority content is best introduced once the trainee is in internship, and that such content has no place in the universal knowledge base of psychology. And when I have pressed for a minority mental health course as a requirement in the clinical doctoral curriculum, I have had intense reactions from my colleagues to the addition of yet one more course among all the other requirements.

That fellow faculty members view ethnic minorities and their perspectives as inferior was exemplified for me in a variety of ways years ago when I explored the interest of faculty in my department in a doctoral training program that would prepare ethnic-minority clinical psychologists. The reactions I received included that of one professor who expressed grave reservations that minority students would be able to satisfactorily complete the statistics requirements. Another colleague suggested a plan for an applied program to train minority psychologists for work in child care settings as an alternative to the traditional research training of the clinical psychologist. These and other reactions in a similar vein persuaded me that my colleagues would have to undergo some attitudinal changes before I would be willing to pursue development of the training program.

Federal funds for training ethnic-minority clinical psychologists then became available, and, despite my reservations, I prepared a proposal that was not funded. I admit that I was relieved, but shortly thereafter, while I was on leave, the proposal was rewritten by one of my colleagues and submitted with my name given as project director. This time the proposal was funded, and I was treated as the nominal director who did the paperwork on the grant and organized the students' training experiences. Important decisions regarding the grant, such as selection of the students to be supported, were controlled by the codirector of the grant, who was an administrator within the department. As an example of the arrangement of parallel structures of participation for minority faculty while withholding power, this situation has few equals.

Resistance to Diversity of Identity

Acceptance by one's white colleagues may also depend upon a shared identity. Earlier in my career, I did extensive mainstream research on conduct-disordered children, which was then an "in" area of work that gave me a positive professional identity among my colleagues in psychology. When, about fifteen years ago, I switched my research interests to minority mental health, a change that I believe established me as a minority in the eyes of other faculty, my colleagues seemed to find themselves at a loss as to how to interact with me. For example, in a transparent attempt to bridge the newly perceived cultural gap, one faculty member developed a habit of referring to a Mexican American relative every time we met. Another development correlated with this switch in research was that my new research was devalued. At one point, the annual evaluation of my performance included a criticism that my research productivity was lacking, despite the fact that I had recently published several empirical papers on minority mental health training in psychology.

The Dynamics of Tokenism

The hiring of one minority faculty member in a training program often is seen as evidence of having met affirmative-action requirements or having fulfilled training needs. As one of my colleagues once put it, "Martha takes care of minority mental health, so there is no need to hire any more minorities." Tokenism in psychology, defined in terms of numerical representation, was supported by data collected in 1990–91 by Bernal and Castro (in press), who found that, in clinical training programs accredited by the APA, 48, or 46 percent of the 104 participating programs had no minority faculty. Among the 56 programs that had minority faculty, two-thirds had only one ethnic-minority faculty member. When a program had more than one minority faculty member, there were two; more than two were quite rare. Jones (1990) has described evidence of such tokenism in data on the representation of minorities in psychology generally; he reported that, in 1989, the percentage of minority graduate students (15 percent), new minority Ph.D.'s in psychology (8 percent), minority APA members (less than 5 percent), and minority faculty members (5 percent) had remained relatively unchanged for an entire decade.

Research on the effects of tokenism has yielded some interesting results that describe the negative, stressful consequences to individuals who are distinct members of a larger group. Solo status is associated with being more noticeable to co-workers, being evaluated more critically in terms of job performance, and being perceived in terms of ethnic and racial stereotypes (Kanter, 1977; Taylor and others, 1981). Co-workers may assume that the minority person was hired to reach affirmative-action quotas and not for his or her competence (Morland, 1965). When tokens have failure experiences, and particularly when they are among the first of their category hired in a given position, such failures may be used by co-workers to reinforce the idea that the tokens were not well suited or capable enough for the job (Gutierrez, Saenz, & Green, in press). Token status also may result in behavioral withdrawal and decreased self-esteem (Yoder, 985), and tokens have been demonstrated to have performance deficits in both memory and problem solving under conditions when they were aware of their difference from majority-group members (Lord & Saenz, 1985; Saenz & Lord, 1989; Saenz, 1992).

Aspects of the work environment such as the formation of in-groups and out-groups also may produce negative consequences for tokens. Consider the finding that, in comparison to out-group members, employees who are in-group members are more likely to be privy to inside information, have greater influence in the making of decisions, and receive more sensitive and supportive treatment from their supervisors (Cashman, Dansereau, Graen, & Haga, 1976; Dansereau, Graen, & Haga, 1975). By extension, when the basis for membership in an in-group or out-group is racial or ethnic incongruence, token minorities may experience poor communication and interaction with their majority-culture co-workers and thus become isolated and excluded from participation in the business of the organization (Gutierrez, Saenz, & Green, in press).

In day-to-day life as a faculty member, the token may experience varying degrees of these effects and consequences associated with solo status, but the causes and processes leading to the effects are likely to be very difficult to sort out. Instead, the individual probably will experience considerable confusion about what exactly is happening to her or him and be unable to determine whether the cause of the personal discomfort is internally or externally generated. While social support may help to sort out these matters, there isn't likely to be another minority faculty member with whom to discuss problems as they arise, and attempts to deal with the discomfort and to correct its course will be largely unsuccessful. In time, a self-fulfilling prophecy will play itself out: the token becomes confused and uncertain and suffers loss of self-esteem and self-confidence; in turn, his or her work begins to suffer, and thus, judgments of the token's incompetence are proven true.

Such was the personal experience of Yoder (1985), who was one of the first female civilian faculty members at a U.S. military academy. She reported that she was isolated during teaching-team meetings and social events, and that she began to withdraw, attending only mandatory meetings and other events. Along with her increasing isolation, she experienced anxiety, sleeplessness, and decreased self-esteem and blamed herself for not being able to get along with others. Over time, my own token status had a similar impact on me. In contrast, when I participated in conferences, consultations, or meetings away from my academic home setting, others communicated their respect and positive evaluation of my worth as a colleague and behavioral scientist, and I felt valued and competent among them.

The Advantages of Collegial Support

The presence of minority colleagues can moderate the negative forces that act on the token. I see the presence of colleagues as a critical factor for minority faculty to consider in job selection. Is there someone to talk to if the aforementioned oppressive processes are encountered? Is there someone who could more objectively assess these situations and create the best coping strategies? Shared professional interests are also important. If I were applying for positions, I would look for colleagues who are working on key mental health issues for Hispanics, or colleagues who could co-teach a minority mental health course. I was confused by my experiences as a token for many years, even after I moved out of the troubling department I was in. And then, one day, Delia Saenz, whose research is on the effects of tokenism, came to give a colloquium as part of a job interview at Arizona State University. When she described the performance deficits, heightened self-consciousness, isolation, and sense of failure experienced by tokens, she was describing my experience as a token in that former academic home. Not only did she help me to understand my confusion, she also became my first female Mexican American colleague.

These impressions point only to the benefits of minority colleagues for token minority faculty. From the point of view of the academic program and department, why is it important to have more than one minority faculty member? The answer to this question is suggested by the relationships that have been reported between minority faculty in a program and critical elements of minority training such as numbers of minority students and minority courses in clinical psychology (Bernal & Castro, in press), in counseling psychology (Hills & Strozier, 1992), and in clinical, counseling, and school psychology (Jones, 1990). In APA-accredited clinical programs, Bernal and Castro (in press) found that the numbers of minority faculty were correlated with numbers of minority students, minority courses, and faculty conducting minority research, and with ratings of the importance the program placed on minority training (Bernal & Castro, in press). While it is only correlational, this pattern of relationships suggests that increasing the number of minority faculty may enhance minority curricular offerings and research training and draw more minority students.

Selection of Minority Students

Every year, new graduate students are admitted and the issue of the selection of minority students is revisited. In many cases, faculty may sense that standard admissions criteria are inappropriate in the evaluation of minority applicants' credentials, or they may be uncertain about criteria to use in minority student selection. Unfortunately, discussion of the issue often has a low priority in the faculty's list of the many things that must be done to keep a department and program operating. In part because of the urgency of screening and evaluating what usually is a very large number of applicants, when admissions committees have to make their decisions, they may end up applying to minority applicants some version of the same criteria that are applied to dominant-culture applicants. They also tend to sweep under the rug all the other important issues that have arisen; these issues will surface again the following year.

Generally, faculty are more comfortable in making admissions decisions about majority-culture applicants than about minority-culture applicants. In the former case, the faculty are guided by their greater experience with white applicants as well as by empirically derived knowledge regarding the predictive validity of test scores and grade-point averages (GPAs) for these students. In the case of minority applicants, their more limited experience inspires less confidence in decision making, as does the relative dearth of data regarding the predictive validity of criteria for ethnic minorities. The selection decision also is complicated by the reality that, in comparison to the larger numbers of white applicants with top academic credentials, minority students with comparable credentials are scarce. (The exception is Asian applicants, who often present outstanding credentials.) The top minority applicants' credentials are not likely to include the very high Graduate Record Exam (GRE) scores (Diaz, 1990) and GPAs from highly rated educational institutions that tend to characterize those of the best white students. Furthermore, their educational, socioeconomic, and cultural backgrounds, as well as their life experiences, may be very different from those of both majority-culture applicants and faculty.

When such differences are great, applicants may not be selected for admission because they are viewed as a "risk." Despite the heavy implications that admissions decisions based on this risk hypothesis have for ethnic minorities, it probably has not been put to the test by application of the very methods that are part of the training of psychologists. I would guess that few programs have heeded the recommendation of the GRE Board, set forth in the *Guidelines for the Use of GRE Scores* (Educational Testing Service, 1989), that graduate departments undertake local studies of the validity of GRE scores to justify selection procedures. Although every program should conduct a local study (and avail itself of the Educational Testing Service's free technical assistance), it should be kept in mind that minority students sometimes fail to complete graduate school because the program fails to marshal the necessary resources to support and facilitate their success, or because of family or financial-support problems. Recent literature on the validity of the GRE in predicting Ph.D. attainment by minority, nonminority, and foreign students (Zwick, 1991) suggests that GRE scores may be problematic. Zwick found that both GRE scores and undergraduate GPA were almost entirely unrelated to the achievement of candidacy and graduation in a sample of five thousand students seeking doctoral degrees from eleven departments in three major universities.

Training Contexts That Foster Cultural Diversity

In the best of all possible worlds, what kind of academic environment would best attract and retain ethnic-minority faculty? The answer to this question is "a setting that fosters cultural diversity." Creating such a setting requires careful self-examination to assess the existing power structure and the ways in which it supports or impedes change. A variety of actual changes in the attitudes and behaviors of administration, faculty, staff, and students may be needed. It might even require a redistribution of power. These changes must occur vertically — that is, from the top administrator down — rather than horizontally, such as across faculty.

The nature of such change is embodied in the following operational definition of the term *cultural diversity* as it might be manifested in a university. Cultural diversity refers to differences among people in their way of thinking and behaving, or worldview, which results from their socialization and education, and in their appearance, which reflects their genetic inheritance. A university that strives to be culturally diverse has the following characteristics. The administration, faculty, and staff of the university are committed to the full realization of the value of cultural diversity in the education of its students and in the life of its community. Such commitment is apparent through the allocation of significant resources toward vigorous efforts to increase the representation of culturally diverse people across the campus in positions at all levels of power, and to promote appreciation and understanding of cultures as well as to foster their uniqueness. A multicultural perspective is represented in the general education curriculum, as well as in specialty graduate training such as psychology. The presence of racism and sexism in its community is recognized, and there are ongoing campus-wide programs to assist everyone in developing antiracist and antisexist attitudes and behaviors. These activities, based on the value of cultural diversity, are maintained on a continuous, ongoing basis, as a way of life.

Associated with these activities is a regular review of their effectiveness and a strengthening of this effectiveness by solicitation from the university community of ideas for continuing improvement. Persico (1990) has discussed the steps required in creating a culturally diverse institution, and various sources are available on the topic of cultural diversity in educational settings (Green, 1989; Vaughn, 1990). While the above description is more representative of an ideal rather than a real setting, a glimpse of the major ingredients of a culturally diverse university provides a frame of reference within which requirements for diversity within an academic department can be understood.

Power, Ideology, and Structure

Within such a university setting, one might expect that the impact of these ingredients of an ideal university climate, singly or in combination, would be reflected at the departmental level. However, university policy at the highest administrative level does not necessarily dictate the ways in which departments function, and vice versa. Thus, members of a department of psychology who are striving to become culturally diverse need to do some groundwork. Identification of goals for creating a culturally diverse setting is the first step. Resistance to change as a major barrier to the participation of minority faculty in academic life needs to be confronted directly. To permit identification of barriers, so that they can be reduced or withdrawn, and of facilitators, so that they can be strategically placed, scrutiny of the people and functions that are potentially capable of such resistance and facilitation is a second task. This task involves examination of the department's power structure to determine who controls the resources for cultural diversity and makes decisions about their allocation, and what ideologies and values guide those who control and decide.

Open discussion of several topics is advisable, with the aim of arriving at some consensus for achieving goals. Topics for discussion include rationales for hiring minority faculty, the implications of bringing such faculty on board, the role of all faculty in the promotion of cultural diversity, expectations of minority faculty, and the contributions that such people can make to the intellectual substance of the training program. Within this discussion, the distinction should be drawn between meeting affirmative-action requirements by recruiting people who are demographically different and therefore look different versus recruiting people who not only look different but have a wide range of ideas, paradigms, and viewpoints that are different and new to the academic setting. This is important because one element of change is a willingness to hear new ideas. Hiring minority faculty who already are assimilated, and who will teach the same ideas and do the same kind of research that their white counterparts already do, will not lead to cultural diversity. A culturally diverse academic environment is one that introduces and is positively responsive to ideological diversity. It recognizes that minority faculty (and administrators) will want to change some things, and it has to be ready to accommodate to such changes. When satisfactory resolution of conflicts among those involved has resulted in a clear commitment that details the department's plans for creating and funding cultural diversity, the next step is to determine how to recruit minority faculty.

In a department that has no minority faculty, the establishment of an unambiguous goal of recruiting more than one minority faculty member within a certain time frame is essential. As Ijima-Hall (1990) has suggested, numbers of minority faculty who are already present within a department, or at least within the college of which the department is a part, are likely to attract diversity. Otherwise, if no minorities are present in a department, and only one is hired, several years may pass before the next minority hire. There may be no overlap in their employment because the first person may have left for the reasons that were described earlier. When writing the announcement of the position, mention should be made of the department's goal of filling a given number of positions with ethnic-minority faculty. A brief but adequate explanation of the department's rationale and plans for developing a culturally diverse setting will help to draw the attention of potential applicants. Also, some statement can be included that communicates the department's desire to recruit faculty who can bring a research program that deals with significant multicultural issues relevant to psychology and/or who can contribute a multicultural perspective to the teaching program.

This contrasts with faculty announcements currently appearing in such publications as the *APA Monitor,* in which the following kinds of statements may be seen: "Applications of minorities and women are strongly encouraged" and "We encourage women and members of minority groups to consider this opportunity to identify themselves when applying." These common statements fail to communicate the character of the setting, nor do they provide the potential applicant with the right reasons for responding to the ad. Such statements make me wary, because some departments use their minority faculty member as a symbol of affirmative action to funding agencies and others — a pawn who bears the responsibility for making the department look as if it is culturally diverse and responsive to the issues of ethnic-minority populations.

The idea is to communicate to applicants that this department is prepared to (1) empower the applicant to help it introduce and nurture cultural diversity within its ranks; (2) work, with the applicant's guidance, toward the integration of multicultural perspectives across the spectrum of its training functions; and (3) recognize the contributions of minority- and majority-culture faculty to these endeavors as being on a par with research and teaching criteria when they are reviewed for tenure and promotion.

Student Issues

Scientific work and research productivity are typically rewarded more highly than any other activity in graduate programs. Nonetheless, it is often expected that minority students and faculty, but not others, should take time away from their research and other work in order to recruit minorities. The recruitment of minority students is part of a larger effort to create cultural diversity. If a high value is placed on this larger effort, and it is recognized as an important contribution to the department, then minority and nonminority faculty and students will seek to do it, and they are likely to be just as creative and successful in creating diversity as they are in conducting their research.

Successful selection of minority students requires appropriate admissions criteria. There are several options for accomplishing this, for example, a standing student selection committee composed of interested faculty that is empowered to consult the available literature and conduct the necessary local research to identify the most valid predictive criteria for selection of minority students. Such work, incidentally, is likely to lead to some worthwhile insights about the selection of nonminority students as well. The student who has adopted the dominant culture and its perspectives, and relinquished her or his ethnic or racial identity, by definition does not add cultural diversity. When such a student applies, and has good academic credentials, that student qualifies for consideration with other dominant-culture applicants.

Conclusion

I have had many letters from undergraduates asking for information about my ethnic identity research and about minority training at my department, as have many of my minority colleagues. Opportunities for realization of these student motivations are likely to be heavily weighed in the students' choice of graduate school. The responsibility of a department of psychology in creating a culturally diverse setting must extend to the attitudes modeled by the faculty, the content that they teach, and the emphasis that they place on the importance of equality, race, ethnicity, gender, and culture. Many have written about what constitutes culturally diverse training, and it is such training that will draw minority students and properly prepare them as leaders in conducting research, teaching, and offering service that will contribute to the welfare of ethnic-minority people. For me, in addition to the aforementioned elements, the essential ingredients of a graduate curriculum are that it incorporate the worldview of different cultural groups, instill a high regard and respect for cultures, expose all students to a standard cultural content that relates to basic competencies in their area of specialization, and planfully coordinate their courses, practica, and research to produce the best integration of multicultural training in science and practice. At present, only a handful of psychology training programs, mostly professional programs, approximate this ideal (Bernal & Castro, in press).

References

Bernal, M. E., & Castro, F. B. (in press). Are clinical psychologists prepared for service and research with ethnic minorities? Report of a decade of progress. *American Psychologist.*

Cashman, J., Dansereau, F., Graen, G., & Haga, W. J. (1976). Organizational understructure and leadership: A longitudinal investigation of the managerial role-making process. *Organizational Behavior and Human Performance, 15,* 278–296.

Dansereau, F., Graen, G., & Haga, W. J. (1975). A vertical dyad linkage approach to leadership within formal organizations: A longitudinal investigation of the role making process. *Organizational Behavior and Human Performance, 13,* 46–78.

Diaz, E. (1990). Barriers to minorities in the field of psychology and strategies for change. In G. Stricker & others (Eds.), *Toward ethnic diversification in psychology education and training* (pp. 77–88). Washington, DC: American Psychological Association.

Educational Testing Service, Graduate Record Exams Board (1989). *Guidelines for the use of GRE scores.* Princeton, NJ: Educational Testing Service.

Green, M. F. (Ed.). (1989). *Minorities on campus: A handbook for enhancing diversity.* Washington, DC: American Council on Education.

Gutierrez, S. E., Saenz, D. S., & Green, B. L. (in press). Job stress and health outcomes among Anglo and Hispanic employees: A test of the person-environment fit model. In G. K. Sauter and S. Sauter (Eds.), *Job stress 2000: Emergent issues.* Washington, DC: American Psychological Association.

Hills, H. I., & Strozier, A. L. (1992). Multicultural training in APA-approved counseling psychology programs: A survey. *Professional Psychology: Research and Practice, 23,* 43–51.

Ijima-Hall, C. C. (1990). Qualified minorities are encouraged to apply: The recruitment of ethnic minority and women psychologists. In G. Stricker, and others (Eds.), *Toward ethnic diversification in psychology education and training* (pp. 105–112). Washington, DC: American Psychological Association.

Jones, J. M. (1990). Invitational address: Who is training our ethnic minority psychologists, and are they doing it right? In G. Stricker and others (Eds.), *Toward ethnic diversification in psychology education and training* (pp. 17–34). Washington, DC: American Psychological Association.

Kanter, R. M. (1977). Some effects of proportions on group life: Skewed sex ratios and responses to token women. *American Journal of Sociology, 82,* 965–991.

Lord, C. G., & Saenz, D. S. (1985). Memory deficits and memory surfeits: Differential cognitive consequences of tokenism for tokens and observers. *Journal of Personality and Social Psychology, 49,* 918–926.

Morland, J. K. (1965). Token desegregation and beyond. In M. Rose & C. B. Rose (Eds.), *Minority problems* (pp. 229–238). New York: HarperCollins.

Persico, C. F. (1990). Creating an institutional climate that honors diversity. In G. Stricker and others (Eds.), *Toward ethnic diversification in psychology education and training* (pp. 55–63). Washington, DC: American Psychological Association.

Saenz, D. S. (1992). *Token status and problem-solving capability: The detrimental effects of non-perceptual distinctiveness.* Unpublished manuscript, Arizona State University, Tempe.

Saenz, D. S., & Lord, C. G. (1989). Reversing roles: A cognitive strategy for undoing memory deficits associated with token status. *Journal of Personality and Social Psychology, 56,* 698–708.

Taylor, S. E., and others (1981). *Solo status as a psychological variable: The power of being distinctive.* Unpublished manuscript, Harvard University, Cambridge, MA.

Vaughn, B. E. (1990). Recruitment and retention of ethnic minority faculty in professional schools of psychology. In G. Stricker and others (Eds.), *Toward ethnic diversification in psychology education and training* (pp. 91–98). Washington, DC: American Psychological Association.

Yoder, J. D. (1985). An academic woman as a token: A case study. *Journal of Social Issues, 41,* 61–72.

Zwick, R. (1991). *Differences in graduate school attainment patterns across academic programs and demographic groups* (A research report of the Minority Graduate Education Project). Princeton, NJ: Educational Testing Service.

19

Creating Social Settings for Diversity: An Ecological Thesis

James G. Kelly, L. Seán Azelton, Rebecca G. Burzette, Lynne O. Mock

Only in the last moment of human history has the delusion arisen that people can flourish apart from the rest of the living world. —Edward O. Wilson, *The Diversity of Life*

What it requires above all is an admission that we are very far away from that ultimate horizon from which the relative worth of different cultures might be evident.
　　—Charles Taylor and A. Gutmann,
　　　Multiculturalism and "The Politics of Recognition"

Diversity is an intriguing concept because it suggests the possibility that people from different cultural or social backgrounds can interact and carry out their daily tasks relatively free of destructive or unproductive social relationships. In this chapter, diversity is viewed as an outcome of creating social settings that enable people to value, embrace, and use differences for their collective good.

The potential meaning of diversity is compromised when we focus exclusively on efforts to train people to be more tolerant (Egan, 1993). Such imposed training programs are often insensitive to the qualities of the social support systems needed to appreciate and understand differences in points of view and

Note: The authors have benefited from the appraisal and feedback generously given about this chapter. We thank the following people for their interest and help: Dina Birman, Meg Bond, Dan Cervone, Jack Glidewell, Steve Goldston, Chris Keys, Stephanie Riger, Dan Romer, Ed Trickett, and Marc Alan Zimmerman.

heritage. Without an appropriate supportive setting, participants can become wary of efforts to be "trained" to appreciate differences (Egan, 1993) and may fall back on even more strongly held beliefs to maintain their differences. In this chapter, the emphasis is on constructing specific social settings that enable people to experience increased understanding of varied cultural, social, or personal histories.

This point of view is referred to as ecological pragmatism. The framework is ecological in that it includes an explicit recognition of context as a supportive resource for understanding personal differences. The approach is pragmatic because it focuses upon concrete ways in which social settings can facilitate mutual understanding among people who are unlike one another.

There is a difference between an idealistic meaning of the concept of diversity and the point of view of ecological pragmatism. An idealistic position often relies on individuals to initiate positive social interactions by themselves in the absence of supportive social structures. Ecological pragmatism emphasizes the active creation of social settings. Constructing social settings to enhance an appreciation of diversity is, however, an undeveloped task. This chapter proposes that this task become a fully explicit and intentionally conscious enterprise.

Premises of This Chapter

Our assumption is that social norms can be created within social settings to enable participants to become interdependent. The term *setting* can be defined broadly to refer to entities such as organizations or more narrowly to refer to specific smaller parts of an organization such as departments or classrooms. In addition, settings can be defined by such factors as cultural or ethnic ties, racial ties, or regional ties. The ecological meaning of the concept of interdependence is that people can be interconnected and mutually interactive in a supportive social setting (Kelly, 1968; Kingry-Westergaard & Kelly, 1990).

Ecological pragmatism places significance on how the social norms of the new setting enable interdependent roles to be performed. An individual may be willing to understand and appreciate diversity, but the way in which the social setting functions can accelerate or limit the learning process. Creating interdependence among the participants is an essential first step. When a social setting has support systems in place, participants have opportunities to redefine their notions about a variety of topics such as race, gender, class, age, sexual orientation, and disability.

Thus, the focus of the chapter is not on the qualities of individuals per se but rather on how the qualities of a supportive context enable individuals to become resources for one another. Attention is given to the properties of social settings — specific social spaces — that promote social norms for cohesiveness and mutual understanding. Creating such settings requires the development of new values, new social norms, and new traditions through which individuals can be resources for one another. In such settings, differences between people are not explained as deviance but as an expression of plausible and valid alternative customs, traditions, and points of view. The learning process in ecologically designed settings is derived from a supportive environment that affirms diversity as an explicit value.

The concept of diversity presented here is based upon two premises regarding the vitality of social settings. The first is that social settings that include a mix of people can create opportunities for the participants to understand the historical basis for differences between them. The second is that social settings that include a mix of people have the potential to establish social norms in which differences emerge as a resource for the participants. Underlying these two assertions is the fundamental assumption that people participate in these settings voluntarily. The thesis of ecological pragmatism is that the construction of settings is not a coercive stratagem (Murray, 1993).

The implication of these premises is that participants in such settings support each other as they begin to understand and appreciate the potential validity of alternative points of view. For diversity to become a practical and meaningful concept, participants need to establish social norms that allow them to become interdependent (Johnson & Johnson, 1991; Kelly, 1968). The concept of interdependence refers to the processes by which people form the social norms that facilitate these working relationships.

This chapter offers four propositions as a start toward creating social settings supportive of diversity. However, this task is difficult because of at least two pervasive social processes: the presence of norms for homogeneity and the absence of cooperative exchanges.

Norms for Homogeneity

Cognitive-consistency theories (for example, Festinger, 1962; Heider, 1958) in social psychological research assume that individuals have a basic need for control and predictability. Norms for homogeneity are viewed as a social process that helps individuals to be in control by reducing perceptions of differences. Such social norms can sanction people from a dominant culture viewing it as a primary reference point, restricting their interactions with people who are different from themselves. To the extent that norms for homogeneity are derived from a culture that is self-contained and exclusionary, members are denied opportunities to experience and appreciate individuals with different and equally valid cultural or social histories. People who are not members of the dominant culture may feel pressured to conform to the dominant culture and forgo their own cultural heritage.

A norm for homogeneity can thus be a limiting social force that reduces the value of diversity for everyone, as the social status and stigma of being different deprives some people of access to acceptance, status, and influence. Being different can reduce opportunities for inclusion in a shared group identity and can inhibit commitments to try out new relationships. In contrast, creating a social setting where the participants value diversity allows them to initiate standards for their behavior that permit interdependence between individuals while also valuing the uniqueness of each individual. Here, participants have opportunities to create settings whose very purpose is to acknowledge and even celebrate variety and differences. A norm for homogeneity is replaced by a norm for heterogeneity.

In order for this new norm of heterogeneity to be implemented, participants create a working structure for personal communication and reciprocal interaction in order to reduce each participant's expectant anxieties about his or her esteem and status as a group member. An operating norm for heterogeneity requires participants to be attuned to their personal need for approval and group membership. When participants are aware of their personal needs, they are expected to feel anchored and be more receptive to differences in other members (Aldag & Fuller, 1993). The operation of a social norm for heterogeneity, in contrast to homogeneity, makes it possible for people from a nondominant culture to be included as valid members and equal participants in the setting.

Absence of Cooperative Exchanges

The second social process that can hinder the creation of supportive settings is the absence of cooperative exchanges between individuals and between social settings (Kahn, 1990; Slavin, 1990). Members of a dominant culture may grow up learning to understand a small number of settings. In the United States, these social settings are likely to advocate norms for individual achievement, competitive exchanges, and a search for dominance by control and submission. The consequence of being a member of such a noncooperative system is that a person may have few opportunities to create interdependent ties or experience reciprocal communication across different types of social settings, thus reducing her or his chances to experience divergent values, norms, and traditions. In addition, those who do take part in another setting may simply bring their previous points of view and attitudes to the new setting without creating ways to understand and appreciate it. Such limitations inadvertently encourage people to invest their energies in the setting they know best; give unrestricted positive acclaim to its merits, rules, traditions, and ways of carrying out tasks; and remain ethnocentric (Deutsch, 1993; Weiner, 1992).

The two social processes — pressures toward homogeneity (everyone being the same or alike) and pressures toward ethnocentrism (staying within one's group) — reduce opportunities to appreciate differences. The remainder of the chapter elaborates four propositions intended to counteract these social processes. Each proposition provides a different focus for creating new social norms that can counter the operation of norms for homogeneity and increase the value for cooperative exchanges.

Creating Social Settings to Facilitate Diversity

The following propositions are guidelines for the creation of social settings to facilitate an understanding of the validity of diversity. Experiences in these four prototypical social settings are expected to enable participants to generate authentic and reciprocal exchanges with others unlike themselves. These four settings emphasize a sequence of integrated experiences that can be planned and arranged to facilitate a generative and constructive experience with diversity.

The first setting establishes opportunities to create social norms where the setting members can establish a sense of being interdependent. The norm establishes a level of cohesiveness that promotes viewing others in a differentiated way.

The second setting is one in which participants learn how to consider and relate to each other as resources. This setting establishes a social norm that values differences as a resource. In this setting there is a conscious effort to create opportunities for people to interact informally across status boundaries. This setting also illuminates how available, yet unused, resources can be drawn upon by the participants.

In the third setting, the participants consciously establish communication channels with other people in other settings and organizations. This setting establishes a social norm that appreciates differences across settings. The process expands access to resources and generates new criteria, new insights, and new processes that allow people outside the immediate group to also become resources.

The fourth setting is a place for reflection and integration. This setting establishes a norm for appraisal of previous experiences. It emphasizes the need for participants to create space and time to integrate their experiences and to create a working definition and appreciation of diversity. This is a setting where people learn about the sources and bases for each other's points of view.

While each of these settings can stand on its own as a prototype, they are presented in a suggested sequence under the assumption that each setting represents a useful stage to experience before going on to the next setting. For example, having a validating experience in creating interpersonal ties in the first setting can provide a positive socialization experience, encouraging an individual to be a contributing member in creating a second setting. In the second setting, the emphasis is on establishing interdependence between people who are occupying roles marked by wide social-status differences. A positive experience in this setting can enhance the likelihood that an individual will take on roles in the third setting, where the participants establish communication between people in different settings. Finally, having meaningful experiences in the third setting can enrich an individual's evaluation and understanding of experiences in the fourth setting.

Creating Social Settings to Enhance Interdependence

This first proposition affirms that social settings can create mediating processes in which diverse group members are linked together in the pursuit of goals. Each member has resources, such as materials or talent, that are needed to meet the goals established by the group. The task is to develop processes that utilize all resources in the setting to further the goals of the group and its individual members. As group members create new social norms and traditions that allow them to be resources for each other, each benefits from the others' success (Johnson & Johnson, 1991, 1992). The more diverse the group and the greater the number of processes facilitating harmonious relationships, the more likely it is that resources and assistance will be exchanged among group members.

Four factors affect how well people learn to be interdependent (Johnson & Johnson, 1992). The first and second factors prescribe the learning of specific interpersonal behaviors. The third and fourth factors are characteristics of the setting that require a conscious effort involving all participants.

The first factor is the opportunity for the people in the setting to have extensive face-to-face interaction. Such a process is necessary to facilitate a working relationship among people in the setting and to generate experiences to nurture it (Johnson & Johnson, 1992). Personal interaction also increases the probability that people will share their personal histories, agendas, problems, and so on in informal, relaxed discussions.

The second factor is the opportunity for the participants to practice a variety of social skills that facilitate cooperative activities (Johnson & Johnson, 1992). Such experiences may make it easier for participants to form a bond of social interdependence. Research on school-based instruction has affirmed that when grade school students have an opportunity to learn in a cooperative way, they can acquire skills that enhance their academic performance. More specifically, children who served as explainers learned more than children who received the elaborated explanations, and children involved in cooperative activities learned more than those who worked alone (Deutsch, 1993; Slavin, 1992; Webb, 1992). This suggests that students who initiated elaborated explanations in particular received confirmation for being cooperative and for discussing their experiences (Tiedt, 1992).

More importantly, such positive and confirmatory experiences can be further enriched if the cooperative experiences have taken place with children who are different in some important way from each other, such as size, ethnic heritage, or physical attractiveness. In such a setting, they may acquire the belief that it *is* possible to develop trust in the process of discovering, and that working together can produce a product that can be more enlightened than a product produced alone.

While the two factors described above focus on interpersonal dynamics, the next two factors are characteristics of the setting. The third factor is the presence of a social norm for individual accountability where the individual's contribution to the group is explicit (Johnson & Johnson, 1992). Each person in the setting has the potential to contribute something unique toward obtaining the goal of the group. As much as possible, the expectations, responsibilities, and obligations of each person's role should be made explicit and negotiable (Sniezek, May, & Sawyer, 1990). Making expectations explicit may also increase the level of commitment to the group, since information about other members' expected roles and commitment level decreases the risks perceived to be associated with interdependence (Sniezek, May, & Sawyer, 1990).

Emphasis on explicit expectations may also counter any *implicit* role expectations that can be detrimental to the formation of group interdependence. These implcit roles may ignore the individual's area of expertise, unique perspective, or explicit role commitment to the group. For example, a person may be ascribed an implicit role based on his or her ethnicity and be expected to speak for that racial or ethnic group regardless of expertise in other areas or lack of expertise in the normative aspects of his or her own culture. To be called upon only to discuss minority issues negates the person as an individual with a specific area of expertise that does not relate to minority status. A more desirable approach may be to make this implicit expectation explicit so that it can be discussed with the individual. Such overt negotiation allows the person to develop a clear, comfortable role that contributes to objectives that are beneficial to the group, thus enhancing the evolving interdependence.

A fourth factor is that the *process* for developing a group goal must be valued. Members of this setting must become committed to exploring alternative ideas and different ways of working toward group goals (Johnson & Johnson, 1992). Making it possible for people to identify how each individual within the setting can contribute toward a *group goal* is an essential social norm. This may be difficult because people do not often value or create opportunities to construct a shared understanding and meaning about what may be a desirable goal.

Creating social settings to enhance interdependence takes on special significance when it is focused explicitly on supporting diversity. Settings with diverse populations have a greater potential for developing new ideas, reevaluating outdated assumptions, and making sense of phenomena. People with different worldviews may have more difficulty coming to a common understanding. However, when understanding is established, the result is likely to have greater complexity and depth because of the dialogue that has occurred. Assumptions and presuppositions are more likely to be challenged, reevaluated, and recast, particularly those that are barriers to positive change.

For example, three of the authors have been involved in a setting as researchers collaborating with African American community leaders. The setting, referred to as the Community Research Panel, allowed researchers and community leaders to discuss the definition and components of community leadership. Over time, this group became committed to creating a contextually and culturally appropriate research protocol for interviewing community leaders. The purpose of the interview was to document the development of the community leaders over time.

The researchers' initial focus was on understanding the personal qualities of individual community leaders. This was primarily the result of prior psychological research that emphasized the importance of the individual characteristics of leaders. The community leaders, on the other hand, valued their experiences of *collective* leadership. One of the participants presented a metaphor of the organization's idea of collective leadership as a soup. Each ingredient in a soup contributes to its texture and taste in such a way that the omission of an ingredient adversely affects the soup. Likewise, each community leader contributed to the vitality of the total group effort in such a way that their absence would have left an important void.

Using the soup metaphor to define community leadership made it possible for all participants to relate to a common understanding of collective leadership. This common understanding allowed the community leadership to fully explore with the researchers their unique experiences and perspectives of community leadership. The metaphor introduced an affective and integrative understanding of this phenomenon (Danzinger, 1990; Leary, 1990), which resulted in modifications in the interview consistent with understanding leadership as a collective phenomenon more so than an individual one.

Creating a norm to enhance positive interdependence thus increases the potential of using all of the resources available in a setting with a diverse population. Doing so requires individuals to learn how to facilitate communication processes among people from different backgrounds (Hecht, Ribeau, & Alberts, 1989). The setting proposed next will address how such communication can be facilitated among diverse members across status boundaries.

Enhancing Informal Social Interactions Across Status Boundaries

One of the limiting conditions in most contemporary social structures is that people in positions of different statuses usually have few day-to-day opportunities to interact informally as equals. Over time, this pattern will result in fewer and fewer opportunities for informal exchanges to occur, trust will either decay or fail to develop, and shared myths or stereotypes may develop about each of the other groups. Research in social categorization and intergroup bias (Wilder, 1986) suggests that in-group members (those who belong to one's own group) are perceived to be more heterogeneous than out-group members (those who belong to some other recognizable group), who are perceived to believe and behave more similarly to one another. Their behaviors are seen as less informative about them as unique individuals and more informative about them as group members. Social categorization results in accentuation of between-group differences and within-group similarities (Stephan, 1985; Wilder, 1986).

Antidotes for this condition are social settings where participants from different status levels have occasion to interact informally — settings that involve the development of norms for heterogeneity. Such interactions create opportunities for people to interact outside their respective formal roles, such as boss, trainee, custodian, secretary, teacher, or student. Interacting in such informal settings diminishes intergroup boundaries through individuation of out-group members — getting to know one another (Stephan, 1985; Wilder, 1986). Informal interactions move the process from an intergroup dynamic to an interpersonal dynamic by providing more opportunities for mutual exchange and interaction and reducing reliance on social categories. By fostering interpersonal comparisons as opposed to intergroup comparisons (Wilder, 1986), they decrease the likelihood of operating on stereotypes of the out-group.

We hypothesize that such experiences provide opportunities to process divergent information about others (Banks, 1992; Pang & Nieto, 1992; Sleeter, 1992). These experiences can generate self-confidence about appreciating differences in contrast to learning that differences are a source of distress and anguish. All participants can then develop beliefs that may more easily include alternative explanations for behavior.

One of the benefits of this setting is that it provides an opportunity for the participants to experience the role of culture in interpreting experience, through the process of informal interactions. Miller (1984) has concluded from her research on everyday social explanations in Indian and American children that "what constitutes objective knowledge of the world . . . is framed in terms of culturally variable concepts acquired gradually over development. Such knowledge then cannot be acquired through processes of autonomous individual discovery but requires the communication of culturally derived conceptual premises for interpreting experience" (p. 975). We expect that such experiences will make it easier to create opportunities for people to go beyond just perceiving features such as gender, age, ethnicity, life-style, and residence and appreciate not only the unique personal qualities and contributions of an individual, but also how she or he uniquely combines features such as those noted above.

This proposition addresses a fundamental feature of organizational life—that both the quality of the individual's participation in an organization and his or her personal beliefs are affected by the duties and responsibilities performed within the organization (Katz & Kahn, 1978). In a confining work situation, few opportunities arise for people in one role to appreciate the unique contextual factors affecting another person in another role. To make any real sense of the qualities of the people occupying these roles, individuals need social settings to express themselves outside of their work roles, thus allowing them to perceive others on dimensions other than those that define work-related roles such as supervisor and subordinate.

Activities such as team sports, picnics, celebrations of birthdays and anniversaries, and acknowledgments of personal and professional achievements, where people of "higher" and "lower" status share new situations and become an interdependent unit, are occasions in which participants interact informally. Here individuals can discover similarities with others on dimensions that were not previously considered and can recognize mutual membership in new social groups (for example, avid reader, lover of the arts, sports fan). Recognition of overlapping group memberships by people of varying statuses is expected to diminish intergroup boundaries and facilitate an appreciation of diversity. Several corporations in the Chicago area, for example, have established company choirs (McIntosh, 1993). Choir members reported a sense of camaraderie and a reduction in work-related stress. They also reported a feeling of equality with co-workers of varying statuses. One choir member stated: "When we're singing, we're all on the same level — we have to be in accord or else our music won't be" (Smart, as cited in McIntosh, 1993, p. 5).

Devine and Monteith (Devine, 1989; Devine & Monteith, 1993; Monteith, 1993) proposed a model of self-regulation of prejudiced behavior that posits that group membership serves as a cue to activate stereotypes that may lead to a prejudiced response to a group member. At the point of stereotype activation, an individual can inhibit the prejudicial response by slowing down and considering a less automatic, belief-based response that may be less prejudiced. Participation in the setting described here may enhance a person's ability to slow down and may strengthen the likelihood of a belief-based, rather than stereotype-based, response.

Similarly, Wilder (1986) stated that intergroup boundaries can be made more flexible and permeable by cultivation of similarities of beliefs and behaviors by members of different groups. Specifically, removing cues of dissimilarity (for example, status differences), introducing cues of similarities (for example, opinion agreement), or both (for example, replacing a competitive relationship with a cooperative one) can diminish intergroup boundaries. We expect that as a result of the setting described here, the process of intergroup boundary reduction will be enhanced and limiting definitions will be reduced as opportunities for new social interactions generate new bases for allegiances. These new allegiances can be stimulated by means of mutual interests and shared experiences. Once individuals in a setting have recognized previously unconsidered similarities and have achieved a reduction in intergroup boundaries, it then becomes critical to return to consideration and appreciation of differences.

Two caveats are in order here. Status boundaries are the result of power differences, particularly in a formal, hierarchical organization. Crossing status boundaries often may be initiated by the higher-status individual. If the gesture is perceived by lower-status individuals as a superficial exercise, it may be seen as condescending and insulting (Stephan, 1985; Tannen, 1986). The empty gesture may also increase the possibility that the lower-status individuals will lose respect for the higher-staus person and will perceive a lack of respect for themselves from the higher-status person. In this event, the psychological and social distance between the groups and between the individuals becomes even greater. Thus, crossing of status boundaries must explicitly affirm and carry with it a genuine commitment to draw on the resources of people beyond the boundaries.

Second, for this setting to be beneficial, participants must beware of "isolating" the events in the setting. That is, there is a danger that rather than rendering intergroup boundaries more flexible and permeable, participants will erect new boundaries and a new hierarchy will be established. The understanding and enlightenment gained in social settings where status boundaries are crossed must be integrated into the original hierarchical setting. If this is not done, then the expected benefits of such status-crossing efforts may not be obtained. Thus, participants need to be committed to using their new understanding in the original setting.

Participation in a setting such as the one described above will provide several benefits. Interacting in informal settings that include people of varying statuses is expected to reduce the individual's experience of being isolated, fragmented, and limited and may enhance development of interpersonal skills. Participation in such a setting may also enhance positive attitudes toward members of other status levels, a key element in achieving bicultural competence (LaFromboise, Coleman, & Gerton, 1993). Participation also is expected to assist participants in viewing individuals, groups, and organizations as interdependent and multifaceted and to reduce the use of stereotypes to guide interactions.

Socialization Processes and Support Systems for Spanning Boundaries

Research from organizational psychology and organizational sociology has suggested that organizations benefit when participants in one setting have an opportunity to represent that setting to participants in other settings (Galaskiewicz, 1979, 1985; Katz & Kahn, 1978; Kelly, Ryan, Altman, & Stelzner, in press, Leifer & Delbecq, 1978). The term *boundary spanning* refers to the actions of people who engage in tasks at one setting while simultaneously relating to people in other settings (Kelly, Ryan, Altman, & Stelzner, in press; Leifer & Delbecq, 1978). The focus here is not on how boundary spanning can benefit the setting directly, but rather on how boundary spanning as a *process* can influence the appreciation of diversity among setting members.

The concept of boundary spanning is applicable to discussions of relations between any two or more settings. For example, high school foreign exchange students engage in a type of boundary spanning. The premise underlying foreign exchange student programs is that students who interact with other students like themselves (that is, similar in age and educational level) but from a different culture are able to use those similarities to overcome the initial barriers of cultural difference. The expected benefit from the exchange program is that both groups will gain a greater understanding and appreciation of their similarities and their differences. The exchange students can then share this newly acquired understanding with students and adults from their own cultural group upon their return home. Similarly, the host family can share their new insights with others in their group. Through boundary spanning, perceived differences between groups and, by extension, diversity among individuals within a group can be reframed as a valuable pool of untapped resources.

In order to effectively perform in the boundary-spanning role, people must understand the languages and conceptual frameworks of each setting, as well as appreciating their differing cultural norms (Katz & Kahn, 1978; Rizzo, House, & Lirtzman, 1970; Tushman & Scanlan, 1981). Also key to successful cross-boundary relationships is a high degree of trust in the boundary spanner by members of each setting (Katz & Kahn, 1978).

One primary benefit of boundary spanning is that resources can be identified and exchanged between settings (At-Twaijri & Montanari, 1987; Azelton, 1992; Galaskiewicz, 1985; Katz & Kahn, 1978; Kelly, Ryan, Altman, & Stelzner, in press). As resources are exchanged, there will be increased opportunities for members of different settings to understand and value the activities and accomplishments of people in other settings. Active boundary spanning should facilitate mutual understanding of alternative beliefs, increase the opportunity to generate alternative ways to carry out tasks, allow people to think differently about who has something to offer, and, hence, facilitate using the diversity of groups as a source of alternative methods for accomplishing goals.

Boundary spanning increases the appreciation of diversity within a system when socialization processes are present that make it possible for a variety of people to observe and interact with each other in different settings. Some factors of this socialization process relate to the individual boundary spanner. These include opportunities to:

- Receive feedback on how he or she is perceived in different settings

- Enter a new social system and interact in different ways within that system
- Develop a new vocabulary and concepts to assess the structures and processes of an unfamiliar system
- Test out her or his own hypotheses about the way different systems function

Other factors of this socialization process relate to the boundary spanner's ability to focus on the processes at work within each setting. These include opportunities to:

- Assess and contrast the informal social processes of different settings
- Identify how the various resources of each system can be noted and exchanged
- Communicate the key defining qualities of each system to participants in another system, without losing the confidence and trust of participants in either system

The effectiveness of the above socialization process is contingent on the presence of a value framework to encourage people who are assuming the boundary-spanning role to bring their experiences back into their own setting (Katz & Kahn, 1978). If this value framework is lacking, the various opportunities of socialization suggested earlier will be confined within the other setting, and the opportunity to facilitate an appreciation for diversity will be greatly reduced. Where this framework exists, however, people in boundary-spanning roles can increase the availability of acceptable responses in a given situation by drawing on a more in-depth and differentiated set of experiences derived from the boundary-spanning role.

Besides the previously mentioned set of socialization processes, other processes within a setting can provide support for boundary spanning. They include:

- Opportunities for group members other than boundary spanners to experience the rewards involved in setting-to-setting interactions

- Formal structures to provide feedback between a setting's primary decision makers and boundary spanners
- Opportunities for informal interaction to occur between a setting's primary decision makers and boundary spanners

In addition, continual evaluation of the exchange process between the settings is needed so that the individuals involved can discuss the benefits and drawbacks of the boundary-spanning process. This evaluation can guard against the "ritualization" of interactions. When interactions become ritualized, the benefits of the process are not appreciated, and the ability to adapt the process to the needs of the setting and/or the needs of those involved is greatly reduced.

The boundary-spanning role may have negative as well as positive outcomes. Some have argued that the multiple roles the boundary spanner must perform can lead to problems and ambiguity (Katz & Kahn, 1978; King & King, 1990; Rizzo, House, & Lirtzman, 1970). Others have emphasized the supportive nature that these multiple roles can have for the boundary spanner (Aldrich & Herker, 1977; Keller & Holland, 1975). Little empirical evidence exists to support either perspective, although one study (Keller & Holland, 1975) found that the correlation between measures of boundary-spanning activity and measures of job satisfaction was higher than the correlation between boundary-spanning and role-conflict measures.

In their review of the literature on biculturalism, LaFromboise, Coleman, and Gerton (1993) posit that as a person's control over his or her relationship with the majority culture increases, the negative effects associated with the complexity of being in two cultures simultaneously are decreased. In addition, people are able to give equal status to the cultures they are involved with, even if the cultures are not equally valued or preferred (LaFromboise, Coleman, & Gerton, 1993). From this perspective, engaging in boundary spanning is more likely to be positive than stressful. Individuals who can use multiple perspectives to redefine their setting from an obstacle to a resource are expected to have a greater sense of satisfaction in their role as well as an increased ability to define differences within each setting as potential resources.

Creating Social Settings to Integrate Diverse Experiences

The fourth proposition focuses on a particular type of social setting where the goal is to appraise and review the kinds of experiences generated in the previous three propositions. This particular social setting involves the creation of social norms that encourage reflection and integration of experiences (Glidewell, 1976); it is an example of a "safe place" where a person can think out loud and create, in the presence of others, a new framework for organizing their shared experiences.

The purpose of this setting is to make it possible to process and evaluate personal experiences so that the observations about these experiences can become resources for others. This process of consensual understanding, while difficult, is expected to generate a workable structure for understanding diversity. Essential to achieving this understanding are the social norms that establish standards and expectations for social interaction and that sanction the open expression of diverse views and concerns. These social norms also create support among participants for elaborating the meanings of interactions both inside and outside the setting.

One prototype for such an integrative setting consists of the seminars and forums that have been initiated at the University of Massachusetts–Boston; Princeton University in Princeton, New Jersey; and Mount St. Mary's College in Los Angeles, which are participants in the Ford Foundation's Campus Diversity project (Beckham, 1992). Each faculty and student group has created places, occasions, or structures that enable students and faculty from diverse ethnic backgrounds to report, elaborate on, and evaluate their experiences of diversity. Students and faculty in these programs go beyond stereotypes and open up new bases for discourse. They also acquire sensitivities and understandings as they work through a range of feelings and coping strategies stimulated by their experiences with diversity. What takes place in these integrative and reflective settings is the opportunity for the participants to recast and reframe their emotional *and* intellectual understanding of their experiences. Creating an emotional and conceptual connection to what has been learned enables participants to be role models, mentors, or reference points for others who can benefit from this type of setting.

An important function of this type of setting is to allow participants not only to integrate experiences of being different but also to examine their various personal identities. Coughlin (1993) described the various personal identities: "One and the same person, for example, might be an American citizen when he travels abroad, self-consciously white when he moves into an integrated neighborhood, and proudly Irish American on St. Patrick's Day" (p. A8). As Olzak states, "We all have a variety of ethnic and racial boundaries available to us, and we have more or less power to identify according to these boundaries. . . . Sometimes these choices are constrained" (as cited in Coughlin, 1993, p. A8).

The observation by Olzak emphasizes that the integrative setting can be an essential resource to organize the multiple layers of the participants' personal identities. In fact, the experiences gained from the seminars is likely to stimulate the participants' greater awareness about their multiple identities and how they come into play in different types of settings. Those who are clear about the boundaries of their various personal identities are expected to have a more differentiated view of themselves.

The social norms essential for this setting include norms where participants (1) value the processes of exploration and self-discovery and actively sort out their experiences; (2) encourage each other to speak openly about their anxieties when they are engaged in a new cultural experience; (3) struggle out loud, to brainstorm working concepts for themselves; and (4) enable each other to establish an understanding of the experiences they are having. These norms also may facilitate the learning of tolerance (see *Teaching Tolerance*, 1993).

Many groups debrief after an important occasion. In fact, some organizations develop a tradition of evaluating and seeking feedback on an ongoing basis for what has been experienced and accomplished in shared group activities (Katz & Kahn, 1978). Participants in such settings are expected to refine their ability to make sense of their experiences. Talking about the nuances and complexities of their experiences is difficult, yet essential, to obtain an emotional and conceptual understanding of diversity. This proposed social setting establishes a value to help participants pull together, sort out, and refine an array of inconsistencies and contradictions as they work through these experiences.

As previously mentioned, we are involved in creating a setting where community residents design an interview for African American community leaders. During the early part of this research process, we were interested in making sure that community members who missed a meeting knew the date of the next meeting. A member of the community was serving as liaison between the sponsoring community organization and the university research team. What follows is a description of the ways in which integrative settings were used to help clarify cultural differences.

Because the first author was enthusiastic about receiving the comments from community residents on the proposed procedures and desired their feedback on the content of the research topics, he routinely phoned the community residents immediately after the meeting to remind them of the date of the next meeting. When the liaison person would call these same community residents close to the next meeting date, the community residents often would say that the author had already called. The author's view of efficiency was stimulated by a lifelong value "to not let any grass grow under one's feet." The liaison person's view of efficiency was to contact each person shortly before the meeting so that their chance of being at the meeting would be increased. In retrospect, the author's value for efficiency was undermining the liaison person's value for efficiency.

A number of integrative settings enabled the first author and the liaison person to process this issue. Several lunches between them were settings in which the cultural differences between traditional research procedures and the working style within this African American community were discussed. Another setting for the first author was the university research team, where the issue of conducting collaborative research in the African American community while adapting to its cultural norms was discussed.

Presentations at the Midwestern Psychological Association and the American Psychological Association provided two other opportunities to elaborate on the experience. At both meetings, the liaison person formally commented on this experience. She referred to the ambiguity of her role and the way this particular issue clarified her role and increased her investment in performing it.

These settings together provided an opportunity for the first author and the liaison person to deepen their understanding of their roles and philosophies and to develop further mutual respect. The discussions and reflections in these four different settings covered a period of several months. There was no one setting that produced a rapprochement. Instead, it was the cumulative impact of these informal and formal occasions that enabled the issues to be discussed, evaluated, and processed. Without the opportunity for these integrative experiences, the research-and-collaboration process might have been impaired.

We expect several benefits to result from being a participant in such integrative settings. The efforts devoted to this process help people to reevaluate prior assumptions and develop a new style of interaction, thus reducing stereotypes about each other. The participants' new constructions are expected to be of greater differentiation and depth than prior constructions. The participants also can appreciate how contextual factors, such as the presence or absence of dialogue, can constrain or free up understandings. In these integrative settings, the participants create sanctions to openly and freely process information about personal experiences.

To appreciate how differences can become resources, the participants should enter the setting with a belief that there is a definite possibility of being free of discrimination. For the expected benefits to be realized, participants must genuinely believe that opportunities exist for them to develop their own unique perspectives and to express these perspectives. Participants may not wish to be present solely to "teach" others how to reduce their stereotypes (Shea, 1992). The pressure is on all participants in this supportive setting to free up their own stereo-typical notions without asking to be "freed" by another.

If support systems can be operative within these integra-tive settings, the participants will learn to initiate help and ad-vice as they create new pragmatic traditions for the next gener-ation. In this way each participant will learn to draw upon the group as a resource in order to make sense of diversity.

Conclusion

Most efforts to understand experiences of diversity focus on the individual—on increasing her or his capacity to understand cul-tural differences or to learn interpersonal skills that may make it easier to cope with people different from himself or herself. This chapter presented an alternative perspective that empha-sized the construction of social settings that enable people to understand diversity. The assumption has been that social norms can be established to understand, appreciate, and validate ex-periences with diversity. The thesis of ecological pragmatism is that learning contexts are influential in this process.

Four proposed settings focused on appreciating and un-derstanding diversity. These four settings initiate a social process of discovery about diversity. The ecological thesis asserts that people can benefit from social settings in learning how to be interdependent, interacting across status boundaries, interacting with people from other settings, and reflecting and integrating their diverse experiences. Each of these settings was presented as an opportunity for people to have an in-depth experience in understanding differences. Although the settings were presented as distinct, they are interrelated.

The cumulative impact of these four settings is that the participants are expected to create for themselves a workable basis for appreciating and validating diversity. The expectation is that experiences in these four settings can help participants to move beyond gender, ethnicity, class, and life-style and to embrace transcending values such as dignity, justice, and equality.

The spirit of this chapter is that ecological pragmatism is a resource for creating the conditions, atmosphere, and milieu that allow people with diverse social histories to be a resource for other people. There is an absence of one monolithic, paramount, or dominant preferred way of viewing the world and an absence of social norms that define one standard as the only appropriate one. A variety of experiences, points of view, skills, and competencies are acknowledged as valid in their own right. These four settings focus on the pragmatic opportunity for participants in the settings to construct specific cultures that support diversity.

Creating these social settings is not the sole province of professionals. These accessible ideas allow any person in a community to begin the process of creating settings. The latent power of the ecological thesis lies in the immediacy with which each person can create social settings. The pragmatic aspect of the ecological thesis is that the solutions are local and require a minimum of outside technology and expertise. These four social settings are presented as practical ways to construct new realities in order to improve an everyday understanding of cultural and social differences.

References

Aldag, R., & Fuller, S. (1993). Beyond fiasco: A reappraisal of the groupthink phenomenon and a new model of group decision processes. *Psychological Bulletin, 113,* 533–552.

Aldrich, H., & Herker, D. (1977). Boundary spanning roles and organization structure. *Academy of Management Review, 2,* 217–230.

At-Twaijri, M.I.A., & Montanari, J. R. (1987). The impact of context and choice on the boundary-spanning process: An empirical extension. *Human Relations, 40,* 783–798.

Azelton, L. S. (1992, Aug.). Assessing organizational and community interdependences. In J. G. Kelly (Chair), *African-American leaders: Research as a collaborative process.* Symposium conducted at the 100th meeting of the American Psychological Association, Washington, DC.

Banks, J. (1992). Dimensions of multicultural education. *Kappa Delta Pi Record, 29,* 12.

Beckham, E. E. (1992, Winter). Campus diversity: Facing new realities. *Ford Foundation Report,* pp. 8–25.

Coughlin, E. K. (1993, Mar. 24). Sociologists examine the complexities of racial and ethnic identity in America. *Chronicle of Higher Education,* pp. A7–A8.

Danzinger, K. (1990). Generative metaphor and the history of psychological discourse. In D. E. Leary (Ed.), *Metaphors in the History of Psychology* (pp. 331–356). New York: Cambridge University Press.

Deutsch, M. (1993). Educating for a peaceful world. *American Psychologist, 48,* 510–517.

Devine, P. G. (1989). Stereotypes and prejudice: Their automatic and controlled components. *Journal of Personality and Social Psychology, 56,* 5–18.

Devine, P. G., & Monteith, M. J. (1993). The role of discrepancy-associated affect in prejudice reduction. In D. M. Mackie & D. L. Hamilton (Eds.), *Affect, cognition, and stereotyping: Interactive processes in intergroup perception* (pp. 317–344). San Diego, CA: Academic Press.

Egan, T. (1993, Oct. 8). Teaching tolerance in workplaces: A Seattle program illustrates limits. *New York Times,* p. A-12.

Festinger, L. (1962). *A theory of cognitive dissonance.* Stanford, CA: Stanford University Press.

Galaskiewicz, J. (1979). The structure of community organizational networks. *Social Forces, 57,* 1346–1364.

Galaskiewicz, J. (1985). Interorganizational relations. *Annual Review of Sociology, 11,* 281–304.

Glidewell, J. (1976). A theory of induced social change. *American Journal of Community Psychology, 4,* 227–242.

Hecht, M., Ribeau, S., & Alberts, J. (1989). An Afro-American perspective on interethnic communication. *Communication Monographs, 56,* 385–410.

Heider, F. (1958). *The psychology of interpersonal relations.* New York: Wiley.

Johnson, D. W., & Johnson, R. T. (1991). The impact of positive goal and resource interdependence on achievement, interaction, and attitudes. *Journal of General Psychology, 118,* 341–347.

Johnson, D. W., & Johnson, R. T. (1992). Positive interdependence: Key to effective cooperation. In R. Hertz-Lazarowitz & N. Miller (Eds.), *Interaction in cooperative groups: The theoretical anatomy of group learning* (pp. 174–199). Cambridge, MA: Cambridge University Press.

Kahn, R. L. (1990). Organizational theory and international relations: Mutually informing paradigms. In R. L. Kahn & M. N. Zald (Eds.), *Organizations and nation-states: New perspectives on conflict and cooperation.* San Francisco: Jossey-Bass.

Katz, D., & Kahn, R. (1978). *The social psychology of organizations* (2nd ed.). New York: Wiley.

Keller, R. T., & Holland, W. E. (1975). Boundary spanning roles in a research and development organization: An empirical invetigation. *Academy of Management Journal, 18,* 388–393.

Kelly, J. G. (1968). Towards an ecological conception of preventive interventions. In J. W. Carter (Ed.), *Research contributions from psychology to community mental health.* New York: Behavioral Publications.

Kelly, J. G., Ryan, A., Altman, B., & Stelzner, S. (in press). Chapter VII: Understanding and changing social systems: An ecological view. In J. Rappaport & E. Seidman (Eds.), *Handbook of community psychology.* New York: Plenum.

King, L., & King, D. (1990). Role conflict and role ambiguity: A critical assessment of construct validity. *Psychological Bulletin, 107*(1), 48–64.

Kingry-Westergaard, C., & Kelly, J. G. (1990). A contextualist epistemology for ecological research. In P. H. Tolan, C. Keys, F. Chertok, & L. Jason (Eds.), *Researching community psychology: The integration of theories and methods* (pp. 23–31). Washington, DC: American Psychological Association.

LaFromboise, T., Coleman, H.L.K., & Gerton, J. (1993). Psychological impact of biculturalism: Evidence and theory. *Psychological Bulletin, 114,* 395–412.

Leary, D. E. (1990). Psyche's muse: The role of metaphor in the history of psychology. In D. E. Leary (Ed.), *Metaphors in the history of psychology* (pp. 1–78). New York: Cambridge University Press.

Leifer, R., & Delbecq, A. (1978). Organizational/environmental interchange: A model of boundary spanning activity. *Academy of Management Review, 3,* 40–50.

McIntosh, L. (1993, Dec. 12). Office harmony: Choirs help keep employees in tune. *Chicago Tribune,* Sec. 7, p. 5.

Miller, J. G. (1984). Culture and the development of everyday social explanation. *Journal of Personality and Social Psychology, 46,* 961–978.

Monteith, M. J. (1993). Self-regulation of prejudiced responses: Implications for progress in prejudice-reduction efforts. *Journal of Personality and Social Psychology, 65,* 469–485.

Murray, K. (1993, Aug. 1). The unfortunate side effects of diversity training. *New York Times,* p. 5.

Pang, V., & Nieto, J. (1992). Multicultural teaching. *Kappa Delta Pi Record, 29*(1), 25–27.

Rizzo, J., House, R., & Lirtzman, S. (1970). Role conflict and ambiguity in complex organizations. *Administrative Science Quarterly, 15,* 150–163.

Shea, C. (1992, Oct. 12). Students: A campus newspaper confronts emotional issue of how best to incorporate minority students. *Chronicle of Higher Education,* pp. A31–A32.

Slavin, R. E. (1990). *Cooperative learning theory: Theory, research and practice.* Englewood Cliffs, NJ: Prentice-Hall. (177–209).

Slavin, R. E. (1992). When and why does cooperative learning increase achievement? Theoretical and empirical perspectives. In R. Hertz-Lazarowitz & N. Miller (Eds.), *Interaction in cooperative groups: The theoretical anatomy of group learning* (pp. 145–173). Cambridge, MA: Cambridge University Press.

Sleeter, C. (1992). What is multicultural education? *Kappa Delta Pi Record, 29*(1), 4–8.

Sniezek, J., May, D., & Sawyer, J. (1990). Social uncertainty and interdependence: A study of resource allocation decisions in groups. *Organizational Behavior and Human Decision Processes, 46,* 155–180.

Stephan, W. G. (1985). Intergroup relations. In G. Lindzey & E. Aronson (Eds.), *Handbook of Social Psychology.* New York: Random House.

Tannen, D. (1986). *That's not what I meant: How conversational style makes or breaks your relations with others.* New York: Ballantine Books.

Taylor, C., & Gutmann, A. (Eds.). (1992). *Multiculturalism and "the politics of recognition."* Princeton, NJ: Princeton University Press.

Teaching Tolerance (1993). Montgomery, AL: Southern Poverty Law Center.

Tiedt, P. L. (1992). Embracing multicultural teaching. *Kappa Delta Pi Record, 29*(1), 13.

Tushman, M., & Scanlan, T. (1981). Boundary spanning individuals: Their role in information transfer and their antecedents. *Academy of Management Journal, 24,* 289–305.

Webb, N. M. (1992). Testing a theoretical model of student interaction and learning in small groups. In R. Hertz-Lazarowitz & N. Miller (Eds.), *Interaction in cooperative groups* (pp. 102–119). New York: Cambridge University Press.

Weiner, A. (1992, July 22). Anthropology's lessons for cultural diversity: The discipline can help to redefine current debates. *Chronicle of Higher Education,* pp. B1, B2.

Wilder, D. (1986). Social categorization: Implications for creation and reduction of intergroup bias. In L. Berkowitz (Ed.), *Advances in experimental social psychology* (Vol. 19, pp. 291–355). New York: Academic Press.

Wilson, E. O. (1992). *The diversity of life.* Cambridge, MA: Harvard University Press.

Conclusion:
Convergence and Divergence in Human Diversity

Roderick J. Watts,
Edison J. Trickett, Dina Birman

We began the book with a history of the diversity concept, show-ing its movement from a focus on minority status and disen-franchisement to one that increasingly celebrated the contribu-tions of personal and group distinctiveness to U.S. culture. This book broadens existing notions of diversity by including popu-lations whose distinctiveness is not necessarily cultural and deepens understanding by clarifying concepts and paradigms related to context, race, culture, and social injustice. Broaden-ing minority issues and cultural diversity to include theories of context and other populations raises questions about the com-parability of theories and ideas. To what extent does the shared language refer to common phenomena? Does human diversity constitute an emerging field or paradigm, or is it best described as a loosely connected set of interest groups?

To approach this question, we began at the highest level of analysis — paradigms. Included at this level were cross-cultural, ecological, sociopolitical, and population-specific paradigms. At this level we found scholars focused on their own perspectives in their own "home" disciplines with little cross-fertilization by ideas in other areas. Despite this isolation, we discovered evidence of parallel thinking and seemingly common concepts, such as identity. To create the structure for the book, we selected several of the paradigms and three of the cross-cutting concepts that many of the paradigms shared — culture, oppression, and identity. We also sought to highlight perspectives on context and its role in the production of the differences we call diversity. In our view, the divergence between views provided an intellectually stimulating counterpoint to some of the convergence concerning terminology. This complementarity offered opportunities for exchange that would not have been possible if we had organized the book by demographic populations such as women, Asian Americans, or Latinos.

Dialectics and Paradigms of Human Diversity

Cohesiveness and shared ideas offer some advantages for an emerging area, but for human diversity, focusing solely on convergence misses the dialectical interplay between ideas. Jones noted that proponents of new perspectives often sharpen differences in a dialectical way. Consequently, *they distance themselves from one another* as well as from traditional psychology. Part of a psychology of human diversity is tolerating the tension, complexity, and ambiguity that arises from multiple and diverging perspectives. To begin our discussion of the dialectics of diversity, we take some liberties with the words of Dale Berra (see Chapter Two): "There are many shared themes in human diversity, but the similarities are different."

Our starting point is the notion of context, because it exemplifies the dialectic between convergence and divergence. Virtually every author agreed that social, historical, and material context shapes individual differences and the distinctive patterns of behavior seen in many populations. Differences in context, and the disparate transactions people experience in the broader society as individuals and as members of socially meaningful populations, are major forces behind the divergence of ideas. Context is thus a foundation stone for a psychology of human diversity, and its salience reaffirms the need for research and action on people in context. Research must devote more attention to the interactions between human behavior and social markers, social policies, and institutions.

Yet the notion of context is framed in varying ways: ecological pragmatism (Kelly, Azelton, Burzette, and Mock), historical construction of oppression (Prilleltensky and Gonick), worldview (Watts), culture and nationality (Birman, Lonner), and African history and spirituality (Myers and Speight). They provide very different foci on the nature of context and what is important in it. Nonetheless, there was a shared belief in the potency of the context and the way it shapes the accumulation and patterning of experience.

The concepts of context and worldview are important to understanding the paradigms presented in this book. As noted above, authors framed context differently; it referred sometimes to material conditions and at other times to the social context. Both were seen as forces that shape behavior. In contrast, worldview was often used to describe the internal representations of these forces that people in common contexts share. The terms authors used to describe worldviews include *worldview, perspective, culture* (*culture* is used both ways), *orientation, conceptual system,* and *ideology.* These terms are distinguishable from personality characteristics by their level of analysis; they refer to patterns of beliefs and thinking that are *shared* by many members of a population in a common context. At times worldview operates across contexts, as when immigrants bring their pattern of cultural beliefs to a new context. Context also shapes worldview, however. Immigrants in a new cultural context tend to acculturate and alter their original beliefs and values (Birman). Thus, the relationship between context and worldview is complex and interactive.

The interplay of context and worldview is related to two other areas of convergence: (1) acknowledgment of the validity of multiple worldviews and (2) recognition of the embeddedness of worldview in all theory, research, and action. These shared ideas have important implications for human diversity. They define the task and focus of the paradigm as one of clarifying how context interacts with worldview to produce the divergence in human thought and behavior we call diversity. An understanding of context also reveals new strategies for changing it.

For most authors, the recognition of multiple valid world-views led to an endorsement of social constructivism and a critique of efforts to achieve objectivity. In its moderate forms, social constructivism is a hedge against hegemony and an ally of pluralism for at least three reasons. First, it is inherently more inclusive of multiple worldviews because it acknowledges that context and interpretive processes shape worldview. Second, it focuses attention on the interpretive process itself. It questions *why* people take the positions they do, rather than focusing exclusively on the veracity of the positions themselves. Third, it is a useful way of reframing difference as diversity and not as deficit, as has happened historically (Jones, Watts).

However, social constructivism is only one end of an epistemological dialectic. Extreme social constructivism can lead to a world without right or wrong, where everything is relative. Prilleltensky and Gonick warn that if there is no moral, ethical, or empirical high ground, we can easily drift into moral relativism with no higher values, righteous causes, or sense of meaning. Myers and Speight also implicitly reject such postmodern and deconstructionist thinking. They argue that spiritual values can unify the fragmented materialism of Western scientific methods. They call for an integration of psychology and the ancient spiritual values and perspectives that have grounded civilizations for centuries.

The dialectical alternative to social constructivism is a "one truth" epistemology that sharply distinguishes objective from subjective. Here, multiple realities are seen as approximations of objective truth. Subjectivity becomes an impediment to truth-seeking, rather than an essential part of research and a topic of inquiry in its own right. Subject-object dualism encourages discourse that demonstrates the *superiority* of a perspective; it does not typically focus on articulating the *distinctiveness* of a perspective so that others may better understand it. Clearly this extreme is antithetical to human diversity. In our view, an optimal position along this dialectic for the field of diversity is closer to social constructivism but not at its extreme.

As a strategy for managing the constructivist-dualist dialectic in the formation of knowledge, we propose a renewed emphasis on *process*. This means less concern with what reality ultimately gets constructed and more concern with the construction process. To turn an old slogan on its head, "The means justify the ends." The end-result of a just process is a shared understanding of truth and morality. As the perspectives of Rappaport, Tyler and Kelly, Azelton, Burzette, and Mock suggest, this process is communication-intensive; its aims are ecological validity and capturing local meaning (constructions). A process orientation shifts attention from questions of philosophy to questions of procedure and participants: with whom, and in what context, should the process of concept development occur? In adopting a process orientation, the creation of settings and norms becomes a primary concern.

Knowledge and paradigm development will also benefit from greater theoretical clarity about context. Ecological theory (Kelly, Azelton, Burzette, and Mock) is one of the most developed theories, but authors regularly used at least six terms to describe context: *setting, context, environment, ecology, culture,* and *history*. Typically, authors used these terms to denote the material features of context or a socially constructed reality that influenced the members of the setting in predictable ways. For example, *culture* could be used to explain why people in the United States are likely to line up while waiting for a store to open, while Italians in an identical physical setting in Italy would not. In this instance, distinctive behavior is attributed to an implicit, but pervasive, shared pattern of norms and values that influence behavior.

Contexts, as described above, are social or physical forces that shape behavior. In contrast, worldviews are the internal representations of these forces that many share. This shared pattern arises from shared experience in shared contexts over time. To return to the previous example, culture-as-worldview explains why a new Italian immigrant in the United States would initially break U.S. norms (culture-as-context) about queues or fail to see their value because of internalized beliefs and attitudes from Italian cultural contexts. However, ecological theories and other approaches to context would predict that an extensive stay in the U.S. context would produce a change in the immigrant's behavior and worldview. Thus, the relationship between context and worldview is complex and interactive. Context does shape worldview, but as social constructivists, we would argue that context is not absolute; it is subject to interpretation.

Key Concepts in Human Diversity

We based our choice of key concepts such as culture, oppression, and identity on a recognition of this dialectical tension between similarities and differences in their use and the potential for fruitful exchange. Perhaps the best example of "different similarities" is culture. Although Lonner's review of culture showed a lack of consensus on its meaning, its nearly ubiquitous use among scholars of diversity made it one of the earliest cross-cutting concepts for this book. Yet it was used many different ways: authors used it to describe systems (the dominant culture), attributes of people (cultural identity and acculturation), and the dynamics of contact between cultures (cross-cultural theory). Culture is useful at multiple levels of analysis and, despite its ambiguity, it will continue to contribute to convergence.

Oppression played a linking role similar to that of culture. Oppression is a theme in the feminist perspective of Russo and Dabul and the Optimal Theory of Myers and Speight. D'Augelli discussed its role in gay and lesbian identity development, as did Alderfer and Helms in their discussions of racial oppression and racial identity. Gatz and Cotton's discussion of stereotypes of the elderly and Scheer's discussion of people with disabilities also referred to oppression.

In each case, the use of a common language across paradigms produced divergence as well as convergence. Despite wideranging use of the terms *oppression, identity, culture, empowerment,* and *diversity,* variations in the author's worldviews or paradigms produced variations in definitions, emphases, and shades of meaning. Racism, for example, produces a different set of outcomes for oppression (for example, segregation) than sexism (control and exploitation of sexuality). These variations in context contributed to different assumptions, different worldviews, and, ultimately, different paradigms. As Bernal points out, racism and sexism can also occur simultaneously and paradigms that arise from this context produce a unique perspective on oppression. Similarly, language is often a key element of identity for acculturating immigrants, but it is of little importance in gay identity. Again, shared terminology produces common ground and fruitful exchange, but the context and worldview of the terminology leads to important differences in meaning.

However stimulating the differences are, extreme divergence can hamper communication across areas of study and action. Terms like *ethnicity, acculturation* (and its subcategories), *minority, majority, racial categories, dominant-group, group, population, mainstream, Western, setting, environment, society, worldview,* and *ecology,* to name a few, are used differently or not defined at all. This results in part from the multidisciplinary approach we took to this book; differences in academic training added another layer of complexity to differences in worldview. Depending on their background, authors sought to integrate psychology with moral or spiritual values, history, political economy, sociology, or anthropology.

For those of us who were trained in the Western scientific tradition, where the accumulation of knowledge is based on replication and a shared understanding of concepts, this plethora of basic terms without common definitions seems to doom all progress. From this perspective, a priority for this book ought to be to create more convergence — perhaps a dictionary of common definitions to aid in precise communication and orderly, coordinated research.

We believe that this impulse must be restrained, and Reinharz's discussion of voice provides the most compelling support for our position. As she notes, those who have been silenced in the past must find their voice and articulate their worldview for themselves; in our view, this means that socially distinctive populations must find the words, ideas, and methods of expression that are most consistent with their issues of concern. This applies to *ideas* that have been ignored or denigrated as well as to populations, as is the case for oppression, power, and the self in the research process. As populations and ideas find their voice, the particularism and worldview of psychology (as used without modifiers) is revealed. As a result, we gain a better understanding of which phenomena are truly shared and universal and which are unacknowledged population-specific psychologies.

Methodology in Human Diversity

Because this book is multidisciplinary, many perspectives on research methods are represented. Yet many authors shared a concern about the relationship between methods and action. Rappaport, Reinharz, Kelly, Azelton, Burzette, and Mock and Prilleltensky and Gonick called in varying ways for methods that empower participants in research and action; they described the importance of empowering role relationships in research, voice, supportive norms, and democratic participation, respectively. Prilleltensky and Gonick called for a dissolution of the boundaries between theory and praxis, so that the accumulation of knowledge about oppression would always be accompanied by action against oppression.

In translating these ideals into methods, all authors agreed on the importance of *human relationships* in diversity-conscious methods. One part of all our human relationships is the self, but unlike our pen-and-paper instruments, the self is rarely subject to careful scrutiny. Alderfer's discussion of "disciplined subjectivity" and his frank and personal effort to locate himself in his professional work provided an example of how researchers need to cultivate an awareness of self and what they bring to the research-and-action process. Tyler's discussion of "hyphens" highlighted the relationship interfaces of knower-known and fact-value as they influence relationships, data, and action processes. Rappaport argued that qualitative research and action methods are best suited for the relationship-intensive work of human diversity. In-depth interviews, participant-observation, ethnography, and related methods create roles that bind people together. These research methods produce vastly different relationships than a mailed survey where two-way communication is minimal or a laboratory experiment where researchers must control and manipulate participants.

   Alderfer provided a number of suggestions and concepts for a context-sensitive research strategy in describing parallel process and other dynamics of intergroup contact. He also discussed the value of race- and gender-balanced research-intervention teams and of open communication about the influences of one's population memberships in task-related activity. This notion of balance has broad applications for research and action. After assessing the dimensions of diversity of importance in a given setting, researchers can use this information to construct a research team that allows differing and pertinent worldviews to enter the project. Creative management of the tensions and resources of the research group becomes an important part of the endeavor. This approach to research begins to approximate what Jones called "affirmative diversity," where variation and distinctiveness are viewed as assets. Although these strategies, and qualitative methods more generally, do not guarantee meaningful collaboration and communication, they promote these processes. The future of a psychology of human diversity depends on the continued development of democratic, egalitarian methods.

Creating Settings for the Work: Structure and Process

Often approaches to human diversity neglect questions about the context of the work. In a world still ambivalent about the value of diversity, it is unwise to assume that existing norms and institutions will support productive connections among scholars and activists who could contribute to the field. The remaining pages draw from one of the most compelling theories of context, ecological psychology, as a means of generating practical ideas for productive settings. Again, we define settings broadly; they can be social as well as material. Institutions, departments, project teams, freestanding organizations, net-

works that have ongoing contact in conferences, and joint research activity all qualify as settings. What follows are some of
the key ecological concepts involved in creating diverse settings,
as adapted from the chapter by Kelly, Azelton, Burzette, and
Mock:

- Opportunities to understand the historical basis of diversity
  and the meaning of specific differences. Of particular concern are past and present antagonisms and injustice that
  produce distrust.
- Social norms where differences are resources and interdependence and uniqueness are valued (both boundary spanning
  and a within-group focus are rewarded).
- A focus on the *process* for developing a psychology of human
  diversity. Members must become committed to exploring
  alternative ideas and action in the pursuit of a psychology
  of all people. The spiritual perspective of Myers and Speight
  serves to remind us of humanity's fundamental unity and
  the illusory nature of socially constructed "differences." This
  commitment and awareness of unity become the glue that
  holds a setting together as people struggle with their emotional and intellectual experience.

    Implicit in the above list but worthy of specific attention
is the issue of social power and its relationship to various diversity markers (for example, associations between power and
gender, race, and class). As Alderfer describes in intergroup
theory, the social power and privilege associated with population memberships (regardless of one's *personal* power) influence
the dynamics of intergroup contact. Society and mass culture
tend to reinforce the established social roles and status associated
with certain population memberships. If it is true that power
concedes nothing without a struggle, then all members of the
setting must be open to dialogue about power and the risk of
a parallel process that mirrors society's unjust power relations.

    The creation of this book represents an example of the
complexities, difficulties, and benefits of taking on the issues of
diversity raised throughout the book. The editors themselves

differed in age, gender, race, ethnicity, culture, worldview, and seniority. Trickett is a white male who has devoted many years to developing an ecological perspective on behavior, beginning in the 1960s and reflecting the zeitgeist of that period. Watts is an African American man, more junior in the field, whose early interests were in race and worldview and whose more recent involvements center on linking psychological theory to liberation. Birman, a woman and a refugee from the former Soviet Union, is of ethnically mixed Russian and Jewish origin. She is a recent Ph.D., and she is interested in the interface between culture, oppression, and gender. That such a group would themselves reflect some aspects of the differences discussed in the book was certain. Less certain was the way in which these differences would influence the process of working on the book or how clearly such differences would be available for discussion. The ideological and conceptual glue for the project was our shared belief in the importance of social context, oppression, and culture as key and interacting influences on human behavior.

This glue kept the project whole, but clear differences in perspective and emphasis emerged when we were writing joint chapters such as this one and when we were deciding what topics to include. They influenced how we read each other's drafts of chapters, decided how sharply or subtly to phrase a controversial idea, and even determined what constituted a controversial idea. Although some of this reflected population membership and intergroup dynamics, it would be an oversimplification to link these differences exclusively or, perhaps, primarily, to such factors. But it would be more naive to believe that the editors' personal attributes were unrelated to the issues mentioned above, or to the more general content, tone, preferences for conflict resolution, and imagined audiences we had in mind when discussing issues with each other and making decisions. Because the creation of settings implies an explicit attention to process over time, as suggested above, we tried to be explicit about the values, politics, and perspectives underlying our work on the book. For example, we each felt ourselves, at different times and over different issues, the most appropriate person for dealing with a topic or an author. We each felt ourselves reflecting on how points of debate were best understood when others adopted our worldview or we adopted theirs.

Once the project was under way, managing the process became the challenge. Usually, a respect for differences took precedence over a pressure to build consensus. Few compromises were sought when we had differences of opinion over ideas worthy of chapter-long attention. This choice of pluralism over consensus was operationalized by creating domains or sections of the book that allowed each editor considerable latitude. These quasi-independent domains institutionalized diversity in the project. The operative value in this decision was tolerance; we committed time and energy to ideas we did not fully agree with in the interest of the larger project.

These efforts did not eliminate disagreements, but over time, we learned to understand each other's perspective better as we recognized the traps of terminology. As we talked, we influenced each other, and incremental convergence occurred in our ideas. The insight we gained from this process is that changes in worldview should occur from within, through insights by its adherents, rather than by pressure from efforts of outsiders with very different frames of reference. Rather than being static, worldviews should grow and develop in response to new demands and knowledge. This position makes many more demands on participants, however; everyone must engage in an ongoing program of self-criticism and critique. Knee-jerk support of one's worldview can quickly undermine the larger process and encourage rigidity and dogma rather than growth. Once again, an awareness of divergence and convergence is useful.

To allow for divergence, settings may benefit from multiple domains or bases of power that allow all members of the setting to ground themselves in a worldview that is distinct from the common worldview the setting as a whole is laboring to create. On the other hand, efforts to *sustain* a setting benefit from convergence; settings that include shared experience, nominally shared language, commitment to tolerance and pluralism, and collaborative processes are more likely to endure. History suggests that the more resources that are at stake, and the less these resources are fairly distributed at the outset, the more challenging the effort to create pluralistic settings becomes.

By pulling together theories of context, cross-cutting concepts, and discourse on socially meaningful populations, this book highlighted some key concerns for a psychology of human diversity. Future development will benefit from continued parallel development, based on the demands of varying contexts, but more rapid development will depend on better connections between parallel and diverging paths of development. As we have stressed, a call for connections should not be a mandate for convergence. But as with all the complex dialectics of diversity, a process must be established that maintains an optimal balance between shared and distinctive ideas. We believe that a better understanding of context, specific populations, and nominally shared ideas will create the best common intellectual ground for advancing human diversity in psychology.

Name Index

Subject Index

CPSIA information can be obtained at www.ICGtesting.com
262145BV00007B/80/A

9 780787 900298